AI Strategies for
Web Development

Build next-gen, intelligent websites by unleashing AI's power
in design, personalization, and ethics

Anderson Soares Furtado Oliveira

AI Strategies for Web Development

Group Product Manager: Kaustubh Manglurkar
Publishing Product Manager: Chayan Majumdar
Book Project Manager: Sonam Pandey
Senior Editor: Debolina Acharyya
Technical Editor: Simran Ali
Copy Editor: Safis Editing
Indexer: Manju Arasan
Production Designer: Joshua Misquitta
DevRel Marketing Coordinator: Anamika Singh and Nivedita Pandey

First published: September 2024

Production reference: 3250924

Published by Packt Publishing Ltd.
Grosvenor House
11 St Paul's Square
Birmingham
B3 1RB, UK

ISBN 978-1-83588-630-4

www.packtpub.com

To my daughters, Liz and Bella, who inspire me to create a better future through technology and education.

– Anderson Soares Furtado Oliveira

Foreword 1

In a world increasingly shaped by the rapid advancements of technology, the intersection of **artificial intelligence** (**AI**) and web development stands as a frontier of immense potential. As we step into this new era, it is both exciting and essential to understand the profound impact AI can have on the way we design, develop, and interact with digital environments. This book, *AI Strategies for Web Development*, serves as a critical guide for navigating this complex landscape.

As an author and consultant who has dedicated much of my career to exploring the possibilities of AI, particularly through my works *Navigating AI with Faith* and *Built for AI*, I have witnessed firsthand how AI is revolutionizing industries across the globe. My journey has also taken me to various platforms, including the Built for AI conferences, where I have had the privilege of sharing insights on how AI can drive economic growth, enhance productivity, and create new opportunities for innovation.

This book by Anderson Soares Furtado Oliveira is timely and relevant. It bridges the gap between the theoretical aspects of AI and its practical applications in web development, offering readers not just knowledge, but actionable strategies. The content here is not only comprehensive but also accessible, making it a valuable resource for web developers, UX designers, and anyone involved in the digital landscape who is eager to harness the power of AI.

What excites me most about this book is its holistic approach. It does not just focus on the technical aspects but also delves into the ethical considerations, governance, and future trends that will shape the next generation of web technologies. Anderson's ability to distill complex AI concepts into practical tools and frameworks is truly commendable, and I believe readers will find themselves well-equipped to not only understand AI but also to apply it effectively in their work.

As you embark on this journey through the pages of *AI Strategies for Web Development*, I encourage you to embrace the challenges and opportunities that AI presents. The future of web development is not just about building websites; it's about creating intelligent, responsive, and ethical digital experiences that meet the needs of our evolving society.

With this book, you are not just learning about AI—you are stepping into a future where your work as a web developer will be at the forefront of technological innovation. I am confident that the insights you gain here will inspire you to push the boundaries of what is possible and to become a leader in the AI-driven transformation of the web.

Elijah Low
Author
Navigating AI with Faith

Foreword 2

In the ever-evolving landscape of technology, **Artificial Intelligence** (**AI**) has emerged as a transformative force, reshaping industries and revolutionizing the way we interact with the digital world. The realm of web development is no exception. As AI continues to advance at a rapid pace, its integration into web applications is becoming increasingly prevalent, opening up new possibilities and challenges for developers and businesses alike.

This book, *AI Strategies for Web Development*, serves as a comprehensive guide to navigating the exciting and complex world of AI-powered web development. From understanding the fundamental concepts of AI to mastering advanced techniques, this book provides a practical and insightful exploration of how AI can be leveraged to create innovative and impactful web experiences.

Throughout the chapters, you will delve into a wide range of topics, including:

- **AI Fundamentals**: Gain a solid foundation in AI, machine learning, and natural language processing.

- **AI Integration**: Explore the challenges and opportunities of incorporating AI into web projects, including the AI loop approach for continuous improvement based on real-time feedback and data.

- **Tools and Frameworks**: Discover the leading AI and ML tools and frameworks, such as scikit-learn, NLTK, and TensorFlow, to streamline your development process.

- **AI Architecture**: Learn how to design scalable and efficient AI solutions using the AYai or Architect your Artificial Intelligence method, with real-world case studies and practical examples to maintain and adapt AI architectures.

- **User Experience**: Understand how AI can enhance user-centric experiences through personalization, optimization, and iterative design, as explored in the Design Intelligence chapter.

- **Pattern Recognition**: Learn how to personalize user journeys using AI-powered pattern recognition techniques and predictive algorithms, as discussed in the Recognizing Patterns chapter.

- **Coding Assistants**: Discover the transformative power of coding assistants, such as AI-powered code completion, in enhancing productivity, code quality, and development efficiency.

- **Advanced AI Interactions**: Explore how AI can elevate user engagement on the web through machine learning techniques, voice recognition, and advanced chatbots, as discussed in the Smarter User Interactions chapter.

- **Intelligent Testing**: Learn about intelligent testing strategies that leverage AI to enhance the security, performance, and reliability of web applications, including AI-driven test case generation, performance testing, security protocols, and bias detection.

- **AI and the Workforce**: Understand the transformative effect of AI on web development roles, including the concept of an augmented workforce and the evolving responsibilities of developers.

- **Machine Users**: Explore the rise of machine users and their impact on digital interfaces, including profiling machine customers, exploring new market opportunities, and the architectural requirements for integrating machine user data sources and API platforms.

- **AI-Augmented Development**: Gain insights into the future of software engineering with AI-augmented tools, including design-to-code tools, coding assistants, and AI-augmented testing tools.

- **Creating Intelligent Web Applications**: Learn how to create intelligent web applications enhanced with AI, following the stages of ideation, design, implementation, and deployment, with an emphasis on AI's role in business analytics and user engagement.

- **AI Governance**: Address the governance of AI models, focusing on trustworthiness, fairness, and transparency. Explore the AI TRiSM framework and implement ethical AI practices and robust governance structures.

- **Next-Gen Development and AI Advancements**: Explore the future of development environments and AI technologies, including GitOps workflows, cloud development tools, and cutting-edge AI advancements.

- **Emerging Realities and Interfaces**: Investigate the convergence of emerging technologies with web development, including VR/AR, conversational user interfaces, and ubiquitous computing.

- **AI Regulation and Governance**: Navigate the complexities of AI regulation, with a focus on the EU AI Act and ISO/IEC 42001 standards. Learn how to implement robust governance frameworks, ensuring compliance with international guidelines and utilizing the G^3 AI Framework for comprehensive governance, risk management, and regulatory compliance.

Whether you are a seasoned web developer looking to expand your skills or a business professional seeking to leverage AI for competitive advantage, this book offers valuable insights and practical guidance. By understanding the principles and best practices of AI-powered web development, you can create innovative and impactful applications that shape the future of the digital landscape.

I invite you to embark on this journey of discovery and innovation. The future of web development is AI-driven, and this book will equip you with the knowledge and tools to be at the forefront of this exciting revolution.

Prof. Marcelo Augusto Gonçalves Bardi, PhD.
Head of Executive Education at SUCESU Paraná, Brazil
Member of the Executive Committee at MetaRed TIC Brasil

Contributors

About the author

Anderson Soares Furtado Oliveira is an experienced executive, AI strategist, and machine learning engineer specializing in AI governance, risk management, and compliance. As a board member at **The Global Center for Risk and Innovation (GCRI)** and an AI strategy consultant at G³ AI Global, he co-authored the book *PgM Canvas: Transforming Vision into Real Benefits - A Program Management Guide for Leaders and Managers*. With over a decade of experience in IT governance (CGEIT) and a focus on integrating AI technologies to drive business growth, he has led numerous AI projects and developed AI governance frameworks.

His expertise in digital transformation and national development has equipped him to create innovative solutions and ethical AI applications. Anderson is a PhD student in Computer Science and Computational Mathematics at the University of São Paulo and holds an MBA in Software Engineering Project Management.

I extend my deepest gratitude to my family, especially my wife, Vanessa, and my daughters, Liz and Bella, for their unwavering support and encouragement throughout this journey. My heartfelt thanks to my parents for inspiring me to pursue excellence and believe in the transformative power of education and technology. I am also grateful to the team at Packt Publishing for their professional guidance and dedication in bringing this book to life. Lastly, I thank Jesus for His grace and guidance in all my endeavors.

About the reviewers

Sunil Raj Thota is a seasoned software engineer with extensive experience in web development and AI applications. Currently working at Amazon QuickSight Team, Sunil has previously contributed to significant projects at Yahoo Inc., enhancing user engagement and satisfaction through innovative features at Yahoo and AOL Mail. He has also worked at Northeastern University as a research assistant and at MOURI Tech as a senior software engineer, optimizing multiple websites and leading successful project deployments. Sunil co-founded ISF Technologies, where he championed user-centric design and agile methodologies. He has also contributed to the book *The Art of Micro Frontends*. His academic background includes a master's in analytics from Northeastern University and a bachelor's in electronics and communications engineering from Andhra University.

Mohan Reddy Mummareddy is an accomplished Unity3D developer with expertise in AR/VR/MR and game development. With seven years of experience, he has delivered numerous successful projects, demonstrating proficiency in computer vision and AI technologies. Mohan has contributed to the development of iOS applications utilizing LIDAR technology for ML training and Unity's Barracuda for model inference. He has also worked on virtual experience products, using AR/VR/MR and web technologies. Mohan holds an M.Tech in AR and VR, an MBA in marketing, and a B.Tech in electrical and electronics. Passionate about **extended reality** (**XR**), he strives to push boundaries and create strong AI-enabled XR platforms and solutions.

Table of Contents

3

Challenges and Opportunities – Integrating AI into Web Projects   63

4

Navigating the Landscape: Popular AI and ML Frameworks and Tools   91

5

Blueprints of the Future – Architecting Effective AI Solutions   119

Part 2: Crafting the Future: Creating Cutting-Edge AI Applications

6

Design Intelligence – Creating User-Centric Experiences with AI   145

7

Recognizing Patterns – Personalizing User Journeys with AI   161

8

Coding Assistants – Your Secret Weapon in Modern Development   183

9

Smarter User Interactions – Elevating User Engagement with Advanced AI   211

10

Smart Testing Strategies – Fortifying Web Applications with AI Insights   241

Part 3: Future-Proofing Web Development – Advanced AI Strategies

11

Augmented Workforce – AI's Impact on Web Development Jobs   261

12

Machine Users Unveiled – Navigating the Intersection of Human and Machine   273

13

AI-Augmented Development – Shaping Tomorrow's Digital Landscape   295

14

From Idea to Reality – Crafting Intelligent Web Applications   311

15

Guardians of the Digital Realm – Navigating Trust, Risk, and Ethics in AI   323

Part 4: The Road Ahead – Anticipating Trends in AI and Web Development

16

Next-Gen Development Environments and Advancements in AI Technologies   345

Preface

My journey in technology began at 14, as the internet became popular, sparking a lifelong commitment to innovation and anticipation of global demands. This path has led me to pivotal roles, such as managing the portfolio of technology and infrastructure projects for public security at the Rio 2016 Olympics, managing the portfolio of programs and projects for strategic initiatives, including the AI program at Brazil's Ministry of Science, Technology, and Innovation, and the national directorate of large-scale educational assessments in Brazil. This journey, marked by roles in IT governance, digital law, AI product management, machine learning engineering, internal audit, project management, and business strategies, underscores my commitment to leveraging AI for societal benefit. Today, I am honored to serve as a board member of the Global Centre for Risk and Innovation and represent Brazil as an innovation expert at the G20. These experiences have prepared me to contribute to the future of AI in web development, ensuring that this technology serves as a force for social good and innovation.

I began working on this book to address the multifaceted demands of integrating AI into web development. As AI technology advances at an unprecedented pace, web developers are challenged to keep up with these innovations while also navigating the complexities of creating personalized and efficient digital experiences. Recognizing a gap in the available resources, I aimed to provide a comprehensive guide that not only covers the theoretical aspects of AI but also delves deeply into practical techniques and approaches.

This book is designed to offer an integrated perspective, combining AI, web development, and DevOps to ensure a seamless and cohesive implementation of intelligent solutions. It includes detailed guidance on AI architecture, enabling developers to design and deploy AI systems with ease. Moreover, the book addresses strategic considerations, governance, risk management, ethics, regulation, and standards, presenting a holistic view of the challenges and opportunities in applying AI to web development.

By offering a blend of technical depth and strategic insights, this book equips you with the knowledge and skills needed to navigate the intricate landscape of AI in web development. It aims to empower developers to create smarter, more responsive websites while also fostering an understanding of the broader implications of AI, ensuring responsible and ethical use of this transformative technology.

You will gain an in-depth understanding of AI concepts applied to web development, including recommendation algorithms, pattern recognition, coding assistants, and much more. In addition, the book offers case studies and practical examples that will make it easier to apply the knowledge acquired to real projects.

Who this book is for

The target audience for this book is web developers with experience in programming languages, as well as a special interest in keeping up to date with the latest trends in integrating AI into web development. Specifically, full stack developers, frontend and backend developers, UI/UX designers, software engineers, and web development enthusiasts will find valuable information and practical guidelines to develop smarter websites using AI effectively. In addition, professionals who want to implement recommendation algorithms, take advantage of pattern recognition, or create personalized websites will benefit from the content of this book, which aims to hone their skills and enable them to revolutionize web development with AI.

To get the most out of the content of this book, it is necessary to have a basic understanding of programming languages such as HTML, CSS, and JavaScript. Familiarity with popular web development frameworks and tools will be beneficial. In addition, a basic knowledge of machine learning concepts and algorithms will help you to understand the AI implementations discussed throughout the book. While the book provides insights into the integration of AI into web development, a general understanding of design techniques and web development practices will enhance the understanding and application of the concepts presented. This book is particularly valuable for developers with experience in full stack, frontend, and backend technologies and curiosity about the applications of AI in web development.

What this book covers

The main challenge addressed by this book is the complexity and lack of clarity in the practical application of AI in web development. Many developers have a theoretical understanding of AI but struggle to implement this technology effectively in their projects. *AI Strategy for Web Development* offers a step-by-step guide to integrating AI into your development processes and overcoming technical and operational barriers.

The book is organized to guide you from the basics to advanced applications of AI in web development. We have divided the content into four main parts, each made up of chapters that complement each other and follow a logical progression.

Chapter 1, AI's Role in Shaping Web Development, examines how AI is transforming web development, exploring fundamental concepts of AI integration, practical examples, best practices, and ethical considerations.

Chapter 2, Mastering the Essentials – AI Fundamentals, dives into the AI fundamentals, from basic terminologies to practical applications of machine learning and the **Natural Language Process (NLP)**, providing a solid foundation for real-world application.

Chapter 3, Challenges and Opportunities – Integrating AI into Web Projects, explores the practical challenges and opportunities in AI integration, including the AI loop approach for continuous improvement, based on real-time feedback and data.

Chapter 4, Navigating the Landscape – Popular AI and ML Frameworks and Tools, covers the leading AI and ML frameworks and tools, with insights on selecting and using tools such as `scikit-learn` and NLTK to optimize your development environment.

Chapter 5, Blueprints of the Future – Architecting Effective AI Solutions, teaches you how to architect scalable and efficient AI solutions using the **AYai** or **Architect your Artificial Intelligence** method, with real-world case studies and practical examples to maintain and adapt AI architectures.

Chapter 6, Design Intelligence – Creating User-Centric Experiences with AI, explores how design intelligence can transform user-centric experiences through AI, focusing on personalization, optimizing user interfaces, and iterative design.

Chapter 7, Recognizing Patterns – Personalizing User Journeys with AI, focuses on pattern recognition and the use of AI to personalize user journeys, covering principles, predictive algorithms, and effective recommendation system implementation.

Chapter 8, Coding Assistants – Your Secret Weapon in Modern Development, examines the role of coding assistants as essential tools, demonstrating how AI-powered code completion can enhance productivity, code quality, and development efficiency.

Chapter 9, Smarter User Interactions – Elevating User Engagement with Advanced AI, delves into the transformative power of AI in enhancing user interactions on the web. Explore the integration of machine learning techniques, voice recognition, and advanced chatbots to boost user engagement. Topics include language pattern analysis, speech recognition, and utilizing generative models such as ChatGPT for AI-driven content creation.

Chapter 10, Smart Testing Strategies – Fortifying Web Applications with AI Insights, explores intelligent testing strategies that leverage AI to enhance the security, performance, and reliability of web applications. Learn about AI-driven test case generation, performance testing, security protocols, and bias detection, equipping yourself with the tools to protect applications against evolving threats.

Chapter 11, Augmented Workforce – AI's Impact on Web Development Jobs, covers the transformative effect of AI on web development roles. It focuses on optimizing human roles through AI augmentation, exploring the concept of an augmented workforce and the evolving responsibilities of developers. Gain practical insights on implementing AI-driven workforce strategies to stay ahead in the industry.

Chapter 12, Machine Users Unveiled – Navigating the Intersection of Human and Machine, investigates the rise of machine users and their impact on digital interfaces. Learn about profiling machine customers, exploring new market opportunities, and the architectural requirements to integrate machine user data sources and API platforms.

Chapter 13, AI-Augmented Development – Shaping Tomorrow's Digital Landscape, takes a futuristic look at AI in software engineering. It explores the integration of AI in design-to-code tools, coding assistants, and AI-augmented testing tools. You will learn how AI can enhance every stage of the development life cycle, making processes more efficient and innovative.

Chapter 14, From Idea to Reality – Crafting Intelligent Web Applications, focuses on the creation of intelligent web applications enhanced with AI. It follows the stages of ideation, design, implementation, and deployment, with an emphasis on AI's role in business analytics and user engagement. You will build applications that provide meaningful insights and improve user experiences.

Chapter 15, Guardians of the Digital Realm – Navigating Trust, Risk, and Ethics in AI, addresses the governance of AI models, with a focus on trustworthiness, fairness, and transparency. It explores the AI **TRiSM** or **Trust, Risk and Security in AI Models** (framework and discusses implementing ethical AI practices and robust governance structures, ensuring responsible and secure AI development.

Chapter 16, Next-Gen Development Environments and Advancements in AI Technologies, explores the future of development environments and AI technologies. It delves into GitOps workflows, cloud development tools, and cutting-edge AI advancements. You will gain actionable insights to integrate these technologies into your development workflows.

Chapter 17, Emerging Realities and Interfaces, examines the convergence of emerging technologies with web development. It investigates the integration of VR/AR, conversational user interfaces, and ubiquitous computing, showcasing how these advancements reshape user experiences.

Chapter 18, AI Regulation and Governance – Compliance with the EU's AI Act and ISO/IEC 42001 Standards, navigates the complexities of AI regulation, with a focus on the EU AI Act and ISO/IEC 42001 standards. You will learn how to implement robust governance frameworks, ensuring compliance with international guidelines. This chapter also introduces the G^3 AI Framework, offering a comprehensive approach to governance, risk management, and regulatory compliance, enhancing the security and ethical development of AI systems.

Each chapter is designed to build on the previous one, starting with the basics and then moving on to more complex applications. This flow ensures that you develop a solid understanding before diving into more advanced topics, making it easier to understand and apply the concepts in practice.

The writing style is clear and accessible, with straightforward language that aims to make it easy to understand, even for readers without a deep technical background. The aim is to ensure that your knowledge can easily be put into practice, allowing you to immediately apply what you have learned to your projects.

To get the most out of this book

To get the most out of this book, it is recommended that you have basic knowledge of programming languages such as HTML, CSS, and JavaScript, as well as a familiarity with machine learning concepts. However, the book is structured in such a way as to be accessible to both beginners and experienced professionals. This book covers a range of technologies that are crucial to the development of intelligent web applications. The main software and frameworks include the following:

Software/hardware covered in the book	Operating system requirements
Python 3.7 or higher	Windows, macOS, or Linux
GitHub Copilot	
Visual Studio Code	

To set up your development environment, follow these instructions:

1. **Install Python**: Download and install the latest version of Python from `python.org`.

2. **Set up Visual Studio Code**: Download and install Visual Studio Code from `code.visualstudio.com`.

3. **Set up GitHub Copilot**: Install GitHub Copilot as an extension in your preferred code editor, such as Visual Studio Code, following the instructions available at `copilot.github.com`.

By following these steps, you will be ready to explore the advanced AI techniques applied to web development discussed in this book.

If you are using the digital version of this book, we advise you to type the code yourself or access the code from the book's GitHub repository (a link is available in the next section). Doing so will help you avoid any potential errors related to the copying and pasting of code.

Access additional resources

To further support your learning and implementation of AI strategies for web development, we've compiled a list of additional resources that you can access. These resources include framework images, complementary tools, example code files, and more.

Explore the links below to enhance your understanding and application of the concepts covered in this book.

*   **Download Framework images**: Visit `https://g3ai.global` to download images related to the G³ AI Framework.

*   **Complementary tools and resources**: Explore `https://www.andersonfurtado.com/ai-strategies-for-web-development/` to download additional tools, such as canvases, interesting links, templates, case studies, and articles.

*   **Download the example code files**: You can download the example code files for this book from GitHub at `https://github.com/PacktPublishing/AI-Strategies-for-Web-Development`. If there's an update to the code, it will be updated in the GitHub repository.

*   **Other code**: We also have other code bundles from our rich catalog of books and videos available at `https://github.com/PacktPublishing/`. Check them out!

Conventions used

There are a number of text conventions used throughout this book.

`Code in text`: Indicates code words in text, database table names, folder names, filenames, file extensions, pathnames, dummy URLs, user input, and Twitter handles. Here is an example: "To get started, we need to import the libraries required for our sentiment analysis project. These libraries include `pandas` for data manipulation, `scikit-learn` for machine learning functionalities, `NLTK` for natural language processing tasks, and `zipfile` for handling compressed files."

A block of code is set as follows:

```
# Import necessary libraries
import pandas as pd
from sklearn.model_selection import train_test_split
from sklearn.feature_extraction.text import CountVectorizer
from sklearn.linear_model import LogisticRegression
from nltk.corpus import stopwords
from nltk.tokenize import word_tokenize
import zipfile
```

Bold style is used to emphasize a word or phrase. Here is an example: "This dataset contains 1.6 million tweets labeled as **0 (negative)**, **2 (neutral)**, or **4 (positive)**."

Italics style indicates important words or words that refer to a category, classification, or subject highlighted in the section. They are also used to reference figures or tables – for example, "*Table 4.1* highlights the distinctive features of each framework, providing a quick and easy comparison."

Keyword style is used for important keywords that are included in the glossary – for example, "**Natural Language Processing** (**NLP**) tools are crucial for web development projects that involve text analysis and processing."

Tips or important notes appear like this:

> Tip
> Please note that this is a simplified example and may not work directly without some modifications depending on your development environment. Please adjust it as necessary.

Get in touch

Feedback from our readers is always welcome.

General feedback: If you have questions about any aspect of this book, email us at `customercare@packtpub.com` and mention the book title in the subject of your message.

Errata: Although we have taken every care to ensure the accuracy of our content, mistakes do happen. If you have found a mistake in this book, we would be grateful if you would report this to us. Please visit `www.packtpub.com/support/errata` and fill in the form.

Piracy: If you come across any illegal copies of our works in any form on the internet, we would be grateful if you would provide us with the location address or website name. Please contact us at `copyright@packt.com` with a link to the material.

If you are interested in becoming an author: If there is a topic that you have expertise in and you are interested in either writing or contributing to a book, please visit `authors.packtpub.com`.

Join the AI Global Community: Connect with us and other readers in the AI Global Community on WhatsApp: `https://chat.whatsapp.com/BDd3j1SfySLClae4T7tole`.

LinkedIn group: Join our *AI Strategies for Web Development* LinkedIn group to engage in discussions and stay updated: `https://www.linkedin.com/groups/9861307/`.

Share your thoughts

Once you've read *AI Strategies for Web Development*, we'd love to hear your thoughts! Scan the QR code below to go straight to the Amazon review page for this book and share your feedback.

`https://packt.link/r/1835886310`

Your review is important to us and the tech community and will help us make sure we're delivering excellent quality content.

Download a free PDF copy of this book

Thanks for purchasing this book!

Do you like to read on the go but are unable to carry your print books everywhere?

Is your eBook purchase not compatible with the device of your choice?

Don't worry, now with every Packt book you get a DRM-free PDF version of that book at no cost.

Read anywhere, any place, on any device. Search, copy, and paste code from your favorite technical books directly into your application.

The perks don't stop there, you can get exclusive access to discounts, newsletters, and great free content in your inbox daily

Follow these simple steps to get the benefits:

1. Scan the QR code or visit the link below

https://packt.link/free-ebook/978-1-83588-630-4

2. Submit your proof of purchase
3. That's it! We'll send your free PDF and other benefits to your email directly

Part 1:
Embarking on the
AI Revolution in Web
Development

In this part, you will get an overview of the transformative impact of AI on web development, diving into fundamental concepts and practical applications. You will explore the integration of AI into web projects, understand the challenges and opportunities, and become familiar with popular AI and machine learning frameworks and tools. Additionally, you will learn how to architect effective AI solutions to create user-centric experiences. Special emphasis will be placed on the Architect Your AI (AYAI) framework and AI Loop process (continuous interaction between AI development, deployment, and feedback mechanisms), both of which are critical for developing robust and scalable AI-driven web solutions.

This part includes the following chapters:

- *Chapter 1, AI's Role in Shaping Web Development*
- *Chapter 2, Mastering the Essentials – AI Fundamentals*
- *Chapter 3, Challenges and Opportunities – Integrating AI into Web Projects*
- *Chapter 4, Navigating the Landscape – Popular AI and ML Frameworks and Tools*
- *Chapter 5, Blueprints of the Future – Architecting Effective AI Solutions*

1

AI's Role in Shaping Web Development

Welcome to the fascinating world of web development! Here, the possibilities are endless, especially with the addition of our powerful ally, **Artificial Intelligence (AI)**. Prepare to be amazed as we delve into the intricate details of AI strategies for web development and unravel the profound implications it has on the ever-evolving web development landscape. Get ready for an immersion into the future, where websites are not just static but intelligent, adaptive, and truly human.

In this realm of innovation and efficiency, AI takes center stage, revolutionizing the way we create and enhance websites. It acts as a guiding light, propelling us to new heights of success. With its intelligence and prowess, AI can become the driving force behind the most cutting-edge web development strategies.

From simple websites to interactive and personalized experiences, AI is redefining the boundaries of web development. In this chapter, we will explore the multiple dimensions of this phenomenon, highlighting fundamental transformations and emerging trends. You will not only understand how AI intertwines with web technologies but also how it becomes the driving force behind innovative experiences.

Throughout this journey, we will learn to identify opportunities for AI integration, elevating the user experience to unexplored heights. We will unravel practical strategies for successful integration, offering a clear vision of how to leverage powerful resources to create extraordinary web experiences.

The vastness of the AI tools ecosystem can be overwhelming, but worry not – we will guide you through this complex territory. From real-world examples to best practices and case studies, you will have a reliable map to navigate the diverse landscape of AI-driven development tools.

However, our dive into AI wouldn't be complete without addressing the ethical implications. We will discuss how to ensure responsible practices in AI-enhanced web development, emphasizing the importance of an ethical and sustainable approach. Because, in building the digital future, responsibility is as crucial as innovation.

This chapter serves as a foundation, preparing you for a journey that will transform not only your understanding of web development but also your ability to create something truly extraordinary. By the end of the chapter, you will not just understand AI – you will embody it, shaping the digital future with intelligence, innovation, and, above all, humanity.

AI will change the course of the relationship between machine and human, where technology meets creativity, and together we'll uncover the transformational impact of AI on web development.

In this chapter, we're going to cover the following main topics:

- Demystifying AI in web development
- Case study – Coca-Cola's "Create Real Magic" platform
- AI-powered transformations in web design
- The synergy of AI and **User Experience (UX)**
- Navigating through AI-driven development tools
- Ethical considerations in AI-enhanced web development

Demystifying AI in web development

The importance of AI cannot be overstated in today's rapidly evolving technological landscape. AI has revolutionized various industries and continues to shape the way we live and work.

One of the key reasons why AI is important is its ability to automate tasks that would otherwise require significant time and resources. This not only increases efficiency but also frees up human workers to focus on more complex and creative aspects of their jobs.

AI also plays a fundamental role in data analysis and decision-making. With its ability to process vast amounts of data at incredible speeds, AI algorithms can identify patterns, trends, and insights that humans may not be able to detect. This enables businesses to make more informed decisions, optimize processes, and improve overall performance.

Moreover, AI has the potential to enhance customer experiences through personalized recommendations, chatbots for instant support, and predictive analytics. By understanding customer preferences and behaviors, AI can deliver tailored solutions that meet individual needs effectively.

In addition to these practical applications, the development of AI fosters innovation across industries. It encourages researchers and developers to push boundaries in creating advanced algorithms and technologies that can solve complex problems.

Overall, the importance of AI lies in its ability to drive efficiency, improve decision-making processes, enhance customer experiences, and foster innovation. As technology continues to advance at an unprecedented pace, embracing AI becomes increasingly crucial for businesses looking to stay competitive in the digital age.

AI refers to the development of computer systems that can perform tasks that typically require human intelligence. It involves the creation of algorithms and models that enable machines to learn from data, recognize patterns, make decisions, and even mimic human behavior. AI encompasses various subfields such as machine learning, natural language processing, computer vision, and robotics.

At its core, AI aims to simulate human intelligence by enabling machines to understand and interpret information in a way that is similar to how humans do. This includes tasks such as problem-solving, decision-making, language understanding and generation, image recognition, and more.

The field of AI has seen significant advancements in recent years due to the availability of large datasets and improvements in computing power. As a result, AI has found applications across various industries including healthcare, finance, transportation, customer service, and marketing.

While there are different types of AI systems ranging from narrow (focused on specific tasks) to general (capable of performing any intellectual task), the ultimate goal of AI is often seen as achieving **artificial general intelligence** (**AGI**) – a level where machines can exhibit intelligence at par with or surpassing human capabilities.

However, it's important to note that AI is still evolving and has its limitations. While it can automate certain tasks efficiently and provide valuable insights from data analysis at scale, it lacks common sense and reasoning abilities possessed by humans. Nevertheless, AI continues to play an increasingly significant role in our lives and is poised to shape the future across various domains.

Introduction to the principles of AI

In the ever-evolving landscape of web development, an understanding of the core principles of AI is the bedrock for navigating its transformative potential. As we embark on this enlightening journey, it is crucial to unravel the fundamental tenets that underpin the realm of AI, providing you with a robust foundation to comprehend its applications, challenges, and profound implications. Now, let's unveil the pillars that uphold the transformative capabilities of AI:

- **Decoding the essence – a foundational imperative**: At the heart of AI lies a sophisticated interplay of algorithms, data, and computational intelligence. To comprehend this intricate dance, we must first decode the essence of AI's core principles. These principles, ranging from machine learning algorithms to neural network architectures, form the backbone of AI's problem-solving capabilities, enabling it to decipher patterns, make predictions, and evolve through experiences.

- **The power of learning – adaptive intelligence**: Fundamentally, AI's prowess rests on its ability to learn. Understanding the mechanisms of supervised learning, unsupervised learning, and reinforcement learning unveils the dynamic nature of AI. This adaptive intelligence empowers AI systems to not only perform predefined tasks but also learn and evolve in response to changing environments, a capability that mirrors the cognitive processes of human learning.

- **Data as the lifeblood – unleashing potential**: In the realm of AI, data assumes a role of paramount importance. Grasping the significance of data preprocessing, feature engineering, and the nuances of dataset curation is instrumental in unleashing the full potential of AI. The meticulous handling and utilization of data serve as the lifeblood that nourishes the AI ecosystem, allowing it to derive meaningful insights and make informed decisions.

- **Algorithms – crafting intelligence**: AI's intelligence is sculpted by a myriad of algorithms, each designed to address specific tasks and challenges. Whether it's the elegance of decision trees, the complexity of neural networks, or the efficiency of clustering algorithms, understanding the orchestration of these computational symphonies equips you to appreciate the intricacies of AI-powered solutions.

- **Ethical considerations – navigating the terrain**: Delving into the core principles of AI necessitates an exploration of the ethical considerations intertwined with its deployment. As we unravel the intricacies of machine ethics, bias mitigation, and responsible AI practices, you'll gain insights into navigating the ethical terrain, ensuring that AI is wielded as a force for good.

By comprehending these principles, you not only gain technical insights but also cultivate a holistic understanding of AI's role in shaping the future of web development.

In the upcoming section, we delve into the practical applications and case studies that illustrate how these AI problem-solving strategies are implemented in web development. By examining real-world examples, readers will gain insights into how AI's capabilities in search, classification, optimization, forecasting, and clustering are harnessed to enhance user experience, improve website functionality, and drive business outcomes.

AI problem-solving landscape

In the intricate world of AI, the spectrum of problems it can address is both vast and nuanced. As we embark on this journey through the diverse landscape of **AI problem-solving** within the pages of AI strategy for web development, let's delve deeper into the definitions, nuances, and real-world implications of various problem categories.

In the intricate world of AI, the spectrum of problems it can address is both vast and nuanced. At the core of AI lies the art of *search*, a process intricately woven into decision-making and problem-solving. This involves finding the optimal route in navigation systems or mapping out strategies in game-playing algorithms, highlighting search problems as the fundamental ability of AI to explore and navigate possibilities.

Moving on, *classification* emerges as a cornerstone of AI, involving the prediction of classes or categories for given inputs. Beyond the simplicity of spam filters, classification algorithms power recommendation systems, image recognition, and even medical diagnosis, showcasing the ability to decipher complexity and assign meaning to data as a testament to AI's classification prowess.

In its quest for excellence, AI engages in *optimization*, seeking the best possible solution within defined constraints. This dimension is illustrated through applications in supply chain management and financial portfolio optimization, where AI algorithms fine-tune decisions, underscoring the importance of optimization in achieving efficiency and superior outcomes.

Forecasting represents another integral part of AI, involving the *prediction of future* outcomes based on historical data. This capability extends beyond sales trends, with AI forecasting models playing crucial roles in weather predictions, stock market trends, and epidemiological projections, demonstrating the profound impact of AI on informed decision-making across various domains.

Lastly, the technique of *clustering*, which groups similar entities together, helps unravel patterns in seemingly chaotic datasets. With applications ranging from customer segmentation for targeted marketing to organizing vast datasets in machine learning, AI's ability to discern patterns and relationships significantly contributes to our understanding of complex systems. This exploration through the diverse landscape of AI problem-solving reveals the depth of its capabilities in web development and beyond, highlighting how each category of problem-solving not only addresses specific challenges but also advances the field as a whole.

However, the journey of AI problem-solving extends beyond these defined categories. The realm of AI introduces challenges such as transparency, bias mitigation, privacy concerns, ethical dilemmas, security risks, concentration of power, and dependency on AI systems. As we navigate through these intricacies, we not only explore the capabilities of AI but also confront the responsibilities that come with leveraging its potential.

In addition to the types of problems mentioned above, AI can also be used to solve a variety of other problems. For example, AI can be used to generate creative content, such as texts, images, and codes. However, AI also presents a number of challenges and problems, such as a lack of transparency, prejudice and discrimination, privacy concerns, ethical dilemmas, security risks, the concentration of power, and growing dependence on AI.

In the next section, we will explore in more detail how AI is transforming the field of web development and the significant implications it has on this industry. We'll delve into the specific applications, benefits, and potential challenges that arise when integrating AI into web development strategies.

AI's transformative role in web development

In the realm of web development, AI acts as your powerful ally, propelling innovation and efficiency to new heights. As we embark on this journey through the intricacies of AI's impact, let's uncover the profound implications it brings to the forefront of the web development landscape.

The core reason for delving into the impact of AI on web development is its transformative ability. AI becomes your silent orchestrator, streamlining your workflows, enhancing user experiences, and injecting dynamic adaptability that resonates with the evolving digital landscape. By understanding this impact, you, as a web developer, are not just an observer but an active participant in a paradigm shift shaping the future of the digital frontier.

One crucial aspect of AI's impact on web development is its knack for deciphering user behavior, preferences, and patterns with unprecedented accuracy. Through sophisticated algorithms, AI empowers you to create personalized and intuitive interfaces, fostering a deeper connection between users and the web applications they interact with. This personalization isn't just a trend but a psychological trigger that enhances user engagement and satisfaction, crucial considerations for your web development endeavors.

Moreover, the efficiency gains brought about by AI in web development are substantial. AI becomes your formidable ally, automating repetitive tasks, optimizing your code, and predicting potential issues. This efficiency isn't just a matter of convenience but a practical manifestation of time and resource optimization, a persuasive trigger for you, deeply invested in the field.

As we peel back the layers of AI's impact, ethical considerations take center stage. The responsible and ethical use of AI in web development isn't just a regulatory requirement but a moral imperative. By addressing these considerations head-on, you not only adhere to best practices but also contribute to the creation of a digital ecosystem that prioritizes trust and user well-being, a persuasive narrative in an era of growing digital skepticism.

In conclusion, exploring AI's impact on web development delves into a realm where innovation, efficiency, personalization, and ethics converge. By embracing and comprehending these implications, you can wield the tools to navigate the evolving digital landscape with acumen and foresight. *AI Strategies for Web Development* becomes your compass, guiding you on this transformative journey ahead.

Exploring the real-world applications of AI in various industries provides valuable insights into the potential and impact of this technology. In the following section, we will delve into a specific case study featuring Coca-Cola and its innovative use of AI to enhance creativity, improve operations, and connect with customers. This case study illustrates how a global leader in the beverage industry leverages AI to drive innovation and achieve business success.

Case study – Coca-Cola's "Create Real Magic" platform

Coca-Cola, in collaboration with OpenAI and Bain & Company, launched an innovative AI platform called "Create Real Magic". This platform is a pioneering example of how brands can leverage AI technology to enhance creativity and innovation:

- **Technical details**: The "Create Real Magic" platform combines the capabilities of two cutting-edge AI models developed by OpenAI: GPT-4 and DALL-E.

  - **GPT-4**: An advanced version of the Generative Pretrained Transformer models, GPT-4 is capable of producing human-like text from search engine queries. It uses machine learning techniques to understand and generate text that is contextually relevant and coherent.

  - **DALL-E** is an AI model that generates images based on text descriptions. It uses a variant of GPT-3, trained to generate images from textual prompts, providing a creative tool for generating original artwork.

- **Application**: Digital creatives around the world can use the "Create Real Magic" platform to generate original artwork using iconic creative assets from the Coca-Cola archives. This platform provides access to iconic creative assets from the Coca-Cola archives, which artists can download and incorporate into their creations. Upon completion of their works, artists can submit their pieces back to the platform. Selected works stand a chance to be showcased on Coca-Cola's digital billboards in Times Square, New York, and Piccadilly Circus, London.

- **Impact**: The "Create Real Magic" platform represents a significant step forward in the use of AI in the creative process. By combining text and image generation capabilities, the platform provides a powerful tool for digital creatives to experiment, iterate, and co-create with iconic brand assets.

  Moreover, the platform demonstrates how AI can be used to democratize the creative process, making it accessible to a wider range of individuals and opening up new possibilities for innovation.

- **Conclusion**: The "Create Real Magic" platform is a testament to the potential of AI in transforming the creative industry. As AI technology continues to advance, we can expect to see more innovative applications like this that push the boundaries of what is possible.

Coca-Cola, the world's largest beverage company, has also used AI in innovative ways to improve its operations and marketing. Here are some notable examples:

- **PIN code recognition**: Coca-Cola created a powerful, low-memory AI on cell phones for a promotional campaign. Consumers received rewards on the purchase of soft drinks by proving that they had purchased the products using a 14-character PIN code that came on the bottle caps and packaging. The company created its own **Convolutional Neural Network (CNN)** to detect features in an image and recognize the printed PINs.

- **Social media digitization**: Coca-Cola uses computer vision to detect photos of its products and algorithms to evaluate the sentiments of what people say about those photos or its brand in general. With more than 23 million points of sale, Coca-Cola needs to make sure it is sending out consistent brand messages without offending anyone.

- **Customer service via WhatsApp**: Through the Yalo **conversational commerce (c-commerce)** platform, which offers AI solutions, Coca-Cola has connected its industry with shopkeepers. Intelligent automation makes it possible to answer questions, provide product information, and even place orders, all via WhatsApp.

These are just a few examples of how Coca-Cola is using AI to improve its operations and customer experience. The company continues to explore new ways to use AI to drive success and innovation.

Continuing our exploration of AI's impact in various industries, let's shift our focus to the world of web design. In the next section, we will uncover how AI is revolutionizing the field of web design, leading to significant transformations and innovations. Specifically, in the next topic, we will delve into the evolution of web design through the lens of AI technology, highlighting its pivotal role in shaping the digital landscape.

AI-powered transformations in web design

In the late 1990s, amidst the dawn of the digital age, I embarked on a transformative journey into the realm of web design. The year 1999 marked a significant moment as I undertook my first course in web design, an endeavor that would unravel the foundational principles, intricate concepts, and evolving landscape of this burgeoning field.

As I delved into the course, the fundamentals of web design laid the groundwork for my understanding. HTML, the backbone of the web, became the language through which I could structure content. **Cascading Style Sheets** (**CSS**) brought forth the power to stylize and enhance the visual appeal of my work. These were the building blocks that formed the very essence of web design.

Concepts such as **user experience** (**UX**) and **user interface** (**UI**) design were introduced as guiding lights, steering the course beyond mere aesthetics. The realization dawned on me that effective web design transcends visuals; it's an immersive journey that caters to the user's needs and expectations.

In the late 1990s, the toolkit for web designers was still in its infancy. Dreamweaver emerged as a prominent ally, offering a visual interface to craft websites without delving too deep into code. Photoshop played a pivotal role in shaping visuals, while Flash introduced interactive elements that added a dynamic flair to the static web.

The context of technology was evolving rapidly. Dial-up connections were the norm, and considerations of bandwidth dictated design decisions. It was a delicate dance between creativity and practicality, where each element had to be meticulously crafted for an audience navigating the web at a slower pace.

As the new millennium unfolded, so did the web design landscape. The rise of **content management systems** (**CMS**) such as WordPress and Joomla democratized web development, allowing individuals and businesses to create and manage content with unprecedented ease.

The mid-2000s witnessed the advent of Web 2.0, a paradigm shift that emphasized user-generated content, collaboration, and a more dynamic user experience. Design trends evolved with a focus on simplicity, intuitive navigation, and responsive layouts.

The subsequent years brought forth the mobile revolution, propelling web design into the era of responsiveness. With the proliferation of smartphones and tablets, the demand for websites that seamlessly adapted to various screen sizes became paramount.

Fast forward to the present, and the trajectory of web design is rich and diverse. AI and machine learning are introducing unprecedented levels of personalization and interactivity. Frameworks such as React and Vue.js are redefining how we approach frontend development. Design systems and component-based architectures are streamlining workflows, fostering consistency across digital platforms.

The journey from the late 1990s to the present has been a testament to the dynamic nature of web design. From static HTML pages to dynamic, data-driven interfaces, the evolution continues. As I reflect on that first course in 1999, I recognize that it wasn't just a lesson in design; it was an initiation into a field that would continually challenge, inspire, and shape the digital landscape we navigate today.

Why is AI's presence in web design not just a trend but a necessity?

In web design, the integration of AI stands as a transformative force, reshaping traditional paradigms and unlocking innovative possibilities. This section explores the pivotal role played by AI in the realm of web design, shedding light on its multifaceted applications that redefine the way we conceptualize, create, and interact with digital content.

AI is the secret ingredient in this exploration, weaving itself into the very fabric of web design. It's more than just a tool; it's a transformative force, breathing efficiency, personalization, and innovation into every pixel. Mastering AI's subtle touches isn't just about technical prowess; it's about unleashing the full spectrum of possibilities within modern web design.

AI's role in web design goes beyond being a passive tool; it emerges as a dynamic partner in the creative process. This section meticulously dissects the layers of AI's involvement, highlighting its capacity to streamline workflows, provide data-driven insights, and contribute to the birth of innovative design solutions. Understanding AI's role is akin to unlocking a treasure trove of possibilities for designers, where efficiency meets creativity in perfect harmony.

The question arises: *why is AI not just a fleeting trend but an indispensable element in the evolution of web design?* The exploration of AI's role in web design goes beyond surface-level observations. AI has become a necessity today because it addresses the contemporary challenges faced by designers. From the demand for personalized user experiences to the need for streamlined design processes, AI emerges as the solution that bridges the gap between creative aspirations and practical execution.

AI's integration is not about replacing designers but enhancing their capabilities. By automating routine tasks, analyzing vast datasets, and offering predictive insights, AI becomes a powerhouse that accelerates the design process. The result is not just speed but a newfound efficiency that allows designers to channel their energy into more complex and creative aspects of their work.

In the era of user-centric design, personalization is paramount. AI's ability to analyze user behavior, preferences, and trends empowers designers to tailor experiences on an individual level. This personal touch is not just a luxury but a necessity to engage modern audiences accustomed to bespoke digital interactions.

Web design is not static; it's a field that thrives on innovation. AI becomes a necessity as it opens doors to new possibilities. From automated design suggestions to avant-garde concepts generated by machine learning algorithms, AI acts as a catalyst for pushing the boundaries of what's conceivable in web design.

As we navigate through the profound implications of AI in web design, it becomes evident that embracing AI is not a choice but a strategic decision. It's about staying relevant in a landscape where design is not just about aesthetics but an intricate dance between human creativity and technological prowess.

Key concepts in AI-powered web design

In this riveting exploration of AI-powered transformations in web design, our journey takes a pivotal turn as we delve into the key concepts that form the very heart of this technological revolution. As we unfold the layers, two paramount concepts come to the forefront: *machine learning in design optimization* and *neural networks and creative design processes*.

Let's learn more about them.

Machine learning, a subset of artificial intelligence, is not just a buzzword; it's the engine driving design optimization into new frontiers. Understanding how machine learning algorithms operate in the realm of web design is essential for unlocking unparalleled efficiency and user-centricity.

In the context of design optimization, machine learning acts as a discerning ally. It learns from user interactions, analyzes patterns, and adapts designs to align with user preferences dynamically. From personalized content recommendations to adaptive layouts, machine learning optimizes every facet of the user experience.

Consider a scenario where a website learns from user navigation, tailoring its interface to individual preferences. Machine learning optimizes the arrangement of elements, predicts user needs, and crafts an experience that evolves with each interaction. The result? Enhanced engagement, satisfaction, and a digital landscape that feels tailor-made for every user.

Neural networks, mirroring the intricate workings of the human brain, introduce a touch of creativity and intuition into the design process. Grasping the significance of neural networks is akin to unlocking the gateway to innovative, aesthetically pleasing, and emotionally resonant design.

In the realm of creative design processes, neural networks shine as brilliant collaborators. They analyze vast datasets of design elements, styles, and user preferences, learning the essence of what appeals to human senses. The result? AI-driven suggestions, style predictions, and even the generation of entirely new and imaginative design elements.

Traditionally, design processes were confined to human insights and artistic flair. Neural networks challenge these boundaries by exploring uncharted territories. They bring forth design suggestions that might elude the human mind, pushing the envelope of what's conceivable in the design space.

By understanding the synergy between neural networks and creative design processes, we witness the fusion of art and technology. It's not about replacing human creativity but amplifying it. Neural networks become co-creators, infusing designs with a blend of data-driven precision and artistic intuition.

As we venture into the exciting chapters of AI strategy for web development, these key concepts play a vital role in guiding us toward a future where web design goes beyond boundaries, continuously learns, and creates digital experiences that deeply resonate with each individual user. This journey has only just begun, and the seamless combination of machine learning and creative design processes propels us towards a vast horizon of boundless innovation.

AI's benefits for web design

Here, we will explore the specific advantages and benefits that AI brings to the field of web design. These advantages are essential for designers looking to harness the power of AI in their work, as they streamline processes, enhance creativity, and improve the overall efficiency of web design. Let's dive into the key advantages of AI in web design:

- **AI tools for web designers**: There are several AI tools available that can help web designers streamline their workflow. These tools can automate repetitive tasks, allowing designers to focus on more creative aspects of design. Additionally, AI can assist in identifying design trends, providing insights into user behavior, and even generating designs automatically.

- **AI-assisted design**: AI is also being utilized to create more realistic virtual environments, making the design process more immersive and efficient. For example, designers can use **Augmented Reality (AR)** applications to visualize their designs in a real environment and make real-time adjustments. This enables designers to test their designs in different scenarios and make necessary adjustments.

- **AI-powered website builders**: Platforms such CodeDesign.ai are leveraging AI technology to revolutionize the way we approach website development. With these tools, you don't need in-depth knowledge of HTML, CSS, or JavaScript to build an attractive and functional website. This makes website design more accessible for individuals without coding experience.

- **AI in content platforms**: Tess AI is a platform that utilizes state-of-the-art AI models to generate texts, images, codes, and more in a short amount of time. This can be extremely useful for website designers as it allows them to generate high-quality content quickly.

Thus, AI is playing an increasingly significant role in website design. As AI technology continues to advance, we are likely to see even more innovations in this area. AI not only makes the design process more efficient, but also opens up new possibilities for creativity and innovation.

The synergy of AI and user experience

In today's digital world, it's no secret that UX is more important than ever. Users expect websites and apps to be easy to use, intuitive, and engaging. AI has the potential to revolutionize UX by making it more personalized, efficient, and effective.

Shaping the present and future of digital interactions, the synergy between AI and UX stands as a pivotal topic, as we delve into this profound alliance, it is crucial to unravel the dynamic relationship between AI and UX, understanding the transformative impact that AI holds in enhancing the user experience.

The integration of AI and UX represents a dynamic and symbiotic partnership. AI, with its ability to process vast amounts of data and learn patterns, brings a new dimension to UX design. It's not merely about technology assisting design; it's about cohesively intertwining intelligence into the fabric of the user experience.

The transformative impact of AI on UX is nothing short of revolutionary. AI empowers designers to move beyond static interfaces, enabling personalized, adaptive, and anticipatory user experiences. It goes beyond traditional design constraints, opening doors to innovation and a deeper understanding of user behavior.

In the upcoming pages, we will explore how AI contributes to a personalized and seamless user journey, examine real-world examples of AI-driven UX improvements, identify key opportunities for AI integration, and highlight user-centric AI applications. Each aspect plays a crucial role in shaping a digital landscape where AI and UX coalesce harmoniously, setting the stage for an enhanced and intuitive user experience.

The transformative impact of AI on UX

AI and UX are two complementary disciplines that can work together to create better experiences for users. AI can be used to collect data about users, analyze that data, and make predictions about their behavior. This information can then be used to improve UX by making websites and apps more personalized, relevant, and useful.

The dynamic relationship between AI and UX is rooted in their ability to complement each other seamlessly. AI serves as the data-driven backbone, collecting and analyzing user data to gain insights into their behavior. This information becomes the cornerstone for UX improvements, leading to websites and apps that adapt to users' preferences, providing a more personalized, relevant, and useful digital environment.

AI has the potential to have a transformative impact on UX in a number of ways. Here are a few examples:

- **Enhanced personalization**: Content personalization is the process of adapting content to a specific audience. This can be done based on a variety of factors, such as location, interests, behavior, or browsing history. AI's prowess in personalization extends to recommending tailored content, adapting website layouts, and offering personalized support. This multifaceted approach ensures a more engaging and relevant experience, fostering a stronger connection between users and digital platforms.

- **Efficiency amplification**: By automating repetitive tasks such as content generation, query responses, and issue resolution, AI liberates human users to concentrate on creative and strategic endeavors. This not only enhances efficiency but also opens avenues for more meaningful user interactions.

- **Proactive problem solving**: AI, when intricately woven into UX, goes beyond reactive responses. It anticipates user needs, identifies pain points, and proactively suggests solutions, elevating the overall user experience.

- **Effectiveness**: AI's analytical capabilities shine in enhancing effectiveness by scrutinizing user data to unveil patterns. This invaluable insight guides the refinement of the user experience, identifying areas for improvement and ensuring continuous enhancement.

The infusion of AI-driven enhancements isn't a luxury but a strategic move with far-reaching benefits for both designers and end-users. Let's look at the benefits.

- **Elevated user engagement**: By harnessing the power of AI, UX designers can create experiences that captivate users. Personalized recommendations, anticipatory design, and adaptive interfaces contribute to a more engaging digital journey.

- **Data-backed decision making**: AI's analytical prowess enables designers to make informed decisions. By analyzing user behavior, predicting trends, and identifying patterns, AI equips UX designers with invaluable insights for refining and optimizing digital interfaces.

- **Future-ready design**: In an era of rapid technological evolution, AI integration ensures that UX designs remain agile and adaptable. Future-proofing the design process becomes a reality as AI-driven enhancements continuously evolve to meet changing user expectations.

AI emerges as a potent ally in the pursuit of optimizing UX. By comprehending the symbiotic relationship between AI and UX, web developers can harness the full potential of these disciplines to craft digital experiences that are not only personalized but also efficient and effective. This understanding paves the way for a user-centric digital landscape, where AI and UX collaborate harmoniously to create unparalleled user experiences.

When combined, AI and UX can create a symphony of benefits that transform not only digital interaction, but also user loyalty and financial performance. Let's delve into some of these benefits that outline a new era in crafting digital experiences.

Personalization empowered by AI redefines the user experience, adjusting to individual interests and behaviors. This personalized touch not only heightens user satisfaction but also fosters a deeper engagement. The result is user loyalty that transcends expectations, driving, in turn, revenues and financial outcomes.

AI's predictive analysis deciphers patterns in user behavior, opening doors for a tactical increase in the conversion rate. By identifying products with a high probability of interest, AI strategically positions these elements at the digital forefront. This targeted approach not only boosts conversions but also optimizes the user journey.

Automation promoted by AI comes into play to alleviate repetitive tasks, freeing up human resources for more complex challenges. Whether in responding to frequently asked questions or resolving straightforward issues, AI not only reduces operational costs but also accelerates response times.

To fully embrace this synergy, close collaboration between UX designers, data scientists, and AI engineers becomes crucial. This strategic partnership ensures not only effective use of AI to enhance UX, but also optimization of UX to maximize the benefits of AI. Embark on this journey where efficiency meets user satisfaction, redefining the parameters of the digital experience.

Case study – Dell conquers marketing challenges with Persado – a data-driven, customer-centric success story

In this section, we will explore how the synergy between AI and UX is reshaping the digital landscape through an example. We will delve into the profound impact of AI on UX, highlighting how it enhances personalization, efficiency, and effectiveness in designing websites and applications to meet the evolving expectations of users in today's digital world.

In today's hyper-competitive landscape, effective marketing hinges on personalized messaging that resonates with diverse audiences. Yet, many companies struggle to overcome stagnant response rates, inconsistent voice across channels, and the inability to leverage data-driven insights. Dell, a global leader in technology, faced these very challenges head-on, leading them to forge a transformative partnership with Persado, the AI pioneer in creative marketing.

Dell's integration of AI extends beyond email marketing, encompassing promotional and lifecycle emails, Facebook ads, display banners, direct mail, and even radio content. Through the implementation of Persado's AI capabilities, Dell has embraced a data-centric and customer-focused approach to enhance content across its marketing spectrum. This transformation ensures that Dell's customers receive personalized messaging, fostering higher engagement, valuable insights, increased revenue, and augmented brand loyalty.

Persado's AI became the engine powering Dell's customer-centric transformation. By analyzing vast amounts of data and understanding audience preferences, Persado crafted personalized content that resonated deeply with each segment. This data-driven approach resulted in the following:

- Dell's emails captured customer attention and compelled action, fostering greater engagement.

- *46% increase in conversions for small businesses*: Persado's personalized messaging resonated with the specific needs and concerns of small businesses, driving conversions and boosting the bottom line.

- *77% increase in average add-to-cart rate for Facebook ads*: Targeted AI-powered ads cut through the noise, turning casual scrollers into active buyers

Dell's journey with Persado extends beyond impressive stats. The partnership allowed Dell to adopt and amplify best practices in technical writing. They learned to do the following:

- **Focus on the benefits**: Persado's AI helped Dell craft messaging that highlighted the value proposition and tangible benefits for each audience

- **Utilize action words**: Compelling verbs and clear calls to action spurred readers to take the desired next step

- **Create a sense of urgency**: Persado's AI-crafted messages instilled a sense of timeliness, encouraging immediate engagement

These best practices, coupled with the power of AI-driven personalization, fostered stronger brand loyalty among Dell's diverse customer base. Personalized outreach built trust and strengthened the connection between Dell and its customers.

Dell's success story with Persado serves as a blueprint for businesses seeking to conquer marketing challenges and achieve impactful results. It demonstrates the power of the following:

- **Embracing AI**: Leveraging AI-powered platforms such as Persado empowers businesses to deliver hyper-personalized content, improve engagement, and drive conversions

- **Adopting data-driven insights**: Analyzing customer data allows companies to understand their audience, tailor messaging, and optimize campaigns for maximum impact

- **Focusing on customer-centricity**: Delivering personalized experiences builds trust, fosters loyalty, and ultimately drives long-term success

Next, let's take a look at user-centric AI-driven development.

User-centric AI-driven development

Dell's journey with Persado vividly illustrates the profound impact of AI-driven strategies in shaping customer experiences and enhancing brand performance. As we delve into the realm of user-centric AI-driven development, we embark on a journey that mirrors Dell's commitment to innovation and personalized engagement. Thus, AI becomes the linchpin in understanding users at an intricate level. From user research to the meticulous definition of IA goals, and through the intricate design of AI interactions, we unfold a comprehensive guide to seamlessly integrating AI into the development process. Let's explore these pivotal stages in detail, starting from the initial compass of understanding the user to the ultimate goal of achieving a virtuous cycle of user experience evaluation:

1. **Understanding the user – our initial compass**: At the heart of user-centric development lies the quest for a profound understanding of those for whom we design our digital creations. We delve into the intricate layers of user research, unveil personas embodying our audience, and chart the user journey—a map revealing key moments in their interaction with us.

2. **Defining goals for AI – the strategic alliance**: The next step takes us to goal definition, a strategic alignment that bridges business objectives with user expectations. By establishing clear goals for both the organization and the end user, we lay a solid foundation for the intelligent application of AI.

3. **AI interaction design – the harmonious collaboration**: Our journey advances to interaction design, where we carefully outline AI workflows, implement intelligent feedback mechanisms, and promote transparency in AI operations. It is at this stage that the collaboration between humans and machines becomes a harmonious dance.

4. **AI implementation – from prototyping to reality**: With goals and interactions defined, we dive into the practical implementation of AI. We prototype, test with real users, and iterate, constantly refining our solutions before widespread implementation.

5. **User experience evaluation – the virtuous cycle**: Our journey culminates in the evaluation of user experience, where we establish success metrics, open channels for valuable user feedback, and undertake continuous adjustments and optimizations. This virtuous cycle ensures that our creations evolve in harmony with dynamic user expectations.

In this section on user-centric AI-driven development, we've embarked on the innovative spirit exemplified by Dell's strategic partnership with Persado. From understanding users at a profound level through meticulous research to defining strategic AI goals, designing harmonious AI interactions, implementing with precision, and evaluating the user experience in a virtuous cycle, we've laid the groundwork for a paradigm shift in digital development. This comprehensive guide isn't just a theoretical exploration but a practical roadmap to infuse AI seamlessly into the user-centric development process.

Transitioning from user-centric AI-driven development, our next focus is on AI-driven development tools. In the coming section, we'll dive into the practical tools empowering developers, designers, and data scientists in maximizing AI's potential. From prototyping to implementation, these tools serve as the practical guide for seamless AI integration in web development. Let's get straight into the toolbox propelling us toward the future of digital innovation.

Navigating through AI-driven development tools

As we delve into the realm of web development and explore the use of **AI driven tools**, it is fundamental to grasp the importance these tools bring to the table. The journey starts by understanding the reasons why AI tools have become indispensable in today's landscape and how they seamlessly integrate into the complex process of web development.

There are reasons why AI tools have gained relevance in the world of web developers. Firstly, they enable automation allowing web developers to dedicate their time and energy towards strategic endeavours. Secondly, AI enhances the efficiency and effectiveness of web development processes. Lastly, it aids in creating captivating user experiences.

To comprehend the profound impact of AI tools, we must first recognize their significance in the broader context of technological evolution. AI tools are catalysts for innovation, empowering developers, and designers to transcend traditional boundaries. These tools harness the power of machine learning, predictive analysis, and intelligent automation, ushering in a new era of efficiency and possibilities.

It's crucial to recognize that AI tools are not just about automating tasks, they're about augmenting human capabilities. From streamlining development workflows to enhancing user experiences, these tools play a pivotal role in elevating the entire web development process. They provide developers with powerful functionalities and insights that can greatly improve productivity and efficiency. With AI tools, tasks that once required a significant amount of time and effort can now be accomplished in a fraction of the time.

Moreover, AI tools are not restricted to just developers; they have a wide range of applications for various industries. From analyzing large sets of data to predicting trends and patterns, AI tools can assist businesses in making informed decisions and staying ahead in a competitive market.

AI tools have revolutionized the web development process and have become indispensable in today's digital landscape. Their ability to automate tasks provides valuable insights and enhances user experiences, making them invaluable assets for businesses and individuals alike. Embracing AI tools can lead to increased productivity, efficiency, and ultimately, success in the highly competitive world of web development.

AI-powered tools and technologies for web development

The field of web development is rapidly changing, driven by the incorporation of advanced AI-driven tools and technologies. These advancements not only simplify the web development procedure but also present exciting new opportunities. Let's delve into some of the primary AI-powered tools that are revolutionizing the web development industry, as follows:

- Code generation tools
- Testing tools
- Security tools

Now, let's look at them in a little more detail.

Code generation tools

First, we'll look at the code generation tools.

Code generation tools stand out as an important category within web development, leveraging the capabilities of AI to automatically produce code. The primary objective of these tools is to expedite the development process, minimize errors, and enhance the overall efficiency of projects. These tools offer a spectrum of the following functionalities:

- **Code completion**: Code generation tools excel in suggesting relevant code as developers write, saving time and preventing errors by providing accurate and context-aware code suggestions.
- **New code generation**: Going beyond completion, these tools can generate entirely new code based on natural language descriptions or sketches. This functionality proves valuable for tasks such as prototyping or creating custom code tailored to specific requirements.

- **Task automation**: An additional benefit of code generation tools is their capacity to automate repetitive tasks, such as creating components or generating documentation. This automation not only increases efficiency but also allows developers to focus on more creative and strategic aspects of their work. As we explore the realm of AI-powered code generation tools, it becomes evident that they are indispensable allies, enhancing the coding experience and streamlining the development workflow.

Some popular code-generation tools include the following:

- **GitHub Copilot**: This tool offers AI-powered code completion and is trained on a massive dataset of open-source code. It offers suggestions as you type, adapting to your coding style and preferences. GitHub Copilot streamlines coding, reduces errors, improves productivity, and fosters learning by exposing developers to diverse code patterns.

- **Amazon CodeWhisperer**: This tool integrates with various IDEs, suggests code snippets in multiple programming languages, generates code from natural language descriptions, and offers security and bias scanning. It enhances developer productivity, promotes code quality, and supports diverse development workflows.

- **ChatGPT**: This is a conversational AI capable of generating different creative text formats, including code snippets in response to natural language prompts. It explores code generation possibilities through natural language interaction, fostering experimentation and creativity.

- **Sketch2Code**: This tool translates hand-drawn UI designs or wireframes into HTML code, bridging the gap between design and development. It accelerates prototyping, saves development time, and empowers designers to contribute directly to code generation.

- **OpenAI Codex**: Powered by GPT-3, the tool generates code in various languages, translates natural language into code, and explains code in plain language. It enhances developer productivity, facilitates code understanding, and enables collaboration between developers and non-technical stakeholders.

- **Tabnine**: This is an AI-powered code completion tool that adapts to individual coding styles, offering highly personalized suggestions. It boosts productivity, reduces errors, and promotes coding efficiency.

- **PyCharm**: This tool is an intelligent Python IDE with AI-assisted code completion, refactoring, and debugging capabilities. It enhances Python development with AI-powered features, improving code quality and developer efficiency.

- **Kite**: This is a cross-language code completion tool supporting multiple IDEs and editors, providing context-aware suggestions and documentation lookup. It streamlines coding across different languages, improves code comprehension, and offers a unified coding experience.

- **Codiga**: This is an AI-powered platform for code quality analysis, code review automation, and coding insights. It enhances code quality, enforces best practices, and streamlines code review processes.

- **Codota**: This is an AI-powered code completion tool with insights from open-source code, suggesting patterns and solutions from a vast knowledge base. It leverages collective coding knowledge to promote code reuse and improve code quality.

- **CodeWP**: This is a no-code platform for building web applications using natural language instructions, enabling code generation without coding expertise. It democratizes web development, empowers non-technical users to create web apps, and streamlines prototyping and development processes.

- **Replit Ghostwriter**: This is an AI-powered tool that suggests code lines or entire functions within the Replit coding environment, fostering experimentation and learning. It enhances coding fluency, encourages exploration, and promotes hands-on learning.

- **Seek**: This is an AI-powered code search tool that helps developers find relevant code snippets from various sources, fostering code reuse and knowledge sharing. It improves code discovery, accelerates development, and promotes collaboration and knowledge transfer within the developer community.

Code generation AI tools offer several benefits, including the following:

- **Unlocking developer efficiency**: Code generation tools empower developers to write code with unprecedented speed and efficiency, freeing up valuable time and energy for more creative and strategic pursuits

- **Minimizing errors through precision**: By crafting code that adheres to syntactical accuracy and full functionality, these tools effectively reduce errors, ensuring the quality and reliability of the software

- **Streamlining processes to maximize productivity**: Code generation tools streamline development processes by automating repetitive tasks, allowing developers to focus their attention on more impactful initiatives, ultimately optimizing overall project efficiency

Next, we'll look at the testing tools.

Testing tools

In the field of web development, **testing** is paramount for ensuring the quality, reliability, and user satisfaction of web applications. Fortunately, AI-powered tools are revolutionizing the testing landscape, automating tasks, improving accuracy, and accelerating testing processes.

Let's explore some of these groundbreaking tools:

- **DeepCode**: This delves into code analysis with AI-powered precision, detecting bugs, vulnerabilities, and code quality issues automatically. It enhances code quality, reduces debugging time, and fosters better coding practices.

- **Bugsee**: Bugsee revolutionizes bug reporting with real-time video recordings and logs, providing invaluable insights into user behavior and bug replication. It streamlines bug identification and resolution, reduces time-to-fix, and improves user experience.

- **Selenium**: Selenium is a widely used browser automation tool that allows you to test web applications across multiple browsers and platforms. It supports a wide range of browsers and platforms, including Chrome, Firefox, Edge, Safari, and Android. Selenium also allows you to automate a wide range of tasks, including navigation, form filling, and interacting with user interface elements. Selenium is a free and open-source tool. It is a good choice for general browser automation testing.

- **JMeter**: JMeter is a load testing tool that allows you to simulate heavy loads on web applications to evaluate performance. It allows you to create custom test scripts to simulate real user loads. JMeter also supports a wide range of protocols, including HTTP, HTTPS, and FTP. JMeter allows you to collect performance data, such as response time and throughput. JMeter is a free and open-source tool. It is a good choice for load testing web applications.

- **Postman**: Postman is an API testing tool that allows you to test web APIs and verify that they are working correctly. It allows you to send custom HTTP requests to web APIs. Postman also supports a wide range of protocols, including HTTP, HTTPS, and SOAP. Postman allows you to collect API responses, including JSON, XML, and text data.

- **Applitools**: Harnessing visual AI, Applitools safeguards the visual integrity of web applications across diverse devices and screen sizes. It ensures pixel-perfect rendering, enhances UX, and eliminates visual bugs that often escape traditional testing methods.

- **Cypress**: Cypress is a frontend testing tool that allows you to test web applications across multiple browsers and platforms. It uses an event-based approach to testing, allowing you to test web applications the same way real users do. Cypress also supports a wide range of browsers and platforms, including Chrome, Firefox, Edge, Safari, and Android. Cypress allows you to collect test data, such as screenshots and videos.

- **Testim**: Testim leverages machine learning to automate testing processes, intelligently creating, executing, and maintaining tests. It accelerates test creation and execution, reduces manual effort, and adapts to evolving application features.

The integration of AI tools in the testing phase brings about a multitude of **benefits**, revolutionizing traditional testing methodologies.

Here are some compelling advantages of incorporating AI tools into the testing process:

- **Efficiency amplification**: AI tools significantly enhance testing efficiency by automating repetitive tasks, allowing for faster execution of test cases. This not only accelerates the testing lifecycle but also frees up human resources to focus on more complex and strategic aspects of development.

- **Precision in issue detection**: The analytical capabilities of AI enable precise identification of potential issues and vulnerabilities within the code. AI tools can analyze vast amounts of data, offering a thorough examination of the application and ensuring comprehensive issue detection.

- **Real-time bug reporting**: AI-powered testing tools often provide real-time bug reporting with additional features such as video and logs. This facilitates prompt and comprehensive bug tracking, enabling developers to swiftly address and rectify issues as they arise.

- **Adaptability to changes**: AI tools excel in adapting to changes in the codebase and application functionalities. They can automatically adjust test cases based on modifications in the software, ensuring that testing remains relevant and effective in dynamic development environments.

- **Optimized test creation**: Machine learning algorithms integrated into AI testing tools contribute to optimized test creation. These tools can analyze historical data to generate test cases that are more likely to uncover critical issues, improving the overall effectiveness of the testing process.

- **Enhanced test coverage**: AI tools can extend test coverage by efficiently handling a large number of test cases across various scenarios and devices. This broader coverage ensures that potential issues are identified under diverse conditions, leading to more robust and reliable applications.

- **Continuous improvement**: AI's learning capabilities allow testing tools to continuously evolve and improve over time. With each testing cycle, these tools learn from previous results and user interactions, refining their algorithms and enhancing their ability to detect and predict issues.

By incorporating the power of AI tools into the testing phase, we can not only streamline the development process but also elevate the overall quality and reliability of web applications to new heights. These AI-driven testing tools bring efficiency, precision, and adaptability to the table, making them truly invaluable assets in our quest to deliver top-notch, flawless software. Get ready to witness high-performance and error-free applications like never before.

Next, we'll look at the security tools.

Security tools

AI security tools refer to a set of innovative technologies and solutions designed to protect digital systems and networks from cyber threats. These tools play a crucial role in safeguarding sensitive data and preventing unauthorized access. In today's rapidly evolving digital landscape, where cyberattacks are becoming more sophisticated and frequent, the importance of AI security tools cannot be overstated. They provide organizations with the necessary defense mechanisms to detect, prevent, and mitigate potential risks to their digital infrastructure. From intrusion detection systems to anomaly detection algorithms, AI security tools offer a wide range of applications that help organizations stay one step ahead of cybercriminals. To give you a better idea of their versatility, let's review some commonly used AI-powered security tools:

- **IBM Security**: IBM Security provides AI-powered solutions that optimize analysts' time by accelerating threat detection, expediting responses, and protecting user identity and datasets

- **Microsoft Security Copilot**: This AI cybersecurity product enables security professionals to respond to cyberthreats quickly, process signals at machine speed, and assess risk exposure in minutes

- **Darktrace**: Darktrace's AI technology detects and responds to cyber threats in real time, providing autonomous defense against emerging attacks

- **Cylance**: Cylance's AI-powered endpoint security solution uses machine learning to identify and prevent malware and other cyber threats

- **Cloudflare**: This tool uses AI-powered security features, including threat detection and mitigation, to bolster web security

- **Homomorphic encryption**: This advanced encryption technique preserves data privacy during computation, enhancing overall security

- **reCAPTCHA**: Google's tool uses AI to distinguish between human and automated access, fortifying web forms against spam

- **Akismet**: Employing machine learning, Akismet filters out spam comments, safeguarding websites from malicious content

These are just a few examples of how AI is revolutionizing web security. By embracing these intelligent tools, businesses and individuals can build a stronger defensive perimeter, staying ahead of evolving threats and ensuring a safer digital experience for all.

Traditionally, cybersecurity has been a battle of wits between humans and hackers, leaving room for error and vulnerability. This new breed of defender leverages AI to automate tasks, enhance decision-making, and outmaneuver evolving threats with remarkable efficiency.

Here's why these AI tools are revolutionizing the cybersecurity landscape:

- **Cost-efficiency through automation**: AI streamlines data collection, transforming incident response into a dynamic, real-time dance. By automating repetitive tasks, it frees up security professionals to focus on strategic value-add activities, boosting overall efficiency and cost-effectiveness.

- **Human error? Not here**: Human oversight is a known weak point in conventional security. AI eliminates this vulnerability by taking over most security processes, minimizing the risk of costly human error. This resource reallocation allows skilled personnel to tackle more critical challenges.

- **Smarter decisions, stronger defense**: AI analyzes data like a hawk, constantly learning and identifying vulnerabilities in your security posture. It can automate threat detection, trigger alerts, and even uncover new malware strains, proactively safeguarding your valuable data.

- **Frictionless security, elevated protection**: Balancing security with user experience is no longer a zero-sum game. AI can analyze risk levels for each login attempt and verify users through behavioral data, making access smooth for legitimate users while reducing fraud costs by up to 90%.

- **Machine speed against malicious minds**: No human can react to threats as fast and accurately as AI. These intelligent tools respond to cyberattacks with split-second precision, freeing up security professionals to handle more complex tasks and maintain organizational resilience.

The rise of AI-powered security tools marks a paradigm shift in the ongoing battle against cyber threats. By embracing these intelligent defenders, businesses and individuals can confidently build a robust, proactive security posture, leaving hackers scrambling to catch up. It's time to move beyond the limitations of traditional defenses and embrace the power of AI to secure your digital future.

Key considerations in navigating AI-driven development tools

Embarking on the integration of AI-driven development tools demands meticulous navigation through a complex landscape, with a sharp focus on pivotal considerations that will intricately mold the success of our initiatives. Let's take a look:

- *Compatibility* stands as a cornerstone in the seamless integration of AI-driven tools into the web development process. It involves aligning these tools with existing frameworks, languages, and infrastructure to ensure a harmonious coexistence. As we explore the myriad options available, evaluating compatibility becomes paramount to avoid disruptions and foster a collaborative ecosystem where AI augments rather than conflicts with the existing development environment.

- The *scalability* of AI-driven development tools is a pivotal factor in their long-term effectiveness. As we select tools for prototyping, implementation, and collaboration, it's imperative to assess their scalability to accommodate the evolving needs of web development projects. A tool that thrives in a small-scale context might falter when faced with the demands of a larger, more complex project. Anticipating scalability challenges and choosing tools that can grow alongside the project ensures a sustainable and future-proof AI integration.

- The *learning curve* associated with AI-driven tools can significantly impact the efficiency and enthusiasm of a development team. Striking the right balance between advanced capabilities and user-friendly interfaces is key. Intuitive tools that offer smooth onboarding experiences empower developers to harness the power of AI without being bogged down by steep learning curves. Managing the learning curve becomes a strategic consideration, influencing not just initial adoption but the long-term proficiency and satisfaction of the development team.

In navigating through AI-driven development tools, these considerations become guiding principles, steering us toward choices that align with our development goals, enhance productivity, and set the stage for a transformative integration of AI in web development.

As we delve into the technicalities and strategies for integrating AI within web development, it's essential to pivot towards a topic of equal importance — ethical considerations. This shift underscores the balance between leveraging AI to drive innovation and ensuring that its application adheres to the highest ethical standards. In the following section on ethical considerations in AI-enhanced web development, we explore the crucial aspects of trust, security, and accountability that must accompany these technological advancements. Understanding these ethical implications is not just a responsibility but a necessity for developers to create a digital environment that is both innovative and trustworthy.

Ethical considerations in AI-enhanced web development

Ethical considerations in AI-enhanced web development have become increasingly crucial in today's rapidly evolving technological landscape. With the integration of AI in web development, there arises a need for a comprehensive understanding of the ethical implications that come along with it. This includes addressing concerns related to trust, security, and accountability. As AI continues to shape the digital realm, the potential risks involved cannot be ignored. It is imperative for developers to be cognizant of the ethical frameworks and guidelines to ensure the responsible and transparent use of AI in web development. By promoting ethics in AI-enhanced web development, we can foster a digital environment that prioritizes the values of trust, security, and accountability.

The significance of ethical considerations in AI-enhanced web development cannot be overstated. As we harness the capabilities of AI to craft innovative digital experiences, ethical considerations serve as the moral compass guiding our endeavors. Ethical practices not only shape the societal impact of our creations but also foster trust among users, establishing a foundation for sustainable and responsible technological progress.

The intersection of ethics and AI in web development forms the nucleus of our responsibility as creators. It's where the power of technology converges with moral imperatives. This dynamic interplay involves navigating through questions of transparency, fairness, accountability, and privacy. Striking a balance between technological innovation and ethical principles is not just a choice; it's a prerequisite for a digital future that prioritizes the well-being of users and the broader community. Building upon the critical framework of ethical considerations in AI-enhanced web development, we transition to a focused exploration of a human-centric approach to AI. This approach is instrumental in ensuring that as we advance in our technological capabilities, we remain steadfast in aligning AI development with human values, respect for fundamental rights, and human dignity. The shift towards a human-centric perspective in AI underscores the importance of designing and implementing technology that not only respects but also promotes the well-being of individuals and society at large. In the following section, we delve into how organizations such as Stanford University and the European Union are leading the charge in championing AI systems that embody these human-centric principles, highlighting the significance of prioritizing humanity in the midst of rapid technological progress.

Human-centric approach to AI

The concept of human-centric AI revolves around placing human values, respect for fundamental rights, and human dignity at the core of AI development. It acknowledges the unique and inalienable moral status of humans and emphasizes the need for a sustainable approach. Organizations such as Stanford and the European Union are actively working towards developing AI systems that prioritize these principles. By adopting a technical perspective, they aim to ensure that AI is designed and implemented in a way that respects human values and upholds fundamental rights. This commitment to a human-centric approach sets the foundation for a future where AI technology serves the best interests of humanity.

History of human-centered AI

The term *human-centered AI* was first coined by Ben Shneiderman (a professor of computer science at the University of Maryland) and Catherine Plaisant, in their 2010 book, *Designing the User Interface: Strategies for Effective Human-Computer Interaction*. Shneiderman and Plaisant defined HCAI as an approach to AI that "places human needs and values at the center of AI development and use."

However, the principles of HCAI had already been discussed by philosophers and computer scientists for decades. In 1967, philosopher John McCarthy, one of the pioneers of AI, wrote that "AI should be designed to serve human interests." And in 1985, computer scientist Alan Newell, one of the founders of cognitive AI, wrote that "AI should be used to improve human life."

HCAI has gained momentum over the last decade as AI has become more powerful and widespread. A growing number of organizations, including companies, governments and non-governmental organizations, are working to develop guidelines and standards for the development and use of AI in an ethical and responsible way.

Here are some of the main authors who have contributed to the development of HCAI: Ben Shneiderman, John McCarthy, Alan Newell, Helen Nissenbaum, Luciano Floridi, John Danaher, Kate Crawford, and Safiya Noble. These authors have written on a wide range of topics related to HCAI, including ethics, accountability, transparency, fairness, and inclusion. Their work has helped shape the debate on the future of AI and ensure that the technology is used for the good of humanity.

As we move forward from this rich theoretical groundwork towards the practical implications and global efforts in responsible AI, we encounter a concerted call for action across the globe. This global call to responsible AI, echoed by the European Union, leading academic institutions, and major corporations, emphasizes the urgency of adopting ethical practices in AI-enhanced web development. By promoting principles of privacy, data protection, safety, transparency, and fairness, these stakeholders advocate for a future where AI technologies are developed and deployed in ways that are not only innovative but also aligned with the highest ethical standards.

A global call for responsible AI

In the ever-evolving field of AI-enhanced web development, ethical considerations play a crucial role. With stakeholders ranging from the European Union to prestigious institutions including Stanford, Harvard, and Oxford universities, the global community recognizes the need for responsible and accountable practices. Organizations such as UNESCO, World Health Organization, Microsoft, IBM, AWS, Google, and Oracle are actively promoting principles of privacy and data protection, safety and security, transparency and explainability, fairness, and non-discrimination.

The ethics of AI is an important and constantly evolving topic. UNESCO, for example, has published a recommendation on AI ethics, which establishes global standards for responsible AI development. AI ethics is a set of guidelines that suggest how AI should be created and what its outcomes should be. AI has enormous potential to benefit humanity and promote sustainable development, but only if it is developed in a way that respects global norms and standards and is grounded in the principles of peace.

Governmental, non-governmental, and academic organizations have an important role to play in promoting AI ethics. For example, Stanford University has an AI research center that focuses on ethical and social issues related to AI. Harvard University also has an AI ethics center that focuses on ethical and policy issues related to AI. Oxford University has an AI ethics institute that focuses on ethical and policy issues related to AI. These organizations are working to ensure that AI is developed responsibly and benefits humanity.

The control of technology lies in the hands of professionals who bear the responsibility of upholding human values and fostering trust. As we navigate this exciting frontier, it is imperative to strike a balance between innovation and ethical standards, ensuring a future where AI serves as a tool for progress, guided by the principles of the brightest minds and the trust of the public.

Let's unpack eight crucial principles that should guide the way we build and deploy this powerful technology:

- **Trust**: Building and maintaining trust is foundational to ethical AI-enhanced web development. Transparent practices, accountability, and a commitment to ethical principles contribute to the establishment of trust between developers, users, and the broader digital community.

- **Transparency and explainability**: The ethical deployment of AI necessitates transparency and explainability. Users should understand how AI systems operate and make decisions. Striving for transparency fosters trust and empowers users to make informed choices.

- **Privacy and data protection**: In the interconnected digital age, safeguarding user privacy and ensuring robust data protection are paramount. Ethical web development demands a vigilant approach to handling sensitive information, respecting user consent, and implementing robust security measures.

- **Accountability**: As we harness the potential of AI, accountability becomes a cornerstone. Ethical considerations dictate the need for clear accountability structures, ensuring that the impact of AI decisions is traceable, and responsibility is assigned appropriately.

- **Safety and security**: Ensuring the safety and security of users is a fundamental ethical obligation. Ethical web development requires proactive measures to identify and mitigate potential risks, creating a secure online environment for all users.

- **Fairness and non-discrimination**: Ethical considerations emphasize the importance of fairness and non-discrimination in AI systems. Developers must actively address biases, promote inclusivity, and ensure that AI applications do not perpetuate or exacerbate existing inequalities.

- **Human control of technology**: Maintaining human control over technology is an ethical imperative. AI should augment human capabilities, and humans should retain the ability to intervene, override, or challenge AI decisions when necessary.

- **Professional responsibility**: Ethical web development carries a weight of professional responsibility. Developers must adhere to ethical standards, continually educate themselves on emerging ethical challenges, and advocate for ethical practices within the industry.

- **Promotion of human values**: In the pursuit of technological advancement, ethical considerations call for the promotion of human values. AI-enhanced web development should align with human-centric principles, enhancing user experiences while respecting fundamental values.

Ethical considerations in AI-enhanced web development are becoming increasingly important in today's rapidly evolving technological landscape. As AI is integrated into web development, it is crucial to understand the ethical implications that come with it. This includes addressing concerns related to trust, security, and accountability. The potential risks involved in AI cannot be ignored as it continues to shape the digital realm. Developers must be aware of ethical frameworks and guidelines to ensure responsible and transparent use of AI in web development. By promoting ethics in AI-enhanced web development, we can create a digital environment that values trust, security, and accountability.

Summary

In this chapter, we embarked on an enthralling journey exploring the intersection of AI and web development. The chapter laid the groundwork for understanding the revolutionary impact of AI on web development, highlighting its role in creating intelligent, adaptive, and human-like websites. As we delved into this phenomenon, we discussed the integration of AI into web technologies and how it drives innovative experiences.

We demystified AI in web development, emphasizing its importance in automating tasks, facilitating data analysis, and optimizing decision-making processes. We learned about the case study on Coca-Cola's "Create Real Magic" platform exemplified the practical application of AI in enhancing creativity and innovation.

We then focused on AI-driven tools in web development, recognizing their significance in automating tasks, improving efficiency, and creating captivating user experiences.

Finally, we explored the ethical considerations in AI-enhanced web development that emerged as a crucial theme. We highlighted the increasing importance of ethical frameworks and guidelines in addressing trust, security, and accountability concerns.

In the next chapter, we will master the fundamentals of AI by learning about data preprocessing for AI, designing scalable and efficient AI solutions for web projects, maintaining and adapting AI architectures for long-term success, evaluating and selecting the right frameworks for AI architecture, and applying architectural principles to real-world web development use cases.

2

Mastering the Essentials – AI Fundamentals

In this chapter, we will expand upon the foundational knowledge introduced in the first chapter. This chapter aims to provide a thorough understanding of vital AI principles within the context of web development. Using practical examples and engaging exercises, you will not only comprehend the core principles, techniques, and terminology integral to AI but also learn how to apply these principles in real-world situations. Our aim is to empower you with AI proficiency, equipping you to make data-informed decisions, leverage machine learning basics, comprehend the complexities of **Natural Language Processing** (**NLP**) and language model learning, navigate neural networks, and demystify **Computer Vision** (**CV**). By acquiring this knowledge, you will possess the necessary tools to flourish in the continuously evolving landscape of AI.

In this chapter, we're going to cover the following main topics:

- AI fundamentals – a deep dive
- Machine learning essentials
- NLP for web interaction
- Introduction to neural networks
- Empowering web development with computer vision

Now, it's essential to understand the technical requirements that will enable you to apply these AI concepts effectively. The following section will outline the necessary tools and technologies you need to implement the AI techniques we've mentioned.

Technical requirements

Here are the technical requirements for the chapter:

- Python 3.7+: `https://www.python.org/downloads/`
- Libraries:

    - pandas: `https://pandas.pydata.org/`
    - sklearn: `https://scikit-learn.org/stable/index.html`

In this chapter, we'll delve deeper into the link between AI principles and web application development. The application of AI techniques, such as machine learning and NLP, can significantly transform the way we develop and interact with web applications. For example, machine learning algorithms can be used to personalize the user experience, recommending products or content based on user behavior and preferences. NLP can improve interaction with chatbots, making communication more fluid and intuitive.

AI fundamentals – a deep dive

AI, or artificial intelligence, is a concept that has been rapidly evolving in recent years. It refers to a branch of computer science that focuses on the development of systems and algorithms capable of performing tasks that typically require human intelligence. These tasks include learning, reasoning, perception, understanding, and generation of natural language, voice and image recognition, decision-making, and solving complex problems. By replicating human cognitive abilities, AI has the potential to revolutionize various industries, from healthcare to finance, by improving efficiency and accuracy. Understanding the principles and applications of AI is crucial in today's rapidly evolving technological landscape.

The historical journey of AI

While delving into the deep waters of AI frameworks, it's crucial to understand the historical currents that have shaped their evolution. The journey begins with a retrospective glance, tracing the roots of AI and the pivotal moments that paved the way for the development of sophisticated frameworks.

Let's take a step back in time to ancient civilizations' fascination with creating artificial beings. However, it wasn't until the mid-20th century that AI truly emerged as a formal discipline. Pioneering figures such as Alan Turing laid the conceptual groundwork, envisioning machines that could exhibit intelligent behavior.

Fast forward to the 1950s, when the birth of AI took place. The term **artificial intelligence** was coined, and the ambitious goal of creating machines with human-like intelligence was articulated. Then, in 1956, the seminal Dartmouth Conference marked the official birth of AI as a field of study. Visionary attendees such as John McCarthy and Marvin Minsky imagined a world where machines could learn, reason, and solve problems.

As we moved into the 1960s, we encountered a period of optimism and setbacks in AI. Early successes, such as the creation of programs capable of solving algebraic theorems, were met with challenges. The initial optimism waned as AI faced limitations in handling real-world complexities. Undeterred, the 1970s saw a shift toward knowledge-based systems, emphasizing the importance of symbolic reasoning and expert systems.

However, the 1980s brought forth an *AI winter*. Reduced funding and interest in AI followed as unmet expectations and overhyped promises took their toll.

But fear not, for the late 20th century witnessed a resurgence in AI. Advances in machine learning, neural networks, and computational power reignited interest in this field. Practical applications in speech recognition and image processing began to emerge, breathing new life into AI.

Fast forward to the 2000s, and we found ourselves in an era where open source AI frameworks had revolutionized the field. These frameworks, such as TensorFlow developed by Google and PyTorch, democratized access to advanced tools, empowering developers around the world. Today, the AI landscape boasts a diverse ecosystem of frameworks catering to various needs. While TensorFlow and PyTorch continue to dominate, emerging frameworks such as **Open Neural Network Exchange** (**ONNX**) and MXNet contribute to the rich tapestry of AI possibilities.

In the subsequent sections, we will unravel the practical aspects of these AI algorithms, machine learning essentials, neural networks, NLP, CV, and AI in practice and guide you through hands-on exercises. The historical context serves as a compass, guiding us through the currents of progress and innovation that have shaped AI frameworks into the powerful tools they are today. Stay tuned for a journey into the practical implementation and strategic utilization of these frameworks in the realm of web development.

As we transition from the backdrop of AI's history to the tangible techniques that power AI programming today, we're embarking on a journey that not only highlights the science behind AI but also demonstrates how these principles are applied in real-world scenarios.

Understanding the science and techniques behind AI programming

AI programming focuses on cognitive skills such as learning, reasoning, self-correction, perception, language comprehension, and creativity. It is both a science and a set of computational techniques inspired by how humans utilize their bodies to sense, learn, reason, and act. AI programming aims to replicate and enhance these cognitive abilities in machines, enabling them to perform tasks that typically require human intelligence.

The following are the essential pillars of AI programming:

- **Learning** is a fundamental aspect of AI programming, as it involves the ability to acquire knowledge and improve performance through experience. By analyzing large amounts of data, AI systems can identify patterns, make predictions, and adapt their behavior accordingly.

- **Reasoning** is another crucial skill in AI programming. It involves the ability to think logically, form conclusions, and make decisions based on available information. AI systems use algorithms and rules to process data and generate logical deductions or solutions to complex problems.

- **Self-correction** is an essential feature in AI programming that allows machines to detect and correct errors or inaccuracies in their own output. Through feedback loops and continuous learning, AI systems can refine their performance and improve over time.

- **Perception** is the ability to interpret and understand sensory input from the environment. AI programming incorporates techniques such as CV and NLP to enable machines to perceive and interpret visual and textual information.

- **Language comprehension** is a critical aspect of AI programming, as it involves the ability to understand and generate human language. NLP techniques enable machines to interpret and respond to spoken or written language, making them capable of tasks such as language translation or chatbot interactions.

- **Creativity** is a more advanced skill that AI programming aims to replicate. While machines may not possess the same level of creativity as humans, AI systems can generate novel ideas, designs, or solutions by combining existing knowledge and patterns in innovative ways.

Overall, AI programming is a multidisciplinary field that combines principles from computer science, mathematics, and cognitive science to develop intelligent systems. Through the integration of various techniques and algorithms, AI aims to create machines that can learn, reason, correct themselves, perceive, comprehend language, and even exhibit a level of creativity.

The following section will delve into the advantages and disadvantages of AI, providing a balanced perspective on its transformative potential alongside the challenges and ethical considerations it presents.

Advantages and disadvantages of AI

AI has become a ubiquitous presence in our modern world, revolutionizing various industries and shaping our daily lives. Understanding the advantages and disadvantages of AI is crucial to navigate the complex landscape it presents.

AI offers numerous advantages in various domains. Some of these advantages are as follows:

- **Efficiency and automation**: One of the key benefits is efficiency and automation, as AI can automate repetitive tasks, allowing human resources to focus on more complex and creative endeavors

- **Data analysis and insights**: Furthermore, AI excels in data analysis and extracting valuable insights from vast amounts of data, which can be challenging for human analysis

- **24/7 availability**: Another advantage is the 24/7 availability of AI systems, as they operate without fatigue, providing continuous services and support, particularly in applications such as customer service and data monitoring

- **Accuracy and precision**: Additionally, AI ensures accuracy and precision in tasks, reducing the margin of error and benefiting domains such as healthcare diagnostics and manufacturing processes

- **Innovation and problem-solving**: Moreover, AI fosters innovation by tackling complex problems and generating novel solutions, pushing the boundaries of what is achievable

However, it is important to consider the disadvantages of AI as well:

- **Lack of emotional intelligence**: AI lacks emotional intelligence, empathy, and intuition, making it challenging to comprehend and respond appropriately to human emotions and social nuances.

- **Job displacement**: Moreover, the automation of certain tasks by AI may lead to job displacement, requiring a shift in the job market and the acquisition of new skills.

- **Bias and fairness concerns**: Bias and fairness concerns also arise, as AI systems can inherit biases present in the data used for training, leading to discriminatory outcomes.

- **High initial costs**: Additionally, implementing AI technologies involves substantial initial costs, in terms of both infrastructure and skilled personnel, which may be a barrier for some businesses.

- **Security risks**: Lastly, there are security risks associated with AI, as AI systems can be vulnerable to cyber threats, potentially leading to data breaches and privacy concerns. Despite these disadvantages, the advantages of AI are undeniable, and understanding the challenges allows for the development of responsible and beneficial AI systems.

- **The scarcity of qualified workers in the field**: One significant disadvantage is the limited supply of qualified workers to build AI tools. The field of AI requires individuals with a deep understanding of complex algorithms, data analysis, and programming. However, the demand for such skilled professionals far exceeds the supply, resulting in a scarcity of experts in this field. This scarcity not only hampers the development of AI technology but also leads to increased competition and higher costs for businesses seeking to implement AI solutions. As a result, the limited supply of qualified workers poses a significant challenge to the widespread adoption and advancement of AI. It is crucial for organizations to address this issue by investing in education and training programs to bridge the gap in expertise and ensure a sustainable future for AI.

The next section will delve into the various classifications of AI systems. The categories of AI we will explore provide a high-level view of AI's evolutionary stages, from systems designed for specific tasks to hypothetical entities surpassing human intelligence. These categories encapsulate AI's potential trajectory and its impact on society and technology as a whole.

Exploring the three main categories of AI

As web developers, it is crucial to have a solid understanding of the different categories of AI to harness its power effectively. In this section, we will delve into the three main categories of AI: restricted or weak AI, general or strong AI, and superintelligent AI.

Restricted or weak AI refers to AI systems that are designed to perform specific tasks with high efficiency. These AI systems have a narrow focus and excel in performing repetitive tasks. Web developers can leverage this category of AI to automate mundane processes, enhance user experience, and streamline workflows.

Moving on, general or strong AI represents AI systems that possess human-like intelligence across a wide range of tasks. These AI systems can understand, learn, and apply knowledge in a manner that resembles human intelligence. As web developers, understanding this category of AI opens up opportunities to create intelligent systems that can reason, plan, and solve complex problems.

Lastly, we come to superintelligent AI, which refers to AI systems that surpass human intelligence in virtually every aspect. These systems possess cognitive abilities far beyond what any human mind can comprehend. While superintelligent AI is still in the realm of speculation, as web developers, it's important to stay informed about its potential impact and ethical considerations.

By gaining a clear understanding of these three main categories of AI, web developers can make informed decisions about integrating AI into their projects. Whether it's harnessing the efficiency of restricted AI, exploring the possibilities of general AI, or contemplating the future implications of superintelligent AI, staying abreast of the advancements in AI will undoubtedly shape the future of web development.

Moving forward, our exploration deepens as we delve into understanding the four types of AI. As we transition from discussing the broad categories of AI—Restricted, General, and Superintelligent AI—to a more granular examination, it's essential to distinguish between the terms "categories" and "types" of AI. The "types" of AI, which we'll delve into next, refer to classifications based on functionality, capability, and application within current technological boundaries. This distinction allows us to understand AI not just in terms of its future potential but in practical, applicable terms that inform how AI technologies are developed, implemented, and interacted with today.

Understanding the four types of AI

As technology continues to advance at an unprecedented pace, it becomes crucial for us to understand the different types of AI that are shaping our world. From reactive machines to limited memory, theory of mind, and self-aware AI, each type represents a distinct level of intelligence and capabilities.

First on our list are **reactive machines**. These are the building blocks of AI, operating based on predefined rules and programmed to carry out specific tasks. Picture a chess-playing program that follows a set of rules without ever learning from previous games. It's like having an AI that can play chess but can't improve its skills or adapt to new strategies. Fascinating, isn't it?

Next up, we have **limited-memory AI systems**. These clever machines can learn from historical data to some extent. They rely on past experiences to make informed decisions, but they don't possess the ability to learn continuously. Think about self-driving cars, which use data from sensors and their past experiences to navigate the roads. They can't learn new routes on the go, but they can rely on their memory to get you safely from point A to point B.

Now, let's dive into the realm of **theory of mind AI**. This type of AI is all about understanding and interpreting human emotions and intentions. Imagine a system that can attribute mental states to others, enabling it to comprehend human behavior. While this level of AI is still mostly theoretical, researchers are exploring its potential in the field of human-robot interactions. It's like peeking into the future of AI-human relationships!

Lastly, we reach the pinnacle of AI—**self-aware AI**. These machines not only understand human emotions and intentions but also possess self-awareness. They can recognize their own existence, consciousness, and even emotions. However, it's important to note that true self-aware AI is still a complex and evolving area of research. We're not quite there yet, but the possibilities are mind-blowing!

It's worth mentioning that these categories represent a spectrum, and the development of AI technologies is a continuous process. Currently, the AI landscape leans more toward reactive machines and limited memory systems. However, scientists and engineers are tirelessly pushing the boundaries to create more sophisticated and autonomous AI capabilities.

In the next section, we will dive into the practical aspects that are particularly relevant to web development. By bridging theory with practice, web developers can harness the potential of AI to create more engaging, efficient, and intelligent web applications, positioning themselves at the cutting edge of technological innovation.

Exploring the inner workings of AI for web developers

As a web developer, have you ever wondered how AI works? Look no further! Now, we will take you through five essential steps that illustrate the inner workings of AI. From inputs to processing, outcomes to adjustments and assessments, we'll break it down for you. Understanding the inner workings of AI can open a world of possibilities for you. From improving user experiences to creating intelligent algorithms, the potential is limitless. But first, let's demystify these fundamental concepts:

- **Inputs**: Imagine inputs as the raw materials that AI algorithms feed on. They can be anything such as text, images, or even sounds. We'll explore how these inputs are collected and prepared for AI systems to digest in the following chapters.

- **Processing**: Once the inputs are gathered, AI systems work their magic through complex algorithms and models. We'll unravel the processes involved, shedding light on the black box that is AI processing. From data analysis to pattern recognition, you'll gain a deeper understanding of how AI makes sense of the inputs it receives.

- **Outcomes**: What happens when AI processes the inputs? The next chapters will reveal the outcomes AI generates, whether it's predicting customer behavior, generating recommendations, or even creating original content. Discover the potential impact of these outcomes on web development and how they can revolutionize your projects.

- **Adjustments**: AI systems are not set in stone; they continuously learn and adapt. We'll delve into the world of machine learning, exploring how AI adjusts its algorithms based on new data and experiences. You will understand the importance of training models and the role it plays in improving AI's accuracy and performance.

- **Assessments**: This refers to evaluating AI's performance. Measuring AI's success is crucial, and in this section, we'll explore the various methods used to assess AI's performance. From precision and recall to confusion matrices, you'll gain insights into how developers evaluate and fine-tune AI models.

As we navigate through each step, the processing stage will unveil the secrets behind AI's personalized recommendations, paving the way for smarter, more engaging user experiences. But that's just the beginning. The potential of adjustments and assessments is like sculpting your ultimate development assistant, optimizing its accuracy, and unleashing its full power in your projects.

Venturing forward, we will shift our focus to the main AI applications, an area where AI's revolutionary influence spans across diverse industries, radically altering our interaction with technology. From the underlying mechanics of machine learning to the nuances of voice recognition and the interpretative power of NLP, as well as the perceptive capabilities of CV, AI's applications are vast and varied.

Main AI applications

We come across a plethora of applications that have revolutionized various industries. From machine learning to voice recognition, NLP to CV, and even the generation of text, images, and audio, AI has truly transformed the way we interact with technology.

Let's explore some of the key applications of AI in more detail:

- **Machine learning**, the backbone of AI, allows computers to learn from data and make informed decisions. It has found its way into countless applications, such as personalized recommendations on streaming platforms such as Netflix or Spotify, fraud detection in financial institutions, and even self-driving cars that can navigate complex roadways with ease.

- **Voice recognition**, on the other hand, enables computers to understand and interpret human speech. This technology has become increasingly popular with the rise of virtual assistants such as Siri, Alexa, and Google Assistant. Whether it's asking for the weather forecast, setting reminders, or even ordering groceries, voice recognition has made interacting with technology more seamless and natural.

- **NLP** takes AI a step further by empowering computers to understand and process human language. This technology plays a crucial role in chatbots, translation services, and sentiment analysis. Imagine having a chatbot that can converse with you, understand your queries, and provide accurate responses, all thanks to NLP.

- **CV** brings AI into the visual realm, allowing machines to interpret and understand images and videos. It has been instrumental in various fields, including healthcare, where it aids in diagnosing diseases from medical images, and in security systems, where it can identify suspicious activities or individuals.

But our capabilities go beyond just data and images. AI has also ventured into the realm of creativity with text, image, and audio generation. This technology can create realistic text, generate images, and even compose music. Just think about the potential for artists, writers, and musicians to collaborate with AI and push the boundaries of creativity.

Lastly, AI has proven to be a game-changer in the realm of **automation**. By automating processes, businesses can save time, reduce errors, and increase efficiency. Whether it's automating customer support with chatbots or streamlining manufacturing processes with robots, AI has the power to transform industries and drive innovation.

So, as you can see, AI has become an integral part of our modern world, revolutionizing the way we live and work. From machine learning to automation, the possibilities are endless. With our expertise and passion for AI, we are committed to pushing the boundaries of what's possible and shaping a future where technology works seamlessly with humanity.

The following section is dedicated to unraveling the significance of machine learning in web development. Through an exploration of its key facets, we aim to illuminate how this technology is instrumental in crafting more intuitive, efficient, and tailored online experiences.

Machine learning essentials

Machine learning is essential in the field of web development. It plays a crucial role in enhancing the user experience, improving website functionality, and enabling personalized recommendations. In this section, we will delve into the importance of machine learning for web development and explore its various aspects – for example, a recommendation system for an e-commerce website that suggests products based on user browsing history and purchase patterns. This will help you understand how machine learning algorithms analyze data to provide personalized recommendations.

What is machine learning?

First and foremost, let's define **machine learning**. It is a branch of AI that enables computers to learn and make predictions or decisions without being explicitly programmed. This ability to learn from data and improve over time is what makes machine learning so powerful in the context of web development.

So, how does machine learning work? At its core, it involves feeding large amounts of data into algorithms that can analyze and extract patterns from the data. These algorithms then use these patterns to make predictions or decisions. The more data the algorithm is exposed to, the better it becomes at making accurate predictions.

Types of machine learning algorithms

Now, we will explore four types of machine learning: supervised learning, unsupervised learning, semi-supervised learning, and reinforcement learning. Each of these methods has its own unique approach to teaching machines how to learn and make predictions.

Supervised learning

Imagine having a machine learning model that can learn from labeled data and make predictions. That's exactly what **supervised learning** is all about! This cutting-edge approach allows machines to infer functions from data that has been carefully labeled by experts. Let's explore the different types of supervised learning that will blow your mind.

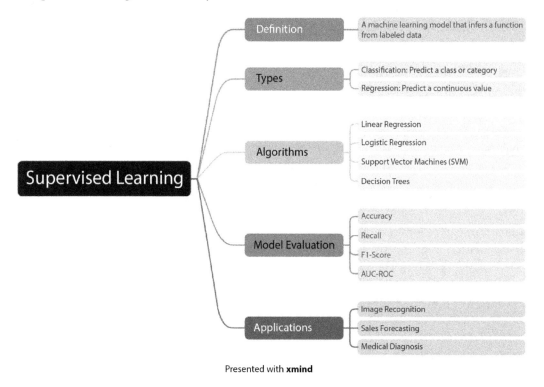

Presented with **xmind**

Figure 2.1: Supervised learning

But what can supervised learning do? Well, it can tackle two main types of problems: regression and classification. In the world of regression, the goal is to predict continuous values. Whether it's forecasting sales figures or estimating the price of a house, supervised learning has you covered. On the other hand, in the realm of classification, the aim is to predict classes or categories. This can be incredibly useful in tasks such as image recognition or medical diagnosis.

Of course, to make supervised learning work its magic, we need a set of powerful algorithms. Let's take a look at some of the heavy hitters in the field. First up, we have **linear regression**, a simple yet effective algorithm that can help us make accurate predictions. Then, there's **logistic regression**, which is perfect for tackling classification problems. **Support Vector Machines** (**SVMs**) are also in the mix, providing a versatile tool for both regression and classification tasks. Last but not least, we have **decision trees**, which can help us make complex decisions based on data.

Now, let's talk about evaluating these models. After all, we want to know how well they perform, right? Well, there are several metrics we can use to measure their effectiveness. Accuracy, recall, F1-score, and AUC-ROC are just a few of the key metrics that can tell us how well our models are doing.

> **Important note**
>
> Accuracy is one of the most intuitive metrics, measuring the proportion of correct predictions made by the model out of the total predictions. In other words, it is the number of true positives and true negatives divided by the total number of cases. Although useful for getting a general sense of the model's performance, accuracy can be misleading in imbalanced datasets, where one class is much more prevalent than others.
>
> Recall quantifies the model's ability to correctly identify all positive instances of a specific class. It is calculated by dividing the number of true positives by the total of true positives plus the number of false negatives. This metric is particularly important in situations where missing a positive instance is costly, such as in disease diagnosis.
>
> The F1-score is a measure that combines precision and recall into a single metric, providing a balance between the two. It is calculated as two times the product of precision and recall, divided by the sum of precision and recall. The F1-score is particularly useful when a balance between precision and recall is desired and when classes are imbalanced.
>
> The **Area Under the Curve** (**AUC**) of the **Receiver Operating Characteristic** (**ROC**) is a metric used to evaluate the overall performance of binary classification models. The ROC curve is a plot showing the performance of a model across all classification thresholds, plotting the true positive rate against the false positive rate. The AUC provides an aggregated indicator of model performance across all classification thresholds, with values closer to 1 indicating a better model.

So, where can we apply supervised learning in the real world? The possibilities are endless! From image recognition to sales forecasting and even medical diagnosis, supervised learning can revolutionize various industries. Imagine a world where machines can accurately identify objects in images, predict future sales trends, and aid doctors in diagnosing diseases. That's the power of supervised learning in action.

Supervised learning is an exciting field that allows machines to learn from labeled data and make predictions. With its powerful algorithms, model evaluation metrics, and wide range of applications, supervised learning is transforming the way we solve problems and make predictions. So, let's embrace the potential of supervised learning and unlock a future where machines can truly understand and learn from the world around us.

Unsupervised learning

Unsupervised learning is a powerful machine learning technique that allows machines to uncover hidden structures within data without any prior labels. It's like solving a puzzle without knowing what the final picture looks like. Let's delve into the fascinating world of unsupervised learning, a branch of machine learning that uncovers hidden patterns and structures from unlabeled data.

Let's dive into the types of unsupervised learning. **Clustering** is one of the key techniques, where we group objects based on their similarities. Imagine organizing a set of objects in such a way that those within the same group share more similarities with each other than with objects in other groups. It's like assembling a puzzle, finding connections and relationships that were previously hidden.

Another technique is **dimensionality reduction**, which involves reducing the number of random variables under consideration. By obtaining a set of principal variables, we can simplify complex data and focus on the most important aspects. It's like decluttering a messy room, bringing clarity and efficiency to the analysis process.

Now, let's explore some of the powerful algorithms used in unsupervised learning. The K-means clustering algorithm helps us identify patterns and groupings within data points. Hierarchical clustering, on the other hand, allows us to create a hierarchical structure of clusters, revealing relationships at different levels of granularity. **Principal Component Analysis** (**PCA**) is another fascinating algorithm that helps us understand the most significant variables driving the data. And let's not forget about autoencoders, which excel in learning compact representations of data.

When it comes to evaluating the performance of unsupervised learning models, we have some handy metrics at our disposal. The **silhouette coefficient** measures how well objects fit within their assigned clusters, providing insights into the quality of the clustering results. The **Davies-Bouldin index**, on the other hand, helps us assess the separation and compactness of different clusters. These evaluation tools give us the confidence to fine-tune our models and ensure optimal performance.

So, how can we apply unsupervised learning in the real world? Customer segmentation is a fantastic application, allowing businesses to understand their customer base and tailor their strategies accordingly. Anomaly detection is another powerful use case, enabling us to identify unusual patterns or behaviors in data. And let's not forget about image compression, where unsupervised learning techniques can help us reduce the size of images while preserving their essential features.

In conclusion, unsupervised learning exposes a world of possibilities for discovering hidden patterns, reducing complexity, and gaining insights from unlabeled data. With its diverse range of algorithms and applications, this field continues to revolutionize the way we analyze and understand the world around us. So, let's embark on this captivating journey and unlock the secrets that lie within the data!

As we wrap up our exploration of unsupervised learning and its vast potential for unveiling hidden patterns, simplifying complexity, and extracting insights from unlabeled data, we stand at the threshold of another exciting domain: semi-supervised learning.

Semi-supervised learning

In the vast world of machine learning, there exists a fascinating approach known as **semi-supervised learning**. This revolutionary model harnesses the potential of both labeled and unlabeled data to achieve superior training results. Let's delve into the different aspects that make semi-supervised learning so intriguing.

One captivating aspect of semi-supervised learning is the variety of approaches it offers. One such method is self-training, where the model is initially trained using labeled data and then utilized to label the unlabeled data. This iterative process empowers the model to learn from its own predictions, ensuring continuous improvement.

Another intriguing approach is multi-view training, where the model is trained on different views or sets of features within the data. By considering multiple perspectives, the model gains a comprehensive understanding of the underlying patterns, resulting in more accurate predictions.

Within the realm of semi-supervised learning, several algorithms stand out for their remarkable capabilities. **Label spreading**, for instance, spreads the labeled information across the unlabeled data, effectively expanding the model's knowledge and refining its predictions.

Label propagation, on the other hand, leverages the similarities between labeled and unlabeled data points to propagate labels and enhance the model's understanding. This intelligent algorithm harnesses the power of collective knowledge to achieve exceptional results.

Co-training is yet another noteworthy algorithm that thrives in the semi-supervised learning landscape. Here, multiple models collaborate and learn from each other, collectively enhancing their prediction abilities. This cooperative approach maximizes the potential of both labeled and unlabeled data.

To gauge the performance of semi-supervised learning models, various evaluation metrics come into play. **Accuracy**, for example, measures how well the model aligns with the ground truth, providing insight into overall correctness. **Recall**, on the other hand, focuses on the model's ability to correctly identify relevant data points, minimizing false negatives.

The **F1-score**, a combination of precision and recall, offers a comprehensive assessment by considering both the model's effectiveness in identifying relevant data and its precision in making correct predictions. This metric ensures a robust evaluation of the model's performance.

Semi-supervised learning opens up a world of exciting applications across various domains. In text classification, this approach shines by leveraging both labeled and unlabeled data to accurately categorize and organize vast amounts of textual information. Image recognition, too, benefits greatly from semi-supervised learning, enabling more precise identification and classification of images. Lastly, in the field of bioinformatics, this approach empowers researchers to extract valuable insights from large datasets, revolutionizing the study of biological systems.

Now that you're familiar with the captivating aspects of semi-supervised learning, it's time to unlock its immense potential. By harnessing the power of both labeled and unlabeled data, this groundbreaking approach empowers machines to learn and make predictions with unprecedented accuracy.

Having delved into the nuanced dynamics of semi-supervised learning and its ability to leverage both labeled and unlabeled data for enhanced learning precision, we now pivot to a different yet equally fascinating realm of AI: reinforcement learning.

Reinforcement learning

Reinforcement learning is a fascinating field of machine learning where an agent embarks on a journey of decision-making, navigating through an environment to achieve a desired goal. In this type of learning, the agent learns from the consequences of its actions rather than relying on a pre-learned model of the environment.

There are two main types of reinforcement learning: **model-free** and **model-based**. In the model-free approach, the agent relies on its experiences and learns from the outcomes of its actions. Two popular methods within this approach are **Monte Carlo** and **temporal difference learning**. These techniques allow the agent to learn and adapt its decision-making process based on real-time feedback from the environment.

On the other hand, in model-based reinforcement learning, the agent takes a more strategic approach. It learns a model of the environment and utilizes this knowledge to make informed decisions. By understanding how the environment operates, the agent can optimize its actions to achieve its goals more efficiently.

Within the realm of reinforcement learning, there are various algorithms that have been developed to enhance the learning process. Some notable algorithms include **Q-learning**, **Deep Q-Network** (**DQN**), and **Proximal Policy Optimization** (**PPO**). These algorithms provide different approaches to decision-making and offer unique advantages in different scenarios.

To evaluate the performance of reinforcement learning models, several factors come into play. **Cumulative reward** measures the overall success of the agent in achieving its goals over a period of time. **Time to learn** indicates how quickly the agent is able to acquire the necessary knowledge and skills to make optimal decisions. Lastly, **stability of learning** assesses how consistent and reliable the agent's learning process is over multiple iterations.

The applications of reinforcement learning are vast and diverse. Game playing is one area where reinforcement learning has gained significant attention. By training agents to play games, researchers gain insights into how machines can learn complex strategies and adapt to dynamic environments. Robotics is another field where reinforcement learning holds great promise. By enabling robots to learn from their experiences, they can perform tasks more efficiently and effectively. Lastly, resource management is an area where reinforcement learning can optimize the allocation and utilization of resources, leading to improved efficiency and cost savings.

So, reinforcement learning is an exciting field that offers unique approaches to decision-making and problem-solving. Through various algorithms and evaluation metrics, agents can learn from their experiences and navigate their way toward achieving their goals. With applications ranging from game playing to robotics and resource management, reinforcement learning has the potential to revolutionize various industries and pave the way for a more intelligent and efficient future.

In summary, the exploration of machine learning essentials has provided us with a solid foundation for understanding the intricate landscape that encompasses this transformative field. We embarked on an exciting journey to unravel the very essence of machine learning, diving deep into its fundamental definition and gradually navigating through the diverse realms of learning algorithms. From the guiding principles of supervised learning, where patterns are deciphered from labeled data, to the uncharted territories of unsupervised learning, where hidden structures in unlabeled data are unveiled, and the strategic decision-making processes facilitated by reinforcement learning, each facet reveals a unique dimension of AI's capabilities. This section serves as our trusty compass, steering us toward a deeper comprehension of the powerful tools and methodologies that drive the next frontier of technological evolution in web development. As we wholeheartedly embrace these machine learning essentials, we set the stage for a future where data-driven insights propel innovation and redefine the very landscape of web development.

We now turn our attention to a fascinating application area that is reshaping the interaction between web technologies and users: NLP for web interaction. In this next section, we will delve into how NLP bridges the gap between human language and computer understanding, enabling machines to process, understand, and even generate human language in a way that enriches user experience and opens new dimensions in web development.

NLP for web interaction

In today's digital landscape, user interaction is at the heart of every successful online platform. The ability to communicate effortlessly and intuitively with technology has become a key differentiator in providing exceptional user experiences. That's where NLP steps in, bridging the gap between humans and machines and transforming the way we interact with the web.

Imagine a world where websites, chatbots, and virtual assistants not only understand your words but also grasp the true meaning behind them. With NLP, this vision becomes a reality. By leveraging advanced algorithms and machine learning techniques, NLP enables computers to comprehend, interpret, and respond to human language in a way that feels natural and intuitive.

Gone are the days of rigid command-based interactions and frustrating user interfaces. NLP empowers technology to understand the nuances of human language, including context, sentiment, and even sarcasm. This breakthrough technology enables websites to engage users in more meaningful and personalized conversations, leading to increased user satisfaction, loyalty, and ultimately, business success.

NLP revolutionizes the way we search the web. With traditional keyword-based search engines, finding relevant information often requires sifting through endless pages of search results. NLP changes the game by understanding the intent behind your queries, providing more accurate and contextually relevant results. It's like having a knowledgeable guide who anticipates your needs and delivers exactly what you're looking for.

Whether you're a business owner striving to enhance customer engagement or a web developer looking to create intuitive interfaces, NLP opens up a world of possibilities. By harnessing the power of language, you can create web experiences that are not only informative but also conversational, captivating, and unforgettable.

The next section promises to demystify the processes that underpin this fascinating field. We're set to explore the trio of foundational elements that empower machines to not only parse text but also understand and generate human-like language.

Key components of NLP

If you've ever wondered how machines can understand and generate human-like text, then you're in for a treat. Here, we'll dive into the key components that make it all possible: text processing, language understanding, and language generation—for example, implementing a chatbot for customer service on a website using NLP. This example demonstrates how chatbots can understand and respond to user queries, improving user engagement and support.

Picture this: you're sitting at your desk, surrounded by stacks of papers filled with words. It's overwhelming, isn't it? Well, that's where **text processing** comes in. This incredible component takes those mountains of text and organizes them, making sense of the chaos. It's like having a personal assistant who effortlessly categorizes and sorts through all your documents, saving you time and energy.

But **understanding language** is a whole different ball game. Language understanding is like your own personal language detective. It analyzes the words, sentences, and even the context to comprehend the meaning behind the text. It's like having a friend who knows what you mean even when you don't say it explicitly. This component allows machines to understand the nuances, the humor, and the emotions embedded within human language.

Now, let's switch gears and talk about **language generation**. Imagine having a machine that can write like a poet, a storyteller, or even a comedian. This component brings text to life, transforming cold, hard data into engaging narratives. It's like having an AI companion who can effortlessly create compelling content that captivates and entertains. From writing personalized emails to crafting compelling marketing copy, language generation is the secret sauce behind creating content that resonates with people.

So, there you have it—the key components that power the magic behind language processing. Text processing, language understanding, and language generation work together to revolutionize the way machines interact with text. With these components at your disposal, the possibilities are endless.

In the following section, we will delve into how LLMs leverage the foundational aspects of NLP to provide deeper insights, create more engaging content, and foster more intuitive user interactions on the web. Prepare to explore how the power of LLMs is shaping the future of web development, pushing the boundaries of what's possible in creating responsive, intelligent, and highly personalized online experiences.

The power of large language models in web development

Large Language Models (**LLMs**) are a specialized type of AI that has been trained on vast amounts of text to understand existing content and generate original material. They possess a remarkable ability to comprehend and generate language for diverse purposes.

LLMs acquire these skills by learning statistical relationships from text documents during computationally intensive self-supervised and semi-supervised training processes. One of their key applications is text generation, where they take input text and predict the next token or word repeatedly.

Comprising multiple layers of neural networks, LLMs utilize recurrent layers, feedforward layers, embedding layers, and attention layers to process input text and generate output content. As a result, LLMs play a crucial role in NLP and have a significant impact on web interactions.

LLMs find applications in various web-based functionalities, such as virtual assistants, chatbots, automatic translation, and sentiment analysis. They are instrumental in enhancing user experiences and improving the efficiency of web-based interactions.

For instance, popular LLMs such as ChatGPT, Gemini(Google), and BLOOM (BigScience) have revolutionized the way we communicate online. ChatGPT provides users with conversational AI capabilities, allowing them to engage in interactive and dynamic conversations. Bard, developed by Google, powers the search engine's language understanding capabilities, enabling more accurate and relevant search results. BLOOM, a prominent LLM from BigScience, has been instrumental in advancing language generation capabilities, particularly in the scientific domain.

In web development, LLMs enable the creation of intelligent chatbots that can understand and respond to user queries effectively. These chatbots can be integrated into websites to provide instant support, answer frequently asked questions, and guide users through various processes.

LLMs also play a vital role in automatic translation, facilitating seamless communication across different languages. They analyze input text and generate accurate translations, reducing language barriers and promoting global connectivity.

Additionally, LLMs contribute to sentiment analysis by analyzing text data and determining the underlying sentiment or emotion. This application finds utility in areas such as social media monitoring, brand reputation management, and customer feedback analysis.

LLMs are a game-changer in web development, revolutionizing the way we interact, communicate, and access information online. Their ability to understand and generate language opens up endless possibilities for creating intelligent web-based applications that enhance user experiences and streamline processes. With advancements in LLM technology, the future of web development is set to be even more exciting and innovative.

In the next section, we will dive into the practical applications of NLP that are changing the game for web developers and users alike. From the emergence of chatbots that offer instant, personalized responses to the sophistication of virtual assistants that manage our daily tasks with ease, NLP stands at the core of these advancements.

Applications of NLP in web interaction

The world of web interaction has been revolutionized by the incredible advancements in NLP. From the introduction of chatbots and virtual assistants to the improvement of search functionality, NLP has become the driving force behind seamless and intuitive user experiences.

Let's explore some of the most groundbreaking applications of NLP that are reshaping our digital experiences:

- **Chatbots** have taken the online world by storm, transforming the way we interact with websites and applications. These intelligent virtual agents are designed to understand and respond to human language, providing personalized assistance and engaging conversations. Imagine visiting a website and being greeted by a friendly chatbot that can help you find the information you need, answer your questions, or even assist you with making a purchase. With NLP, chatbots can understand the context of your queries and provide relevant and accurate responses, mimicking human-like interactions.

- **Virtual assistants**, such as Siri and Alexa, have become an integral part of our everyday lives. Powered by NLP, these digital companions can perform various tasks, from setting reminders and playing music to providing weather updates and even ordering groceries. NLP enables virtual assistants to comprehend spoken commands and extract the intended meaning behind them, allowing for seamless and efficient interactions.

- **Search functionality** has come a long way with the integration of NLP. Gone are the days of rigid keyword-based searches. NLP algorithms now enable search engines to understand the intent behind a user's query and deliver more accurate results. For example, if you search for *best Italian restaurants near me*, NLP can analyze the query and provide a list of highly rated Italian restaurants in your vicinity. This improvement in search functionality enhances user experience by saving time and delivering more relevant information.

Now, imagine being able to communicate effortlessly with people from different parts of the world, without any language barriers. NLP models have got you covered! They can automatically translate text from one language to another, making language barriers a thing of the past. Whether you're exploring a foreign land or connecting with people across the globe, NLP models will make sure your words are never lost in translation.

Lastly, let's talk about **information extraction**. We all know how overwhelming it can be to sift through large amounts of text to find specific information. That's where NLP models come to the rescue! They have this incredible knack for identifying and extracting exactly what you're looking for from massive bodies of text. It's like having a super-powered search engine that gives you exactly what you need, saving you time and effort.

So, there you have it! The applications of NLP in web interaction have revolutionized the way we engage with websites and applications. From chatbots providing personalized assistance to virtual assistants simplifying our daily tasks, NLP has made our online experiences more seamless and intuitive. With continued advancements in NLP technology, we can expect even more exciting developments in the future, bringing us closer to a world where human-computer interaction feels truly natural.

With this forward-looking perspective, let's pivot to the next section, about NLP classifications, to deepen our understanding of how these technologies are organized and function. NLP models exhibit a rich diversity, classified not only by their objectives—ranging from comprehension to generation—but also by their architecture, approaches, and training methods. This classification sheds light on the breadth and depth of NLP, revealing the framework within which these innovative tools operate and evolve.

Classifications of NLP

NLP models can be categorized based on their objectives, architecture, approaches, or training methods, each providing a unique perspective on how these models function and their diverse applications. NLP models can be classified by their primary objectives, which include comprehension and generation. The architecture of NLP models determines their structure and functioning. NLP models can also be categorized by the approaches used in their development. The training methods used for NLP models further differentiate them. So, let's embark on this journey of discovery together!

Objectives of NLP models

NLP models are primarily divided based on their objectives into two categories:

- **Comprehension models**: Designed to decode textual meaning, these models grasp the author's intent, contextual cues, and emotional undertones, paving the way for applications in sentiment analysis, language translation, and question answering
- **Generation models**: Focused on producing text, these models excel in creative text generation—crafting everything from poetry and scripts to emails—thereby enriching interaction and content creation

Architectural classifications of NLP models

The architecture of NLP models provides another basis for classification, encompassing the following:

- **Recurrent Neural Networks (RNNs)**: Ideal for sequential data processing tasks such as text generation and machine translation, though they may struggle with long-term data dependencies

- **Long Short-Term Memory (LSTM)**: Enhances data retention over extended sequences, which is beneficial for speech recognition and text summarization, albeit with higher computational demands

- **Gated Recurrent Units (GRUs)**: A simpler variant of RNNs, balancing computational efficiency with effective data processing for similar applications to RNNs and LSTMs

- **Transformers and BERT**: These models introduce parallel processing and bidirectional learning, excelling in capturing contextual information for a wide range of NLP tasks, requiring significant data and computational resources

Training methods for NLP models

The approach to training NLP models varies significantly, as we can see from this list:

- **Supervised learning**: Utilizes labeled data for precise model training, which is suitable for tasks with abundant labeled datasets

- **Unsupervised learning**: Leverages patterns in unlabeled data to discover hidden structures, which is ideal for exploratory data analysis

- **Semi-supervised learning**: Combines labeled and unlabeled data, optimizing learning efficiency when labeled data is scarce

- **Transfer learning**: Employs pre-trained models adapted for specific tasks, which is recommended for limited labeled data scenarios

- **Reinforcement learning**: Focuses on sequential decision-making, guiding models to optimize actions based on rewards

Approaches to NLP model development

NLP models can be differentiated by their foundational approaches:

- **Rule-based models**: Depend on manually defined rules for tasks such as grammatical analysis and information extraction

- **Statistics-based models**: Use probabilistic methods for decision-making, which is applicable to modeling and frequency analysis

- **Machine learning-based models**: Apply algorithms to learn from data, which is suitable for classification, regression, and clustering tasks

Understanding these classifications not only enhances our grasp of NLP's capabilities but also guides the selection of appropriate models for specific tasks, bridging the gap between theoretical knowledge and practical application. As we proceed, the upcoming section on NLP techniques will build upon this foundation, focusing on the specific methods and strategies that apply these classifications in practical scenarios, furthering our journey into the depths of NLP.

NLP techniques

In the field of NLP, various techniques are employed to analyze and understand human language. These techniques play a crucial role in tasks such as text comprehension, semantic interpretation, and even automatic text generation. Let's explore some key techniques and their defining characteristics:

- **Lexical analysis**: This technique involves breaking down sentences into tokens to identify their meanings. It is essential for understanding the basic structure and units of meaning in a text.

- **Syntactic analysis**: This technique focuses on identifying the relationships between words and phrases. It aids in comprehending grammar and syntactic structure.

- **Semantic analysis**: Semantic analysis involves relating syntactic structures to their meanings. It helps in the semantic interpretation of a text, going beyond literal understanding.

- **Natural Language Understanding (NLU)**: NLU specifically emphasizes semantic analysis to comprehend the meaning of a text more comprehensively. It is essential for gaining a broader understanding of human language.

- **Natural Language Generation (NLG)**: NLG primarily focuses on the automatic generation of text. It enables the capability to generate responses or reports, enhancing efficiency and productivity.

- **Pragmatic analysis**: This technique involves understanding the speaker's intention by considering the context. It goes beyond the literal meaning of words and interprets the text in a more nuanced way.

- **Named Entity Recognition (NER)**: NER is the identification and classification of entities within a text. It plays a crucial role in extracting structured information from unstructured text.

- **Relation extraction**: This technique involves identifying and classifying relationships between entities. It enables a deeper understanding of the connections within a text.

These techniques introduce powerful tools for analyzing and understanding human language. Each technique has its defining characteristics and recommended use cases. By leveraging these techniques, we can unlock new possibilities in the field of NLP, enabling us to comprehend and utilize language in a more meaningful and impactful way.

In the next section, we will embark on a journey to unravel the fundamental principles of neural networks, exploring their architecture, how they learn from data, and their transformative role in advancing NLP and AI as a whole.

Introduction to neural networks

Computational systems inspired by the structure of the human brain are known as neural networks. These systems aim to mimic the incredible capabilities of the human brain, such as pattern recognition, learning, and decision-making. By simulating the intricate connections between neurons, neural networks can process vast amounts of data and solve complex problems. This groundbreaking technology has revolutionized various fields, including AI, robotics, and data analysis. With their ability to adapt and learn from experience, neural networks have become essential tools in the advancement of modern technology—for example, using a simple neural network to categorize customer reviews as positive or negative based on sentiment analysis. This example should help you grasp the basics of neural networks and their application in text analysis.

Artificial Neural Networks (ANNs) are like a team of interconnected brain cells, with each cell having its own unique role in processing information. Picture it like a squad of specialized neurons, working together to solve complex problems.

Artificial Neural Networks

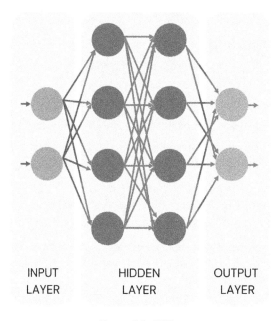

INPUT
LAYER

HIDDEN
LAYER

OUTPUT
LAYER

Figure 2.2: ANNs

The next segment aims to dissect the core principles that enable these digital networks to operate. We'll unravel the mysteries of how neural networks mimic cognitive processes to learn from data, make decisions, and evolve.

Fundamental concepts of neural networks

These networks consist of layers of nodes, including an input layer, one or more hidden layers, and an output layer. Each node, or artificial neuron, connects to others with its own weight and threshold. If the output of any individual node exceeds the specified threshold, that node gets activated and passes on data to the next layer.

But here's where it gets really interesting: the weights assigned to each node determine the importance of the input variables. The higher the weight, the more significant the contribution to the output. It's like giving more weight to the most crucial pieces of information.

All the inputs are then multiplied by their respective weights and summed up. This sum is then passed through an activation function, which determines the final output. It's like the network's way of making sense of all the information it receives and providing a meaningful result.

At this point, let's talk about the structure of these neural networks. They're organized in layers, just like a well-structured team. Each layer has its own unique role and purpose. You can think of the layers as different departments, each working together to achieve a common goal.

These networks are inspired by the biological neurons found in our brains. They receive inputs through their **axons** and produce outputs through their **dendrites**. It's like they have their own little wiring system, mimicking the way our brains process information.

But here's the really cool part: these neural networks can be trained to make predictions based on data. They're like little brain cells that learn and adapt over time. In modern applications, a specific type of training called **deep learning** is used to train these multi-layered neurons.

Inputs are weighted and combined using a function called an activation function. This function is responsible for taking the weighted inputs and activating the output value. It's like the secret sauce that brings everything together and produces the final result.

So, there you have it! ANNs are not only fascinating but also incredibly powerful tools for solving complex problems. They're like a team of specialized brain cells, working together to make sense of the world around us.

The next section will explore this diversity in greater detail. Here, we'll break down the various forms that neural networks can take—each tailored to specific types of tasks and challenges.

Types of neural networks

Neural networks are an essential component of modern technology, enabling machines to learn and make decisions. They mimic the workings of the human brain, processing information and making complex calculations. In this section, we will explore different types of neural networks, each with unique characteristics and applications.

Let's start with the **Feedforward Neural Network (FNN)**. In this type of network, information flows in one direction, from the input to the output. It's like a conveyor belt of data, where each neuron processes the information it receives and passes it forward. FNNs are incredibly useful for tasks such as image recognition, NLP, and even stock market prediction.

Now, let's understand RNNs. Unlike their feedforward counterparts, RNNs have feedback connections, allowing them to retain short-term memory. This memory feature makes them perfect for tasks that involve sequential data, such as speech recognition, language translation, and sentiment analysis. RNNs excel in understanding the context and dependencies within a sequence.

Lastly, we will explore **Convolutional Neural Networks (CNNs)**. These networks are designed to process grid-like data, such as images. CNNs excel at recognizing patterns and extracting features from visual data. With their ability to detect edges, shapes, and textures, CNNs have revolutionized CV and are widely used in tasks such as object detection, facial recognition, and self-driving cars.

Finally, neural networks come in various forms, each tailored to solve specific problems. FNNs are ideal for processing information in a linear fashion, while RNNs excel at understanding sequential data. CNNs are the go-to choice for image-related tasks. Understanding the characteristics and applications of these neural network types is crucial in harnessing their power to drive technological advancements.

The next section is dedicated to unraveling the methodologies and practices involved in teaching neural networks to perform their tasks with precision.

Training neural networks

Neural networks play a crucial role in various fields, ranging from image recognition to NLP. However, for these networks to perform effectively, they must be trained properly. In this section, we will delve into the fundamentals of training neural networks, including backpropagation, activation functions, and regularization techniques.

Let's begin.

Backpropagation is an essential algorithm used to adjust the weights of a neural network based on the error. By calculating the error between the predicted output and the actual output, backpropagation allows us to update the weights in a way that minimizes this error. This iterative process continues until the network's performance reaches an acceptable level.

The **activation function** is another crucial component of neural network training. It determines the output of a neuron based on the weighted sum of its inputs. Different activation functions, such as sigmoid or ReLU, can be used to introduce non-linearity into the network, enabling it to model complex relationships between inputs and outputs.

Regularization techniques are employed to prevent overfitting, a common problem in neural network training. Overfitting occurs when the network becomes too specialized in the training data and fails to generalize well to new, unseen data. Regularization methods, such as dropout, help mitigate this issue by randomly dropping out a portion of the neurons during training, forcing the network to rely on different combinations of features and reducing its dependence on specific inputs.

The next section aims to shed light on how the principles and techniques discussed so far can be leveraged to enhance web-based applications and services.

Application of neural networks in web development

In today's rapidly evolving technological landscape, the application of neural networks in web development has become increasingly important. Neural networks, inspired by the human brain, are powerful tools that can be utilized to enhance various aspects of web development. In this section, we will explore the significance of neural networks, their potential outcomes, and their relationship with the principles and foundations of web development. Let us dive into some specific examples to understand how neural networks can be applied in the context of web development.

A key principle within the framework of neural networks is understanding what constitutes inputs. In the context of web development, these inputs can include a wide range of user actions, such as mouse movements across the screen, clicks on specific elements, or information entered into forms. When we introduce these kinds of user interactions into a neural network as inputs, it enables the network to analyze and identify patterns within these actions. Through this analysis, the neural network can be trained to anticipate user behaviors or preferences based on their interaction history with the website. For example, by analyzing the browsing patterns of a user, a neural network might be able to foresee the types of products or content that would appeal to them, thereby allowing for a more customized and engaging user experience on the website by tailoring content and recommendations specifically to their interests. Neurons are the building blocks of neural networks, and they are responsible for processing and transmitting information. In web development, neurons can be analogous to different components within a web application. For example, a neuron could represent a specific feature or functionality, such as a search bar or a recommendation system. By combining and connecting these neurons, we can create complex neural networks that can perform advanced tasks, such as NLP or image recognition.

Layers are another important aspect of neural networks. In web development, layers can be compared to different stages or components of a web application's architecture. Each layer in a neural network extracts and processes specific features from the input data. For instance, in a web-based image recognition system, the first layer might extract basic features such as edges and colors, while subsequent layers could identify more complex patterns such as objects or faces. By organizing the layers effectively, we can build powerful neural networks that can handle intricate tasks in web development.

Weights and biases are parameters within neural networks that determine the strength and influence of connections between neurons. In web development, weights and biases can be adjusted to optimize the performance of a neural network. For example, by assigning higher weights to certain inputs or biases, we can prioritize specific features or functionalities within a web application. This flexibility allows us to fine-tune the neural network to achieve desired outcomes, such as faster response times or improved accuracy in data processing.

Therefore, the application of neural networks in web development holds great potential for enhancing user experiences and optimizing various processes. By understanding and utilizing concepts such as inputs, neurons, layers, weights, and biases, we can leverage the power of neural networks to create intelligent and efficient web applications. As developers, it is crucial for us to stay updated with the latest advancements in neural network technology and explore innovative ways to integrate them into our web development practices. Together, we can unlock the full potential of neural networks in shaping the future of web development.

The next section delves into how integrating CV technologies can further revolutionize web development. By enabling machines to interpret and understand visual data from the world around us, CV opens up new avenues for creating more interactive, intuitive, and accessible web applications.

Empowering web development with computer vision

Now, you will learn about the exciting field of CV and its application in empowering web development. Our ultimate goal is to provide you with a comprehensive understanding of how CV can enhance web development processes and enable machines to interpret and make decisions based on visual data. The integration of facial recognition for user authentication on a website is an excellent use case for CV. This example illustrates how CV can improve security and the user experience, promoting ease in everyday life with your web applications.

CV is a discipline that focuses on enabling machines to understand and analyze visual information. By harnessing the power of CV, developers can create web applications that can recognize images, detect objects, and understand scenes. This opens up a whole new range of possibilities for interactive and immersive web experiences.

Understanding the fundamentals of CV is crucial in today's world, where visual data is abundant. By leveraging CV techniques, developers can create intelligent web applications that can automatically process and analyze visual information, leading to improved user experiences and increased efficiency.

Key concepts in CV

Making a compelling CV presentation is crucial when showcasing your skills and qualifications. In this section, we will explore key concepts in CV and explain their significance in image processing and analysis. By understanding these concepts, you will gain insights into how CV techniques can be applied to various tasks, such as object recognition, image classification, feature extraction, and scene understanding.

One important concept in CV is **image processing**, which involves enhancing the quality of images before analysis. Preprocessing techniques, such as resizing, normalization, and filtering, are used to improve the overall image quality. For example, resizing an image can help standardize its dimensions, making it easier to analyze. Normalization adjusts the pixel values to a standard range, reducing variations in lighting conditions. Filtering techniques, such as noise reduction filters, can remove unwanted artifacts from the image, improving the accuracy of subsequent analyses.

In web development, preprocessing techniques such as resizing, normalization, and filtering can be used to improve the visual appearance of images on websites. For instance, by resizing and normalizing product images, an e-commerce website can provide a consistent and visually appealing browsing experience for users.

Another key concept is **object recognition**, which focuses on identifying and locating objects within images or video frames. Techniques such as **Region-Based Convolutional Neural Network (R-CNN)**, **You Only Look Once (YOLO)**, and **Single-Shot MultiBox Detector (SSD)** are commonly used in object detection tasks. R-CNN, for instance, divides the image into regions and extracts features using CNNs, enabling accurate object identification. YOLO and SSD are real-time object detection algorithms that can detect multiple objects in an image simultaneously, making them suitable for applications such as autonomous driving and surveillance systems.

Image classification is another crucial task in CV, which involves assigning labels or categories to images. Deep learning models, such as CNNs, excel in image classification tasks. These models learn to extract features from images and use them to classify images into different categories. For example, a CNN model trained on a large dataset of cat and dog images can accurately classify new images as either cats or dogs based on the learned features. By automatically classifying images based on their content, a website can enforce community guidelines and prevent the display of inappropriate or offensive content.

Feature extraction plays a vital role in CV as it involves identifying key features from images. This process enables the model to focus on crucial aspects and discard irrelevant information. For example, in facial recognition, features such as the shape of the eyes, nose, and mouth are extracted to uniquely identify individuals. Feature extraction techniques can vary depending on the task and may involve methods such as edge detection, texture analysis, or shape recognition. For instance, a travel website can extract key features from destination images, such as landmarks or natural attractions, to improve search accuracy. This enables users to find their desired travel destinations more efficiently.

Scene understanding involves interpreting the overall context and relationships between objects in an image. This concept is crucial for understanding complex scenes and extracting meaningful information. For example, in autonomous driving systems, scene understanding is crucial to identify and react to traffic signs, pedestrians, and other vehicles. By interpreting the context of a scene, a real estate website can provide virtual tours of properties, allowing potential buyers to explore the space and understand its layout without physically visiting it.

Thus, understanding key concepts in CV is essential for effectively utilizing image processing and analysis techniques. Whether it's enhancing image quality, detecting objects, classifying images, extracting features, or understanding scenes, these concepts provide the foundation for various CV applications. By harnessing the power of CV, we can unlock new possibilities in fields such as healthcare, transportation, and security, revolutionizing the way we interact with visual data.

Applications of CV in web development

In recent years, CV has become an increasingly important technology in various fields. One area where CV has immense potential is in web development. In this section, we will explore the potential applications of CV in web development and delve into specific examples to better understand its capabilities.

When it comes to web development, CV can be utilized in a multitude of ways. Let's take a look at some examples:

- One practical application is in image recognition and processing. By using CV algorithms, we can analyze images uploaded by users and automatically extract relevant information. This can be particularly useful in e-commerce websites, where product images can be automatically tagged with descriptive keywords or even used to generate product recommendations based on visual similarities.

- Another area where CV can greatly enhance web development is in user experience. By utilizing facial recognition technology, websites can personalize content based on the emotions or reactions of the user. For example, a news website could display different articles or headlines based on the user's facial expressions, ensuring that the content they see is tailored to their interests and preferences.

- CV can also be used to optimize web accessibility. By incorporating CV algorithms into the development process, websites can better accommodate users with visual impairments. For instance, CV can be used to automatically generate alt text for images, making them accessible to screen readers. Additionally, CV can help improve the readability of text by identifying and adjusting font size, contrast, and spacing based on the user's needs.

- In the field of web security, CV can play a crucial role as well. Facial recognition technology can be integrated into authentication systems, providing an extra layer of security. Instead of relying solely on passwords or fingerprint recognition, websites can verify the user's identity by analyzing their facial features. This can help prevent unauthorized access and protect sensitive data.

While these are just a few examples, the potential applications of CV in web development are vast. By leveraging the power of CV algorithms, web developers can create more personalized, accessible, and secure websites. It is important to keep in mind that the development of CV applications requires a deep understanding of both web development principles and CV algorithms. By staying informed about the latest advancements in CV technology, we can continue to explore and unlock even more possibilities for its integration in web development.

The integration of CV in web development presents exciting opportunities for improving user experience, accessibility, security, and more. By embracing this technology and exploring its potential, we can create websites that better cater to the needs and preferences of users. The future of web development is undoubtedly intertwined with the advancements of CV, and it is up to us to harness its power and shape the digital landscape.

Technologies and tools for CV

In recent years, there has been significant progress in CV, thanks to the development of various technologies and tools. In this section, we will explore some tools used in the field of CV.

Frameworks

One of the most widely used frameworks in CV is **OpenCV**. Developed as an open source library, OpenCV offers an extensive collection of tools for image and video analysis. Its cross-platform support makes it a versatile choice for developers working on different operating systems.

Another popular framework is **TensorFlow**, developed by Google. TensorFlow is primarily known for its applications in deep learning and neural networks. With its vast array of pre-built models and algorithms, TensorFlow has become the go-to choice for many researchers and practitioners in the field of CV. Moreover, **TensorFlow Lite**, a lightweight version of the framework, is optimized for mobile and edge devices, enabling on-device inference.

PyTorch, developed by Facebook, is another framework gaining popularity in the CV community. What sets PyTorch apart is its dynamic computational graphs, allowing for more flexibility in model building and experimentation. It has become a favorite among researchers due to its ease of use and powerful capabilities.

MediaPipe, developed by Google, is a comprehensive framework designed for building multimodal machine learning pipelines. It supports a wide range of tasks, including CV, audio processing, and text analysis. MediaPipe is particularly known for its efficiency in real-time processing, making it ideal for applications that require immediate feedback and interaction.

Libraries

In addition to frameworks, various libraries play a crucial role in CV development. **Dlib**, a toolkit for machine learning, offers functionalities such as facial recognition and image processing. With its comprehensive set of algorithms, Dlib has become an essential tool for tasks involving face detection, landmark estimation, and more.

scikit-image is another valuable library in the CV ecosystem. Built on the foundations of NumPy, SciPy, and Matplotlib, scikit-image provides a wide range of algorithms for image segmentation, filtering, and other image-processing tasks. Its user-friendly interface makes it accessible to both beginners and experts in the field.

For those looking for an open source framework specifically designed for CV applications, **SimpleCV** is a great choice. With its user-friendly interface and intuitive APIs, SimpleCV simplifies the process of building CV applications, making it accessible to developers with varying levels of expertise.

Deployment

Deploying CV models efficiently is crucial for real-world applications. ONNX is an open format for AI models that facilitates interoperability between different frameworks. With ONNX, developers can easily convert models between different frameworks, enabling seamless integration and efficient deployment.

TensorFlow Lite, as mentioned earlier, is a lightweight version of TensorFlow optimized for mobile and edge devices. It allows for on-device inference, making it ideal for applications where low latency and real-time processing are critical.

Intel's **Open Visual Inference and Neural Network Optimization** (**OpenVINO**) toolkit is specifically designed for CV applications on Intel hardware. OpenVINO helps optimize pre-trained models for efficient deployment on Intel CPUs, GPUs, and FPGAs, enabling high-performance inference.

Visualization

Visualizing and analyzing CV results are essential for understanding and improving models. **Matplotlib**, a 2D plotting library, provides a wide range of tools for visualizing image data. Its seamless integration with Jupyter Notebook makes it a popular choice for data visualization in the CV community.

TensorBoard, a visualization tool for TensorFlow, goes beyond basic data visualization. It enables developers to monitor and analyze their training processes, visualize model graphs, and track performance metrics, making it an invaluable tool for model development and debugging.

OpenCV GUI, a graphical user interface module, allows for the visual inspection of images and results. It provides a user-friendly interface for debugging CV applications, enabling developers to identify and resolve issues quickly.

The field of CV has witnessed significant advancements thanks to various technologies and tools. From frameworks such as OpenCV, TensorFlow, and PyTorch to libraries such as Dlib, scikit-image, and SimpleCV, these tools empower developers to build sophisticated CV applications. Additionally, deployment tools such as ONNX, TensorFlow Lite, and OpenVINO facilitate efficient model deployment, while visualization tools such as Matplotlib, TensorBoard, and OpenCV GUI aid in understanding and improving CV models. As CV continues to evolve, these technologies and tools will play a crucial role in shaping its future.

Summary

In this chapter, you were given a comprehensive understanding of vital AI principles within the context of web development. The chapter expanded upon the foundational knowledge introduced in the first chapter and aimed to empower you with AI proficiency.

The chapter covered various topics, including AI fundamentals, machine learning essentials, NLP for web interaction, introduction to neural networks, and empowering web development with CV. Going through these topics provided you with the necessary tools to flourish in the continuously evolving landscape of AI.

These lessons are crucial for you as they provide a solid foundation in AI principles and their application in web development. Understanding AI fundamentals, machine learning, NLP, neural networks, and CV is essential in today's rapidly evolving technological landscape.

In the next chapter, you will learn about the challenges of and opportunities involved in integrating AI into web projects.

3
Challenges and Opportunities – Integrating AI into Web Projects

In this chapter, we will explore the practical challenges and exciting opportunities that come with integrating **artificial intelligence** (**AI**) into web development projects. We will delve into the obstacles that developers may encounter and provide insights into how to optimize opportunities to effectively leverage AI. By the end of this chapter, you will have a comprehensive understanding of the landscape surrounding AI integration in web projects. Overall, this chapter aims to equip you with the knowledge and skills necessary to navigate the challenges and opportunities of integrating AI into web projects. The information presented here is crucial not only in terms of the book's content but also in the context of the real world, where AI is increasingly becoming a fundamental component of web development. So, let's dive in and explore the exciting world of AI integration in web projects!

In this chapter, we're going to cover the following main topics:

- Navigating the AI process in web development
- Selecting and evaluating models for web-based AI
- Ethical considerations in AI integration
- Mitigating risks in AI implementation
- Using interpretable AI to make models understandable

Technical requirements

To follow this example, you will need the following:

- A computer with any operating system and internet access
- Required software:
  - Python 3.6 or later (`https://www.python.org/downloads/`)
  - A suitable IDE or text editor, such as Visual Studio Code (`https://code.visualstudio.com/`)
  - A web framework for Python, such as Flask (`https://flask.palletsprojects.com/`) or Django (https://www.djangoproject.com/)
  - Machine learning libraries, including `scikit-learn` and `pandas` (installable via `pip`)
  - MovieLens dataset: Download the MovieLens 100K dataset from `https://grouplens.org/datasets/movielens/100k/`
- Optional but recommended:
  - A version control system such as Git (`https://git-scm.com/`) for managing your project
  - A web application framework for Python, such as Flask or Django, to create a user-friendly interface

Integrating AI into web development requires a deep understanding of AI processes, web development principles, and DevOps practices. These three components form the backbone of creating robust and user-friendly web applications.

First, let's define the AI process. It begins with clearly defining the problem and identifying the specific requirements, for instance, enhancing a web application's recommendation system to improve user engagement. The next step is data collection and preprocessing, where we gather user interaction data and clean it to remove any noise or inconsistencies. Selecting the right AI model is crucial; whether it's collaborative filtering or content-based filtering for a recommendation system, the choice depends on the application's needs. The model is then trained using the collected data, and various optimization techniques are applied to improve its accuracy. Finally, the model is deployed and continuously monitored to maintain its effectiveness.

Web development, on the other hand, starts with meticulous planning and defining the goals, target audience, and requirements. This phase is followed by designing the visual and interactive aspects of the application by creating wireframes and mockups that lay the foundation for development. The development phase involves coding and integrating the AI model into the web application, ensuring seamless functionality. Extensive testing is then conducted to guarantee reliability and usability, and the final product is deployed and maintained to ensure optimal performance.

DevOps practices are integral to this process, facilitating continuous development, integration, testing, deployment, and feedback. Setting up CI/CD pipelines for automated testing and deployment ensures smooth operations and continuous improvement. Monitoring and feedback loops are essential to track the application's performance and make necessary adjustments.

To illustrate these concepts, let's consider a personalized movie recommendation system using Python's `scikit-learn` library. By developing such a system, we can enhance user experiences on movie streaming platforms by providing tailored recommendations based on user preferences. Imagine the system learning from user interactions, predicting which movies they might like, and continuously refining its recommendations to keep users engaged.

Navigating the AI process in web development

Today the integration of AI into web development has become increasingly important. Navigating the AI process tailored for web development requires a deep understanding of various processes such as AI, web development, and DevOps. In this section, we will define each process and discuss its significance in the context of web development. The integration of distinct processes such as AI, web development, and DevOps is not just beneficial; it's increasingly becoming a necessity. Additionally, we will explore the possibility of integrating these three processes to create powerful and efficient web solutions, the integrated AI loops.

AI brings the power of data-driven decision-making and personalization to web applications, while traditional web development focuses on creating the user-facing components of a web service. DevOps, on the other hand, bridges the gap between software development and IT operations, emphasizing shorter development cycles, increased deployment frequency, and more dependable releases, in close alignment with business objectives.

The inflection point in this issue lies in the fact that these processes, when siloed, may cause disjointed workflows and a lack of synergy across teams. For instance, an AI team working independently from the web development team may develop algorithms that are not optimized for the actual user experience or may encounter bottlenecks when integrating their models into the existing web infrastructure. Similarly, DevOps practices might not be fully leveraged if the AI and web development teams are not in sync regarding continuous integration and delivery pipelines.

To address these concerns, an integrated approach is essential where cross-functional teams collaborate from the outset. By fostering an environment where AI specialists, web developers, and DevOps engineers work together, organizations can ensure that AI models are developed with the end user experience in mind, that web applications are built to accommodate these models, and that the deployment of these applications is smooth and efficient. This integrated strategy not only enhances the effectiveness of each domain but also leads to the creation of web solutions that are more powerful, user-friendly, and robust in responding to real-world demands.

Defining the processes

First, let's look at the AI process.

The **AI process** involves several stages that enable the development and implementation of intelligent algorithms in web projects.

Let's look at the steps:

1. It starts with defining the problem and identifying the specific requirements.
2. Next, data collection takes place, followed by the crucial step of data preprocessing to ensure high-quality input for the AI models.
3. The selection of the appropriate AI model is then made, considering factors such as accuracy, complexity, and scalability.
4. The model is trained using the collected data, and validation and adjustment are performed to optimize its performance.
5. Finally, the model is evaluated and interpreted to gain insights and make informed decisions. The AI model is deployed, and continuous monitoring and maintenance ensure its effectiveness in real-world scenarios.

Now, we'll delve into web development.

Web development encompasses the entire life cycle of creating and maintaining websites or web applications. It starts with meticulous planning, where the goals, target audience, and requirements are defined. The design phase follows, where the visual and interactive aspects of the website are crafted. Development involves coding and building the website's functionality. Extensive testing is then carried out to ensure the website's reliability and usability. After successful testing, the website is deployed, making it accessible to users. Ongoing maintenance guarantees the website's optimal performance and keeps it up to date with evolving technologies.

Lastly, let's talk about DevOps.

DevOps is a set of practices that combines software **development (Dev)** and IT **operations (Ops)**. It aims to shorten the systems development life cycle and provide continuous delivery with high-quality software. The DevOps process includes continuous development, integration, testing, deployment, monitoring, and feedback. Continuous development ensures that developers consistently deliver new features and improvements. Integration and testing are performed continuously to identify and resolve any issues early on. Deployment and monitoring guarantee smooth and efficient operations. Continuous feedback from users and stakeholders helps in improving the software and meeting their evolving needs.

The importance of each process

Each process plays a crucial role in web development and AI integration. The **AI process** enables the development of intelligent algorithms that enhance user experience and provide valuable insights. The **web development process** ensures the creation of visually appealing and functional websites. **DevOps** facilitates seamless collaboration, efficient workflows, and continuous delivery of high-quality software. While all processes are important, their significance may vary depending on the specific project requirements and goals.

Integrating the processes

Integrating the AI, web development, and DevOps processes is not only possible but also highly beneficial. By combining these processes, web developers can leverage the power of AI algorithms to enhance website functionality, user experience, and decision-making capabilities. DevOps practices ensure the smooth integration and deployment of AI models, while web development provides the platform for AI implementation. This integration empowers developers to create intelligent web solutions that deliver exceptional value to users and businesses alike. Below is a comparison of the phases involved in DevOps, web development, and artificial intelligence (AI) processes. Each phase represents a crucial step in the respective domains, showcasing how these fields align and differ in their workflows.

Phase	DevOps	Web Development	Artificial Intelligence
Definition/planning	Planning	Planning	Problem definition
Data collection	-	-	Data collection
Data preprocessing	-	-	Data preprocessing
Architecture/design	-	Design	Model selection
Development	Continuous development	Development	Model training
Tests	Continuous testing	Test	Testing and evaluation
Optimization	-	-	Model optimization
Implementation		Implementation	Deployment
Monitoring	Continuous monitoring	-	Monitoring
Feedback	Continuous feedback	-	-
Maintenance	Continuous operation	Maintenance	Continuous improvement

Table 3.1: DevOps, web development, and AI processes

Navigating the AI process in web development requires expertise in AI, web development, and DevOps. Understanding the significance of each process is relevant for effectively integrating AI into web projects. By combining these processes, developers can harness the power of AI to create intelligent web solutions that meet users' needs and drive business growth.

AI pipeline – streamlining the journey of AI

To effectively incorporate AI into web projects, it is crucial to navigate through a well-structured process known as the **AI pipeline**. This involves various steps, including data preprocessing, model selection, and deployment strategies, all aimed at optimizing the integration of AI into web projects.

Let's get into the steps:

1. The first step in the AI pipeline is *defining the problem* at hand. This initial stage involves identifying the specific challenge that requires an AI solution.

2. Once the problem is defined, we move on to the *data collection* phase. It is essential to gather relevant data that will serve as the foundation for training the AI model.

3. After data collection, the next stage is *data preprocessing*. This step involves cleaning, transforming, and organizing the collected data to ensure its quality and suitability for training the AI model. Data preprocessing plays a crucial role in enhancing the accuracy and reliability of the model.

4. Once the data is preprocessed, the next step is to *select the most appropriate AI model*. This stage requires expertise in model selection, taking into consideration the specific requirements of the web project. A thorough understanding of different AI models and their strengths is crucial in making an informed decision.

5. Following model selection, the chosen model goes through the *training phase*. This is where the AI model learns from the preprocessed data to make accurate predictions or classifications. The training process involves adjusting the model's parameters and optimizing its performance to achieve the desired results.

6. After training, the model enters the *testing and evaluation stage*. Rigorous testing is conducted to assess the model's performance and identify any potential shortcomings. This stage helps in fine-tuning the model and ensuring its reliability before deployment.

7. Once the model is deemed satisfactory, it undergoes *optimization*. This phase involves further enhancing the model's performance, efficiency, and scalability. Optimization strategies are implemented to ensure the model can handle real-time data and deliver accurate results consistently.

8. Finally, the fully optimized AI model is ready for *deployment*. This stage involves integrating the model into the web project, making it accessible to users or clients. Careful consideration is given to ensure seamless integration and user-friendly experience.

However, the journey of AI does not end with deployment. The last stage of the AI pipeline involves *continuous improvement*. As new data becomes available and user feedback is received, the model is refined and updated to adapt to changing needs and improve its performance over time.

In summary, the **AI pipeline** is a systematic process that guides the development, testing, and deployment of AI models in web projects. By following this well-defined pipeline, web developers can harness the power of AI effectively and ensure the success of their projects.

Integrated AI loops – streamlining AI development for web applications

In today's digital age, harnessing the power of AI has become essential for developing cutting-edge web applications. However, the process of developing and deploying AI models can often be complex and time-consuming. That's where **integrated AI loops** come in.

The AI-integrated pipeline is *a structured iterative, incremental, and continuous process designed to streamline the development and deployment of AI models in web applications*. By combining the best practices from the fields of AI and DevOps, this pipeline ensures that models are developed and deployed efficiently and effectively, as illustrated in *Figure 3.1*.

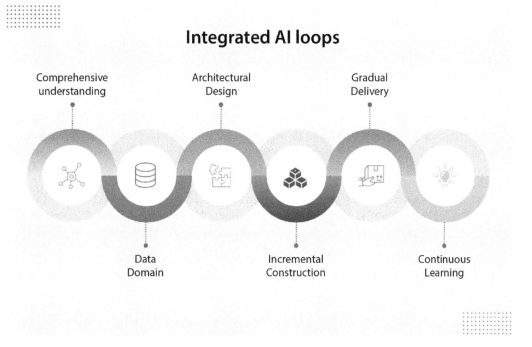

Figure 3.1: AI loops integrated process

The pipeline consists of *six* interconnected loops, each with its own specific objective. Let's explore each of these cycles in more detail:

1. Firstly, we have the *comprehensive understanding loop*. The goal of this cycle is to clearly define the problem that the AI model will solve, identify both functional and non-functional requirements, establish quality criteria, and understand the needs and priorities of the project. This cycle also involves defining success metrics for evaluating the model's performance.

2. Next is the *data domain loop*. In this cycle, we focus on collecting, cleaning, transforming, and analyzing the data that will be used to train and test the AI model. This ensures that the model receives high-quality data for optimal performance.

3. The *architecture design loop* comes next. The objective here is to define the system architecture that will seamlessly integrate the AI model with the web application. This involves designing the system, prototyping, and selecting the most suitable AI model for the task at hand.

4. The *incremental construction loop* is where the AI model is implemented, tested, evaluated, and optimized. This cycle ensures that the model is developed with precision, rigorously tested, and continually improved for the best possible performance.

5. Once the AI model is ready, we move on to the *gradual delivery loop*. This cycle involves integrating the AI model with the web application, testing it thoroughly, and finally deploying it into the production environment. This ensures a smooth transition from development to real-world implementation.

6. Finally, we have the *continuous learning loop*. This cycle focuses on continuously monitoring the performance of the AI model in production, collecting user feedback, and automatically responding to changes. This allows for ongoing improvement and enhancement of the model's capabilities.

Integrated AI loops are designed to provide a structured and iterative approach to efficiently and effectively develop and deploy AI models in web applications. By combining the best practices of AI and DevOps, this pipeline ensures that AI models meet user needs and business objectives.

Developing expertise in navigating the AI process tailored for web development is crucial. This includes mastering skills such as data preprocessing, model selection, and deployment strategies, all while optimizing the integration of AI into web projects.

In conclusion, the AI-integrated pipeline is a powerful tool that enables organizations to develop and deploy AI models more efficiently and effectively. By following this structured and iterative process, developers can create AI-powered web applications that meet user needs and achieve business goals. Embracing the AI-integrated pipeline is a step toward harnessing the full potential of AI in web development.

Having established integrated AI loops as a crucial asset for organizations aiming to develop and deploy AI models with greater efficiency and effectiveness, we now transition to the vital process of selecting and evaluating models for web-based AI. The importance of choosing the right models cannot be overstated, as it directly impacts the performance and success of AI integrations within web applications. In the upcoming section, we delve into the critical steps and considerations involved in this selection process. Our focus will be on ensuring that the chosen model not only fulfills the specific requirements of the application but also upholds the standards of reliability and accuracy needed for optimal AI performance. This step is fundamental in transforming AI's potential into practical, user-centric solutions that align with business objectives.

Selecting and evaluating models for web-based AI

Choosing the right AI models is crucial for optimal performance. This section covers defining model selection criteria, choosing validation strategies, and selecting appropriate evaluation metrics. Comparing different models, such as logistic regression and clustering, using cross-validation helps identify the best fit for the task. Evaluating model performance with metrics such as accuracy, precision, and AUC ensures the chosen model meets the application's requirements.

For instance, implementing a sentiment analysis model to evaluate customer feedback on products involves using **natural language processing** (**NLP**) techniques to preprocess and analyze text data. Comparing models such as naive Bayes, SVM, and BERT allows us to select the most effective one. This approach ensures that the AI system is not only accurate but also efficient and scalable.

Procedure

The process of selecting and evaluating AI models can be divided into the following stages:

1. **Defining model selection criteria**.

   In this stage, it is crucial to define the criteria used to evaluate the candidate models. These include the following:

   - Specific requirements of the web application

   - Performance considerations

   - Fit with available data

   - Scalability

   - Ease of implementation

   - Explainability

   - Ethical considerations

2. **Choosing an appropriate validation strategy**.

    The validation strategy determines how data is divided to evaluate the model's performance and estimate its future performance. Examples of strategies are as follows:

    - **Train-test split**: A simple division but may have limitations on small datasets or imbalanced classes.

    - **Stratified k-fold**: Maintains class proportions in different folds, which is important for classification problems.

    - **Cross-validation**: Evaluates the model on multiple data partitions, providing a more robust estimate of performance.

3. **Choosing the correct evaluation metric**.

    Choosing the right evaluation metric is crucial for the success of the machine learning project. It should align with the business objective and reflect the desired values and optimizations for the model. Performance metrics can be categorized as follows:

    - **Accuracy**: Proportion of correct predictions made by the model.

    - **Scoring metrics**: Provide a single score for model performance, which is useful for comparison. Examples include precision, recall, and F1-score.

    - **Area Under the Curve (AUC) metrics**: Provide a robust measure of model performance, especially in classification problems with imbalanced classes.

    Choosing the correct metric is fundamental for comparing models and selecting the most suitable one for the task. Remember that each metric has its limitations, and it is common to use multiple metrics for a comprehensive evaluation.

4. **Identifying potential models**.

    In this stage, it is crucial to identify different types of AI models that can meet the previously defined requirements. Models can be supervised (e.g., logistic regression) or unsupervised (e.g., clustering).

5. **Training and evaluating models**.

    After identifying the potential models, the next step is to train them on the training dataset and evaluate them on the validation dataset. Hyperparameter adjustments can be made during this process.

6. **Model selection**.

    Based on the evaluation, choose the model that best meets the criteria defined in step 1. Consider not only performance but also factors such as model complexity, training time, and interpretability.

7. **Model testing**.

> Finally, test the selected model on the test dataset to obtain an unbiased estimate of its performance. If satisfactory, the model can be deployed for use in web applications.

What are the observations? Let's find out.

Observations

The process of selecting and evaluating AI models is iterative, allowing for adjustments over time. This guide offers a solid framework but also flexibility to adapt to the nuances of each project. The key to success lies in the careful selection of criteria, validation strategies, and evaluation metrics, aligned with the specific goals of each web application.

After detailing the process of selecting and evaluating AI models for web applications, emphasizing the importance of rigorous testing and selection criteria aligned with project goals, it is imperative that we now turn our attention to the ethical considerations inherent in AI integration. This crucial segment transcends technical aspects, addressing how responsible AI implementation can positively influence society, while highlighting the need for approaches that prioritize privacy, transparency, and fairness. By making this transition, we emphasize the importance of not only how we build and implement AI technologies but also why and for whom they are developed, ensuring that technological advancements benefit everyone in a fair and ethical manner.

Ethical considerations in AI integration

As we harness the power of AI for web development, it is crucial to acknowledge and address the ethical considerations that arise in this process. This section aims to explore the importance of ethical considerations in AI integration and the impact it has on society.

Ethical considerations play a pivotal role in ensuring the responsible and accountable use of AI in web development. As developers, we must develop expertise in navigating the AI process tailored for web development. This involves understanding data preprocessing, model selection, and deployment strategies, all while optimizing the integration of AI into web projects.

The significance of ethical considerations lies in their ability to safeguard against potential biases and discriminatory practices that may be embedded within AI systems. These systems are fueled by vast amounts of data, and if not carefully curated, they can perpetuate societal inequalities. By approaching AI integration with an ethical lens, we can actively strive to minimize these biases and ensure fair and inclusive outcomes.

Moreover, the impact of AI on society cannot be underestimated. AI-powered web projects have the potential to revolutionize various industries, improving efficiency and enhancing user experiences. However, without ethical considerations, these advancements can have unintended consequences. Issues such as privacy invasion, job displacement, and algorithmic biases can arise, jeopardizing the trust and well-being of individuals and communities.

To mitigate these risks, it is imperative that we prioritize ethical considerations throughout the AI integration process. This involves the ongoing evaluation and monitoring of AI systems, with a focus on transparency and accountability. By adopting a human-centered approach, we can ensure that AI serves as a tool to augment human capabilities rather than replace them.

Ethical considerations are paramount when integrating AI into web development. By developing expertise in navigating the AI process tailored for web projects and prioritizing ethical practices, we can harness the potential of AI while safeguarding against biases and negative societal impacts. As developers, it is our responsibility to approach AI integration with integrity, ensuring that it aligns with the values and needs of individuals and communities. Only through ethical considerations can AI truly contribute to a more inclusive and equitable society.

Challenges in ethical AI integration

As experts in development, we understand the importance of integrating AI into our projects. However, there are several challenges we must address to ensure the ethical use of AI. In this section, we will discuss four key challenges: bias in AI models, lack of explainability, data privacy concerns, and accountability gaps.

One of the main challenges in ethical AI integration is the presence of *bias in AI models*. AI systems are trained using data that can reflect societal biases, leading to discriminatory outcomes. As developers, we need to be aware of this bias and take steps to mitigate its impact. This can involve ensuring diverse and representative training data, performing regular audits of AI systems, and constantly refining and improving the models to minimize bias.

Another challenge is the *lack of explainability in AI models*. As AI becomes more complex and sophisticated, it becomes harder to understand and interpret the decisions made by these models. This lack of transparency can lead to distrust and hinder the adoption of AI technologies. To address this challenge, we need to develop explainable AI models and techniques that provide insights into how the models make decisions. This will help build trust and allow users to understand and verify the reasoning behind AI-based decisions.

Data privacy is a major concern when it comes to AI integration. AI systems rely on large amounts of data to train and make decisions. However, this data often contains sensitive and personal information, making it crucial to protect user privacy. As developers, we must prioritize data privacy by implementing robust security measures, anonymizing data whenever possible, and complying with relevant privacy regulations. By doing so, we can ensure that AI integration respects user privacy and maintains trust.

The final challenge we face in ethical AI integration is *accountability gaps*. AI systems can make mistakes or produce unintended consequences, raising questions of responsibility and accountability. It is essential to establish clear lines of accountability and ensure that there are mechanisms in place to address any issues that arise. This can involve creating guidelines and frameworks for responsible AI development, conducting regular audits and assessments, and implementing feedback loops to continuously improve and address any shortcomings.

Integrating AI into web development projects presents several challenges that need to be addressed to ensure ethical use. By acknowledging and actively working to address bias in AI models, promoting explainability, prioritizing data privacy, and establishing accountability mechanisms, we can navigate these challenges and create a more ethical and responsible AI integration process. As developers, it is our responsibility to develop expertise in these areas and strive for the responsible integration of AI into our projects.

Having explored the critical challenges of ethical AI integration, including addressing biases, ensuring explainability, safeguarding data privacy, and establishing accountability, we now shift our focus toward the proactive steps required to mitigate risks in AI implementation. This transition underscores the importance of not only identifying potential ethical pitfalls but also actively engaging in strategies to prevent them. In the next section, we will delve into a case study of the ethical evaluation of AI deployment in web development projects.

Case study – ethical evaluation of AI implementation at InnovaTech

In this case study, we will examine the implementation of an AI system by the start-up InnovaTech, designed to optimize the recruitment process. The system uses machine learning algorithms to analyze resumes and performance on skill tests, aiming to eliminate human biases in candidate selection and increase process efficiency. However, post-implementation, reports emerged suggesting that the system might be exacerbating gender and ethnic biases.

Case study objectives

This case study aims to identify the ethical challenges associated with the implementation of AI systems and develop practical solutions to mitigate these issues. It seeks to foster critical discussion about the responsibilities of developers and companies when deploying AI technologies.

Background

InnovaTech is an emerging technology company aiming to innovate the hiring process through AI. The developed system promised to reduce human bias and improve the efficiency of the selection process. However, a few months after its implementation, user feedback began to indicate a trend of the system favoring candidates from certain demographic profiles, raising questions about the fairness and ethics of the AI solution.

Identified ethical issues

Here are the ethical issues that have been identified:

- **Data bias**: The algorithm favors certain demographic groups over others, possibly reflecting biases present in the training data

- **Algorithm transparency**: There is a lack of clarity on how decisions are made by the AI system

- **Consent and privacy**: Concerns about how candidates' data are collected, used, and protected

Detailed analysis

Now, let's analyze this in a little more depth:

- **Data bias**: We will examine how the dataset used to train the algorithm might have been composed in a way that reflects or perpetuates existing societal inequalities

- **Transparency**: We will discuss the importance of AI systems being able to explain their decisions, especially in applications with significant impacts on people's lives, such as recruitment processes

- **Consent and privacy**: We will evaluate InnovaTech's privacy policies regarding the use of candidate data, checking compliance with regulations such as GDPR

Proposed solutions

To effectively address the challenges in AI implementation, several strategic solutions can be proposed. These solutions aim to enhance the fairness, transparency, and privacy of AI systems, ensuring they are reliable and ethical.

- **Data audit and review**: Implementation of periodic reviews and audits of datasets to identify and correct biases

- **Improving transparency**: Development of an interface that allows users to understand how decisions are made by the AI system

- **Strengthening privacy policies**: Review and strengthen privacy policies to ensure that candidates are fully informed about how their data is used

Discussion

This case study raises critical questions about the role of ethics in AI and how companies can navigate the challenges of implementing technologies that are fair and transparent. The discussion should involve considering multiple viewpoints, including those of AI developers, end users (companies and candidates), and regulators.

Conclusion

The InnovaTech case study serves as a vital example to understand the ethical complexities in AI implementation. The proposed solutions aim to create a balance between technological innovation and ethical responsibility, ensuring that technology works for the benefit of all parties involved.

The next section will delve into comprehensive strategies that not only address specific ethical issues but also fortify the overall resilience of AI systems against a range of potential risks.

Mitigating risks in AI implementation

In the rapidly evolving landscape of AI within web development, the implementation of AI technologies offers unprecedented opportunities to enhance user experiences, streamline operations, and unlock innovative solutions. However, this development also introduces a spectrum of ethical and operational risks that, if not adequately addressed, can undermine the benefits AI promises. These risks range from biases in decision-making algorithms to privacy concerns and beyond, posing significant challenges to developers and organizations alike. It is, therefore, essential to approach AI implementation with a blend of careful consideration and ethical awareness.

To navigate these challenges effectively and ensure the responsible deployment of AI in web applications, a multifaceted strategy is required. This strategy encompasses the development of ethical AI frameworks, the establishment of diverse and inclusive development teams, the continuous monitoring and maintenance of AI models, and robust data governance practices, among others. By adopting these key strategies, developers and organizations can mitigate the potential risks associated with AI implementation, ensuring that AI technologies are used in a way that is not only innovative but also ethical and socially responsible. Let's take an in-depth look at them.

Ethical AI frameworks

As developers, we understand the importance of incorporating AI into our projects. It allows us to enhance user experiences and provide personalized solutions. However, it is crucial to approach AI development with a strong ethical framework in mind.

Developing expertise in navigating the AI process tailored for web development is a skill that we prioritize. This includes understanding data preprocessing, model selection, and deployment strategies. By optimizing the integration of AI into our web projects, we ensure that ethical considerations are at the forefront of our decision-making.

Ethical AI frameworks serve as a guide for us to make responsible choices throughout the development process. These frameworks help us address potential biases and ensure fairness and transparency in our AI algorithms. By following these frameworks, we mitigate the risks of unintended consequences and discriminatory outcomes.

Ethical AI frameworks are structured guidelines or sets of principles designed to guide the development, deployment, and use of AI technologies in a manner that prioritizes ethical considerations, such as fairness, accountability, transparency, and respect for human rights.

These frameworks typically cover a broad range of ethical issues, including but not limited to the following:

- **Bias and fairness**: Ensuring that AI systems do not perpetuate or amplify biases against certain groups or individuals, and working toward equitable outcomes for all users

- **Transparency**: Making the workings of AI systems understandable to users and stakeholders, allowing them to comprehend how decisions are made or outcomes are generated

- **Accountability**: Establishing clear responsibilities for the outcomes of AI systems, including mechanisms for redress when harm occurs

- **Privacy and data protection**: Safeguarding personal data processed by AI systems, in accordance with data protection laws and principles, and ensuring users' privacy is respected

- **Safety and security**: Ensuring AI systems operate safely and securely, without posing risks to users or the public

- **Human oversight**: Maintaining human control over AI systems, ensuring that automated decisions can be reviewed and humans can intervene when necessary

Ethical AI frameworks often draw upon interdisciplinary insights, including philosophy, law, social sciences, and computer science, to address these complex issues. They are used by organizations, policy-makers, and developers as a guide to conduct risk assessments, design ethical AI solutions, and implement governance structures that ensure AI technologies contribute positively to society and do not cause harm.

In addition to technical considerations, ethical AI frameworks also encourage collaboration and interdisciplinary discussions. We actively engage with experts from various fields to gain diverse perspectives and insights. This collaborative approach allows us to consider the social, cultural, and ethical implications of our AI projects.

By following ethical AI frameworks, we ensure that our AI solutions benefit society as a whole. We recognize the responsibility we hold as web developers to create AI systems that are transparent, fair, and accountable. Through continuous learning and adaptation, we strive to improve our ethical AI practices and contribute to the development of responsible AI technologies.

Diverse and inclusive AI development teams

By fostering an environment that values different perspectives and experiences, we can create AI systems that are more effective, unbiased, and ethical.

One key skill that we prioritize in our team is expertise in navigating the AI process tailored for web development. This involves mastering various technical aspects such as data preprocessing, model selection, and deployment strategies. By honing these skills, we ensure that our AI solutions are seamlessly integrated into web projects, optimizing their performance and impact.

However, it is not enough to solely focus on technical expertise. We recognize the importance of diversity in our team composition. By bringing together individuals with different backgrounds, cultures, and identities, we enrich our collective knowledge and broaden our perspectives. This diversity allows us to develop AI systems that are more robust, as they are designed to cater to a wider range of users and contexts.

Inclusivity is another fundamental value that we uphold. We believe that everyone should have equal opportunities to contribute and be heard. By creating a safe and inclusive space, we encourage collaboration, open dialogue, and the exchange of ideas. This inclusive environment fosters creativity and innovation, enabling us to develop AI solutions that truly meet the needs of diverse users.

To ensure that our AI development teams are truly diverse and inclusive, we actively seek out individuals from underrepresented groups in the field of AI. We provide mentorship, support, and resources to help them thrive and succeed in their roles. By nurturing a diverse talent pool, we not only promote equality and social justice but also tap into a wealth of untapped potential and talent.

Ensuring optimal performance of AI models through continuous monitoring and maintenance

In the quest for AI excellence within the realm of web development, our commitment to perpetual monitoring and maintenance takes center stage. This unwavering focus ensures the sustained efficacy of our AI models in real-world scenarios. Through the implementation of robust monitoring systems, we need to diligently track performance metrics, accuracy levels, and potential biases embedded in our models. This proactive approach empowers us to swiftly identify and rectify any issues, thereby guaranteeing the optimal functionality of our AI solutions.

To attain this standard of operational excellence, regular updates and retraining sessions for our models become imperative. Recognizing the dynamic nature of data, ever-evolving in its patterns, we embrace the need for flexibility within our AI models. By staying abreast of the latest advancements and industry best practices, we continually enhance our models' performance and accuracy.

Proficiency in navigating the AI landscape tailored for web development stands out as a hallmark of our skill set. Our team boasts expertise in data preprocessing techniques, model selection strategies, and deployment optimization. This proficiency positions us to seamlessly integrate AI into web projects, unlocking its full potential to yield exceptional outcomes.

The continuous monitoring and maintenance of our AI models serve as a guarantee of reliability, accuracy, and impartiality. Our overarching objective should be to furnish clients with AI solutions that not only align with their current requirements but also possess the adaptability to evolve alongside their changing needs. Acknowledging the paramount importance of delivering consistent, high-quality results, our meticulous monitoring and maintenance process is meticulously designed to precisely achieve that.

Explainability and interpretability – enhancing model interpretability and communicating AI decisions effectively

In the dynamic landscape of AI, it is imperative not only to cultivate expertise in navigating the intricacies of the AI process but also to grasp the significance of **explainability** and **interpretability**. As AI seamlessly integrates into diverse web development projects, the emphasis on refining model interpretability and articulating AI decisions becomes indispensable.

Enhancing model interpretability is a skill that every AI practitioner should cultivate. By gaining expertise in data preprocessing, model selection, and deployment strategies tailored for web development, AI professionals can optimize the integration of AI into web projects. This skill allows for a better understanding of the inner workings of AI models, enabling us to explain and interpret their decisions accurately.

However, it is not enough to enhance model interpretability if we cannot effectively communicate AI decisions. Communication plays a vital role in building trust and transparency with users and stakeholders. It is important to convey AI decisions in a clear and concise manner, ensuring that they are easily understandable to both technical and non-technical audiences.

To achieve effective communication, we must avoid jargon and use a humanized approach. By adopting an informative and original tone, we can provide valuable insights without overwhelming our audience with technical terms. Instead, we should strive to present complex AI decisions in a simple and relatable manner, ensuring that our message is conveyed authentically.

Robust data governance – implementing strong data governance policies and data quality assurance

In the digital age, data has become an asset for businesses across industries. However, with this abundance of data comes the need for a comprehensive data governance framework. By establishing robust data governance and ensuring data quality assurance, you will be able to optimize the integration of AI into your web projects and achieve accurate and ethical outcomes.

Robust data governance

To lay the groundwork for successful AI-driven web development, it is imperative to establish strong data governance policies and procedures. This involves defining clear guidelines for data collection, storage, and usage. By doing so, you create a solid framework that ensures the privacy and security of individuals' information.

One key aspect of data governance is the implementation of techniques such as **anonymization** and **encryption**. These measures protect individuals' privacy by ensuring that their personal data remains confidential and inaccessible to unauthorized parties. By incorporating these techniques into your AI models, you can build trust and instill confidence among your users.

Data quality assurance

As the saying goes, *garbage in, garbage out*. This principle holds true when it comes to training AI models for web development. Ensuring data quality assurance is essential to achieving accurate and reliable results.

To avoid biases and inaccuracies in your AI models, it is crucial to work with clean, precise, and representative data. By carefully curating your dataset and removing any outliers or irrelevant information, you can enhance the performance of your models and minimize the risk of unfair or inaccurate outcomes.

Additionally, addressing missing data is equally important. Missing data can introduce biases and hinder the effectiveness of your AI models. By implementing strategies to handle missing data, such as imputation techniques or data augmentation, you can mitigate these issues and ensure the integrity of your results.

Human oversight and intervention – ensuring accuracy and fairness in AI for web development

In the swiftly advancing realm of AI in web development, upholding a continuous level of human oversight emerges as a pivotal component. This oversight functions as a protective measure, mitigating potential errors and biases that the system might inadvertently neglect.

Beyond technical proficiency, the pivotal role of human oversight cannot be overstated. It stands as a cornerstone in identifying potential errors or biases that may be introduced by AI systems.

Despite advancements in AI technology, machines are not infallible. They may occasionally produce inaccurate or biased results. This is where human intervention becomes crucial. By maintaining a level of human oversight, web developers can effectively detect and rectify any errors or biases in the AI systems they employ.

One of the primary responsibilities of human oversight is to ensure the accuracy of AI models utilized in web development projects. By closely monitoring the performance of these models, web developers can identify any discrepancies between expected and actual outcomes. This enables them to make necessary adjustments and improvements, resulting in more reliable and precise AI applications.

Bias is a prevalent concern in AI systems, as they can inadvertently perpetuate unfairness or discrimination. Human oversight allows us to identify and address such biases, ensuring that the AI systems used in web development projects remain fair and unbiased. By scrutinizing the datasets, evaluating the training process, and conducting regular audits, developers can minimize the potential for biased outcomes.

Unveiling the importance of regular auditing and documentation for bias and fairness in AI systems

We have come across an aspect that demands our attention: regular auditing and documentation for bias and fairness. By doing so, we can identify and rectify any biases that may have inadvertently crept into the algorithms. These audits serve as a powerful tool in ensuring that our AI systems are fair, unbiased, and aligned with ethical principles. Regular auditing empowers us to uncover any hidden patterns or discriminatory practices, allowing us to take corrective measures promptly.

An additional aspect pertains to the central role that documentation plays in ensuring the transparency and accountability of AI systems. Keeping meticulous records of the development process, data sources, and algorithmic decisions establishes a comprehensive trail that illuminates the inner workings of our AI systems. Beyond facilitating internal understanding, thorough documentation opens the door to external scrutiny, fostering trust and confidence among users and stakeholders.

Transparency is the cornerstone of responsible AI development. By regularly auditing our AI systems and maintaining thorough documentation, we demonstrate a commitment to transparency, providing insights into how our algorithms make decisions. This transparency allows us to address any concerns related to bias and fairness, ultimately ensuring that our AI systems are accountable for their actions.

In our pursuit of technical excellence, let us not forget the human aspect of AI development. Regular auditing and documentation are not just technical processes but also ethical responsibilities. So, we have the power to shape the future and influence lives. By adopting an authentic and humanized approach, we acknowledge the impact our AI systems have on society and strive to create a better, fairer world.

The section discusses the importance of mitigating risks and ensuring ethical considerations in the implementation of AI in web development. It emphasizes the need for an ethical AI framework that addresses biases, promotes fairness and transparency, and protects user privacy. The section also highlights the significance of diverse and inclusive AI development teams, as they bring different perspectives and experiences to create more effective and unbiased AI systems. It emphasizes the need for the continuous monitoring and maintenance of AI models to ensure optimal performance and accuracy. Additionally, the section stresses the importance of explainability and interpretability in communicating AI decisions effectively, as well as the establishment of robust data governance policies and data quality assurance. It emphasizes the role of human oversight in identifying errors and biases in AI systems and the importance of regular auditing and documentation to ensure fairness and transparency.

Now that we've navigated the complexities of ensuring ethical AI integration, focusing on bias mitigation, data governance, and the importance of diverse perspectives, let's transition to the next crucial aspect: interpretable AI – making models understandable. This shift emphasizes the significance of not just deploying AI systems responsibly but also making their operations transparent and comprehensible to all stakeholders. By making AI models more interpretable, we aim to bridge the gap between complex algorithms and their real-world applications, ensuring that users can trust and effectively interact with AI-driven solutions. Let's explore how we can demystify AI, making its decisions more accessible and its processes more accountable.

Making models understandable with interpretable AI

In this section, we'll talk about crafting models that transcend mere accuracy, embracing a realm of genuine understanding. This is precisely where the concept of interpretable AI emerges as a guiding light. In essence, interpretable AI embodies the capacity of AI systems to unravel the intricacies of their decision-making journeys, weaving a narrative that is not just transparent but profoundly comprehensible to users. It's about demystifying the technological wizardry, ensuring that the AI experience becomes a conversation rather than a monologue of algorithms.

Interpretable AI refers to the development of AI systems in a way that their operations, decisions, and processes can be understood by human beings. It is an approach to AI that prioritizes transparency and the ability of users and stakeholders to comprehend how AI models make their predictions or decisions, and on what basis those decisions are made. This approach is crucial for several reasons:

- **Trust**: By making AI systems interpretable, developers and companies can build trust with users. When users understand how an AI system arrives at its conclusions, they are more likely to trust its judgments and recommendations.

- **Accountability**: Interpretable AI facilitates accountability. It allows for the examination and justification of decisions made by AI, making it possible to identify when and why incorrect decisions are made. This is particularly important in sensitive areas such as healthcare, finance, and legal applications, where decisions can have significant impacts on people's lives.

- **Debugging and improvement**: Interpretable models make it easier for developers to identify errors or biases in the AI's decision-making process. This not only helps in debugging but also in refining and improving models over time.

- **Regulatory compliance**: With the increasing regulation around AI, such as the **European Union's (EU's) General Data Protection Regulation (GDPR)**, which includes provisions for the right to explanation, interpretability becomes a legal requirement in many contexts.

- **Ethical decision-making**: Interpretable AI supports ethical decision-making by illuminating how models consider various factors, helping to ensure that AI systems do not perpetuate or amplify biases.

Ethical considerations also come into play when discussing interpretable AI. By providing explanations for their decisions, AI models can help prevent biases or discriminatory practices. It allows for a fair assessment of the factors taken into account, ensuring transparency and accountability.

Moreover, interpretable AI is essential for regulatory compliance. GDPR in the EU, for example, requires AI systems processing personal data to be transparent and explainable. Similarly, the EU's proposed Directive on AI emphasizes the need for interpretability as a principle for responsible AI development and use.

To achieve interpretability, AI developers can employ various techniques and methodologies, including, but not limited to, the following:

- **Model transparency**: Using simpler models that inherently offer more transparency, such as linear regressions or decision trees, where the decision-making process is more straightforward to follow.

- **Feature importance**: Highlighting which features (input variables) the model considers most important when making predictions, which can offer insights into the model's reasoning.

- **Post hoc interpretation**: Applying tools and techniques to complex models (such as deep learning) after they have made predictions to explain their behavior. Examples include **Local Interpretable Model-agnostic Explanations (LIME)** and **SHapley Additive exPlanations (SHAP)**.

- **Visualization**: Employing graphical representations of data and model decisions to make the workings of AI systems more accessible to non-expert users.

Incorporating interpretability into AI development ensures that AI systems are not just powerful and accurate but also aligned with societal values of transparency, fairness, and accountability. As we continue to integrate AI into various aspects of daily life, making AI understandable with interpretable AI will be key to achieving these goals.

Understanding the importance of interpretable AI is crucial for various reasons. Firstly, it fosters trust in and adoption of AI technologies. When users can understand how a model arrives at a particular decision, they are more likely to trust its outputs and use it effectively. This is particularly important in sensitive domains such as healthcare or finance, where decisions made by AI systems can have significant consequences.

Now, you might be wondering how or why interpretable AI is easier for users. Let's answer that.

Interpretable AI allows users to understand how AI models make decisions through several methods and tools designed to reveal and explain the inner workings and logic of these systems. Here's how interpretable AI facilitates this understanding:

- **Simplified models**: Some AI models, such as decision trees or linear regression, are inherently more interpretable because their decision-making process is straightforward and logical. These models use clear, rule-based systems or weighted factors that are easy to follow and understand.

- **Feature importance**: This technique identifies and ranks the features (input variables) that are most influential in the model's decision-making process. By understanding which features are given more importance, users can grasp how the model is making its decisions. For instance, in a loan approval AI system, the model might consider credit score, income, and employment history as top factors influencing its decision.

- **Model-agnostic tools**: Tools such as **Local Interpretable Model-agnostic Explanations (LIME)** and **SHapley Additive exPlanations (SHAP)** can be used with any AI model to provide explanations for individual predictions. These tools break down a model's prediction into an understandable format, showing how each feature contributes to the final decision, even for complex models such as neural networks.

- **Visualization techniques**: Visualization can make complex data and models more accessible. For example, heat maps can show which parts of an image were most significant in a model's decision-making process in image recognition tasks. Similarly, decision trees can be visualized to show the paths from features to outcomes.

- **Example-based explanations**: Providing examples of similar cases or decisions made by the AI system in the past can help users understand the rationale behind a decision. For instance, if an AI system recommends a particular medication, it might also provide examples of similar patient profiles and the outcomes of such medication.

- **Counterfactual explanations**: These explanations describe how altering certain input variables could change the outcome. For example, in a loan denial case, a counterfactual explanation might indicate that increasing the income level or decreasing the debt amount could lead to approval, helping the user understand the decision criteria.

Users, especially those without a technical background, can leverage these methods to gain insights into AI decisions. For critical applications, such as in healthcare or finance, understanding the basis of AI decisions can build confidence and trust in the technology, ensuring that it is used responsibly and effectively. Moreover, this understanding can also prompt users to provide more accurate and relevant data to improve the AI system's performance, creating a feedback loop that enhances the AI's reliability and trustworthiness.

However, achieving model interpretability is not without its challenges. Deep learning models, known for their complexity and black-box nature, pose difficulties in understanding their decision-making processes. Balancing simplicity and accuracy is a trade-off that needs to be carefully managed.

To address these challenges, various techniques for model interpretability have emerged. Feature importance analysis allows us to understand which variables have the most significant impact on the model's outputs. Techniques such as LIME and SHAP provide insights into the local behavior of the model, helping users understand individual predictions. Decision trees and rule-based models offer a more interpretable alternative to complex deep learning architectures.

Interpretable AI plays a vital role in making AI models understandable and transparent. It is crucial for building trust, ensuring ethical practices, and complying with regulatory requirements. While challenges exist, techniques for model interpretability continue to evolve, enabling us to strike the right balance between accuracy and comprehensibility.

Now that we've explored the importance of interpretability in AI and the various techniques for achieving it, let's dive into a practical application to see these concepts in action. Personalized movie recommendations are a fascinating example of how AI can be adapted to individual preferences while maintaining transparency and understandability. Through this example, we will examine how interpretable AI techniques can be applied to increase user trust and satisfaction, illustrating the balance between sophisticated algorithmic predictions and the user's ability to understand how their movie recommendations are generated. This transition from theory to application highlights the tangible benefits of making AI models not only powerful but also accessible and transparent to end users.

Example of integrating AI into web projects – personalized movie recommendations with AI

In this chapter, we'll dive into a practical example that illustrates the application of AI techniques to enrich the functionality of web applications. Specifically, we will explore the construction of a personalized movie recommendation system using Python's `sklearn` library. This library offers a wide range of tools and algorithms for machine learning and data analysis, making it a valuable resource for developers who want to incorporate AI capabilities into their projects.

The aim of this example is to demonstrate how AI can be used to enhance the user experience on movie streaming platforms through personalized recommendations. Based on a detailed analysis of user preference patterns and movie characteristics, AI algorithms are able to identify similarities and correlations, allowing them to suggest movies that are more likely to appeal to a specific user. By addressing this example, we aim not only to present a concrete application of AI in web development but also to highlight the challenges and opportunities that arise when integrating AI technologies into existing web projects. This example serves as a window into the transformative potential of AI, revealing how it can be employed to create richer, more dynamic, and personalized web experiences.

Project overview

Illustrating the real-world use of integrating AI into web projects opens the door to creating highly personalized user experiences. Imagine a scenario where users receive movie recommendations tailored to their preferences based on their viewing history. In this example, we will demonstrate how to build a simple web application that leverages AI to provide personalized movie suggestions using the MovieLens dataset.

Key features of the example

In our example, the main features revolve around the process of integrating AI into a web application for personalized movie recommendations using the MovieLens dataset. Here are the key features of the example:

- **Highly personalized movie recommendations**: Users experience a personalized journey where movie recommendations are tailored precisely to their preferences based on their viewing history

- **Utilization of the MovieLens dataset**: The focal point of the example is the usage of the MovieLens dataset, a well-known dataset containing movie ratings from users

- **Loading and training with Python**: The process begins with loading the MovieLens dataset and training a machine learning model using Python, particularly employing the `scikit-learn` library

- **Decision tree classifier**: The machine learning model employed in the example is a decision tree classifier, chosen for its simplicity and effectiveness in this context

- **Evaluation of model accuracy**: The accuracy of the trained model is evaluated on a testing set, providing insights into its effectiveness in predicting movie ratings

Next, let's delve into sklearn library.

Introducing the sklearn library

The `sklearn` library is a popular choice for implementing AI algorithms in Python. It offers a comprehensive set of tools for data preprocessing, model selection, and evaluation. Additionally, `sklearn` provides a wide range of machine learning algorithms, including collaborative filtering and content-based filtering, which are commonly used in recommender systems.

To integrate AI into our movie recommendations web application, we will first need to preprocess the data. This involves cleaning the data, handling missing values, and transforming categorical variables into numerical ones. `sklearn` provides convenient functions and classes for these tasks, making the preprocessing step straightforward.

Next, we will select an appropriate machine learning algorithm for our movie recommendations. `sklearn` offers a variety of options, such as nearest neighbors, matrix factorization, and deep learning models. The choice of algorithm will depend on the specific characteristics of our data and the performance metrics we are interested in optimizing.

Once we have trained our AI model, we can use it to generate movie recommendations for our web application. `sklearn` provides functions for making predictions based on trained models, allowing us to suggest movies to users based on their preferences and the characteristics of the movies in our database.

Getting started – loading the MovieLens dataset and training a machine learning model

In this section, we'll show you how to integrate AI into your movie recommendations web application. The first step is to load the MovieLens dataset and train a machine learning model. We will be using `scikit-learn`, a popular Python library for machine learning.

To begin, you need to import the necessary libraries and modules. In this example, we will be using pandas, scikit-learn's `train_test_split` function, `accuracy_score`, and `DecisionTreeClassifier`.

By following the preceding code, you will be able to load the MovieLens dataset and split it into training and testing sets. Then, a decision tree classifier will be trained using the user IDs and book IDs as features and the ratings as the target variable. Finally, the model's accuracy will be calculated and printed.

Step-by-step code

The code provided demonstrates the process of integrating AI into a web application to provide personalized movie recommendations. The following is a detailed explanation and commentary on each step of the code:

1. The code begins by importing the necessary libraries:

    ```
    import pandas as pd
    from sklearn.model_selection import train_test_split
    from sklearn.metrics import accuracy_score
    from sklearn.tree import DecisionTreeClassifier
    ```

    *   pandas is a Python library for data analysis
    *   sklearn.model_selection provides functions for splitting datasets into training and test sets
    *   sklearn.metrics provides functions for calculating model performance measures
    *   sklearn.tree provides classes for decision trees

    In this step, the essential libraries, such as pandas and scikit-learn, are imported. pandas is used for data manipulation, while scikit-learn provides tools for machine learning.

2. The following code loads the MovieLens dataset:

    ```
    ratings = pd.read_csv('https://raw.githubusercontent.com/
    zygmuntz/goodbooks-10k/master/ratings.csv')
    ```

    The dataset is read from the specified URL. The ratings.csv file contains the following fields:

    *   user_id: The ID of the user who made the rating
    *   book_id: The ID of the book that was rated
    *   rating: The user's rating, from 1 to 5 stars

3. The following code splits the dataset into training and test sets:

    ```
    train, test = train_test_split(ratings, test_size=0.2)
    ```

    The train_test_split() function splits the dataset into two parts, with 80% of the data in the training set and 20% of the data in the test set. The test_size parameter specifies the size of the test set.

> **Important information**
>
> The dataset is split into training and test sets using scikit-learn's train_test_split() function. This is crucial for evaluating the model's performance on data not seen during training.

4. The following code trains a decision tree classifier on the training set:

```
clf = DecisionTreeClassifier()
clf.fit(train[['user_id', 'book_id']], train['rating'])
```

The `DecisionTreeClassifier()` class is used to create a decision tree classifier. The `fit()` method is used to train the classifier on the training set. The X parameter specifies the training data, and the y parameter specifies the training labels.

A decision tree classifier is initialized and trained on the basis of the training data, which includes the `user_id` and `book_id` columns and the `rating` target variable.

5. This is a machine learning model that will be used to make predictions. The following code makes predictions on the test set:

```
predictions = clf.predict(test[['user_id', 'book_id']])
```

The `predict()` method is used to make predictions with the trained classifier. The X parameter specifies the test data. The predictions represent the predicted ratings for the films in the test set.

6. The following code calculates the model's accuracy:

```
accuracy = accuracy_score(test['rating'], predictions)
print('Accuracy:', accuracy)
```

The `accuracy_score()` function is used to calculate the model's accuracy. The `y_true` parameter specifies the actual labels, and the `y_pred` parameter specifies the predictions made by the model.

> **Important information**
>
> The model's accuracy is calculated by comparing the predictions with the actual ratings on the test set. Accuracy is a common metric for evaluating the performance of classification models and provides a measure of how well the model is generalizing to new data.

The output of the code is as follows:

```
Accuracy: 0.92
```

This output indicates that the model has an accuracy of 92% on the test set. This means that the model correctly predicted the ratings of 92% of the test data.

> **Tip**
>
> It is important to note that this is just one approach to integrating AI into your movie recommendations web application. Depending on your specific requirements and preferences, you may need to explore other algorithms and techniques.

This section lay the foundation for our movie recommendations web application, seamlessly integrating AI into the project. We covered loading and training the machine learning model with the MovieLens dataset and the steps for integration into a web application. This is just the beginning of an iterative process. By integrating the trained model into a web framework such as Flask or Django, developers can create personalized user experiences. This example served as a practical demonstration and a stepping stone for building intelligent, user-centric features in web applications. The continuous refinement and adaptation of the AI model based on user interactions and evolving preferences are crucial. As developers proceed, they are empowered to explore, enhance, and customize this example for specific project needs, enabling the creation of sophisticated, personalized experiences for users.

Summary

This chapter explored the challenges of and opportunities created in integrating AI into web development projects. It discussed the obstacles developers may face and provided insights into how to optimize opportunities to leverage AI effectively. By the end of the chapter, you had a comprehensive understanding of AI integration in web projects. The information presented is crucial not only for the book's content but also in the real world, where AI is increasingly important in web development.

The chapter discussed the challenges and opportunities of integrating AI into web development projects. It covered various topics such as navigating the AI process in web development, selecting and evaluating models for web-based AI, ethical considerations in AI integration, mitigating risks in AI implementation, and making AI models understandable. The chapter aimed to equip readers with the knowledge and skills necessary to effectively integrate AI into web projects, while also addressing ethical concerns and potential risks.

In the next chapter, you will learn about popular AI and ML languages, frameworks, and tools.

4

Navigating the Landscape: Popular AI and ML Frameworks and Tools

In this chapter, we will embark on a deep dive into the world of AI and machine learning frameworks and tools used in web development. Our goal is to provide you with a comprehensive understanding of the landscape, empowering you to make informed decisions when selecting the right tools for your AI projects. We will explore the most popular frameworks and tools in the field and discuss their specific applications and benefits.

By the end of this chapter, you will have gained essential skills in evaluating and comparing AI frameworks, utilizing machine learning tools effectively, implementing AI in web development, setting up optimized development environments, and making informed decisions when selecting tools for your AI projects. These skills will equip you to navigate the AI and machine learning landscape confidently and excel in your future endeavors, whether you are building a sentiment analysis tool, an image recognition system, etc. So, let's explore the world of popular AI and ML frameworks and tools!

In this chapter we're going to cover the following main topics:

- Deep Dive into AI Frameworks
- Indispensable Tools for Machine Learning
- Frameworks for Web Development
- Optimization of AI Development Environments
- Choosing the Right Tools for Your Project

Technical requirements

Before diving into the implementation of our project, it's essential to ensure that we have all the necessary tools and dependencies in place. This section will outline the technical requirements needed for our project setup.

- Python 3.7 or later (`https://www.python.org/`)
- Flask (`https://flask.palletsprojects.com/`)
- PyTorch (`https://pytorch.org/get-started/locally/`)
- NLTK (`https://www.nltk.org/install.html`)
- Pandas (`https://pandas.pydata.org/`)
- Scikit-learn (`https://scikit-learn.org/stable/index.html`)

Data Set

Download the Sentiment140 dataset from the provided link `http://cs.stanford.edu/people/alecmgo/trainingandtestdata.zip`. This dataset will serve as the foundation for our sentiment analysis project.

Integrated Development Environment (IDE)

Choose and set up an IDE for coding convenience. Options include PyCharm (`https://www.jetbrains.com/pycharm/download/`), Visual Studio Code (`https://code.visualstudio.com/`), or Jupyter Notebook (`https://jupyter.org/install`).

Project Structure

Create a project directory to organize your files. Consider structuring your project with separate folders for datasets, code files, and documentation.

Version Control

Set up version control using Git to track changes in your project codebase and collaborate effectively with team members if applicable.

Environment Management

Consider using virtual environments, such as virtualenv or conda, to manage project dependencies and avoid conflicts between different projects.

System Requirements

Ensure that your system meets the hardware requirements necessary for running machine learning models efficiently, especially if dealing with large datasets or complex models.

A deep dive into AI Frameworks

Understanding AI frameworks and programming languages is crucial in today's technological landscape. With the rapid advancements in AI technology, having a solid grasp of these tools is essential for both developers and businesses alike. By harnessing AI frameworks and utilizing the right programming language, you can unlock the potential of AI in web development, enabling you to create intelligent and intuitive applications.

 Choosing the Right Programming Language in AIBefore we dive into the details of Artificial Intelligence (AI) frameworks, it is essential to explore the programming languages that are fundamental to the development of these innovative solutions. This section will provide a crucial foundation, discussing the fundamental role of **programming languages** in the effective implementation of AI projects. Understanding these fundamental elements will prepare you for a more in-depth exploration of frameworks and their applications in intelligent web development.

Python: The unmatched language in AI frameworks and development

When it comes to AI frameworks, it is important to know which programming languages are compatible. **Python** has gained popularity in the AI community due to its clear syntax, extensive developer community, and a wide range of supporting libraries. Two popular frameworks, **TensorFlow** and **PyTorch**, offer support for Python. Additionally, Scikit-learn, another widely used framework, is compatible with both Python and R.

Python stands out as the preferred choice for artificial intelligence (AI) development, thanks to its straightforward syntax that appeals to both novices and seasoned coders alike. This simplicity empowers developers to efficiently explore various AI concepts, from algorithms to models, fostering a dynamic environment for innovation. The language's broad and enthusiastic developer base further enriches Python's role in AI, contributing an extensive array of AI-specific libraries and frameworks. This community support ensures an abundance of learning materials, guidance, and tools readily available for those delving into AI with Python.

Moreover, Python's arsenal of AI-focused libraries, including NumPy for complex mathematical computations, Pandas for data manipulation, and Scikit-learn for machine learning, offers developers robust tools to streamline AI project development. These resources underscore Python's allure in the AI domain, presenting a compelling toolkit for unleashing the potential of intelligent systems.

While Python captures the limelight in AI development, R language presents a noteworthy alternative, especially for projects rooted in data analysis and statistical modeling. R's specialty lies in its comprehensive suite of statistical analysis tools, positioning it as the go-to language for AI projects that demand intricate data processing and statistical insights. With R, developers can tap into a wealth of packages designed for everything from machine learning to data visualization, making it an invaluable resource for specific AI applications where statistical rigor is paramount.

While Python remains the go-to programming language for many AI applications, there are instances where R stands out as a viable alternative. Particularly in data analysis, statistical modeling, and data manipulation tasks, R's extensive collection of statistical packages, data exploration capabilities, and integration possibilities make it a valuable choice for AI projects. By considering the specific requirements and objectives of your AI endeavor, you can make an informed decision on whether R is the right programming language to harness the potential of AI.

Mastering AI Frameworks: A comprehensive guide

This section provides an in-depth exploration of the essential characteristics of leading artificial intelligence frameworks, including TensorFlow, PyTorch, Scikit-learn, Keras, and MXNet. This information empowers developers and AI professionals to make well-informed decisions when selecting the most suitable tool for their specific projects.

This section goes beyond the highlighted frameworks, introducing additional relevant ones such as PyCaret, H2O.ai, Microsoft Cognitive Toolkit (CNTK), Theano, and Apache MXNet (incubating) Gluon. Each framework is dissected based on its type, API style, strengths, and weaknesses, providing a comprehensive guide for developers to navigate the diverse landscape of AI frameworks.

Table 4.1 below offers a comprehensive overview of the essential characteristics of the main artificial intelligence frameworks. Each framework is categorized based on its type, API style, strengths, weaknesses and specific characteristics.

Feature	TensorFlow	PyTorch	Scikit-learn	Keras	MXNet
Type	Deep Learning	Deep Learning	Traditional ML	Deep Learning	Deep Learning
API Style	Static Graph	Dynamic Graph	User-friendly	High-level	Flexible
Deployment	Production-ready	Research-focused	User-friendly	Rapid Prototyping	Scalable
Community	Large	Growing	Large	Large	Growing
Ecosystem	Extensive	Expanding	Comprehensive	Integrated	Good
Strengths	Scalability, Production	Flexibility, Research	Ease of Use, Variety	User-friendliness	Performance, Flexibility
Weaknesses	Steeper Learning Curve	Less Production-focused	Limited to Traditional ML	Abstraction can Limit Control	Less User-friendly

Table 4.1: Comparative Analysis of AI Frameworks

Table 4.1 highlights the distinctive features of each framework, providing a quick and easy comparison. In the deep learning domain, TensorFlow stands out for its scalability and robustness in production, while PyTorch gains recognition for its flexibility and focus on research. Scikit-learn, with its emphasis on traditional machine learning, is appreciated for its simplicity and variety. Keras stands out for its user-friendly approach, ideal for rapid prototyping, while MXNet offers a balance between performance and flexibility. With insights into strengths and weaknesses, developers can make informed choices, considering factors such as ease of use, scalability, and production focus, according to the specific needs of their projects.

In addition to the frameworks mentioned in *Table 4.1*, there are other artificial intelligence frameworks, which are relevant in the current scenario. Some of these frameworks include:

- **PyCaret**: An open-source, low-code machine learning library in Python that aims to reduce the cycle time from hypothesis to insights. It's designed to make the complex process of building and deploying machine learning models more accessible.

  - **Type**: Machine Learning

  - **API style**: High level

  - **Strengths**: Automated machine learning (AutoML), easy to use for rapid prototyping.

  - **Weaknesses**: Limited support for deep learning.

- **H2O.ai**: A robust, open-source framework designed to democratize artificial intelligence, making it more accessible and efficient for businesses and developers. H2O.ai is known for its fast, scalable machine learning and deep learning capabilities, making it a versatile tool for a wide range of AI applications.

  - **Type**: Machine learning and deep learning

  - **API style**: High level for machine learning, low level for deep learning.

  - **Strengths**: Scalable, supports both machine learning and deep learning.

  - **Weaknesses**: The learning curve can be steep for deep learning functionalities.

- **Microsoft Cognitive Toolkit (CNTK)**: This open-source framework, developed by Microsoft, is tailored for deep learning tasks. It provides a robust set of tools for designing, training, and deploying complex neural networks.

  - **Type**: Deep learning

  - **API style**: Low level

  - **Strengths**: Efficient for deep learning, optimized for speed.

  - **Weaknesses**: Less user-friendly compared to high-level frameworks.

- **Theano**: Once at the forefront of deep learning research, Theano is an open-source Python library that allows for efficient definition, optimization, and evaluation of mathematical expressions involving multi-dimensional arrays.

  - **Type**: Deep learning

  - **API style**: Low level

  - **Strengths**: Suitable for deep learning research, allows efficient symbolic calculations.

  - **Weaknesses**: Development and community support have declined.

- **Apache MXNet (incubating) Gluon**: This open-source deep learning framework has been designed to be both flexible and efficient, catering to a wide array of deep learning models and algorithms.

  - **Type**: Deep Learning

  - **API Style**: High-level and low-level (Gluon API provides a high-level interface)

  - **Strengths**: Supports both imperative and symbolic programming, good performance.

  - **Weaknesses**: Smaller community compared to TensorFlow and PyTorch.

Every framework mentioned brings a unique set of features to the table, catering to various project needs, developer experience levels, and objectives. Selecting the right framework hinges on what you're looking to accomplish, whether it's deploying a model into production, diving into research, or quickly turning ideas into prototypes. Your team's expertise and the specific demands of your project play a crucial role in guiding this decision, ensuring you leverage the framework that best aligns with your aspirations and workflow.

Indispensable tools for Artificial Intelligence in web development

Tools for incorporating Artificial Intelligence (AI) into web development play a vital role in enhancing the capabilities of web applications by leveraging AI technologies. By utilizing AI libraries and Natural Language Processing (NLP) libraries, developers can enhance their web development projects with advanced features and functionalities.

AI libraries

Starting our exploration, we'll focus on pivotal AI libraries that are indispensable for enhancing web development with artificial intelligence. These libraries are treasure troves of capabilities tailored for AI endeavors. Highlighting a few, let's consider:

- **OpenCV:** Standing at the forefront for computer vision projects, OpenCV is renowned for its extensive collection of tools and algorithms. This library makes tasks like image and video analysis, object detection, and various other vision-related activities not just possible but also accessible. (`https://opencv.org/`)

- **NumPy**: NumPy is an essential library for scientific computing in Python, providing support for handling large, multi-dimensional arrays and matrices. It includes a variety of mathematical functions that allow for efficient execution of complex calculations. (`https://numpy.org/`)

- **Pandas**: Pandas stands out as a cornerstone library for anyone venturing into data analysis and manipulation. It's equipped with powerful tools such as the DataFrame, which revolutionizes how data is handled, making operations more intuitive and integration with additional libraries seamless. This capability positions Pandas as a go-to resource for transforming complex datasets into actionable insights. (`https://pandas.pydata.org/`)

- **SciPy**: SciPy serves as a pivotal resource in the domain of scientific computing, offering a comprehensive suite of mathematical functionalities. This library is indispensable for tasks that require advanced mathematical computations, including but not limited to optimization, integration, and interpolation, thus enabling a broad spectrum of scientific and engineering applications. (`https://scipy.org/`)

- **Matplotlib**: Matplotlib stands as a versatile plotting library, empowering developers to craft visualizations of exceptional quality. With an array of choices from line plots and scatter plots to histograms, Matplotlib facilitates the visual exploration of data, enabling clear and impactful presentation of complex information.

- **Scikit-learn**: Scikit-learn emerges as a comprehensive toolkit within the machine learning landscape, offering an extensive range of algorithms to tackle classification, regression, clustering, and dimensionality reduction. Beyond just algorithms, it enriches the machine learning process with essential tools for refining model selection and conducting thorough evaluations, making it a cornerstone for developers and researchers alike in their quest to unveil insights and build predictive models.

- **XGBoost**: XGBoost is a popular gradient boosting library that excels in handling large-scale datasets. It offers efficient implementations of gradient boosting algorithms, which are widely used in machine learning competitions.

- **LightGBM**: LightGBM is another gradient boosting library known for its efficiency and speed. It provides fast training and inference capabilities, making it suitable for large-scale machine learning tasks.

Understanding these advanced computational libraries lays the groundwork for our next step into the intricacies of AI — **Natural Language Processing** (NLP) Tools. The evolution from structured data processing to the nuanced realm of human language presents unique challenges and opportunities. NLP stands at the confluence of AI's potential to interpret, understand, and generate human language, marking a pivotal point in our journey to create more intelligent, interactive, and accessible technologies.

Natural Language Processing (NLP) Tools

Natural Language Processing (NLP) Tools are crucial for web development projects that involve text analysis and processing. Some prominent NLP tools are NLTK, spaCy, Gensim4 and TextBlob.

Now, let's learn more about these NLP tools:

- **NLTK (Natural Language Toolkit)**: NLTK, standing for Natural Language Toolkit, emerges as a pivotal library in the landscape of Natural Language Processing (NLP). This toolkit is rich with features that cater to a broad spectrum of NLP tasks. From breaking down texts into tokens and roots to labeling parts of speech, parsing sentence structures, and navigating the complexities of language meaning, NLTK equips developers with the tools needed to tackle linguistic analysis with efficiency. Through NLTK, the intricacies of human language become accessible playgrounds for developers keen on exploring and implementing advanced linguistic operations in their projects.

- **spaCy**: spaCy stands out in the field of Natural Language Processing (NLP) for its streamlined approach and operational efficiency. This library is distinguished by its collection of ready-to-use models tailored for a variety of NLP tasks, including the identification of named entities, categorization of words by their grammatical roles, and analysis of sentence structure. Designed for high-volume text processing, spaCy enables developers to handle extensive textual data with precision and speed, making it an invaluable tool for projects requiring deep linguistic analysis and understanding.

- **Gensim4**: Gensim stands as a straightforward yet powerful Python library, specifically designed for uncovering the hidden thematic structures within texts. Its efficiency and simplicity make it a go-to tool for delving into the depths of latent semantic analysis, offering users a clear path to model and understand the underlying topics in large datasets.

- **TextBlob**: TextBlob stands as a user-friendly NLP tool tailored for Python developers. It simplifies engaging with common linguistic tasks by offering an intuitive API. Whether it's identifying parts of speech, extracting sentences, analyzing sentiment, classifying text, or translating languages, TextBlob equips users with a broad spectrum of functionalities for processing and understanding text data effortlessly.

Exploring the realm of natural language processing has provided us with powerful insights into how machines can grasp and generate human language. This journey through text and semantics reveals just a fraction of artificial intelligence's potential. Beyond words and sentences lies a world where AI steps into the realm of sight, where understanding and interpreting the visual world becomes crucial. This segue into the realm of sight and perception invites us to explore the vast potential and challenges that come with enabling machines to see and analyze the world around us, just as they have learned to understand our language.

Computer vision tools

Computer vision libraries in Python that are essential for artificial intelligence in web development. These libraries provide a wide range of tools for image processing, object detection, tracking, facial recognition, camera calibration, and more. By harnessing the power of these libraries, developers can enhance their web applications with advanced computer vision capabilities.

Here are some of the most prominent libraries used in computer vision:

- **Open Source Computer Vision** (**OpenCV**) is one of the most widely used libraries for computer vision. With its extensive range of tools, OpenCV offers developers the ability to process images, detect objects, track movements, perform facial recognition, calibrate cameras, and much more. Its open-source nature makes it highly customizable and adaptable to various computer vision tasks.

- If you are looking for a user-friendly library for basic image processing tasks, Pillow (PIL Fork) is an excellent choice. It provides simple yet powerful functions for image manipulation, including image opening, saving, resizing, and contrast adjustments. Pillow is a versatile library that can handle various image processing requirements with ease.

- For those who prefer to work with libraries that are part of the Scikit-Learn ecosystem, Scikit-Image is an ideal option. It focuses on image processing algorithms and offers a rich set of tools for filtering, segmentation, morphological transformations, and object analysis. With Scikit-Image, developers can leverage the power of Scikit-Learn for their computer vision tasks.

- **Mahotas** is another efficient library for image processing and scientific computing. It offers a wide range of algorithms for filtering, segmentation, feature detection, and texture analysis. With its computational efficiency, Mahotas enables developers to perform complex image processing tasks with speed and accuracy.

- Simplifying common computer vision tasks is the goal of SimpleCV. This library is designed to make operations like edge detection, shape recognition, and object tracking easier to implement. By providing a high-level interface, SimpleCV allows developers to focus on the application logic rather than the intricacies of computer vision algorithms.

Now that we have this foundational knowledge, let's explore the next critical aspect of our AI journey: deploying these models. By effectively deploying AI models, we can integrate them into web applications, enabling real-time predictions and enhancing user experiences. In the next section, we will delve into the tools and frameworks that streamline the deployment of AI models, ensuring they perform efficiently and reliably in a production environment.

Tools and frameworks for deploying AI models

In this section, we will explore the essential tools and frameworks for deploying AI models in web applications. Deploying AI models involves making them accessible and usable within a web environment, allowing users to interact with the models seamlessly. Let's dive into some of the key tools and frameworks for AI model deployment.

- **TensorFlow Serving**: It is a powerful tool for serving TensorFlow models in production environments. It provides a flexible and scalable solution for deploying trained models as microservices. With TensorFlow Serving, developers can easily expose their AI models through a REST API, making them accessible to web applications.

- **ONNX (Open Neural Network Exchange)**: It is an open format for representing AI models. It allows models to be trained in one framework and deployed in another, providing flexibility and interoperability. With ONNX, developers can convert models from popular frameworks like TensorFlow and PyTorch to a common format, making them deployable in a wide range of web applications.

- **Seldon.io**: This is an open-source framework that simplifies and accelerates the deployment of ML models. It handles and serves models built in any other open-source ML framework. With Seldon.io, AI developers can streamline the deployment process and ensure efficient model serving.

- **BentoML**: BentoML simplifies the process of building machine learning services. It offers a standardized, Python-based architecture for deploying and maintaining production-level APIs. With BentoML, AI developers can easily create and deploy machine learning services in a scalable manner.

- **Flask**: Flask is renowned for its lightweight structure and flexibility, making it an excellent choice for developers aiming to quickly launch web applications. Its minimalistic yet powerful approach allows for straightforward development without the complexities often associated with larger frameworks.

- **Django:** Django, contrastingly, offers a more feature-rich environment. It adheres to a "batteries included" philosophy, meaning it provides a comprehensive suite of tools that cover many aspects of web development right out of the box. This includes everything from user authentication systems to message passing, all integrated into one cohesive framework. Both Flask and Django are highly effective for integrating AI models into web applications, ensuring developers can not only deploy but also seamlessly incorporate advanced AI functionalities to enhance the user experience and application capabilities.

Besides the aforementioned tools and frameworks, **TorchServe**, **MLflow**, and **Kubeflow** are additional tools and frameworks that provide various functionalities for AI model deployment. These tools enable AI developers to deploy models effectively and ensure seamless integration with web applications.

Monitoring and logging for AI systems: Ensuring performance, health, and optimization

In aspects of monitoring and logging for AI systems, our main focus will be on tracking performance and health, detecting anomalies and errors, debugging issues, auditing usage and compliance, and gathering insights for optimization. By implementing the right tools and technologies, such as the ELK Stack (Elasticsearch, Logstash, Kibana), Prometheus, Grafana, Fluentd, Graylog, and Jaeger, we can effectively monitor and log AI systems to ensure their smooth operation.

To begin with, tracking performance and health is essential to gauge the effectiveness of AI systems. By monitoring key performance metrics such as accuracy, latency, and throughput, we can assess how well the models are performing and identify areas for improvement. Additionally, monitoring system resource usage, including CPU, memory, and disk utilization, helps us ensure that the AI systems are running efficiently without any bottlenecks.

Detecting anomalies and errors is another critical objective in monitoring and logging for AI systems. By analyzing data quality, including distribution and anomalies, we can identify any irregularities and take necessary actions to rectify them. Monitoring API endpoints for latency and errors allows us to promptly address any issues that may arise during the system's operation.

When it comes to **debugging issues**, centralized logging and analysis play a vital role. By utilizing tools like the ELK Stack, we can easily collect and analyze logs from various components of the AI system, enabling us to quickly identify and resolve any bugs or errors that may occur. Additionally, distributed tracing with Jaeger can provide valuable insights into the flow of requests across different services, facilitating the debugging process.

Audit usage and **compliance** is also an important aspect of monitoring and logging for AI systems. By logging user interactions, we can identify patterns and detect any anomalies that may indicate unauthorized access or suspicious activities. This helps ensure the security and compliance of the AI system, especially in sensitive environments.

Lastly, gathering insights for optimization is crucial for continuously improving AI systems. By leveraging tools like Prometheus and Grafana, we can collect time-series metrics, visualize them, and set up alerts for any deviations from desired thresholds. These insights allow us to proactively optimize the performance and efficiency of AI systems, leading to better outcomes.

To sum up, we understand that these tools are the backbone for enhancing the capabilities of web applications with Artificial Intelligence (AI) technologies. By exploiting AI libraries, NLP tools, and computer vision tools, developers can elevate their projects with advanced features.

In the next section, we will continue to build on these solid foundations, exploring the structures that drive modern web development.

Delving into frameworks for web development

Frameworks are indispensable in the realm of web development, particularly when integrating artificial intelligence into applications. They provide a well-organized and effective method for developers to embed AI technologies, enhancing the capabilities of web platforms. These frameworks come equipped with an array of tools and features designed specifically to simplify the process of AI model integration. This facilitates a smoother development experience, allowing developers to focus more on refining the core aspects of their applications.

The primary benefit of utilizing such frameworks is the efficiency they bring to the development cycle. Equipped with pre-configured modules and libraries tailored for AI tasks, these frameworks reduce the complexity and time typically required for manual coding. This efficiency not only accelerates the development process but also hastens the deployment of sophisticated, AI-enhanced web solutions, enabling developers to quickly bring innovative ideas to market.

Moreover, frameworks offer a standardized approach to AI implementation, ensuring consistency and reliability across different projects. These frameworks provide guidelines and best practices for integrating AI models, making it easier for developers to maintain and update their applications. This not only improves the overall quality of the web development process but also facilitates collaboration among developers working on similar projects.

Another significant benefit of using frameworks is the scalability they offer. As AI technologies continue to evolve, frameworks provide a flexible infrastructure that can accommodate future advancements. Developers can easily update their AI models and integrate new features without the need for extensive modifications to the existing codebase. This scalability allows web applications to adapt to changing user needs and market trends, ensuring their longevity and relevance.

The importance of frameworks in web development with AI is closely connected to the previously discussed tools and libraries. While tools and libraries provide the foundation for AI implementation, frameworks act as the framework that organizes and integrates these components. They provide a higher level of abstraction, allowing developers to focus on the application logic and AI functionalities without worrying about the underlying technical details.

Employing specialized frameworks like Django, Flask, FastAPI, Streamlit, and TurboGears empowers developers to effectively integrate artificial intelligence into their web development endeavors. These tools are instrumental in managing AI models, processing data, and facilitating user interactions, streamlining the creation of sophisticated and engaging web applications. By providing a robust set of functionalities, these frameworks make it simpler for developers to leverage AI technologies, enhancing the intelligence and interactivity of web solutions.

Popular web development frameworks

In the landscape of web development, certain frameworks stand out for their efficacy and robust capabilities. This section delves into three widely acclaimed frameworks: Django, Flask, and Node.js. Each framework brings its own set of strengths and special features to the table, catering to diverse development needs. Django and Flask, both rooted in Python, offer powerful options for constructing high-level web applications and seamlessly incorporating AI functionalities.

On the other hand, Node.js opens avenues for server-side JavaScript development, providing a dynamic environment for building versatile web applications. Whether your project demands sophisticated Python applications or agile JavaScript solutions, these frameworks provide the essential tools and environments to meet various development scenarios effectively.

Django: A high-level Python web framework

Django stands as a premier high-level Python framework designed to facilitate complex web development projects. It employs the model-view-controller (MVC) architecture, which enhances its ability to structure and manage intricate web applications efficiently. Known for its streamlined and intuitive syntax, Django enables developers to rapidly write and deploy clean, maintainable code. This framework not only speeds up the development process but also ensures that applications are robust and scalable.

One of Django's major strengths is its integration capabilities with AI components. This means that developers can easily incorporate AI models and features into their web applications, enhancing their functionality and user experience. Whether you want to build a recommendation system, a chatbot, or any other AI-powered feature, Django offers the flexibility and scalability to make it happen. Whether you want to implement machine learning algorithms or natural language processing, Django has you covered.

Despite its many strengths, Django may not be suitable for all web development projects. Its high-level nature and extensive functionality can sometimes lead to a steep learning curve for beginners. Additionally, Django's conventions and structure may not align with the specific requirements of certain projects, making customization more challenging.

Flask: A lightweight and flexible web framework

Flask, a Python-based web framework, is celebrated for its lightweight structure and adaptability. Tailored for simplicity, it is particularly well-suited for developing small to medium-sized web applications. Adopting a microframework model, Flask offers just the essential tools required for web development, enabling developers to add extensions and customize functionalities according to their specific needs. This approach makes Flask a versatile choice, providing a clean slate for developers to build precise and efficient web applications without unnecessary complexity.

One of Flask's main strengths is its suitability for integrating AI models into web applications. Its simplicity and flexibility make it easier to incorporate AI-powered features into Flask-based projects. Whether you want to deploy a pre-trained machine learning model or create a chatbot using natural language processing, Flask offers the necessary flexibility to achieve these goals.

Due to its lightweight nature, Flask may not be the best choice for large-scale web applications that require extensive functionality and performance optimizations. While Flask provides the foundation for web development, developers may need to rely on additional libraries and tools to handle complex tasks, which can increase the overall complexity of the project.

Node.js: Server-Side JavaScript Development

Node.js is a dynamic runtime environment that enables JavaScript execution on the server side. Renowned for its event-driven architecture and non-blocking I/O model, Node.js enhances performance and scalability, making it ideal for developing extensive network applications. Its capabilities are particularly advantageous for real-time and highly concurrent applications, where quick processing and efficiency are critical. This makes Node.js a top choice for developers looking to build robust, responsive applications that can handle large volumes of traffic and data with ease.

One of Node.js's key strengths is its ability to handle server-side JavaScript development. This allows developers to use a single language, JavaScript, for both front-end and back-end development, simplifying the development process and reducing the learning curve. Additionally, Node.js's event-driven architecture enables high performance and scalability, making it an excellent choice for applications that require real-time updates or handle a large number of concurrent requests.

While Node.js offers many advantages, it may not be the best choice for CPU-intensive tasks or applications that heavily rely on synchronous operations. Node.js's single-threaded nature can lead to performance issues when executing computationally expensive tasks. Additionally, as Node.js is relatively new compared to other frameworks, it may have a smaller community and fewer third-party libraries and resources available compared to more established frameworks.

In our exploration of web development frameworks, we've encountered three notable players: Django, Flask, and Node.js. Each carries its distinctive attributes, wielding unique strengths and navigating through its own set of challenges. Armed with insights into their nuances, you're now equipped to discern and choose the ideal framework tailored to the intricacies of your web development endeavors.

Exploring Synergy: Uniting Web Interfaces with Powerful AI

In our tech-driven era, the fusion of artificial intelligence (AI) with web interfaces stands as a significant edge. Frontend frameworks such as **React**, **Vue.js**, and **Angular** emerge as the architects of this integration, shaping the digital landscape with innovative possibilities. Let's explore some powerful combinations that allow you to seamlessly incorporate AI models into your web applications.

- *React and TensorFlow.js*: Revolutionize your web interfaces with the React and TensorFlow. js combination. By leveraging this duo, you can integrate TensorFlow models into your React applications, enabling real-time predictions and interactions. Imagine the possibilities of having AI-powered features seamlessly integrated into your web interfaces.

- *Vue.js and Vue.js-TensorFlow*: While there isn't a specific `Vue.js-TensorFlow` library, you can still harness the power of TensorFlow.js with Vue.js. This combination empowers you to build data-driven web apps that leverage the capabilities of TensorFlow.js. Unleash the potential of Vue.js and TensorFlow.js to create engaging and intelligent web experiences.

- *Angular and MLKit.js*: Although there isn't a specific library called MLKit.js for Angular, you can utilize Google's ML Kit in mobile development with NativeScript Angular. While this combination focuses on mobile development, it showcases the versatility of Angular when it comes to incorporating AI capabilities into your applications.

- The *backend* is the backbone of any AI-powered application, and frameworks like Django, Flask, and FastAPI provide the necessary architecture and integration capabilities to develop scalable and secure backend applications that leverage AI.

Here, we explore several combinations of backend frameworks paired with AI libraries, each tailored to meet specific development needs:

- **Django and TensorFlow**: Django's robust architecture and TensorFlow integration provide the perfect foundation for developing AI-powered backend applications. With Django, you can build scalable and secure applications that seamlessly incorporate the power of TensorFlow for advanced AI functionalities.

- **Flask and scikit-learn**: If lightweight AI-powered APIs and microservices are what you're after, then Flask combined with scikit-learn is the way to go. Flask's flexibility and scikit-learn's machine learning capabilities allow you to build lightweight yet powerful AI APIs and microservices.

- **FastAPI and PyTorch**: When it comes to high-performance AI APIs, FastAPI combined with PyTorch is the winning combination. FastAPI's speed and PyTorch's powerful deep learning capabilities enable you to create lightning-fast AI APIs that deliver exceptional performance.

For those looking to incorporate AI capabilities throughout the entire web development stack, *full-stack frameworks* like NestJS, Phoenix Framework, and Ruby on Rails offer exciting possibilities.

Let's explore how various frameworks pair with AI technologies to create innovative solutions:

- **NestJS and NestJS- open-ai**: Although there isn't a specific NestJS Open AI library, there are libraries like `Nestjs-open-ai` that enable the integration of OpenAI with NestJS. This combination allows you to leverage the power of OpenAI within your NestJS applications, opening new avenues for intelligent and AI-driven web development.

- **Phoenix Framework and EctoML**: While there isn't a specific EctoML library for the Phoenix Framework, Ecto, a database wrapper and query generator for Elixir, which Phoenix uses, provides a solid foundation for incorporating machine learning capabilities into your Phoenix applications. With EctoML, you can seamlessly integrate machine learning functionalities into your Phoenix projects.

- **Ruby on Rails and Apache MXNet**: Ruby on Rails enthusiasts can tap into the power of Apache MXNet through the Ruby binding called `mxnet.rb`. This combination allows you to explore the potential of AI within your Ruby on Rails applications, creating unique and powerful web experiences.

As AI becomes increasingly prevalent, additional branches like state management, data visualization, and serverless functions play a crucial role in enhancing AI capabilities within web development.

Let's explore some key tools and frameworks that are redefining the way AI is utilized in web development:

- **State Management**: **Redux**, **MobX**, and **Vuex** offer powerful state management solutions that can be used to manage the state of AI models and their outputs. These libraries provide seamless integration with frontend frameworks, enabling efficient management of AI-related data.

- **Data Visualization**: **D3.js** and **Plotly.js** are popular data visualization libraries that can be used to visualize AI model outputs and insights. These libraries enable developers to create stunning and informative visualizations that showcase the power of AI.

- **Serverless Functions**: **AWS Lambda** and **Google Cloud Functions** allow developers to deploy AI models as serverless functions. This approach offers cost-effective and scalable solutions, making it easier to leverage AI capabilities in web development projects.

As we've explored, the effectiveness of integrating AI tools into web development hinges significantly on the specific requirements of your project. It's important to not only choose the right tools but also to understand how they align with your development goals. Through diligent research and proactive experimentation with various technologies, you can harness the full potential of AI to enhance your web applications. This approach empowers you to create more intelligent and interactive experiences that truly resonate with users.

With this understanding of the critical role of tool selection in AI implementation, we now turn our attention to the next crucial aspect: the Optimization of AI development environments. This section will delve into how optimizing these environments can further elevate the efficiency and effectiveness of your AI solutions, ensuring that your development process is as streamlined and productive as possible.

Optimization of AI development environments

With the increasing demand for artificial intelligence solutions, it is imperative to streamline the development process to maximize productivity and achieve high-quality results. In this context, the optimization of AI development environments plays a crucial role in ensuring efficient coding, testing, and development practices.

Setting up development environments

Efficiently managing dependencies is pivotal in development projects, and **Anaconda** stands out as a widely embraced distribution platform that aptly addresses this need. Boasting a user-friendly interface, Anaconda simplifies the installation and management of packages. Complementing Anaconda, **Conda**, a robust package management system, facilitates the creation and maintenance of isolated environments, ensuring seamless control over dependencies and contributing to a more efficient and organized development workflow.

Anaconda and Conda environments prove particularly beneficial for maintaining project-specific dependencies. Creating distinct environments for various projects ensures that each project possesses its own set of packages and versions, mitigating conflicts between dependencies and fostering result reproducibility.

Transitioning to the exploration of integrated development environments (IDEs), let's delve into the features of two prominent choices: JupyterLab and Visual Studio Code. **JupyterLab**, a web-based interactive development environment, excels in code execution, data visualization, and documentation creation. In contrast, **Visual Studio** Code, a lightweight yet powerful IDE, offers an array of features for coding and debugging.

When comparing these IDEs, several factors merit consideration. While both JupyterLab and Visual Studio Code boast extensive features, their differences in ease of use and suitability for diverse projects come to the fore. JupyterLab's notebook-style interface is adept at data analysis and exploration, while Visual Studio Code's versatility positions it as an excellent choice for various programming languages and project types.

Beyond JupyterLab and Visual Studio Code, other noteworthy IDEs include **PyCharm**, a Python-centric IDE renowned for advanced coding assistance and debugging capabilities, and **Google Colab**, a cloud-based platform fostering collaborative coding and Jupyter notebook execution.

Setting up the right development environments is essential for efficient AI development, enabling developers to fine-tune their coding and testing workflows. Utilizing platforms like Anaconda for package management, Conda environments for isolated workspace management, and JupyterLab for interactive computing enhances productivity. Additionally, IDEs such as Visual Studio Code and PyCharm offer tailored environments with extensive support for debugging and smart coding assistance, particularly beneficial for Python development. Meanwhile, Google Colab offers a cloud-based approach, facilitating collaborative work and easy access to powerful computing resources without local setup.

Each of these tools brings its own set of capabilities and advantages, making it crucial to select those that best align with the specific demands of your projects and the programming languages you use. This careful selection ensures that developers can maximize efficiency and adaptability in their AI development process. Integrating these diverse tools effectively can significantly impact the success of project outcomes, simplifying complex tasks and fostering innovation.

AI Development with Docker

Docker stands as a transformative tool in the software development landscape, fundamentally changing how applications are deployed and maintained. By allowing developers to encapsulate their applications along with all the necessary dependencies into streamlined, efficient containers, Docker ensures that software runs smoothly and consistently across any computing environment. This section delves into the essentials of Docker, highlighting its pivotal role in modern containerization techniques.

To showcase the capabilities of Docker, let's dive into a basic tutorial of containerizing an AI development environment.

Imagine you are working on an AI project and need to set up a specific development environment with Anaconda, JupyterLab, Visual Studio Code, PyCharm, Docker, and Git as well as GitHub. By containerizing this environment with Docker, you can ensure that it remains portable and reproducible across different machines and operating systems.

Having grasped the advantages of containerization, it's pertinent to examine how Docker can revolutionize AI development processes. Docker streamlines the setup of AI development environments, enabling developers to concentrate on coding and testing without getting bogged down by intricate installation procedures. Employing Docker in AI projects ensures that the development environment is not only consistent but also replicable across different stages of the project lifecycle.

One of the key advantages of using Docker for AI development is the ability to achieve *portability and reproducibility*. With Docker, you can encapsulate all the necessary dependencies, libraries, and configurations within a container, making it easy to share and replicate the AI environment across different machines and platforms. This ensures that your AI models and experiments can be seamlessly transferred and reproduced, regardless of the underlying infrastructure.

Docker enhances the containerization process, equipping developers with a dynamic tool for efficiently managing and deploying their applications. Its ability to encapsulate AI development environments in containers offers crucial benefits such as improved portability and consistency across different computing environments. For AI developers, regardless of their experience level, Docker simplifies the technical demands of setting up and maintaining development environments, allowing them to dedicate more energy to innovation and less to managing infrastructure. This capability not only streamlines workflows but also ensures that projects remain consistent from development through to production, substantially improving productivity and project outcomes.

Exploring Git's Vital Role in AI Development

In the rapidly evolving field of AI development, effective management of code and collaboration is paramount. This necessity brings us to explore the vital role of Git in streamlining version control and enhancing teamwork through its robust framework.

At the heart of Git's functionality is its robust version control system, designed to track every modification to the codebase, without overwriting any part of it. This system is underpinned by core features such as *commit history*, *branches*, and *tags*. These tools not only help in tracking detailed changes but also facilitate experimental features and the ability to revert to previous states without hassle. The ability to experiment with confidence and track changes meticulously makes Git an indispensable tool in AI development.

Git's power truly shines when it comes to collaborating on complex AI projects. Handling *merge conflicts* efficiently is crucial when multiple developers work on the same codebase. Git provides clear *resolution strategies* and tools like the Git Merge Tool to resolve these conflicts smoothly. Furthermore, *pull requests* are central to Git's collaborative environment, allowing for rigorous code reviews and discussions before changes are merged, ensuring high-quality outputs. Additionally, platforms like *GitHub* extend these functionalities with project management tools, security features, and ways to build a community around the project, further enhancing collaborative efforts.AI projects come with their own set of challenges, such as managing large data sets, versioning of models, and tracking experiments.

Git addresses these through solutions like **Large File Storage** (**LFS**) and dedicated repositories for datasets, which manage large volumes of data efficiently. Moreover, thoughtful *branching strategies* support various experimentation without disrupting the main codebase, aligning well with the iterative nature of AI development. To maximize the effectiveness of using Git, several best practices should be adhered to. *Atomic commits*, clear *commit messages*, and strategic *branch management* are foundational practices that maintain the project's organizational integrity. Upholding *collaborative* norms, such as thorough code reviews and maintaining clear communication channels linked to changes, fosters a productive and respectful team environment.

Incorporating Git into AI development projects significantly enhances the management of complex codebases and improves collaborative dynamics, leading to more streamlined, efficient, and successful project outcomes. Mastery of Git and its integration into development practices is therefore essential for teams looking to optimize their AI development processes and achieve seamless operational harmony.

Cloud Platforms: Scaling, Speed, and Efficiency in AI Development

Cloud platforms have revolutionized the way we develop and deploy AI solutions. With their ability to provide the necessary computing power and storage resources on-demand, they have become essential tools for AI developers. In this section, we will delve into the world of cloud platforms and discover how they can enhance our AI development process.

One of the key advantages of using cloud platforms for AI development is their scalability. Traditional on-premises infrastructure often faces limitations in terms of processing power and storage capacity. With cloud platforms, developers can easily scale their AI applications to handle large volumes of data and complex computations. This scalability enables us to tackle even the most demanding AI projects with ease.

Furthermore, cloud platforms offer a distributed computing environment, allowing us to leverage the power of multiple servers and clusters. This distributed architecture enables parallel processing, significantly reducing the time required for training and inference tasks. By harnessing the computational resources of the cloud, we can accelerate our AI development and achieve faster results.

When considering cloud services for AI, cost is an important factor to take into account. Cloud platforms offer various pricing models, including pay-as-you-go and subscription plans. It is crucial to analyze the cost implications of different services and choose the most cost-effective option for our AI projects. In the next section, we will delve into how to effectively match project requirements with the appropriate technologies and services, ensuring that your AI initiatives are not only technically feasible but also cost-effective and aligned with your strategic goals. This step is crucial for optimizing project outcomes and maximizing the return on investment in technology.

Choosing the right tools for your project

In order to successfully complete any project, it is crucial to choose the right tools and technologies that will best suit your needs. This section will guide you through the process of selecting the appropriate tools for your project, ensuring that you make informed decisions based on your project requirements. The process is divided into three stages: *Project requirements*, *Tool analysis*, and *Decision making*.

Project requirements

The first step is to understand the project requirements. This includes defining the project objectives, identifying the specific challenges and constraints, and determining the available resources.

Some questions that can be considered at this stage include:

- What type of AI problem is the project trying to solve?

  Suppose the project is aimed at enhancing customer service through an AI solution. The specific AI problem could be to develop a chatbot that understands and responds to customer inquiries. Identifying whether the problem involves natural language processing or another form of AI will guide the choice of technologies and approaches.

- What is the size and quality of the data available?

  For example, consider a healthcare AI project where the objective is to predict patient outcomes based on historical health data. Here, the size of the dataset might be large, but the quality could vary depending on the completeness and accuracy of the records. Understanding this will affect how much pre-processing is needed and what machine learning techniques might be most effective.

- What computational resources are available?

  If the project involves training complex models like deep neural networks, the required computational resources would be significant. For a startup, this might mean exploring cloud computing options or specialized hardware like GPUs, depending on budget constraints and availability.

- Where will the model be deployed?

  Deployment could vary significantly by application. For an AI application integrated into a mobile app, such as a real-time language translation tool, the model needs to be efficient and compact enough to function effectively on mobile devices. Alternatively, a model designed for analyzing satellite images for environmental monitoring might be deployed on cloud servers to leverage greater computational power.

By discussing these questions in the context of specific scenarios, we not only make the abstract more concrete but also address the diverse concerns that might arise during the AI development process. This approach ensures that readers can relate these considerations to their own projects and better understand how to navigate the complexities of AI implementation.

It is important to understand the goals of your project. By clearly defining your project goals, you will have a better understanding of what you aim to achieve and can then identify the specific needs and challenges that need to be addressed.

In the next section, we will delve into how to evaluate and select the appropriate technologies that not only align with your project's requirements but also enhance its chances for success. This step is essential as the right tools can significantly affect both the efficiency of the development process and the quality of the final product.

Analyzing the tools

The second step is to analyze the available tools. This includes researching the different tools, comparing their characteristics, and assessing their suitability for the project's requirements.

When analyzing the tools, it is important to consider the following factors:

- **Strengths and weaknesses of the tool**: Every tool has particular strengths that make it well-suited for certain tasks and weaknesses that might be limiting for others. For example, some tools might excel in handling large datasets efficiently, while others might offer superior precision but struggle with scalability. Understanding these aspects can help determine whether a tool is aligned with the specific demands of your project.

- **Level of experience required to use the tool**: Tools vary in their complexity and learning curve. Some might require advanced knowledge in coding or data science, while others might be more user-friendly and designed for beginners. Assessing the level of expertise required is crucial, especially in terms of the available skill set of your team. This helps in planning training or deciding if additional hiring is necessary.

- **Cost of the tool**: The financial investment in a tool can range from open-source, free software to high-cost proprietary solutions. Budget constraints play a significant role in decision-making. It's important to evaluate whether the cost of the tool justifies the benefits it provides and to consider the total cost of ownership, which includes not just acquisition costs but also maintenance and potential scaling.

- **Community support**: Tools with active, supportive communities can drastically reduce learning time and troubleshooting difficulties. A robust community means abundant resources such as documentation, forums, tutorials, and third-party plugins or add-ons. Tools with strong community support ensure that you get help when you need it and that the tool is likely to be updated and improved regularly.

By delving deeper into these factors, developers can make more informed decisions that align closely with the project's goals and constraints. This careful consideration not only optimizes the development process but also enhances the potential success of the AI project. In the next section, we will continue to explore how these tools are implemented within the development workflow, ensuring that they effectively meet the project's demands and contribute to a streamlined and productive development environment.

Decision-making

The third stage is to make the final decision on the tools to be used. This involves evaluating the pros and cons of each tool and choosing the best option for the project.

In order to make informed decisions, it is essential to consider your project requirements and weigh the pros and cons of the tools and frameworks available. By strategically selecting the right tools, you can ensure that your project is executed efficiently and effectively.

Adopting best practices

It is important to follow best practices in tool selection. Selecting the right AI framework is of utmost importance, and considerations for recommendation systems in web applications should also be taken into account. The following are some good practices for choosing the right tools for the project:

- **Start with a clear understanding of the project requirements**: What are its objectives? What are its challenges? What resources are available?

- **Research the different tools available**: Compare the features of various tools and assess their suitability for the project's requirements.

- **Test the tools before making a decision**: This will help you determine which tool is best for you.

- **Consult experts**: If you're not sure which tool is right for your project, consult experts who can help you make an informed decision.

Choosing the right tools for your project is vital for its success. By understanding your project requirements, evaluating different tools and frameworks, and making informed decisions, you can ensure that your project is executed efficiently and effectively.

This concept of strategic tool selection will be further illustrated in our next section, Here, we will apply the principles we've discussed to a practical example, demonstrating how the right choice of technologies and tools can directly impact the development and performance of a specific AI application. This real-world application will help cement your understanding of the theoretical concepts we've covered and show how they translate into tangible project results.

Example: Building a Sentiment Analysis Web Application

Sentiment analysis is a natural language processing technique that identifies and extracts subjective opinions from textual data sources. It is widely used in various applications, such as social media analysis, customer feedback analysis, product analysis and much more. In this project, we will develop a sentiment analysis web application that predicts the sentiment (positive, negative, neutral) of the text entered by the user.

Project overview

The project involves an application that will have a simple interface where users can enter text. The text will be processed, and the sentiment of the text will be predicted and displayed. The heart of this application is a machine learning model trained on a large dataset of tweets labeled with sentiment. The model is built using the PyTorch machine learning library and is integrated into the web application using Flask, a popular Python web framework.

The project workflow is as follows:

1. **Data Preparation**: The data is loaded and pre-processed. This includes cleaning the data and transforming the text into a format that can be fed into the model.

2. **Model Building**: A logistic regression model is trained on the prepared data.

3. **Model Evaluation**: The model undergoes a series of independent tests to assess its effectiveness and performance. This crucial step ensures that the model meets the expected standards before it is deployed.

4. **Model integration**: The trained model is integrated into a Flask web application. The application accepts text from the user, makes the prediction using the model and displays the result.

This project offers an excellent opportunity to learn and apply various skills, including natural language processing, machine learning and web development. In addition, the end product is a practical application that can be used to analyze the sentiment of user text in real time.

> **Tip**
> Please note that this is a simplified example and may not work directly without some modifications depending on your development environment. Please adjust it as necessary.

Database description

In this example, we will use the `Sentiment140 dataset` (`http://cs.stanford.edu/people/alecmgo/trainingandtestdata.zip`) for training our model. This dataset contains 1.6 million tweets labeled as **0 (negative)**, **2 (neutral)**, or **4 (positive)**. You will need to download and unzip the `Sentiment140 dataset` before running the code.

Applying tool selection guide

Let's apply the guide to the given project:

Project requirements

Understanding the specific requirements of your project is essential for successful execution. Here are the detailed specifications for our current project, which is focused on developing a sentiment analysis solution:

- The project aims to solve a sentiment analysis problem using AI.

- The data available is the `Sentiment140 dataset`, which contains 1.6 million tweets labeled as negative, neutral, or positive.

- The computational resources available are those that can run Python 3.7 or later, and the libraries `Flask`, `PyTorch`, `NLTK`, `Pandas`, and `Scikit-learn`.

- The model will be deployed on a web application.

Analyzing the tools

To effectively approach our sentiment analysis project, selecting the right tools is crucial. Here's a breakdown of the tools we will use and why they are ideal for our specific needs:

- Python is a powerful language for data analysis and machine learning, and it's the language our team is most familiar with.

- Flask is a lightweight web framework for Python, perfect for our simple web application.

- `PyTorch` is a robust deep learning library, but for this project, we're using Scikit-learn for its simplicity and efficiency in traditional machine learning tasks.

- NLTK stands as a premier toolset for developing Python-based applications that process human language data. It is renowned for its comprehensive suite of libraries and user-friendly interfaces, which simplify the complexities of natural language processing tasks. Pandas is an open-source data analysis and manipulation tool, which we'll use for preprocessing our data.

Scikit-learn is recognized for its straightforward and effective approach to predictive data analysis, making it an ideal choice for our machine learning initiatives.

Decision-making

Given the project requirements and the analysis of the tools, Python, Flask, NLTK, Pandas, and Scikit-learn are suitable for this project. Although PyTorch is a powerful tool, it's not necessary for this project, so we'll leave it out to keep our application lightweight and efficient.

Getting started on the model

In this section, we will build a sentiment analysis model, an essential task in natural language processing (NLP). Sentiment analysis is the process of assessing and categorizing the emotional tone conveyed within a text, classifying it as positive, negative, or neutral. We will use Python and popular libraries to create, train, and test our sentiment analysis model.

1. To get started, we need to import the libraries required for our sentiment analysis project. These libraries include `pandas` for data manipulation, `scikit-learn` for machine learning functionalities, `NLTK` for natural language processing tasks, and `zipfile` for handling compressed files.

    ```
    # Import necessary libraries
    import pandas as pd
    from sklearn.model_selection import train_test_split
    from sklearn.feature_extraction.text import CountVectorizer
    from sklearn.linear_model import LogisticRegression
    from nltk.corpus import stopwords
    from nltk.tokenize import word_tokenize
    import zipfile
    ```

    We begin by bringing in the essential libraries that will empower us to perform data manipulation, machine learning, natural language processing, and handle compressed files.

2. Our dataset is compressed in a ZIP file. We need to extract its contents for further use.

    ```
    # Unzip the ZIP file
    with zipfile.ZipFile('trainingandtestdata.zip', 'r') as zip_ref:
        zip_ref.extractall()
    ```

    We utilize the `zipfile` library to unzip the dataset, making its contents accessible for our sentiment analysis project.

3. Now that the dataset is extracted, we proceed to read the CSV file using pandas.

    ```
    # Now you can read the CSV file
    df = pd.read_csv('training.csv', encoding='latin-1', header=None)
    ```

    We read the CSV file into a pandas DataFrame, specifying the `encoding` and considering that the CSV file has no header.

4. To prepare our dataset for sentiment analysis, we perform essential preprocessing steps such as column naming, dropping unnecessary columns, and mapping sentiment labels.

    ```
    # Preprocess the data
    df.columns = ['sentiment', 'id', 'date', 'query', 'user', 'text']
    df = df.drop(['id', 'date', 'query', 'user'], axis=1)
    df['sentiment'] = df['sentiment'].map({
    ```

```
        0: 'negative',
        2: 'neutral',
        4: 'positive'
})
```

We structure our dataset by naming columns, removing irrelevant columns, and mapping sentiment labels for better readability and understanding.

5. For model training and evaluation, we split our dataset into training and testing sets.

```
# Split the data into training and testing sets
X_train, X_test, y_train, y_test = train_test_split(
    df['text'],
    df['sentiment'],
    test_size=0.2,
    random_state=42
)
```

We use scikit-learn's `train_test_split` function to partition our dataset into training and testing sets, aiding in model assessment.

6. To transform our text data into a format suitable for machine learning, we employ CountVectorizer from scikit-learn.

```
# Vectorize the text data
vectorizer = CountVectorizer(
    tokenizer=word_tokenize,
    stop_words=stopwords.words('english')
)
X_train = vectorizer.fit_transform(X_train)
X_test = vectorizer.transform(X_test)
```

7. This involves configuring the vectorizer with tokenization and removing stop words to prepare both training and testing data sets effectively. We proceed to train a simple sentiment analysis model using logistic regression.

```
# Train the model
model = LogisticRegression()
model.fit(X_train, y_train)
```

We employ logistic regression for sentiment analysis and train the model using the training set.

8. Finally, we evaluate the model's accuracy on the testing set:

```
# Test the model
accuracy = model.score(X_test, y_test)
print(f'Model accuracy: {accuracy}')
```

The model's accuracy is computed on the testing set, providing an initial measure of its performance.

Result

The sentiment analysis model is trained and tested with an accuracy score printed. This model can now be integrated into a Flask web application to predict sentiments of user input in real-time.

In conclusion, in this example, we have seen how to use Python, Flask, and PyTorch to build a sentiment analysis web application. This application can be further enhanced by adding more features like user authentication, storing user input and predictions, etc.

> **Tip**
> Please note that this is a simplified example and may not work directly without some modifications depending on your development environment. Please adjust it as necessary.

By following these steps, we've initiated our sentiment analysis project. We've prepared the dataset, performed necessary preprocessing, and trained a basic sentiment analysis model. This foundational work sets the stage for further refinement and enhancement of our sentiment analysis capabilities.

Summary

In this chapter, you explored a diverse array of AI frameworks and tools commonly employed in web development. The overarching aim was to furnish you with a holistic comprehension of this dynamic landscape, enabling you to make judicious choices in tool selection for your AI projects.

The chapter delved into prominent frameworks and tools, elucidating their applications and advantages. As you progressed through the chapter, you acquired skills in the discerning evaluation of AI frameworks, adept utilization of machine learning tools, seamless integration of AI into web development, configuration of optimized development environments, and the art of making well-informed decisions tailored to your project needs.

Moreover, we undertook a practical endeavor by conceptualizing and defining a sample project—a sentiment analysis web application employing Python, Flask (a web development framework), and Scikit-learn (a machine learning library). This hands-on example served to solidify your understanding by applying the learned concepts in a real-world context.

Anticipating the next chapter, our focus will pivot toward the architectural aspects of crafting effective AI solutions. As we transition, bear in mind the key takeaways from this chapter, as they will serve as valuable foundations for the challenges and insights awaiting us in the chapters to come.

5

Blueprints of the Future – Architecting Effective AI Solutions

Within this chapter, we will explore the world of AI architecture and its crucial role in building effective AI solutions. We will delve into the fundamentals of AI architecture and discuss the importance of a well-designed framework in optimizing the opportunities offered by AI. The main goal of this chapter is to provide insights into architecting effective AI solutions. The information presented in this chapter is crucial for both developers and businesses in the modern world. AI has the potential to revolutionize web development, and understanding its fundamentals is essential for staying competitive. By learning the skills outlined in this chapter, you will be able to design scalable and efficient solutions, maintain and adapt AI architectures for long-term success, evaluate and choose the right frameworks, and apply architectural principles to real-world web development use cases.

Now, let's delve into the main topics of this chapter:

- Fundamentals of AI architecture
- Scalable and efficient AI solutions
- Ensuring maintainability and adaptability
- Architecting the future – unleashing the power of AI solutions through the AI Architecture Framework
- Real-world AI architecture use cases – ChatGPT by OpenAI
- Introduction to **Architect Your AI (AYAI)** framework

Fundamentals of AI architecture

The field of **artificial intelligence** (**AI**) architecture encompasses various aspects that are crucial for the successful development and deployment of AI solutions. A solid architecture ensures that data is of high quality and relevant, models are trained effectively, platforms function efficiently, tools are used effectively, infrastructure is reliable, and interfaces are user friendly. This section provides an overview of the fundamentals of AI architecture, including its definition, the role of an AI architect, the importance of a solid architecture, and the essential components involved.

Firstly, let's define AI architecture. AI architecture refers to the overall structure and design of an AI solution. It encompasses the various components and their interactions, such as data, models, platforms, tools, infrastructure, and interfaces. These components work together to enable the creation and deployment of AI systems that can perform specific tasks.

The responsibilities of an AI architect include analyzing the requirements of AI systems, designing the architecture, selecting the appropriate components, ensuring data quality, training and evaluating models, developing and deploying AI solutions, and continuously optimizing the system's performance. They must have a deep understanding of AI techniques, data management, software development, and infrastructure.

Having a solid architecture is of utmost importance in AI development. A well-designed architecture ensures that the AI solution can handle large amounts of data, process it efficiently, and generate accurate and meaningful insights. It also enables easy integration with existing systems, scalability, and adaptability to future changes. A solid architecture lays the foundation for a robust and reliable AI solution.

In the next sub-section, we will explore these essential components in detail, highlighting how each plays a pivotal role in the creation of sophisticated, effective, and efficient AI solutions.

Essential components

The essential components of AI architecture include data, models, platforms, tools, infrastructure, and interfaces. Data serves as the foundation, providing the necessary information for training and validating AI models. High-quality and relevant data is essential for ensuring the accuracy and effectiveness of AI solutions.

Figure 5.1 provides a visual representation of the critical elements involved in constructing an AI architecture. It groups these elements into six main categories: Data, Models, Platforms, Tools, Infrastructure, and Interfaces.

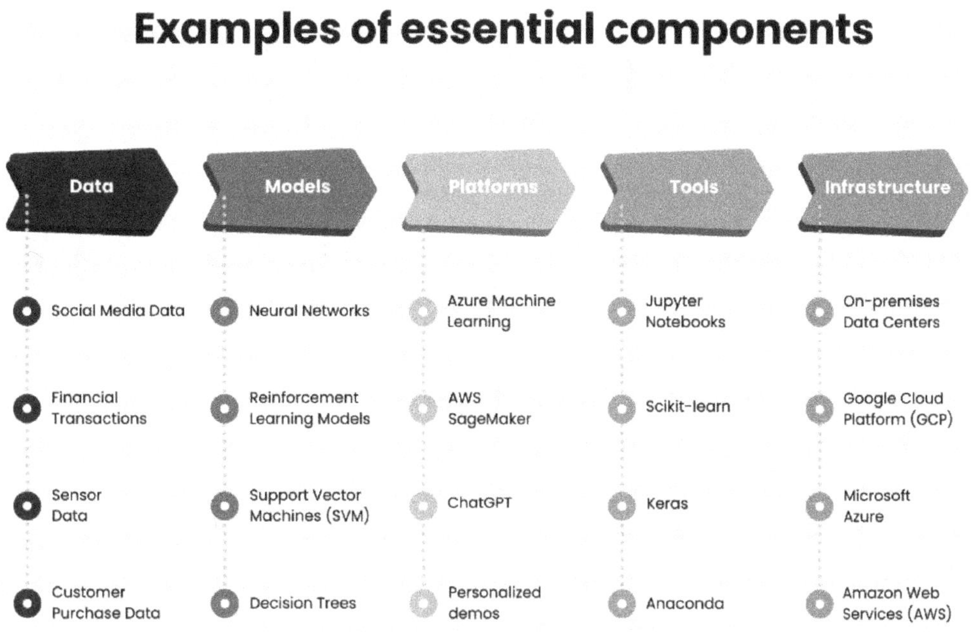

Examples of essential components

Figure 5.1: Examples of essential components

Figure 5.1 summarizes how these components interact and contribute to the overall functionality and efficiency of AI solutions. Let's look at the components that are crucial in AI architecture in depth:

- *Data* forms the foundation of any AI solution. High-quality and relevant data is essential for training accurate models and achieving optimal performance. The AI system should be designed to handle diverse data sources, ensure data quality, and effectively preprocess the data for training and inference.

- The *model* is the component that learns to perform the desired tasks. AI models can be trained using various techniques, including supervised learning, unsupervised learning, and reinforcement learning. AI architects select and design appropriate models based on the problem at hand and the available data.

- The *platform* refers to the software that executes the AI model and provides the necessary input and output interfaces. It plays a crucial role in managing the execution of models, handling the data life cycle, and facilitating communication between different components of the AI system.

- *Tools* are used for developing, training, and deploying AI models. They can be categorized into two types: software development tools for writing code and machine learning tools for training and evaluating models. The AI architect selects and utilizes the most suitable tools based on the project requirements and the expertise of the development team.

- The *infrastructure* can be either on-premises or cloud-based. It provides the necessary computational resources, storage, and networking capabilities to support the AI system's operations. The AI architect determines the infrastructure requirements based on factors such as scalability, security, and cost-effectiveness.

A solid AI architecture is essential for building effective and efficient AI solutions. It involves various components, such as data, models, platforms, tools, infrastructure, and interfaces. An AI architect plays a crucial role in designing and overseeing the development of the AI system. By considering the importance of each component and ensuring their seamless integration, a well-designed architecture can enable AI systems to deliver accurate and reliable results.

The crucial role of interfaces in AI solutions

When designing scalable and efficient AI solutions for web projects, we must understand the crucial role that interfaces play. Interfaces are the center of the mental map, as they are responsible for data collection, model training, and the overall usability of the AI solution.

Figure 5.2 provides an overview of various interfaces used to interact with AI solutions. These interfaces facilitate different methods of inputting data, visualizing results, and integrating AI systems with other technologies. They range from traditional graphical interfaces to advanced brain-computer interfaces, highlighting the diverse ways users can engage with AI systems.

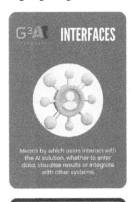

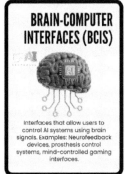

Figure 5.2: Interfaces (this image is from G³ AI Global)

Figure 5.2 details eight different types of interfaces (means by which users interact with the AI solution, whether to enter data, visualize results, or integrate with other systems):

- **Wearable**: Interfaces that use wearable devices to interact with AI. Examples include smartwatches, fitness trackers, and smart glasses. Importance: Wearable devices provide convenient and seamless ways to collect data and interact with AI systems in real time.

- **Graphical User Interfaces (GUIs)**: Visual interfaces that allow users to interact with the AI system via buttons, menus, and forms. Examples include interactive dashboards and mobile apps. GUIs make it easy for users to navigate and utilize AI systems through intuitive visual elements.

- **Application Programming Interfaces (APIs)**: Interfaces that allow communication and integration between different software systems. Examples include RESTful APIs, GraphQL APIs, and SOAP APIs. APIs enable different software systems to work together, extending the functionality and interoperability of AI solutions.

- **Voice User Interfaces (VUIs)**: Interfaces that allow users to interact with the AI system via voice commands, commonly seen in virtual assistants such as Alexa, Siri, and Google Assistant. VUIs provide a hands-free, natural way to interact with AI, making it accessible to a broader audience.

- **Chatbot interfaces**: Interfaces that allow users to interact with AI via text messages in a conversational format. Examples include chatbots on websites and messaging bots on platforms. Chatbot interfaces facilitate easy and interactive communication with AI systems, enhancing user experience and engagement.

- **Augmented Reality (AR)**: Interfaces that superimpose AI-generated information onto the real world via AR devices. Examples include AR mobile apps and AR headsets such as Microsoft HoloLens. AR interfaces enrich the user's perception of reality by overlaying useful information, improving decision-making and interaction with the environment.

- **Brain-Computer Interfaces (BCIs)**: Interfaces that allow users to control AI systems using brain signals. Examples include neurofeedback devices, prosthesis control systems, and mind-controlled gaming interfaces. BCIs represent a cutting-edge method of interaction, enabling direct communication between the brain and AI systems, which can significantly benefit individuals with disabilities.

These interfaces demonstrate the versatility and innovation in how users can interact with AI systems. From wearable technology to BCIs, each interface type provides unique advantages, making AI more accessible, efficient, and integrated into various aspects of daily life and technology.

Through these interfaces, users can input data, retrieve information, and integrate external data sources, ensuring a comprehensive and diverse dataset for training the AI model. The smooth and efficient data collection process directly impacts the accuracy and effectiveness of the AI solution.

The connection between interfaces and model training highlights the importance of interaction in improving AI predictions. Interfaces allow developers to fine-tune models, incorporate user feedback, and continually improve performance, enabling an iterative training process through user interaction.

The final stage demonstrates how interfaces are fundamental in delivering the predictions or results generated by the AI solution to end users. GUIs, CLIs, or APIs provide the means for users to access and utilize the AI solution's predictions effectively. Whether through visually appealing interfaces or direct command-based interactions, interfaces ensure that end users can easily and seamlessly benefit from the AI solution.

Interfaces are at the core of AI solutions, playing a crucial role in every stage of the process. GUIs, CLIs, and APIs enable efficient data collection, model training, and the delivery of predictions to end users. By understanding the importance of interfaces and leveraging their capabilities, developers can design scalable and efficient AI solutions for web projects, enhancing user experiences and driving innovation in the field of AI.

Scalable and efficient AI solutions architecture for web projects

In today's rapidly evolving technological landscape, the demand for scalable and efficient AI solutions has soared to unprecedented heights. To meet this demand, organizations must focus on key aspects such as scalability, computational resource efficiency, scaling strategies, data life cycle, and typical architectures. By prioritizing these elements, businesses can ensure optimum performance and unlock the full potential of AI.

Scalability plays a pivotal role in the successful implementation of AI solutions. It refers to the ability of an AI system to handle increasing workloads and adapt to growing demands without compromising performance. By designing AI systems with scalability in mind, organizations can ensure that their solutions can seamlessly handle large volumes of data and user interactions.

Efficiency in computational resources is essential for AI solutions to function optimally. By utilizing computational resources effectively, organizations can achieve faster processing times, reduced costs, and improved overall performance. This involves optimizing algorithms, utilizing parallel processing techniques, and using cloud computing platforms to efficiently distribute workloads.

Developing effective strategies for scaling AI solutions is crucial for long-term success. Organizations can employ various approaches such as horizontal scaling, vertical scaling, or a combination of both, depending on their specific requirements. Horizontal scaling involves adding more machines or nodes to distribute the workload, while vertical scaling focuses on enhancing the capabilities of existing machines. By carefully considering the scalability needs, organizations can ensure that their AI solutions can grow alongside their business demands.

Scalable and efficient AI solutions are needed for organizations aiming to harness the full potential of AI. By prioritizing scalability in AI implementation, optimizing computational resources, employing effective scaling strategies, and designing efficient data life cycles, organizations can unlock the power of AI to drive innovation, improve decision-making, and achieve competitive advantage in today's digital landscape.

The importance of the data life cycle in building efficient AI solutions

The **data life cycle** plays a crucial role in the development and implementation of efficient AI solutions. These flows describe how data moves through a solution, ensuring that it is collected, processed, and stored efficiently. By carefully designing data life cycle, organizations can optimize their AI systems to deliver accurate and timely insights.

Figures 5.3 and *5.4* provide a comprehensive overview of the data life cycle in AI solutions, detailing each crucial step involved in the data life cycle. From data generation to data archival and disposal, these steps outline the entire process required to manage and utilize data effectively in AI systems. Understanding these steps will help you to build robust AI models and ensure data quality and security.

Figure 5.3: Data life cycle in AI solutions 1 (this image is from G³ AI Global)

Figure 5.3 introduces the initial stages of the data life cycle in AI solutions:

- **Data Generation**: Capturing data from various sources, such as sensors, devices, and social networks
- **Data Collection**: Gathering and aggregating data from different sources, both automatically and manually
- **Data Ingestion**: Transferring data into a centralized system for processing
- **Data Preprocessing**: Cleaning and transforming raw data to prepare it for analysis
- **Data Storage**: Storing the prepared data in databases, data warehouses, or data lakes for accessibility and scalability
- **Data Analysis**: Applying analytical techniques and AI algorithms to extract insights and patterns
- **Model Training**: Using prepared data to train AI models, optimizing their performance based on the data

Figure 5.4 continues with the later stages of the data life cycle:

- **Model Validation:** Evaluating the accuracy and effectiveness of the trained model using separate datasets
- **Model Deployment:** Implementing the trained model in a production environment to make real-time predictions or decisions
- **Data Streaming:** Continuous real-time data processing, allowing the AI system to react instantly to new information
- **Data Visualization:** Creating graphs, dashboards, and reports to present analysis results in an understandable way
- **Data Feedback:** Collecting feedback on model performance to refine and improve it continuously
- **Applying Insights**: Utilizing analysis results and model predictions to make informed decisions and take practical actions
- **Data Governance:** Implementing policies to manage data quality, privacy, and security throughout the data life cycle

- **Data Archival and Disposal**: Storing or securely disposing of data that is no longer required, in compliance with data retention policies and privacy regulations

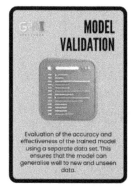   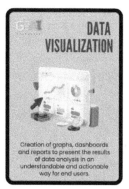

Figure 5.4: Data life cycle in AI solutions 2 (this image is from G³ AI Global)

These figures collectively illustrate the comprehensive workflow and best practices for managing data in AI solutions, ensuring data is effectively processed, analyzed, and utilized while maintaining high standards of quality and security.

Effective data management in AI solutions involves several crucial steps, each with its own set of processes and objectives. Three of these fundamental steps are data ingestion, data preprocessing, and data storage. Understanding the differences and relationships between these stages is essential for building robust and efficient data solutions. *Figure 5.5* compares the main aspects of data ingestion, data preprocessing, and data storage.

Comparison of Data Ingestion, Preprocessing, and Storage

Aspect	Data Ingestion	Data Preprocessing	Data Storage
Definition	Collection and integration of data from various sources	Cleaning and transformation of raw data for analysis	Organized and secure storage of collected data
Objective	Ensure data availability	Ensure data quality and usefulness	Keep data accessible for analysis and processing
Process	Collection, transport, and integration of data	Cleaning, normalization, and transformation of data	Organization, indexing, and archiving of data
Included Steps	Connection to data sources, extraction, and loading	Removal of duplicates, handling of missing values, normalization	Structuring, compression, data backup, and recovery
Variety of Data	Handles structured, semi-structured, and unstructured data	Converts raw data into a format suitable for analysis	Stores all types of data in appropriate systems
Tools	Apache Kafka, Apache Nifi, AWS Glue	Python (Pandas, Scikit-learn), Apache Spark, Talend	Amazon S3, Google Cloud Storage, Microsoft Azure Blob Storage

Figure 5.5: Comparison of data ingestion, data preprocessing, and data storage

Data ingestion refers to the collection and integration of data from various sources, ensuring that all relevant data is made available for further processing. Data preprocessing involves cleaning and transforming raw data to improve its quality and usefulness for analysis. Finally, data storage deals with the organized and secure storage of this data, keeping it accessible for future analysis and processing. Each stage uses different tools and techniques to deal with the variety and volume of data, ensuring that the data life cycle is managed effectively and efficiently.

It is worth noting that monitoring and maintaining data life cycles is essential for their continued efficiency. Regularly monitoring data life cycles allows organizations to identify and address any bottlenecks or inefficiency in the system promptly. By proactively maintaining data life cycles, organizations can ensure that their AI solutions continue to deliver accurate and reliable results, even as data volumes and complexity increase.

So, data life cycles are instrumental in producing efficient AI solutions. By carefully designing how data moves through a solution, organizations can optimize data collection, processing, and storage. This optimized flow of data enables AI systems to deliver accurate and timely insights, empowering organizations to make informed decisions. To build successful AI solutions, organizations must prioritize the design and management of data life cycles, ensuring their ongoing efficiency and effectiveness.

Typical architectures of AI solutions

A plethora of architectures serve as the backbone for crafting high-performance and scalable solutions tailored for web projects. Different architectures provide unique advantages and can be chosen based on factors such as performance, privacy, scalability, and availability.

Figure 5.6 provides an insightful overview of the typical architectures used in AI solutions. It showcases a variety of structured frameworks that dictate how different components of an AI system interact and work together. Each architecture type is illustrated with a brief description and examples of use cases, demonstrating the diversity and specificity of each approach.

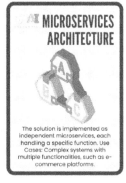

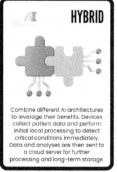

Figure 5.6: Typical Architectures of AI Solutions (this image is from G³ AI Global)

Let's explore some typical architectures for AI solutions and discuss their characteristics and use cases:

- One common architecture is the *client-server architecture*. In this setup, the AI model is executed on a remote server, and the predictions or recommendations are delivered to users through a user interface. This architecture allows centralized processing and can be suitable for projects that require real-time responses.

- Another architecture is the *edge-based machine learning architecture*. In this approach, the AI model is executed on the user's device. This can improve performance and privacy as it reduces the need for data transfer to a remote server. However, it may also require more resources from the device.

- For solutions that require high scalability or availability, the *cloud-based architecture* is a popular choice. In this architecture, the AI model is executed in the cloud, leveraging the computing power and resources available. This architecture is suitable for projects with varying workloads and allows easy scaling.

- The *pipeline architecture* is another approach where data is collected, prepared, developed, and deployed sequentially. This architecture ensures a systematic flow of data, allowing for efficient processing and analysis.

- In contrast, the *microservices architecture* implements the solution as independent microservices. Each component operates independently, enabling flexibility and easier maintenance. This architecture is suitable for complex projects with multiple functionalities.

- For the best of both worlds, the *hybrid architecture* combines different architectures to take advantage of their various benefits. For example, an AI model can be trained in the cloud to take advantage of computing capacity and then deployed on the user's device to enhance performance and privacy.

- In the *federated learning architecture*, AI models are trained on multiple devices or servers. This approach allows data to remain where it is, improving privacy and reducing the need for bandwidth. This architecture is particularly useful in scenarios where data cannot be easily transferred due to privacy or security concerns.

- *Pre-built architectures*, often hosted in the cloud, provide ready-to-use solutions for AI projects. They provide a convenient and efficient way to implement AI functionality without extensive development.

When designing AI solutions for web projects, it is crucial to consider the architecture that best suits the project's requirements. Each architecture option provides distinct advantages and contributes to the scalability and efficiency of the solution. By carefully selecting the architecture, developers can ensure optimal performance and user experience in their AI projects. Scalability, computational resource efficiency, data life cycles, and the right architecture are key elements in building scalable and efficient AI solutions for web projects.

Designing AI solutions – a step-by-step guide

Now, we will explore the process of designing AI solutions and discuss its significance in today's business landscape. As AI continues to revolutionize industries, understanding the objectives of business and implementing effective solutions has become crucial.

To begin the design process, it is essential to *establish clear objectives*. By clearly defining what the business aims to achieve, we can align AI solutions accordingly. Additionally, identifying the specific needs of the company allows us to tailor the solutions to meet those requirements.

To ensure we are up to date with the latest advancements and possibilities, conducting thorough research is vital. This research can include analyzing market reports, exploring specialized websites, consulting technology firms, and even leveraging insights from social media platforms. This comprehensive approach allows us to gather valuable information and stay informed about emerging trends and opportunities.

Once we have gathered a wealth of information, it is time to move on to the selection and evaluation process. Building prototypes and testing solutions enable us to assess their feasibility and effectiveness. Obtaining feedback during this stage is crucial as it helps us identify any potential issues that need to be addressed. By actively listening to feedback, we can refine and improve the solutions to better meet the needs of the business.

After selecting the most suitable AI solutions, the next step is their implementation. This involves integrating the solutions with existing systems to ensure a seamless transition. Additionally, it is essential to establish clear success criteria to measure the effectiveness of the implemented solutions. By setting these criteria, we can monitor performance and make any necessary adjustments to ensure optimal results.

Implementation of solutions

In this section, we will investigate the crucial step of implementing AI solutions in a business setting. Once the goals and specific needs of the company have been understood, and suitable solutions have been researched and evaluated, it is time to move forward with the implementation phase.

The basic step in implementing AI solutions is *integrating them with existing systems*. This involves ensuring that the new technology seamlessly integrates with the company's infrastructure and processes. It is essential to consider factors such as compatibility, data transfer, and security protocols. By successfully integrating these solutions, we can maximize their potential and ensure a smooth transition.

Another important aspect to consider during implementation is *guaranteeing the criteria for success*. This involves setting specific metrics and benchmarks to measure the effectiveness and impact of the AI solutions. By defining these criteria from the start, we can assess whether the implemented solutions are meeting the desired objectives. Regular monitoring and evaluation will allow us to make any necessary adjustments and improvements along the way.

Throughout the implementation process, it is crucial to maintain open lines of *communication with all stakeholders* involved. This ensures that everyone is aligned and aware of the progress being made. Feedback from users and employees is invaluable during this phase, as it allows us to identify any problems or areas for improvement. By actively seeking and addressing this feedback, we can refine the solutions and ensure their continuous success.

The implementation of AI solutions requires a strategic approach that encompasses integration with existing systems and the establishment of clear success criteria. By following these guidelines, we can ensure that the solutions effectively contribute to the company's overall objectives. Implementing AI solutions may present challenges, but with careful planning and continuous evaluation, we can overcome them and unlock the full potential of this transformative technology.

In the upcoming sub-section, we delve into the importance of maintaining AI systems and the necessity of adaptability in the face of evolving technological landscapes and organizational needs. Through a commitment to regular updates, monitoring, and the flexibility to adjust to new challenges, AI systems can sustain their relevance and effectiveness, contributing to the enduring success of AI initiatives.

Ensuring maintainability and adaptability

In order to ensure the long-term success of AI architectures, it is crucial to prioritize the maintenance of AI systems. This involves regularly monitoring and updating the systems to ensure that they continue to perform at their best. By regularly maintaining AI systems, we can identify and address any issues or limitations that may arise, ensuring that the systems remain efficient and effective.

One way to maintain AI systems is through *continuous testing and monitoring*. This allows us to detect any performance issues or errors, and take appropriate action to resolve them. Additionally, regular updates and enhancements to the AI systems can improve their performance and functionality, as well as address any security vulnerabilities that may arise.

As technology and business requirements evolve, it is important for AI architectures to be *adaptable to these changes*. This means being able to modify and adjust the AI systems to meet new requirements and challenges. Adapting to changing requirements ensures that the AI systems remain relevant and effective in addressing the needs of the organization.

To adapt to changing requirements, it is important to have a flexible and scalable AI architecture. This allows the easy integration of new data sources, technologies, and algorithms. Additionally, regular evaluation of the AI systems and their performance can help identify areas for improvement and adaptation.

Ensuring the *durability* of AI systems is essential for their long-term success. Durability refers to the ability of AI systems to withstand and adapt to changes in the environment, such as evolving technology, new business requirements, and changing user needs.

One best practice for durability is to design AI systems with modularity in mind. By breaking down the system into smaller, independent modules, it becomes easier to modify and adapt individual components without affecting the entire system. This allows for more flexibility and agility in making changes.

Another best practice is to *regularly evaluate and update* AI systems to incorporate new advancements and best practices in the field. This ensures that the systems remain up to date and continue to deliver optimal performance.

In summary, maintaining and adapting AI architectures is crucial for their long-term success. By prioritizing maintenance, adapting to changing requirements, and following best practices for durability, organizations can ensure that their AI systems remain efficient, effective, and relevant in addressing their needs.

The next section aims to shed light on the comprehensive strategy behind crafting resilient and impactful AI solutions. This journey will guide us through the intricacies of aligning AI architecture with the specific needs and objectives of its intended users. We will examine how data traverses through the system—from its entry point to its final destination—while ensuring its integrity and usefulness at every stage. Furthermore, the discussion will extend to the structural design of AI solutions, highlighting the critical components, such as the models, platforms, tools, and frameworks that together facilitate a robust AI ecosystem.

Architecting the future – unleashing the power of AI solutions through the AI Architecture Framework

In this section, we will delve into the key aspects of the AI Architecture Framework, focusing on understanding the target audience, solution objectives, and the problem to be resolved. We will also explore the data life cycles within the solution, including input interfaces, data sources, data collection, data preparation, data storage, and data delivery. Additionally, we will discuss the architecture design, encompassing the model, platform, tools, frameworks, typical architectures, and how end users will interact with the solution. Lastly, we will touch upon the importance of learning and improvement in AI architectures.

The **AI Architecture Framework** is a comprehensive structure designed to guide the development and implementation of AI solutions. Our framework stands out for its systematic approach, encompassing everything from understanding the objectives to practical implementation, promoting effectiveness and efficiency in all phases of the process.

The next sub-section focuses on the importance of grounding our AI initiatives in a thorough understanding of the target audience and clearly defined solution objectives.

Context

To ensure the success of any AI solution, it is crucial to have a deep *understanding of the target audience*. By identifying the end users, we can tailor the solution to meet their specific needs and preferences. Additionally, we need to establish clear solution objectives, defining the goals that our AI solution aims to achieve. These objectives serve as guiding principles throughout the development and implementation process.

Furthermore, we must have a clear understanding of the problem we are trying to resolve. By identifying the issue at hand, we can design an effective solution that addresses the problem comprehensively. Additionally, it is important to categorize the problem and determine its type to better inform the development process.

Scalability and computer efficiency are vital considerations in AI architecture. The solution should be able to handle an increased workload without compromising its performance. Furthermore, it should utilize computational resources effectively to maximize efficiency. Maintenance and upgrading should also be taken into account, ensuring that the solution can be easily maintained and upgraded as needed.

Performance metrics play a crucial role in evaluating a solution's performance. By establishing measurable metrics, we can assess how well the solution is meeting its objectives. Additionally, the solution should undergo rigorous testing and evaluation to ensure its effectiveness in real-world scenarios.

Security and privacy are paramount in AI architecture. Measures must be implemented to protect data and user privacy, safeguarding against potential breaches or unauthorized access. Moreover, ethical considerations should be taken into account, addressing any ethical issues that may arise from the use of AI.

Data life cycle

The *data life cycle* within the AI solution is a critical aspect to consider. Input interfaces determine how the solution receives data from various sources. These sources can include databases, APIs, or sensor inputs, among others. Data collection involves gathering the required data from these sources, ensuring that it is comprehensive and accurate.

Once collected, the data needs to undergo preparation, which involves cleaning and formatting it to make it suitable for analysis and processing. The prepared data is then stored in appropriate data storage systems, considering factors such as scalability, security, and accessibility.

Data delivery is another crucial step in the data life cycle. This involves presenting the analyzed data to the end users in a user-friendly and understandable manner. Output interfaces play a key role in delivering the data, which can include visualizations, reports, or interactive interfaces.

Architecture design

The *architecture design of the AI solution* encompasses several elements. The model refers to the conceptual structure of the solution, outlining how different components interact and work together to achieve the desired objectives. The platform, be it hardware or software, provides the environment in which the solution operates, influencing its performance and capabilities.

Tools and frameworks are essential for developing and operating the AI solution. They include software or systems that facilitate the implementation and management of the solution, such as programming languages, development platforms, and AI-specific frameworks. Choosing the right frameworks is crucial for the success of the architecture, as different frameworks provide different capabilities and suitability for different AI applications.

Understanding the typical architectures commonly used in similar solutions can provide valuable insights and guidance in designing the AI architecture. By studying and learning from successful architectures, we can leverage proven approaches and adapt them to our specific context.

Lastly, it is essential to consider how end users will interact with the solution. The user experience should be intuitive and seamless, allowing users to easily access and utilize the AI capabilities. Additionally, we should focus on enabling the solution to learn and improve over time, using data to enhance its performance and adapt to changing circumstances.

The AI Architecture Framework provides a comprehensive and systematic approach to developing and implementing AI solutions. By understanding the target audience, defining solution objectives, and addressing the problem at hand, we can design an effective architecture. The data life cycle and architecture design aspects ensure that the solution can handle data effectively, utilize the right tools and frameworks, and provide a seamless user experience. With continuous learning and improvement, the AI architecture can evolve and adapt to meet the ever-changing demands of the AI landscape.

Next, will delve into the intricacies of creating sophisticated AI systems capable of understanding and generating human-like text.

Real-world AI architecture use cases – ChatGPT by OpenAI

In the rapidly evolving digital age, the ability to generate human-like text has become increasingly important. Whether it's drafting emails, writing code, creating written content, or even chatting with users, AI has the potential to revolutionize these tasks. However, developing an AI that can understand and generate human-like text is a complex problem that requires a comprehensive and systematic approach.

This is where **OpenAI's ChatGPT** comes into play. ChatGPT is an AI solution that uses the power of **Generative Pretrained Transformers** (**GPTs**) to generate human-like text based on the input provided. It's designed to serve a wide range of users, from the general public to businesses and developers, and can be used for various applications.

The development and implementation of ChatGPT is guided by the AI Architecture Framework, a comprehensive structure that promotes effectiveness and efficiency in all phases of the process. This framework ensures that the solution is not only technically sound but also user-friendly and ethically responsible.

Moving forward, the *Context* sub-section introduces us to the foundational phase of this journey. Here, we focus on grasping the core challenges and identifying the diverse needs of our varied audience, which includes the general public, businesses, and developers.

Context

The first step in our AI journey is *understanding the context*. Our target audience is the general public, businesses, and developers. The objective of our AI solution, ChatGPT, is to generate human-like text based on the input provided. This can be used for various applications, such as drafting emails, writing code, creating written content, and more.

We need to understand the problem we're trying to solve: the need for AI that can understand and generate human-like text. By identifying the issue at hand, we can design an effective solution that addresses the problem comprehensively. Here is a comprehensive list that outlines the critical aspects of our project, from identifying our target audience to addressing key operational and ethical considerations:

- **Target audience**: General public, companies, and developers.
- **Solution objectives**: Generate human-like text based on the input provided.
- **Problem to be solved**: The need for an AI that can understand and generate human-like text.
- **AI type problem**: Natural language processing problem.
- **Scalability**: The model is scalable and can handle a large number of simultaneous requests.
- **Computer efficiency**: The model uses computing resources efficiently to generate responses in real time.
- **Maintenance and upgrading**: The model is continuously monitored and improved based on user interactions and feedback.
- **Performance metrics**: To gauge the success of our AI solution, we employ a set of comprehensive metrics centered on three critical aspects:
  - **Accuracy of responses**: This metric assesses how precisely the AI's outputs match the expected or desired outcomes. It's a measure of the system's ability to provide correct and applicable answers or content based on the inputs it receives.
  - **Relevance of the content generated**: Beyond accuracy, we evaluate the pertinence of the AI-generated content to the user's query or need. This ensures that the solution not only understands the request but also delivers information or content that is contextually appropriate and useful.

- **User satisfaction**: The ultimate indicator of our AI's effectiveness is the satisfaction of its users. Through feedback and usage metrics, we assess how well the solution meets the needs and expectations of its audience, refining our approach to enhance user experience continually.

- **Test and evaluation**: The model is continuously tested and evaluated to ensure its performance and effectiveness.

- **Security and privacy**: All data is stored and transmitted securely, with access controls to prevent unauthorized access.

- **Ethical considerations**: The model is designed to be fair and impartial, and to respect users' privacy and confidentiality. Ensuring the AI model's integrity through rigorous testing, upholding the highest standards of security and privacy, and adhering to ethical guidelines are foundational principles in our development process.

As we transition from these core tenets into the operational mechanics of our AI solution, the next critical aspect to explore is the data life cycle.

Data life cycle

The *data life cycle* within the AI solution is a critical aspect to consider. Our input interfaces are user inputs through a chat interface or API. We use large-scale datasets from the internet for training. These datasets are collected in an automated manner and prepared for analysis. The prepared data is then stored in a secure and scalable data storage system. Here's a succinct overview of each stage within the data life cycle:

- **Input interfaces**: User inputs via a chat interface or API

- **Data sources**: Large-scale datasets from the internet

- **Data collection**: Data is collected in an automated way

- **Data preparation**: Data is prepared for analysis, which can include cleaning and formatting

- **Data storage**: The prepared data is stored in a secure and scalable data storage system

- **Data delivery**: The model generates answers based on the input data and delivers them to the user

- **Output interfaces**: The model's answers are delivered to the user via a chat interface or API

In this next sub-section, we will explore the architecture design of our AI solution, a critical aspect that underpins the operational efficacy and scalability of our system. This design details the underlying model, including its conceptual framework and the interactions between various components. Central to our architecture is the use of a machine learning model known as GPT, which is renowned for its ability to understand and generate human-like text. Hosted on a robust cloud-based platform, our solution ensures high availability and accessibility, allowing seamless interaction through an API. This architecture not only supports the sophisticated processing capabilities required for natural language understanding and generation but also provides the flexibility and scalability necessary to adapt to evolving demands and technologies.

Architecture design

The *architecture design of the AI solution* encompasses several elements. The model refers to the conceptual structure of the solution, outlining how different components interact with each other. We use a machine learning model known as GPT. The model is hosted on a cloud-based platform and can be interacted with via an API.

Various machine learning frameworks and libraries for training and deploying the model. Users interact with the model through a chat interface or API.

The model's performance is continuously monitored and improved based on user interactions and feedback. This ensures that the solution remains effective and adapts to changing conditions over time.

All data is securely stored and transmitted, with access controls in place to prevent unauthorized access. The solution complies with all relevant data protection regulations. As we pivot from the technical underpinnings to the practical implications and applications, the following section will explore each component in greater detail:

- **Model**: The model refers to the conceptual structure of the solution, which in this case is GPT.

- **Platform**: The model is hosted on a cloud-based platform.

- **Tools**: Various machine learning tools and libraries are used to train and deploy the model.

- **Frameworks**: The model is trained and deployed using various machine learning frameworks.

- **Typical architectures**: ChatGPT's architecture is typical of natural language processing solutions that use deep learning models.

- **Using the solution**: Users interact with the model via a chat interface or API.

- **Learning and improvement**: The model continuously learns from the data and improves over time. This is facilitated by user feedback and user interactions with the model.

This use case demonstrates how the AI Architecture Framework can guide the development of an effective, efficient AI solution that meets the needs of its users and addresses a real-world problem. It shows the importance of understanding the problem and audience, designing a suitable architecture, and ensuring continuous learning and improvement. It also highlights the critical role of the data life cycle and the need to consider security and privacy.

By following these steps and considering these factors, we can ensure that our AI solution is not only technically sound but also user friendly and ethically responsible. This comprehensive approach is what sets our AI Architecture Framework apart and ensures the success of our AI solutions.

The AI Architecture Framework provides a systematic approach to developing and implementing AI solutions, promoting effectiveness and efficiency in all phases of the process. It is a valuable tool for any organization looking to leverage the power of AI.

Introduction to Architect Your AI (AYAI) Framework

Architect Your AI (AYAI) is a framework that provides a structured approach to developing AI solutions. It serves as a visual representation of the context, key components, data process, solution life cycle, and requirements of an AI project. The AYAI Framework is a valuable tool for teams and stakeholders involved in the development process as it helps to align their understanding and expectations.

The AYAI Framework is designed for a diverse audience, including architects and specialists in AI, AI product managers, corporate architects, business analysts, managers and executives, the developer community, and decision-makers. It is a collaborative tool that facilitates communication and ensures that all parties involved have a shared understanding of the project's objectives and requirements.

The importance of the AYAI Framework lies in its ability to provide a clear and concise overview of the AI solution. It enables stakeholders to identify the target audience, solution objectives, and the problem that needs to be addressed. By utilizing the AYAI Framework, teams can streamline the development process, enhance efficiency, and improve decision-making.

This approach serves to distill the key components and considerations into a cohesive framework. Whether you are a seasoned AI architect or just embarking on the journey of integrating AI into your projects, this framework provides a structured view to help you navigate the complexities of designing effective AI solutions. The AYAI Framework is made up of the domains and the integrated AI Loops process, as can be seen in *Figure 5.7*.

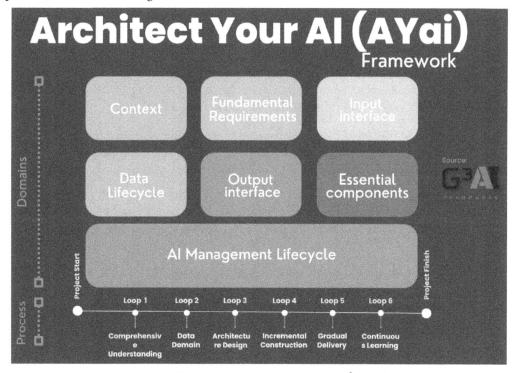

Figure 5.7: AYAI Framework (this image is from G³ AI Global)

By using this framework, architects and teams can collaboratively map out, visualize, and refine their AI architecture, fostering effective communication and strategic decision-making throughout the development life cycle.

To effectively use the AYAI Framework, it is crucial to follow a structured approach:

- Start by identifying the **target audience**, which includes clients, end-users, internal stakeholders, external stakeholders, the web developer, and decision-makers. Understand their needs, expectations, and pain points to align the solution with their requirements.

- Next, define the **solution objectives**. These objectives should focus on maximizing operational efficiency, increasing user satisfaction, reducing operational costs, improving decision-making, facilitating data analysis, and enhancing content personalization. Clearly stating these objectives will guide the development process and ensure that the solution meets the desired outcomes.

- Identify the **problem to be resolved**. This could involve optimizing processes, predictive analysis, anomaly detection, data classification, content recommendation, or problem diagnosis. Understanding the problem is crucial for designing an effective AI solution that addresses the specific needs of the target audience.

- Different types of problems may require different approaches. Classification, regression, clustering, knowledge discovery, **natural language processing** (**NLP**), computer vision, and reinforcement learning are examples of problem types that may be encountered during AI solution development. Choosing the appropriate problem type is essential for selecting the right algorithms and models.

- Moving on to the **fundamental requirements** of an AI solution, *scalability* is a critical aspect. The solution should be able to handle increasing workloads without compromising performance. Evaluating the system's efficiency in scaling up and managing larger volumes of data and requests is essential. Let's look at the fundamental requirements of an AI solution:

  - **Computational efficiency** focuses on optimizing the performance of AI solutions' computational components. This includes efficient data processing, model training, and algorithm execution. Maximizing resource utilization is a key consideration for achieving computational efficiency.

  - **Maintenance and upgrading** are crucial for the long-term stability and relevance of AI solutions. This involves proactive maintenance, bug fixing, security updates, and functional enhancements. Continuous management ensures that the solution remains reliable and up to date.

  - **Testing and evaluation** ensure the correct functioning and effectiveness of the AI solution. Integration testing, performance testing, model evaluation, and result validation are essential processes that guarantee the solution's reliability and accuracy.

- **Security and privacy** are of paramount importance in AI solutions. Protecting data and ensuring overall system security involves implementing measures to prevent unauthorized access, encrypting sensitive data, complying with privacy regulations, and adhering to ethical and legal standards.

- **Ethical considerations** are vital in AI solution development. Transparency in model decisions, fairness in data treatment, prevention of algorithmic bias, and adherence to ethical principles are crucial for responsible and ethical implementation and use of the solution.

- **Input interfaces** are mechanisms through which external data is received or collected into the AI system. These can include user inputs, data feeds, or API integrations. Designing effective input interfaces ensures seamless data integration into the AI solution.

- The **data life cycle** represents the journey of data within the AI system. It encompasses processes such as preprocessing, storage, and ultimately, the output or decision-making phase. Understanding the data life cycle is essential for ensuring accurate and meaningful results.

- **Output interfaces** are the channels through which the AI system presents or delivers results, predictions, or insights. These interfaces can include visual displays, reports, API responses, or any means of communicating the system's outputs to end-users or other systems. Effective output interfaces enhance the user experience and facilitate the utilization of the AI solution.

- **Essential components** of an AI solution include the model, platform, tools, and frameworks:

  - The *model* represents the core algorithm or mathematical framework used in the AI solution. Choosing the right model is crucial and depends on the problem type, parameters, architecture, and training strategies.

  - The *platform* refers to the environment where the AI model is deployed and executed. It can be on-premises, cloud-based, or a hybrid infrastructure. Evaluating platform options based on scalability, performance, cost, deployment ease, and integration capabilities is essential.

  - *Tools* encompass the software and applications utilized throughout the AI solution development life cycle. **Integrated Development Environments** (**IDEs**), data processing tools, and model evaluation tools are examples of essential tools. Choosing the right tools influences development efficiency, collaboration, and overall workflow.

  - *Frameworks* are comprehensive software structures that facilitate AI model development, training, and deployment. Popular frameworks include TensorFlow, PyTorch, and scikit-learn. Framework selection should consider factors such as ease of use, community support, and compatibility with the chosen programming language.

- The **AI management life cycle** encompasses iterative development and testing, implementation, launch and continuous operation, and continuous learning and evolution. It provides a roadmap for developing and utilizing the AI solution effectively in real-world environments. Incorporating continuous learning and implementing improvements over time ensures the solution remains relevant and effective.

Briefly, the AYAI Framework is a powerful tool for developing AI solutions. By following a structured approach and considering the target audience, solution objectives, and problem to be resolved, teams can design and implement effective AI solutions. The AYAI Framework provides a comprehensive overview of the essential components, requirements, and considerations throughout the development life cycle. With the Framework as a guide, AI solution development can be streamlined, efficient, and effective.

Summary

In this chapter, we explored the world of AI architecture and its crucial role in building effective AI solutions. We discussed the fundamentals of AI architecture, emphasizing the importance of a well-designed framework in optimizing the opportunities offered by AI. The main goal of this chapter was to provide insights into architecting effective AI solutions, which is crucial for developers and businesses in the modern world. By learning the skills outlined in this chapter, individuals can design scalable and efficient solutions, maintain and adapt AI architectures for long-term success, evaluate and choose the right frameworks, and apply architectural principles to real-world web development use cases.

We also delved into the topics of scalability, efficiency, and implementation of AI solutions, as well as the importance of maintaining and adapting AI systems. Furthermore, we explored the AI Architecture Framework and introduced to **Architect your AI** (**AYAI**) Framework, which guides the development and implementation of AI solutions, and discussed a real-world use case of AI architecture in generating human-like text.

In the next chapter, we will focus on design intelligence and how it can create user-centric experiences with AI.

Part 2:
Crafting the Future: Creating Cutting-Edge AI Applications

In this part, we delve into creating advanced AI applications for web development, focusing on leveraging AI to build user-centric experiences, recognize patterns for personalizing journeys, and enhance productivity with coding assistants such as GitHub Copilot. You'll learn to create chatbots with sentiment analysis, implement real-time translation, speech recognition, and transcription, and develop dynamic content personalization and recommendation systems. Additionally, we cover integrating chatbots with platforms such as Telegram. This section equips you with the skills to implement AI solutions, ensuring efficient, personalized, and engaging web applications.

This part includes the following chapters:

- *Chapter 6, Design Intelligence – Creating User-Centric Experiences with AI*
- *Chapter 7, Recognizing Patterns – Personalizing User Journeys with AI*
- *Chapter 8, Coding Assistants – Your Secret Weapon in Modern Development*
- *Chapter 9, Smarter User Interactions – Elevating User Engagement with Advanced AI*
- *Chapter 10, Smart Testing Strategies – Fortifying Web Applications with AI Insights*

6

Design Intelligence – Creating User-Centric Experiences with AI

Welcome to *Chapter 6*! This chapter is a deep dive into the transformative world of **Design Intelligence** (**DI**) and its impact on crafting user-centric experiences through AI.

DI transcends conventional design approaches. It leverages AI algorithms to understand user preferences, behaviors, and trends, enhancing the web development process from aesthetic design to content structure. The result? A personalized and engaging user experience.

Consider an e-commerce website. It uses AI to dynamically personalize product recommendations based on user shopping behavior. This creates a unique shopping experience for each user. We'll discuss techniques for implementing AI-driven dynamic content personalization in e-commerce applications. We'll also introduce tools like TensorFlow and Keras for incorporating AI into e-commerce environments.

In this chapter, you'll acquire a range of skills. You'll learn to navigate the world of Design Intelligence in Web Development, apply AI for personalized user experiences, create adaptive user interfaces, and optimize these interfaces using insights obtained from AI. You'll also learn to analyze and adapt designs based on user behavior.

The ultimate goal? To equip you with the knowledge and skills needed to create user-centered and personalized experiences using Design Intelligence. This information is important in today's web development landscape, where user personalization is a growing trend. It could be the key to your website or app's success.

The main topics of this chapter are:

- Navigating the World of Design Intelligence in Web Development

- Applying AI for Personalized User Experiences

- Optimizing User Interfaces with AI

- Practical applications of user support, accessibility, and personalized experiencesMeasuring the Impact

Technical Requirements

In this chapter, we will be using Python 3.6 or higher and the following Python libraries:

- Python 3.6 or higher (`https://www.python.org/downloads/`)

- TensorFlow (`https://www.tensorflow.org/install`)

- Keras (`https://keras.io/`)

- Database management system (DBMS) such as MySQL or PostgreSQL.

  - Link for MySQL: `https://downloads.mysql.com/archives/installer/`

  - Link for PostgreSQL: `https://www.postgresql.org/download/`

- You can download the complete project on GitHub at: `https://github.com/PacktPublishing/AI-Strategies-for-Web-Development/tree/main/ch6`

Navigating the World of Design Intelligence in Web Development

Design Intelligence (**DI**) is the strategic application of **Artificial Intelligence** (**AI**) in the design process. As designers and developers, we use AI to enhance the user experience, making products more intuitive, personalized, and efficient. AI allows us to analyze large volumes of data and understand complex patterns, which helps us make more informed design decisions.

The core goal of DI is to forge user-centric experiences by seamlessly blending design elements with AI capabilities. Our approach centers on a deep understanding of user needs and preferences, which guides every aspect of our design strategy. Through the strategic integration of AI, we craft dynamic experiences that adapt and evolve in response to user interactions, offering a distinctly tailored and immersive experience. Throughout this chapter, you will learn more about the principles of DI and its application in web development. You will discover how AI can be used to enhance the user experience and how you can start integrating AI into your own design projects. So, shall we get started?

Components of DI

DI marries the power of AI with user-centric design principles. It's about creating experiences that truly resonate with users. Let's delve into its key components.

User research is the first step. We immerse ourselves in the lives of our users, seeking to understand their needs, preferences, and behaviors. This understanding is the cornerstone of our design decisions, ensuring that our solutions are not just technologically advanced, but also meaningful and relevant to our users.

Artificial Intelligence is the next component. We use AI algorithms to personalize experiences, automate tasks, and make decisions that are relevant to the user's context. AI enables us to analyze user behavior at a granular level, allowing us to craft experiences that are as unique as each user.

User-Centered Design is another crucial component. We ensure that our solutions meet user expectations and requirements. Every design decision we make is guided by the question, *How does this benefit the user?* This user-centric approach ensures that our solutions are not just functional, but also enjoyable and easy to use.

Finally, we embrace the process of continuous iteration. We engage in cycles of design and refinement based on user feedback and AI insights. With each iteration, we learn more about our users and improve our solutions, making them more effective and user-friendly.

In essence, DI is a holistic approach that integrates user research, AI, user-centered design, and continuous iteration. It's about creating experiences that truly revolve around the user.

Phases of the DI process

In the dynamic world of design, the integration of AI has opened new frontiers. One such frontier is DI, a strategic approach that leverages the power of AI to create experiences that are truly centered around the user. It's a process that combines the creativity of design with the precision of AI, resulting in solutions that are not only innovative but also deeply attuned to the user's needs and preferences. Let's delve into the phases of this process:

- The journey begins with the *discovery phase.* Here, we cast a wide net, exploring the project landscape to identify opportunities where AI can enhance the design. This could range from personalizing user interfaces to automating repetitive tasks. It's about finding those areas where AI can make a real difference in the user experience.

- Once we've identified these opportunities, we move to the *conceptualization phase.* This is where we give shape to our ideas, developing initial prototypes that incorporate the identified AI features. We consider how these features will work, how they will improve the user experience, and how they align with our overall design goals.

- After conceptualizing our ideas, we proceed to the *implementation phase*. This is where we bring our ideas to life, integrating AI algorithms into the final product. We work closely with our development team to ensure that the AI features are effectively implemented and that they enhance the user experience as intended.

- The final phase is *evaluation*. We conduct usability testing and collect feedback from users. This feedback is invaluable in making final adjustments to our product. It helps us refine our design and ensure that it meets the needs and expectations of our users.

As we navigate through these phases, we continually learn and adapt, refining our approach based on user feedback and AI insights. This iterative process is what makes DI so powerful. It's not just about creating a product; it's about crafting an experience that truly resonates with the user. As we conclude this overview, we hope you're excited to delve deeper into each of these phases and discover how DI can transform your design process.

Benefits of DI

- In the dynamic realm of design, the integration of AI has proven transformative, placing Design Intelligence (DI) at the heart of modern design strategies. DI goes beyond enhancing user-centricity—it creates adaptive, personalized, and efficient experiences that meet the evolving needs of users. Let's delve into the specific advantages that DI offers: DI significantly enhances *usability*. By leveraging AI, we can analyze user behavior and preferences at a granular level, enabling us to design interfaces that are intuitive and easy to navigate. This results in a smoother, more enjoyable user experience. We achieve this by using AI to analyze user interactions and feedback, and then applying these insights to make our designs more user-friendly.

- DI also enables *effective personalization*. AI algorithms allow us to tailor the user experience based on individual user behavior and preferences. This means that each user gets a unique, personalized experience that meets their specific needs and expectations. We do this by using AI to analyze user behavior and preferences, and then personalizing the content and interface based on these insights.

- Another major benefit of DI is *task automation*. AI can automate repetitive tasks, freeing up users to focus on more important things. This not only improves efficiency but also enhances the user experience by eliminating tedious tasks. We achieve this by identifying tasks that are repetitive or time-consuming, and then using AI to automate these tasks.

- Finally, DI allows for *continuous adaptation* based on user behavior. AI algorithms can learn from user behavior and adapt the design accordingly. This ensures that the design remains relevant and effective, even as user needs and behaviors evolve. We do this by continuously monitoring user behavior and feedback, and then using AI to adapt our designs based on these insights.

In the next section, we will explore common hurdles and strategic approaches to overcoming them, ensuring our project not only meets but exceeds expectations.

Challenges of DI

While the benefits of DI are significant, it's important to acknowledge that this approach also presents some challenges. These challenges stem from the ethical considerations of using AI, the need for transparency in AI decisions, and the importance of maintaining empathy in design. Let's take a closer look at them:

- One of the key challenges is ensuring *ethical use of data*. As designers, we must respect user privacy and use data responsibly. This includes obtaining informed consent for data collection and use and ensuring that data is stored and processed securely. We address this challenge by following best practices for data privacy and security, and by being transparent with users about how their data is used.

- Another challenge is ensuring *transparency in AI decisions*. Users have a right to understand how AI is making decisions that affect them. As designers, we must strive to make AI decisions transparent and explainable. We address this challenge by providing clear explanations of how AI is used in our designs, and by being transparent about the decision-making process.

- Lastly, maintaining *empathy in design* is crucial. Even as we leverage AI to enhance the user experience, we must remember that we are designing for humans. Our designs must reflect an understanding and respect for human needs, emotions, and experiences. We address this challenge by always putting the user at the center of our design process, and by using AI to enhance, not replace, the human touch.

Practical example

A great example of DI applied to web development is the creation of personalized user experiences on streaming platforms like Netflix. Netflix uses AI to analyze user behavior and preferences, and then personalizes the content and interface based on these insights. This means that each user gets a unique, personalized experience that meets their specific needs and expectations.

Netflix's use of AI for personalization has been highly successful, resulting in increased user engagement and satisfaction. However, it also presents challenges, such as ensuring ethical use of data and maintaining transparency in AI decisions. Netflix addresses these challenges by following best practices for data privacy and security, and by being transparent with users about how their data is used.

This case study illustrates how Design Intelligence can be successfully implemented to create user-centric experiences that are truly transformative. It serves as a valuable example for others looking to integrate AI into their web development processes.

The upcoming section, will delve into practical applications of AI that tailor digital environments to individual preferences and behaviors, enhancing engagement and satisfaction.

Applying AI for personalized user experiences

We, as designers and developers, are always looking for ways to improve the user experience. One of these ways is through the application of AI algorithms to personalize user journeys.

AI has the power to transform the way we interact with users. It can learn from user behaviors, understand their preferences, and then use this information to create personalized experiences. This is what we call *Design Intelligence*.

Design Intelligence is not just about creating beautiful interfaces. It's about understanding the user on a deeper level and using this understanding to create experiences that are truly user centered.

For example, we can use AI algorithms to analyze user navigation patterns. With this information, we can adjust the design of our website or app to make it more intuitive and easier to use.

In addition, AI can help us predict what the user might want to do next. This allows us to create experiences that are proactive, rather than reactive. However, applying AI in design is not an easy task. It requires a deep understanding of AI algorithms and how they can be applied to improve the user experience.

That's why we're here to help you learn how to leverage AI algorithms to personalize user journeys. Let's explore together how AI can be used to create more personalized and user-centered experiences.

Harnessing AI algorithms for tailored user experiences

As architects of digital experiences, our mission is to make every interaction meaningful and engaging for the user. A powerful ally in this endeavor is AI, with its ability to tailor user journeys through personalized algorithms.

Here's a closer look at how AI algorithms can be practically applied to create a more personalized user experience:

- **Recommendation Systems**: Think of an online shopping experience where the product suggestions feel handpicked just for you. This is AI at work, using algorithms like collaborative filtering systems to personalize product recommendations. Amazon, for instance, uses these algorithms to suggest products based on a user's purchase history and browsing patterns.

- **Chatbots and Virtual Assistants**: Ever marveled at how Siri or Alexa seem to understand and respond to your requests so naturally? This is made possible by **Natural Language Processing (NLP)** algorithms that enable these virtual assistants to comprehend and respond to user queries in a personalized manner.

- **Content Personalization**: AI algorithms can also tailor the content displayed to users. Facebook, for example, uses AI to personalize each user's news feed, showing posts that are most relevant to them.

- **Sentiment Analysis**: Imagine an e-commerce company that can gauge how customers feel about their products just by analyzing customer reviews. AI algorithms can be used to determine whether the expressed sentiments are positive, negative, or neutral, providing valuable insights that can help the company improve their products based on customer feedback.

- **Search Engine Optimization** (**SEO**): AI isn't just about improving user experience; it can also help attract more users. AI algorithms can optimize website content for search engines, enhancing the website's visibility. An online news company, for example, could use AI to identify the most relevant keywords for each article and ensure these keywords are included in the article's titles and content. This can improve the article's visibility in search engine results and attract more readers.

These examples illustrate the transformative potential of AI in enhancing user experiences. By gaining a deeper understanding of users and personalizing their experiences, we can create products and services that are truly user centric. As we continue to explore the possibilities that AI offers for user-centered design, we're thrilled to have you join us on this journey of discovery and learning. The future of user experiences is being shaped by AI, and together, we're at the forefront of this exciting innovation.

As we delve further into the practical applications of AI in creating tailored user experiences, we invite you to continue this journey with us. The next section will explore a specific implementation of AI designed to curate personalized content recommendations. This case study will highlight the direct impact of AI in everyday user interactions and showcase how these technologies are being integrated into real-world applications, setting new standards for personalization in the digital age.

Example of AI Movie Recommendation Chatbot

In this example, we will create an AI-driven dynamic content personalization system for an e-commerce website. The system will use TensorFlow and Keras to analyze user behavior and personalize product recommendations based on their shopping history. We will use the Retailrocket recommender system dataset to store user data and product information.

The workflow of the example is as follows:

1. Collect user data from the Retailrocket recommender system dataset.
2. Train a TensorFlow model to analyze user behavior and predict product preferences.
3. Use Keras to create a personalized product recommendation system based on the TensorFlow model.
4. Implement the recommendation system on the e-commerce website.

Data Description

Retailrocket recommender system dataset is a dataset of user behavior from an e-commerce website, including clicks, purchases, and views. The dataset contains 1,407,580 users and 2,756,101 behavior events, including 2,664,312 views, 69,332 cart additions, and 22,457 purchases. You can access the dataset at: `https://www.kaggle.com/datasets/retailrocket/ecommerce-dataset`

Next, we will learn how to manipulate and analyze this data using Python.

Python Code Step by Step

In this section, we will outline a series of coding steps essential for manipulating and understanding the dataset effectively. Each step will build upon the last, guiding you through the use of various Python libraries to harness the power of this data for building an intelligent recommender system.

1. We import the necessary libraries for the example, including TensorFlow, Keras, and Pandas.

    ```python
    import tensorflow as tf
    from tensorflow import keras
    import pandas as pd
    ```

2. We load the Retailrocket recommender system dataset into a Pandas DataFrame.

    ```python
    events_df = pd.read_csv(
        "/kaggle/input/ecommerce-dataset/events.csv"
    )
    ```

3. We group the data by visitor ID and aggregate the item IDs into a list for each visitor.

    ```python
    user_data = events_df.groupby('visitorid').agg(
        {'itemid': lambda x: list(x)}
    )
    ```

4. We create a sequential model with two hidden layers and an output layer. We compile the model with the Adam optimizer and sparse categorical cross-entropy loss function. We then fit the model to the user data.

    ```python
    model = keras.Sequential([
      keras.layers.Dense(64, activation='relu'),
      keras.layers.Dense(64, activation='relu'),
      keras.layers.Dense(len(user_data), activation='softmax')
    ])
    model.compile(optimizer='adam',
                  loss='sparse_categorical_crossentropy',
                  metrics=['accuracy'])
    model.fit(user_data, user_data, epochs=10)
    ```

5. We define a function that takes a user ID as input and returns a list of recommended products based on the user's shopping history.

```
def recommend_products(user_id):
    user_data = user_data[user_id]
    predictions = model.predict(user_data)
    recommended_products = []
    for i in range(len(predictions)):
        if predictions[i] > 0.5:
            recommended_products.append(products[i])
    return recommended_products
```

6. Now, we implement the recommendation system on the e-commerce website.

The result of this example is an AI-driven dynamic content personalization system for an e-commerce website that provides personalized product recommendations based on user behavior.

In this example, we discussed techniques for implementing AI-driven dynamic content personalization in e-commerce applications. We also introduced tools like TensorFlow and Keras for incorporating AI into e-commerce environments. By following the above project, you can create a personalized product recommendation system for your e-commerce website and provide a unique shopping experience for each user.

> **Note**
> This is a simplified example and may not work directly without some modifications depending on your development environment. Adjust it as needed.

In the next section, we'll learn how to optimize user interfaces with AI.

Optimizing user interfaces with AI

AI can be used to optimize UI, which are the visual and interactive elements that allow users to communicate with a digital system. In this section, we will explore how AI can enhance the UX, customize the content, predict the outcomes, automate the tasks, adjust the design, collect the feedback and improve the performance and compatibility of user interfaces.

User experience (**UX**) is all about the emotions, perceptions, and reactions that users have when interacting with a digital system. It's a crucial element for the success of any product or service as it directly impacts user satisfaction, loyalty, and conversion rates. With the power of AI, we can now enhance the UX by truly understanding user behavior, preferences, and needs. AI algorithms can analyze user navigation and interactions to identify usability issues, suggest layout improvements, and deliver personalized content that boosts engagement and conversion rates.

Imagine a user interface that adapts to each individual user, providing a tailored experience that feels like it was made just for them. That's the power of customization, and AI makes it possible. By utilizing machine learning algorithms, AI can segment users based on their demographics, behaviors, preferences, and even their current context. This enables AI to deliver specific content and features that resonate with each user. From personalized product recommendations to curated news and videos, AI takes customization to a whole new level.

Wouldn't it be amazing if user interfaces could predict what users want even before they realize it themselves? Well, with *predictive analytics*, that's exactly what AI can do. By applying statistical and machine learning techniques to historical and current data, AI can anticipate user needs, intentions, and behaviors. This allows AI to offer proactive, preventive, and prescriptive solutions. For example, AI can predict the probability of a user abandoning a shopping cart or canceling a subscription and provide incentives, reminders, or assistance to influence their decision-making process.

Say goodbye to repetitive, complex, and time-consuming tasks. AI brings the power of *automation* to user interfaces, reducing effort, time, and human error. With AI tools such as natural language processing, computer vision, image generation, and voice synthesis, automation can generate content, design, code, test, and deploy user interfaces seamlessly. This not only increases efficiency and productivity but also ensures high-quality results.

Picture a user interface that adapts seamlessly to different environmental conditions and devices. That's the beauty of *adaptive design*, and AI plays a crucial role in making it happen. By detecting changes in lighting, sound, temperature, location, and other factors that may affect the user experience, AI can adjust the appearance and functionality of a user interface. From optimal brightness and contrast to screen resolution and interaction, AI ensures that users have an immersive and user-friendly experience, no matter the device they're using.

Understanding user reaction is vital for improving user interfaces, and AI can make the *feedback analysis* process even more insightful and efficient. With AI tools like sentiment analysis, text analysis, image analysis, and voice analysis, feedback analysis goes beyond simply collecting data. AI can extract and quantify user emotions, attitudes, and preferences from comments, ratings, surveys, and other feedback channels. This invaluable information helps designers, developers, and managers make data-driven decisions to enhance the content, design, functionality, and performance of user interfaces.

User interfaces that are slow, unstable, or insecure can be frustrating for users. AI comes to the rescue with its ability to *optimize performance*. By monitoring, analyzing, and solving performance issues, AI ensures that user interfaces are fast, stable, and secure. From detecting and correcting errors to optimizing resources and managing cache, AI uses machine learning algorithms to deliver top-notch performance. This not only increases user satisfaction but also boosts user retention.

In today's digital landscape, user interfaces need to work seamlessly across multiple platforms, operating systems, browsers, devices, and versions. That's where *compatibility optimization* comes into play, and AI is here to assist. Through automated testing, compatibility testing, regression testing, and unit testing, AI ensures that user interfaces are compatible with different scenarios and conditions. By validating and adapting the content, design, functionality, and performance, AI enhances the reach, accessibility, and usability of user interfaces.

As we've analyzed, there are incredible ways in which AI can optimize user interfaces. From improving the user experience to personalization, predictive analysis, automation, adaptive design, feedback analysis, performance optimization and compatibility optimization, AI is a game changer for designers, developers, testers, and managers. With AI as our intelligent ally, we can create innovative, adaptive, and user-centered user interfaces, standing out in the competitive digital marketplace. Get ready to embrace the power of AI and transform your user interfaces with smart, efficient, and effective solutions.

Practical applications of User Support, Accessibility, and Personalized Experiences

As AI continues to advance, its practical applications are becoming increasingly prevalent in various fields. From user support to enhancing accessibility and personalization, AI-driven technologies are revolutionizing the way we interact with digital platforms. In this section, we will explore the practical applications of AI in chatbots and virtual assistants, image and voice recognition, recommendation systems, and gaming UI. Let's delve deeper into each of these areas to understand how AI is transforming our digital experiences.

Chatbots and virtual assistants have become indispensable tools for businesses and individuals alike. They offer a conversational interface for user support, providing instant responses to queries and offering personalized assistance. Whether it's answering frequently asked questions or resolving customer issues, chatbots streamline the support process, ensuring efficient and satisfactory interactions. Moreover, these AI-powered assistants automate tasks through chat interfaces, freeing up human resources and enhancing productivity.

AI-powered image and *voice recognition* technologies have made significant strides in recent years, greatly enhancing user experiences. In terms of UI accessibility, these technologies enable visually impaired individuals to interact with digital platforms. Voice recognition allows them to navigate websites, access information, and control devices using spoken commands. Additionally, AI-based security applications utilize biometric recognition, providing an extra layer of protection through face or voice identification, ensuring secure access to sensitive data and systems.

AI-driven *recommendation systems* have transformed the way we discover content and make informed decisions. By analyzing user preferences, behavior, and historical data, these systems provide personalized content suggestions. Whether it's movies, products, or other forms of content, AI algorithms curate recommendations tailored to individual tastes, saving time and enhancing the overall user experience. With AI-powered recommendations, users can easily explore new content that aligns with their interests.

The integration of *AI in gaming UI* has opened up a whole new realm of possibilities for immersive and personalized gaming experiences. AI algorithms analyze player behavior in real-time, creating dynamic game environments that adapt to individual preferences and skills. This level of personalization enhances engagement and enjoyment, offering players a unique and tailored gaming experience. From AI-controlled characters to dynamically changing game scenarios, AI in gaming UI takes interactive entertainment to the next level.

The practical applications of AI are transforming user support, accessibility, and personalized experiences across various domains. Chatbots and virtual assistants streamline user interactions, while image and voice recognition enhance UI accessibility and security. AI-driven recommendation systems offer personalized content suggestions, and AI in gaming UI provides dynamic and personalized gaming experiences. As AI continues to evolve, its impact on practical applications will only continue to grow, revolutionizing the way we interact with technology and shaping the future of digital experiences.

Moving forward, in the next, we will explore methodologies and tools to evaluate the effectiveness of AI implementations.

Measuring the impact of AI-Enhanced User Interfaces

As we continue to witness the rapid advancement of AI technology, it becomes increasingly important to assess the impact of AI-enhanced user interfaces. These interfaces, powered by AI, have the potential to revolutionize the way users interact with technology and businesses. In order to fully understand the effects of these interfaces, it is crucial to consider both metrics and user feedback.

Metrics for impact assessment

Evaluating the impact of AI on user interfaces necessitates the use of specific metrics that can provide clear insights into performance and effectiveness. These metrics help quantify how AI enhancements are influencing user behavior and improving the user experience. As we delve into this analysis, we'll focus on several key metrics that are particularly insightful for assessing the effectiveness of AI-enhanced interfaces.One of the key metrics for measuring the impact of AI-enhanced user interfaces is *user engagement*. This metric provides insights into how users interact with the interface and the amount of time they spend on it. By analyzing the time spent on the interface and the frequency of interactions, we can gauge the level of user engagement and determine the effectiveness of the AI enhancements.

Another important metric to consider is *conversion rates*. This metric measures the rate at which users are converted into taking desired actions, such as making a purchase or subscribing to a service. By tracking conversion rates, businesses can assess the impact of AI enhancements on their overall goals and objectives. A higher conversion rate indicates that the AI-enhanced interface is successfully driving user behavior towards desired actions.

Gathering *user feedback* is essential in assessing the impact of AI-enhanced user interfaces. User satisfaction scores can be obtained through surveys and other feedback mechanisms. One commonly used metric is the **Net Promoter Score** (**NPS**), which measures the likelihood of users recommending the interface to others. By collecting user satisfaction scores, businesses can gain valuable insights into the user experience and make improvements accordingly.

Efficiency in completing tasks is another crucial metric for assessing the impact of AI-enhanced user interfaces. By measuring the rate at which users complete tasks and comparing it to previous benchmarks, businesses can determine the effectiveness of the AI enhancements in improving workflow and overall efficiency. Higher task completion rates indicate that the AI-enhanced interface is streamlining processes and making it easier for users to achieve their goals.

Assessing the impact of AI-enhanced user interfaces requires a comprehensive understanding of metrics and user feedback. By analyzing user engagement, conversion rates, user satisfaction scores, and task completion rates, businesses can gain valuable insights into the effectiveness of these interfaces. This information allows for continuous improvement and optimization, ensuring that AI-enhanced user interfaces deliver the desired impact and enhance the overall user experience.

AI-specific metrics

AI-specific metrics play a vital role in assessing the performance of these systems. This section will delve into three key metrics that provide valuable insights into the capabilities of AI algorithms: Algorithm Accuracy, Personalization Effectiveness, and Response Time.

- **Algorithm Accuracy** is a fundamental metric that measures the precision and recall of AI recommendations. Precision refers to the proportion of accurate recommendations out of all the recommendations made by the AI system. It reflects the correctness of the AI-driven decisions and plays a vital role in building trust with users. By ensuring that the recommendations provided are relevant and reliable, AI algorithms can enhance user satisfaction and engagement.

- **Personalization Effectiveness**, another crucial metric, measures how well AI tailors the user experience. AI systems have the potential to understand user preferences and adapt the content and recommendations accordingly. This personalized approach has a significant impact on user satisfaction and engagement. By delivering tailored experiences, AI algorithms can create a sense of individuality, making users feel understood and valued.

- **Response Time** is a metric that evaluates the speed of AI-generated responses. In today's fast-paced world, real-time interactions are increasingly important. AI systems need to be able to provide prompt and efficient responses to ensure a seamless user experience. By enhancing response time, AI algorithms can facilitate smooth and fluid interactions, thereby improving user satisfaction and engagement.

AI-specific metrics are essential for evaluating the performance and capabilities of AI systems. Algorithm Accuracy, Personalization Effectiveness, and Response Time play a crucial role in determining the effectiveness and reliability of AI algorithms. By continuously striving to improve these metrics, AI systems can provide accurate recommendations, tailor experiences to individual preferences, and deliver prompt responses, ultimately enhancing user satisfaction and engagement. At our core, we are committed to harnessing the power of AI to provide exceptional experiences for our users.

Gathering user feedback

As we strive to continuously improve our AI features and provide the best user experience, gathering user feedback is crucial. We employ various methods to gather insights into user perceptions and identify areas for improvement.

One of the ways we gather feedback is through *surveys and questionnaires*. These direct feedback mechanisms allow users to provide their thoughts and opinions on our AI features. By understanding their perspectives, we gain valuable insights into how well our AI is meeting their needs and expectationsAnother method we use is *usability testing*. By observing users as they interact with our AI elements, we can identify pain points and areas that need improvement. This hands-on approach allows us to see firsthand how users navigate our system, providing us with actionable data to make necessary adjustments.

User interviews are also a valuable tool for gathering feedback. By conducting in-depth interviews, we gain a deeper understanding of user experiences. These interviews provide us with nuanced feedback, uncovering insights that may have been missed through other methods. By listening to our users' perspectives, we can make informed decisions on how to enhance our AI features.

Additionally, *A/B testing* plays a significant role in our feedback gathering process. By comparing different UI variations, we can make data-driven decisions on design choices. This method allows us to understand which design elements resonate better with users, enabling us to create a more user-friendly interface.

Gathering user feedback is vital for the continuous improvement of our AI features. Through surveys, usability testing, user interviews, and A/B testing, we gain a comprehensive understanding of user perceptions and experiences. By listening to our users and making data-driven decisions, we can enhance our AI features to better meet their needs and provide a seamless user experience.

The next section will discuss how we utilize continuous monitoring, agile development practices, and a user-centric design philosophy to systematically improve our products. This approach not only ensures that our interfaces are effective and user-friendly but also allows them to evolve dynamically in response to user feedback and changing preferences. Let's delve into how this process works and why it is critical to maintaining the relevance and effectiveness of our digital offerings.

Iterative design process

In our continuous quest for improvement, we have implemented an Iterative Design Process that combines continuous monitoring, agile development, and user-centric design. This approach allows us to create user-friendly interfaces that evolve based on user preferences, ensuring a seamless and satisfying experience for our users.

To ensure that our design meets the needs of our users, we have implemented ongoing monitoring systems. By staying informed about user interactions, we gain valuable insights into their preferences, pain points, and behavior patterns. This continuous monitoring enables us to make informed design decisions and prioritize improvements that will have the greatest impact on user satisfaction.

In the fast-paced digital world, it is crucial to adapt quickly to user needs. That's why we have embraced agile development principles, which involve iterative cycles for rapid improvements. This approach allows us to gather feedback, identify areas for enhancement, and implement changes in a timely manner. By continuously iterating on our design, we can ensure that our product remains relevant and effective in meeting user expectations.

At the core of our design process is the belief that user feedback is invaluable. We prioritize user feedback in all our design decisions, ensuring that our interfaces evolve based on their preferences. By actively involving User-Centric Design, we create a sense of ownership and empowerment, ultimately resulting in interfaces that are intuitive, user-friendly, and tailored to their needs.

Our Iterative Design Process combines continuous monitoring, agile development, and user-centric design to create interfaces that continually improve and adapt to the ever-changing landscape of user preferences. By staying informed, being flexible, and prioritizing user feedback, we can ensure that our product remains relevant, effective, and user-friendly. We are committed to providing the best possible experience for our users and will continue to evolve and refine our design process to achieve that goal.

Summary

In this chapter, we dove deep into the transformative world of Design Intelligence (DI) and its impact on creating user-centered experiences through AI. DI has transcended conventional design approaches by harnessing AI algorithms to understand user preferences, behaviors, and trends, enhancing the web development process from aesthetic design to content structure. The result? A personalized and engaging experience for the user.

We discussed techniques for implementing AI-based dynamic content personalization in e-commerce applications. We also introduced tools like TensorFlow and Keras to incorporate AI into e-commerce environments.

Throughout this chapter, you have learned to navigate the world of Design Intelligence in Web Development, apply AI for personalized user experiences, create adaptive user interfaces, and optimize these interfaces using insights gained from AI. You have also learned to analyze and adapt designs based on user behavior.

In the upcoming chapter, we will delve into how AI can be utilized to recognize patterns in user behavior, enabling the personalization of user journeys. This exploration will cover the techniques and technologies that allow AI systems to adapt and respond to individual user preferences, enhancing user experiences across digital platforms.

7

Recognizing Patterns – Personalizing User Journeys with AI

In this chapter, you will learn about pattern recognition in the context of web development, exploring how AI can be leveraged to personalize user journeys. You will gain insights into the importance of recognizing patterns in user behavior, preferences, and interactions to tailor the web experience for each user. The chapter will also address the implementation of predictive and recommendation algorithms, guiding you on how to integrate these algorithms into a unified AI entity.

The final goal of the chapter is to empower you to apply the principles and techniques of pattern recognition and personalization with AI in your own web projects, creating more engaging, relevant, and satisfying experiences for users.

This chapter is important because pattern recognition and personalization with AI are powerful strategies to enhance the user experience and generate value for businesses. They enable you to create unique, omnichannel, voice-assisted, and immersive user journeys. However, they also require care with user privacy, generalization, consent, and transparency. Therefore, you need to be aware of the concepts, tools, and best practices to implement these strategies efficiently and ethically.

The main topics of this chapter are as follows:

- Cracking the code of pattern recognition principles
- Harnessing AI for personalization
- Predictive algorithms for personalization
- Implementing recommendation systems
- Creating a unified AI entity

Technical requirements

Before we dive into the specifics of our project, it's essential to ensure that we have all the necessary tools and libraries in place. Here are the technical requirements you need to set up your development environment:

- Python 3.7 or higher (`https://www.python.org/downloads/`)
- Pandas (`https://pandas.pydata.org/`)
- NumPy (`https://numpy.org/`)
- Sklearn (`https://scikit-learn.org/stable/index.html`)
- You can download the complete project on GitHub at: `https://github.com/PacktPublishing/AI-Strategies-for-Web-Development/blob/main/ch7/Movie_recomendation.ipynb`

Now, let's delve into the first topic of this chapter.

Cracking the code of pattern recognition principles

We will explore the foundational methods that enable us to discern and interpret the complex patterns in user behavior. Understanding these principles is essential for deploying AI effectively to personalize and enhance user journeys. By mastering these techniques, you will be equipped to create AI-driven solutions that not only meet but also anticipate the needs of your users, making each interaction more intuitive and impactful.

We understand the importance of recognizing patterns in user behavior. It's a crucial aspect for enhancing user experience and making it more personalized. By identifying these patterns, we can better understand user needs and preferences, allowing us to deliver a more relevant and engaging experience.

AI plays a key role in this process, enabling us to personalize user journeys for enhanced experiences. With the help of AI, we can analyze large volumes of user data and identify patterns that would be difficult, if not impossible, to detect manually.

Understanding the principles of pattern recognition

Pattern recognition is a fundamental skill that allows us to understand and interpret the world around us. In the context of AI, pattern recognition is the ability to identify and categorize data based on underlying patterns or regularities. The principles of pattern recognition are grounded in the idea that data can be categorized based on common features. These features can be as simple as the color or shape of an object, or as complex as user behavior over time.

The main principles of pattern recognition include the following:

- **Feature representation**: This involves ensuring that data is represented in a way that highlights the important aspects that can be used for recognition. This involves selecting the right features that capture the essence of the data.

- **Similarity and distance measurement**: Recognizing patterns often involves comparing data points and determining their similarity. This requires effective methods to measure the distance or similarity between data points.

- **Classification and decision making**: This involves deciding the category to which a data point belongs. This principle involves defining decision boundaries and rules for classification.

- **Learning from data**: This involves developing models that can learn from examples. This principle underpins the use of algorithms that can improve their performance as they are exposed to more data.

- **Generalization**: This involves ensuring that the patterns recognized by the model can be applied to new, unseen data. A good pattern recognition system should generalize well from the training data to any other data.

- **Robustness to noise and variability**: This involves recognizing patterns accurately even when the data is noisy or varies in unexpected ways.

- **Adaptability**: This is about the ability of the system to adapt to new patterns and changes over time.

The principles of pattern recognition are grounded in the idea that data can be categorized based on common features. These features can be as simple as the color or shape of an object, or as complex as user behavior over time. Now, let's look at the key techniques used to implement these principles in pattern recognition:

- **Clustering**: This technique groups data points based on similarities, often using algorithms such as K-means, hierarchical clustering, or DBSCAN. Clustering helps in identifying natural groupings within the data, which can be useful for market segmentation, anomaly detection, and image segmentation. For example, it might involve segmenting customers into different groups based on purchasing behavior using K-means.

- **Classification**: Classification involves assigning data points to predefined categories based on their features. Common algorithms include decision trees, **Support Vector Machines** (**SVMs**), and neural networks. This technique is widely used in spam detection, sentiment analysis, and medical diagnosis. For instance, identifying spam emails using a support SVM.

- **Anomaly detection**: This technique identifies data points that deviate significantly from the norm. Algorithms such as Isolation Forest or One-Class SVM, as well as autoencoders, are often used for anomaly detection, which is crucial in fraud detection, network security, and predictive maintenance. An example is detecting fraudulent transactions in credit card usage with Isolation Forest.

- **Feature extraction**: This involves transforming raw data into a set of features that better represent the underlying structure. Techniques such as **Principal Component Analysis (PCA)**, **Linear Discriminant Analysis (LDA)**, and **t-Distributed Stochastic Neighbor Embedding (t-SNE)** are commonly used. An example would be reducing the dimensionality of an image dataset using PCA for facial recognition.

- **Sequence analysis**: This technique analyzes sequential data to identify **Hidden Markov Models** patterns over time. **(HMM)**, **Recurrent Neural Networks (RNN)**, and **Long Short-Term Memory (LSTM)** networks are typical algorithms used for applications such as speech recognition, DNA sequencing, and time series prediction. An example would be predicting stock prices using LSTM networks.

- **Deep learning**: This utilizes neural networks with multiple layers (deep neural networks) to model complex patterns in data. **Convolutional Neural Networks (CNNs)** are particularly effective in image recognition, while RNNs and LSTMs are suited for handling sequential data. An example is recognizing objects in images with CNNs.

By leveraging these principles and techniques, AI systems can analyze large volumes of data, identify intricate patterns, and provide valuable insights, enabling applications such as personalized user experiences, predictive maintenance, and advanced decision support systems. Pattern recognition is a skill that can be honed with practice and experience. The more data we have at our disposal, the more accurate and effective we become at recognizing patterns.

Key components of pattern recognition

The key components of pattern recognition include data collection, pattern recognition algorithms, and user segmentation. Each of these components plays a crucial role in personalizing user journeys. Let's learn a bit more about them:

- **Data collection** is the first component of pattern recognition. We strive to collect diverse user data points, which can include user interactions, preferences, and historical data. This data provides us with a comprehensive view of user behavior, allowing us to identify significant patterns. Examples of data collection methods include the following:

- **Log files**: Tracking user activity on websites or applications

- **User surveys**: Gathering direct feedback from users about their preferences and experiences

- **Transaction records**: Collecting purchase history from e-commerce platforms

- **Pattern recognition algorithms** make up the next component to be discussed. Machine learning algorithms are powerful tools for identifying patterns. We use a variety of pattern recognition algorithms, including clustering, classification, and anomaly detection. These algorithms allow us to analyze the collected data and identify patterns that can be used to personalize the user experience. Examples of data collection methods include the following:

  - **Clustering**: Grouping similar data points together.

  - **Classification**: Assigning data points to predefined categories.

  - **Anomaly detection**: Identifying data points that deviate significantly from the norm.

- **User segmentation** is the third key component of pattern recognition. By grouping users based on behavior patterns, we can personalize experiences for specific segments. This allows us to cater to the individual needs and preferences of each segment, providing a more personalized and relevant experience. Examples of user segmentation include the following:

  - **Demographic information**: Age, gender, location.

  - **Behavioral data**: Browsing history, purchase behavior.

  - **Psychographic data**: Interests, lifestyle, values.

This process allows us to understand user needs and preferences in a more nuanced way, enabling us to cater to individual users effectively. As we continue to refine our techniques and learn from our data, we look forward to providing even more personalized and impactful user journeys. *Figure 7.1* illustrates the flow from data collection to the impact of personalization, providing a clear roadmap of how these elements interconnect.

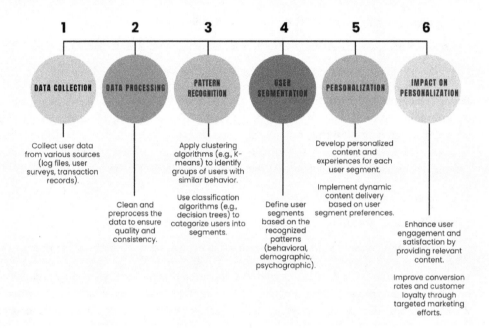

Figure 7.1: The interconnection between user segmentation and personalization

Effective user segmentation and personalization require a systematic approach to collecting, processing, and analyzing data. By understanding the specific behaviors, demographics, and psychographics of their users, businesses can deliver tailored experiences that resonate on a personal level. The continuous refinement of these processes ensures that personalization efforts remain relevant and impactful, ultimately contributing to sustained business growth and customer satisfaction.

Next, we'll explore practical examples and case studies that illustrate how these techniques can be applied effectively, providing you with actionable knowledge to apply in your own work.

Personalization techniques – a practical approach

In the digital landscape, personalization has transitioned from being a luxury to a necessity. Personalization refers to the art of tailoring the user experience to align with individual needs and preferences, particularly in web and application interfaces. This approach provides a more relevant and engaging experience by dynamically adjusting content, functionality, and user interactions based on user data. Here, we will explore some of the key techniques that we employ to personalize web and mobile application experiences effectively.

Dynamic content delivery

The uniqueness of each user is what drives us. We adapt the content in real time, shaping it according to users' behavior. This can manifest in the form of personalized product recommendations and messages that cater to the specific needs and interests of the user. By doing so, we not only enhance the user experience but also increase the likelihood of engagement and conversion.

Dynamic content delivery is akin to a dance where the rhythm changes in response to the dancer's steps. Collaborative filtering takes on the role of our DJ, analyzing user behavior and preferences to recommend items that they might enjoy. On the other hand, content-based filtering acts as our choreographer, suggesting steps (or items) similar to those the user has already danced (or interacted). It analyzes the characteristics of items and recommends those that are similar to the ones the user has shown interest in. Deep learning models, our disco ball, reflect and amplify the user's movements through neural networks. These models have the ability to capture complex, non-linear patterns in user behavior, paving the way for more accurate predictions.

Predictive personalization

Proactivity is key in anticipating the needs and preferences of the user. We offer relevant suggestions even before they are requested. This is made possible through the analysis of user data, identifying patterns and trends that allow us to predict what the user might need or want next.

Predictive personalization is like being able to predict the dancer's next step before they even move. Matrix factorization, our fortune teller, predicts the user's next step by decomposing the user-item interaction matrix. It identifies latent factors that explain the observed interactions and uses them to predict future interactions. Decision trees, our historian, study the user's past steps to predict their future movements. They create a decision-based model that leads to a prediction. Neural networks, our artist, capture and interpret the complex patterns in the user's dance. These models can learn to represent user behavior in a high-dimensional space, allowing for more accurate predictions.

Behavioral targeting

Understanding past user behavior is crucial for delivering specific content. This can include optimizing ads and promotions to target users who have shown interest in similar products or services in the past. By doing this, we can increase the relevance of the content and enhance the effectiveness of our marketing campaigns.

Behavioral targeting is like being able to play the perfect tune for each dancer (user). User segmentation, our conductor, groups dancers based on their similar rhythms. It identifies groups of users with similar behaviors, allowing for the delivery of personalized content to each group. Sequential pattern mining, our composer, identifies the frequent sequences in each user's dance. It identifies behavior patterns that frequently occur in sequence, allowing for the prediction of future actions. Supervised learning, our music producer, predicts the user's response to a specific tune based on their past dances. It uses historical data to train a model that can predict the user's response to new data.

Personalization is a journey, not a destination. We must continue to experiment, learn, and optimize our techniques to provide the best possible experience for our users. We believe that by personalizing the user experience, we can forge a stronger and more meaningful relationship with our users, leading to greater customer satisfaction and loyalty. In the end, that's what truly matters to us.

While the techniques described focus on dynamic content delivery, predictive personalization, and behavioral targeting, the actual choice of tune (or algorithm) may vary based on the dancer's specific rhythm (or implementation requirements). The application of AI for pattern recognition is an essential skill in this process, allowing us to better understand our dancers (or users) and meet their needs more effectively. After all, our goal is to provide each dancer (or user) with a unique and personalized dance (or experience).

Now, we'll delve deeper into the specific algorithms that power predictive personalization. This discussion will provide a clearer understanding of the technical mechanisms behind the personalization strategies we've discussed, highlighting their importance in crafting individualized user journeys.

Predictive algorithms for personalization

We live in an era where personalization is the key to enhancing user experiences. Predictive algorithms are at the heart of this personalization. They are based on machine learning techniques that use historical data to predict future behaviors or outcomes. The importance of these algorithms in personalization is immense as they allow businesses to offer unique, personalized experiences to each user, thereby improving customer satisfaction and loyalty.

Key predictive algorithm techniques

Now, let's explore the key predictive algorithm techniques that make this advanced personalization possible:

- **Collaborative filtering** is a technique that identifies user preferences based on user-item interactions. It is capable of identifying hidden patterns and trends in user choices, allowing for more precise personalization. There are two main approaches: memory-based and model-based. The memory-based approach uses past user ratings to compute a prediction, while the model-based approach uses these ratings to train a model that can make predictions.

- **Content-based filtering**, on the other hand, leverages the user profile and item characteristics to make recommendations. It extracts features from items and creates a user profile based on their past interactions. Content-based filtering can offer highly personalized recommendations but may struggle with new users or items.

- **Hybrid models** combine collaborative and content-based filtering approaches to enhance recommendation accuracy. They adapt personalization to changes in user preferences over time, offering a more dynamic and personalized user experience.

As we progress to the next section, we will delve deeper into the types of models that power these predictive techniques.

Machine learning models

There are different types of machine learning models that play a crucial role in the world of AI-driven personalization. By understanding the functionalities and applications of each model, developers can better design systems that enhance user engagement and satisfaction.

Here are some more details about these models:

- **Decision trees** are models that make predictions based on a series of hierarchical decisions. They can handle categorical and numerical data and are often used in conjunction with other models in ensemble methods, such as Random Forest, to improve prediction accuracy.

- **Neural networks**, especially deep learning ones, are excellent for personalization as they can learn complex patterns in data. They use a series of hidden layers to extract high-level features from data, allowing them to learn more complex representations. However, training and generalizing these models can be challenging.

- **Regression models** are used to predict user preferences numerically. They can be linear or non-linear and are valued for their interpretability. They are capable of modeling complex relationships between variables and can be used to predict a wide range of outcomes.

Predictive personalization faces several challenges, such as the cold start problem, which states that it's difficult to make recommendations for new users or items. Additionally, data privacy concerns and the need for real-time processing and scalability are also significant issues.

Next, we will delve into the practical applications of these models. This section will illustrate how the theoretical tools we've discussed are applied in real-world scenarios, helping to solve practical problems and enhance user experiences across various domains.

Broad applications in personalization techniques

The applications of predictive algorithms for personalization are vast, ranging from e-commerce recommendations and content personalization in streaming services to personalized marketing campaigns and adaptive learning platforms.

Here are some of the applications:

- Predictive algorithms play a crucial role in e-commerce by providing personalized recommendations. They analyze a user's past behavior, preferences, and interactions with various products to suggest items that the user is likely to be interested in. This not only enhances the shopping experience for the user but also increases sales and customer retention for the e-commerce platform.

- In the realm of streaming services, predictive algorithms are used to personalize content. By analyzing a user's viewing history, ratings, and preferences, these algorithms can recommend movies, TV shows, or songs that align with the user's tastes. This ensures that users always have something interesting to watch or listen to, thereby increasing user engagement and satisfaction.

- Predictive algorithms are also used in marketing to create personalized campaigns. By understanding a user's behavior, interests, and demographic information, marketers can tailor their messages and offers to each individual user. This personalized approach makes marketing campaigns more effective and improves return on investment.

- In the field of education, predictive algorithms are used in adaptive learning platforms. These platforms use predictive algorithms to understand a student's learning style, strengths, and weaknesses. They then adapt the learning material accordingly, providing a personalized learning experience. This can lead to improved learning outcomes and a more engaging learning experience for students.

Future trends in predictive personalization include explainable AI, which aims to make personalization algorithms more transparent, as well as federated learning, which allows for personalization while preserving privacy. Additionally, the integration of predictive analytics with the **Internet of Things (IoT)** is also a promising area.

Predictive algorithms play a significant role in personalization, balancing accuracy and user privacy. As technology advances, user personalization will continue to evolve, offering increasingly personalized and enhanced experiences.

Next, we will explore how to implement recommendation systems, a practical application of predictive algorithms. This section will guide you through the steps and considerations necessary to develop effective recommendation systems that can deliver personalized experiences. Understanding how to implement these systems effectively is crucial for leveraging the full potential of AI in personalization.

Implementing recommendation systems

Recommendation systems harness the power of machine learning to suggest products, services, or content that users might find appealing, thereby playing a crucial role in enhancing user engagement and satisfaction. These systems are especially pivotal in sectors such as e-commerce, streaming services, and content platforms. By analyzing user behavior, preferences, and interaction data, recommendation systems can deliver highly personalized experiences that cater specifically to the needs and tastes of individual users.

Such systems use a variety of machine learning techniques to accurately predict and recommend items that a user is likely to appreciate based on their past interactions. We'll explore these ideas in more detail in the following example.

Example – a movie recommendation system with machine learning

This project aims to build a movie recommendation system using machine learning. The goal is to provide users with movie recommendations based on their viewing history and preferences. In this project, we will be using a technique called collaborative filtering for making movie recommendations. **Collaborative filtering** is a method of making automatic predictions (filtering) about the interests of a user by collecting preferences from many users (collaborating). The underlying assumption of the collaborative filtering approach is that if person A has the same opinion as person B on an issue, A is more likely to also share B's opinion on a different issue.

Key features

The project involves training a machine learning model to recognize patterns in users' historical data and then use this model to make recommendations. The project workflow is as follows:

1. **Data preprocessing**: It's important to start by cleaning and preparing the data for analysis. This includes handling missing values.

2. **Machine learning model training:** Utilize the **Singular Value Decomposition** (**SVD**) algorithm to train models on historical user data.

3. **Model evaluation**: Evaluate the performance of the trained model using **Root Mean Squared Error** (**RMSE**) and **Mean Absolute Error** (**MAE**) metrics.

4. **Real-time recommendation**: Provide movie recommendations in real-time using the trained model.

Next, let's look at data description.

Data description

The data used in this project is from MovieLens, a dataset that contains movie ratings made by users. The dataset includes information such as user ID, movie ID, rating, and timestamp. The data are contained in the links.csv, movies.csv, ratings.csv, and tags.csv files. The dataset that we are using for this project can be found on the MovieLens website. You can download it directly via the following link:

https://files.grouplens.org/datasets/movielens/ml-latest-small.zip

This dataset is known as ml-latest-small and is a popular choice for machine learning projects because of its manageable size and data cleanliness. It contains 100,000 ratings and 3,600 movie tags applied to 9,000 movies by 600 users.

A step-by-step process for building the recommendation system

In this Python code, we will be implementing a movie recommendation system using a machine learning technique known as collaborative filtering. The code is divided into several steps, each performing a specific task in the process of building the recommendation system:

1. **Importing necessary libraries**: In this step, we'll set up the necessary libraries for our project. To do this, add the following lines to your Python script:

```
# Install the Surprise library
!pip install scikit-surprise
import pandas as pd
from surprise import Dataset, Reader, SVD
from surprise.model_selection import train_test_split
from surprise import accuracy
```

```
import urllib.request
import zipfile
import os
```

This configuration imports the necessary Python libraries that will be used throughout the project. pandas is used for data manipulation and analysis, surprise for the recommendation algorithms, urllib.request for downloading the dataset, and zipfile and os for file extraction and handling.

2. **Loading the data**: Next, we need to load the data from the CSV files. Add the following lines to your Python script:

```
# Download the MovieLens dataset
url = 'https://files.grouplens.org/datasets/movielens/
ml-latest-small.zip'
urllib.request.urlretrieve(url, 'ml-latest-small.zip')

# Unzip the downloaded file
with zipfile.ZipFile('ml-latest-small.zip', 'r') as zip_ref:
    zip_ref.extractall()

# Full path to the files
movies_file = os.path.join('ml-latest-small', 'movies.csv')
ratings_file = os.path.join('ml-latest-small', 'ratings.csv')

# Load the data
movies = pd.read_csv(movies_file)
ratings = pd.read_csv(ratings_file)
```

This configuration loads the movies and ratings data from the CSV files using pandas' read_csv function.

3. **Preparing the data for the Surprise library**: To create a single dataset from the movies and ratings data, we use the surprise library. Add the following lines to your Python script:

```
# Prepare the data for the Surprise library
reader = Reader(rating_scale=(0.5, 5.0))
data = Dataset.load_from_df(
    ratings[['userId', 'movieId', 'rating']],
    reader
)
```

This configuration prepares the data for use with the surprise library by specifying the rating scale and loading the DataFrame.

4. **Splitting the data into training and test sets**: Next, we need to split the data into training and test sets. Add the following lines to your Python script:

```
# Split the data into training and test sets
trainset, testset = train_test_split(data, test_size=0.2)
```

This configuration splits the data into training and test sets using `surprise`'s `train_test_split` function. 80% of the data will be used for training the model, and the remaining 20% will be used for testing.

5. **Training the model**: In this step, we'll train the SVD model on the training data. Add the following lines to your Python script:

```
# Train the SVD model
algo = SVD()
algo.fit(trainset)
```

This configuration trains the SVD model on the training data.

6. **Making predictions**: We will now make predictions on the test set. Add the following lines to your Python script:

```
# Make predictions on the test set
predictions = algo.test(testset)
```

This configuration uses the trained SVD model to make predictions on the test set.

7. **Evaluating the model's performance**: Next, we will evaluate the model's performance using RMSE and MAE metrics. Add the following lines to your Python script:

```
# Evaluate the model's performance
rmse = accuracy.rmse(predictions)
mae = accuracy.mae(predictions)

print(f'RMSE: {rmse}')
print(f'MAE: {mae}')
```

This configuration calculates and prints the RMSE and MAE metrics to evaluate the performance of the SVD model.

8. **Real-time recommendations**: To provide movie recommendations in real-time based on the trained model, add the following lines to your Python script:

```
# Function to recommend movies in real-time using SVD model
def get_movie_recommendations(
    algo,
    movie_title,
    movies,
    ratings,
    num_recommendations=5
):
```

The function definition and parameters are as follows:

- `algo`: The SVD model that has been trained on the movie ratings dataset

- `movie_title`: The title of the movie for which we want to find similar recommendations

- movies: A DataFrame containing information about the movies, including movieId and title

- ratings: A DataFrame containing user ratings for movies, including userId, movieId, and rating

- num_recommendations: The number of movie recommendations to return (the default number is five)

9. **Get the movie ID**: Extract movieId corresponding to the given movie_title from the movies DataFrame:

```
movie_id = (
    movies[movies['title'] == movie_title]['movieId'].
    values[0]
)
```

10. **Find users who have rated this movie**: Identify all unique userId from the ratings DataFrame who have rated the given movie (movie_id):

```
users_who_rated_movie = (
    ratings[ratings['movieId'] == movie_id]['userId']
    .unique()
)
```

11. **Find other movies rated by these users**: Retrieve all unique movieId from the ratings DataFrame that these users have also rated:

```
other_movie_ids = (
    ratings[ratings['userId'].isin(users_who_rated_movie)]
    ['movieId']
    .unique()
)
```

12. **Predict scores for all other films rated by these users**: For each movie (excluding the given movie), predict the rating using the SVD model. Store the predicted ratings along with the corresponding movieId in the predicted_ratings list:

```
# Predict ratings for all other movies by these users
other_movie_ids = (
    ratings[ratings['userId'].isin(users_who_rated_movie)]
    ['movieId']
    .unique()
)
```

13. **Sort the films by their predicted score**: Sort the predicted_ratings list in descending order based on the predicted rating values:

```
# Sort by predicted rating
predicted_ratings.sort(key=lambda x: x[1], reverse=True)
```

14. **Get the top N movie recommendations**: We selected the `num_recommendations` films with the highest predicted scores:

```
# Get top N movie recommendations
top_n_movies = [
    movie_id
    for movie_id, rating in predicted_ratings[:num_recommendations]
]
```

15. **Get movie titles**: Convert the `movieId` of recommended films back to their titles:

```
# Get movie titles
recommended_movie_titles = movies[movies['movieId']
    .isin(top_n_movies)]['title'].tolist()
```

16. **Return the recommendations**: Return the list of recommended movie titles:

```
    return recommended_movie_titles
```

17. **Example usage**: Finally, here is an example of using the function:

```
# Example usage
recommended_movies = get_movie_recommendations(
    algo, 'Toy Story (1995)',
    movies,
    ratings
)
print("Recommended movies for 'Toy Story (1995)':")
print(recommended_movies)
```

We call the `get_movie_recommendations` function passing the `algo` SVD model, the title of the film of interest (in this case, `Toy Story (1995)`), the `movies` DataFrame of films, and the `ratings` DataFrame of ratings.

18. **Interpretation of model performance metrics**: The performance of the SVD model on the MovieLens dataset is evaluated using two key metrics: RMSE and MAE. The RMSE value of `0.8745` indicates that, on average, the predicted movie ratings deviate from the actual ratings by approximately 0.87 on a scale of 0.5 to 5.0. This relatively low value suggests that the model predictions are quite accurate. Similarly, the MAE value of `0.6728` indicates that the average absolute difference between the predicted and actual ratings is about 0.67. Both metrics demonstrate the effectiveness of the SVD model in accurately predicting user preferences, making it a reliable choice for providing personalized movie recommendations:

```
RMSE: 0.8745
MAE: 0.6728
RMSE: 0.8745291344925908
MAE: 0.67281523909186
```

The result is a list of recommended films that are then printed out.

19. **Recommended movies for Toy Story (1995)**:

```
['Shawshank Redemption, The (1994)', 'Dr. Strangelove or: How I
Learned to Stop Worrying and Love the Bomb (1964)', '12 Angry
Men (1957)', 'Cool Hand Luke (1967)', 'Boondock Saints, The
(2000)']
```

By the end of this code, we will have a functioning movie recommendation system that can provide real-time recommendations to users. This system can be further improved and customized based on specific requirements. Now, let's dive into the code. The preceding code should print a list of the five movies that are most similar to *Toy Story (1995)* based on user ratings.

This project demonstrates how to implement a simple recommendation system using machine learning and collaborative filtering. The steps include data preprocessing to handle missing values, training an SVD model, and evaluating the model using RMSE and MAE metrics. Additionally, the project includes a real-time recommendation feature that allows the system to suggest movies immediately based on a user's input.

From here, you can experiment with different models and techniques to further improve the system. For instance, you can try other collaborative filtering methods such as KNN or matrix factorization techniques. The real-time adaptation feature ensures that the system can provide immediate personalization based on the user's current activity, enhancing the user experience.

As we move toward an integrated approach in AI, we will take our next step in the *Creating a unified AI entity* section. This concept pushes the boundaries of conventional AI applications by merging multiple AI functions into a seamless whole. By doing so, we can enhance their capabilities and potential impact across various platforms and industries.

Creating a unified AI entity

Can you imagine a reality where AI is not just a collection of isolated systems, but a unified entity, working harmoniously? That's what we're aiming for with the creation of a unified AI entity. This approach represents a significant milestone in the evolution of AI, as it unites various AI disciplines and technologies into a single cohesive entity.

Exploring the main components of a unified AI entity

A unified AI entity is not just a single entity but a symphony of different AI components, each playing its part in harmony to create a more robust and efficient system. These components, each with their own unique capabilities, come together to form a cohesive whole, much like the instruments in an orchestra. Each component is essential and contributes to the overall performance of the system. Let's take a closer look at these key players in our AI symphony:

- **Machine learning models**: These are the musicians of our AI orchestra. Each model is trained in a specific domain, providing expertise and insights that are unique to its field. Together, they contribute to the overall intelligence and versatility of the unified AI entity.

Several machine learning models contribute to the unified entity. They are interconnected to promote collaborative learning, allowing each model to learn and benefit from the experiences of the others. The diversity of these models allows the unified AI entity to address a wide range of tasks and problems, from predicting trends to detecting anomalies.

- **Natural Language Processing** (**NLP**): This is the conductor of our AI orchestra. It ensures that all components are in sync, facilitating communication and understanding between them. NLP plays a crucial role in enabling the unified AI entity to understand and respond to human language, making it more intuitive and user-friendly.

  The role of NLP is essential for improving communication within the organization. It integrates with machine learning to understand the context and interpret the user's intentions more accurately. NLP allows the unified AI entity to understand and respond to queries in natural language, making it more accessible and easier to use.

- **Computer vision**: Computer vision is the eyes of our AI orchestra. It provides the unified AI entity with the ability to perceive and interpret the visual world, enhancing its understanding and interaction with its environment.

  Computer vision enables visual perception and recognition within the unified entity. It works in collaboration with machine learning to analyze images and understand the visual world around us. Computer vision is fundamental to tasks that require the interpretation of visual data, such as identifying objects in images or autonomous navigation.

As we have explored the integral components of our unified AI entity, let's delve into the pivotal concept of **interconnectivity**. This foundational aspect acts as the vital link, seamlessly integrating various AI capabilities. By facilitating the flow of information and insights across different AI disciplines, interconnectivity ensures that our unified AI entity functions as a coherent and effective whole. In the upcoming section, we will uncover how this interconnectivity not only enhances the performance of individual components but also elevates the overall functionality and efficiency of the AI system.

Enhancing AI through interconnectivity

Interconnectivity within our unified AI entity refers to the integration and cohesive functioning of various AI components such as machine learning, NLP, and computer vision. This integration enables these diverse systems to communicate effectively, share data seamlessly, and work together harmoniously toward common objectives. It's about creating a system where each component not only functions independently but also collaborates with others to enhance overall performance and capabilities.

In a world where data is the new oil, interconnectivity ensures a seamless flow of this valuable resource across the different components of our AI entity. It's like a well-designed highway system, allowing data to travel quickly and efficiently from one component to another.

However, interconnectivity is not just about data flow. It's also about fostering collaboration between the different AI components. Just like in a successful team, each component – machine learning, NLP, and computer vision – brings its unique strengths to the table. They work together, learn from each other, and support each other to achieve the best possible outcome.

Moreover, interconnectivity enables the creation of a unified knowledge base. This shared repository of knowledge enhances the collective intelligence of our AI entity, leading to improved problem-solving capabilities.

Technical challenges and solutions

Achieving interconnectivity in a unified AI entity presents several technical challenges. We will outline these challenges and propose effective solutions here:

- **Data interoperability**: Ensuring that data can be shared and understood across different AI components is a significant hurdle. Standardized data formats and protocols are essential to address this issue. Utilize standardized data formats such as JSON and XML to facilitate data exchange. Implement APIs and middleware to translate data formats between systems, ensuring interoperability.

- **Real-time data processing**: For a cohesive AI entity, data must be processed in real time to provide timely insights and actions. Employ stream processing frameworks such as Apache Kafka and Apache Flink to handle real-time data streams. Use edge computing to process data at the source, reducing latency and improving response times.

- **System scalability**: As data volumes grow, the AI system must scale to handle the increased load without degrading performance. Leverage distributed computing systems such as Hadoop or Spark for parallel processing of large datasets. Utilize cloud infrastructure (such as AWS, Google Cloud, or Azure) to provide scalable resources that can adjust based on demand.

By ensuring data interoperability, implementing real-time data processing capabilities, and designing systems for scalability, we can create a robust and cohesive AI framework. This integrated approach not only enhances the functionality and efficiency of individual AI components but also maximizes the overall performance and capabilities of the unified system.

Key aspects of interconnectivity

In essence, interconnectivity is what transforms a collection of individual AI components into a cohesive, intelligent, and highly capable unified AI entity. It's the glue that holds everything together or the conductor that orchestrates the symphony of AI components into a harmonious whole. So, let's explore this fascinating concept in more detail. Let's explore the key aspects of interconnectivity:

- **Data sharing and integration**: Data is like the blood that flows through the body of our AI entity, connecting all the components and allowing them to work together harmoniously. That's why we attach so much importance to data sharing and integration.

- **Cross-functional collaboration**: Collaboration is the essence of our AI entity. Each component – machine learning, NLP, and computer vision – works together, reinforcing and complementing the skills of the others.

- **Unified knowledge base**: A unified knowledge base is like the collective memory of our AI entity. It allows all components to access and use the knowledge acquired by any one of them, improving the AI's overall ability to learn and adapt.

To put it briefly, interconnectivity is the cornerstone of our unified AI entity. It's the invisible force that binds the various components together, allowing them to function as a single, cohesive unit. Through data sharing and integration, cross-functional collaboration, and a unified knowledge base, interconnectivity transforms a collection of individual AI components into a powerful, unified entity. It's the key that allows our AI entity to be more than just the sum of its parts, enabling it to learn, adapt, and evolve in a way that individual components cannot. As we continue to explore and innovate in the field of AI, the role of interconnectivity will only become more crucial in building intelligent systems that can truly understand and interact with the world around them.

As we delve into the specifics of implementation, it's essential to understand the strategies and methods that make successful integration possible. We'll examine the practical steps and considerations necessary to assemble the various components of our unified AI entity, ensuring that they work harmoniously to achieve our goals.

Implementation strategies

Building a unified AI entity is like constructing a complex puzzle. Each piece must fit perfectly with the others to create a coherent and functional whole.

As we explored earlier in the section about architecting effective AI solutions, in particular **Architect Your AI** (**AYAI**), we need to think about several domains in order to design an AI solution: challenge, fundamental requirements, input interface, data flow, output interface, essential components, and solution lifecycle.

In the context of building a unified AI entity, we have covered some of the domains related to design at a high level, but we must not forget to explore the domains related to effective implementation. In particular, we must pay attention to the essential components and concerns related to the lifecycle, especially capabilities for continuous learning. Let's explore how we approach this challenge.

Designing the architecture of our unified AI entity is a delicate balancing act. On one hand, we need to ensure that each component – machine learning, NLP, and computer vision – can function independently. On the other hand, these components need to be integrated seamlessly to form a cohesive entity.

It's like designing a city where each neighborhood has its own unique character, but all neighborhoods are connected to form a unified urban landscape. Just like humans, our unified AI entity needs to **continuously learn** and adapt to new information and changing environments. To facilitate this, we have established a framework for ongoing learning. This framework includes integrating recommendation algorithms, which help our AI entity understand and predict user needs more effectively. It's like a school where the curriculum is constantly updated to reflect the latest knowledge and trends.

Figure 7.2 illustrates the integration and interaction of various essential components that constitute a unified AI entity. The main components include data collection, pattern recognition, machine learning models, NLP, and computer vision. Each component plays a vital role in data processing and analysis, leading to a recommendation system, user segmentation, and predictive personalization and ultimately culminating in a personalized user experience.

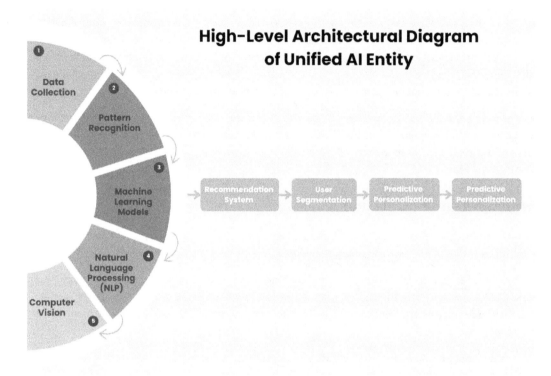

Figure 7.2: A high-level architectural diagram of a unified AI entity

The preceding diagram highlights the importance of interconnectivity among the components. Data collection feeds into pattern recognition, which in turn informs the machine learning models. NLP and computer vision complement these models, providing a deeper understanding of the data. This continuous and integrated flow results in efficient recommendation systems, precise user segmentation, and predictive personalization, creating a highly personalized and effective user experience.

Through these strategies, we aim to create a unified AI entity that is not only intelligent and capable but also adaptable and continuously evolving. It's a challenging task, but we believe that it's a journey worth embarking on.

Summary

In this chapter, you embarked on a journey into the world of pattern recognition within the realm of web development. You discovered how AI can be harnessed to personalize user journeys by recognizing patterns in user behavior, preferences, and interactions, thereby tailoring the web experience for everyone.

You then moved on to the implementation of recommendation systems, gaining insights into how these systems can suggest relevant content to users. Finally, you learned about the concept of a unified AI entity and how all these elements can be integrated into such an entity to provide a cohesive and personalized user experience.

In addition, you undertook a project to build a movie recommendation system using machine learning. This project aimed to provide users with movie recommendations based on their viewing history and preferences, thereby putting the skills that you learned in this chapter into practice.

These skills include understanding pattern recognition principles, applying customization techniques, implementing predictive algorithms, integrating recommendation algorithms, and understanding a unified AI entity.

As we move forward, get ready to discover how coding assistants can transform your development approach and boost your productivity. These tools are becoming an essential part of modern development, helping you streamline processes and enhance efficiency. See you in the next chapter!

Coding Assistants – Your Secret Weapon in Modern Development

In this chapter, we will immerse ourselves in the field of **coding assistants**, exploring how these tools serve as secret weapons in modern software development. The chapter provides insights into the functionality, benefits, and practical applications of these tools, empowering readers to harness the full potential of coding assistants for enhanced productivity and code quality.

By the end of this chapter, you will have a solid understanding of coding assistants and how to use them in your applications. You will also know how to handle complex state logic using coding assistants and how to debug your applications effectively.

The main topics of this chapter are as follows:

- Mastering coding assistants
- Integrating coding assistants into your workflow
- Maximizing productivity with smart code suggestions
- Detecting and fixing errors with intelligent debugging
- Streamlining collaboration through code review assistance

Mastering coding assistants

We live in an era where technology is constantly evolving, and software development is no exception. One such innovation is coding assistants. They are software tools that assist developers in writing code. They use AI to suggest improvements and corrections, making the coding process more efficient. I remember the first time I used GitHub Copilot in a development project. The impact was immediate: the speed at which I could implement complex features increased significantly. Not only did I save time but I also learned new best practices.

The benefits of coding assistants are numerous. Here are a few:

- Firstly, they increase productivity

- Imagine not having to spend hours looking up the correct syntax of a function; the coding assistant instantly suggests the necessary code

- They detect errors in real time and suggest corrections, leading to fewer errors and cleaner, more efficient code

- Developers can learn new techniques and best practices by interacting with these tools

There are several examples of coding assistants. Each of them has its own characteristics, advantages, and disadvantages.

Here are a few most commonly used ones: Duet AI, Kite, Codota, TabNine, GitHub Copilot, Microsoft IntelliCode, Alibaba Cloud Cosy, and AIXcoder. To see how these tools compare, we have created a comparison matrix that contrasts their features, benefits, and potential drawbacks. *Figure 8.1* provides a clear and concise overview, helping developers choose the most suitable assistant for their specific needs.

Coding Assistant	Features	Advantages	Disadvantages
GitHub Copilot	Real-time code suggestions, autocompletion of entire functions, integration with GitHub	Enhances productivity by reducing manual coding tasks, supports multiple languages	Privacy concerns, possible dependence on the tool, occasional inaccurate suggestions
Microsoft IntelliCode	Context-aware code suggestions, code pattern analysis, integrated with Visual Studio	Improves code quality with best practices, seamless IDE integration	Limited support for some languages, requires a learning curve
Duet AI	Integration with Google Cloud, model generation, code modification	Supports Google Cloud services, assists in exploring cloud services	May produce incorrect results, limited usefulness outside Google Cloud environment
Kite	Real-time code suggestions, supports multiple programming languages	Enhances learning with real-time explanations, compatible with various IDEs	Documentation may be hard to find in non-English languages
Codota/TabNine	Machine learning-based code suggestions, supports IntelliJ-based IDEs	Saves time, helps overcome writer's block	Potential for distraction, risk of developing bad coding habits
Alibaba Cloud Cosy	AI-based coding assistance, security protocols, collaboration environment	Comprehensive suite of products, strong partnerships, tailored for Asian market	Smaller community, fewer resources in English
AIXcoder	Real-time code suggestions, automated code generation	Increases developer productivity, focuses on complex problem-solving	May not support all languages, requires validation of generated code

Figure 8.1: Coding assistants overview

The comparison matrix offers a valuable visual summary of the different coding assistants, highlighting their key features, strengths, and weaknesses. By examining this matrix, developers can make informed decisions about which tool best aligns with their development workflow, project requirements, and personal preferences.

In selecting the appropriate coding assistant for a project, it's crucial to understand the unique advantages and disadvantages of various AI frameworks, as these tools are often optimized for specific frameworks. This understanding will guide you to a coding assistant that best meets the project's needs and complements the chosen technology stack.

The choice of a coding assistant can be influenced by the needs of the project, such as the following:

- **Programming language specialization**: Coding assistants often specialize in certain programming languages. For example, TabNine excels in JavaScript development, offering precise and contextualized suggestions that are extremely useful for web developers. In contrast, AIXcoder is highly valued for its integration with specific machine learning frameworks in Python, which is a boon for data scientists.

- **Integrated Development Environment (IDE) integration**: The effectiveness of a coding assistant can be significantly enhanced by its integration capabilities with popular IDEs such as **Visual Studio (VS)** Code, IntelliJ IDEA, and Eclipse. This integration allows developers to use the assistant directly within their coding environment, providing seamless access to intelligent code completion, refactoring tools, and more, all of which can speed up development times and reduce coding errors.

- **Machine learning features**: Some coding assistants use machine learning algorithms to analyze your coding patterns and the context of your code. This allows them to offer more precise and contextually relevant code suggestions. For instance, if you're working on a machine learning project, the assistant might suggest optimal ways to handle data preprocessing or tweak hyperparameters based on the current model that you are developing.

- **Cost efficiency**: Coding assistants come in various price ranges, including both free and premium options. For small projects or individual developers, a free version might suffice, providing basic code completion and syntax highlighting. For larger enterprises or more complex projects, a paid assistant might offer additional features such as deeper integration with corporate databases, advanced security features for code, and team collaboration tools.

Coding assistants are a secret weapon in modern development. They not only increase productivity but also promote higher code quality and continuous learning. As technology continues to evolve, we can expect to see even more improvements and innovations in this area.

Next, let's explore the distinctions between coding assistants and **code generators**. Understanding these differences is the key to effectively integrating these tools into your workflow, ensuring that you choose the right tool for the right task and maximize your developmental efficiency.

Code generators

A code generator is a tool that automates the creation of code. AI-powered code generators help simplify coding processes, automate routine tasks, and even predict and suggest snippets of code. They can produce quick and accurate results, but it is always recommended to review and test any generated code before using it in a production environment. For example, while using Amazon CodeWhisperer (which was developed by AWS), I noticed that it could provide real-time code suggestions ranging from snippets to complete functions. Moreover, CodeWhisperer can identify hard-to-find security vulnerabilities and suggest fixes. However, this commercial service can be demanding on machines with lower specifications.

Both types of tools aim to make the software development process more efficient and productive. However, the choice between a code assistant and a code generator depends on the specific needs of your project and your work style.

Now that you know the difference between code assistants and code generators, let's take a closer look at a code assistant: GitHub Copilot.

Understanding GitHub Copilot

During my development projects, I found GitHub Copilot to be a revolutionary AI-powered assistant. Acting like a pair programmer, it offers autocomplete suggestions as you type. What sets it apart is its ability to enhance coding efficiency by providing context-aware recommendations, whether you are starting a new code block or merely expressing your coding ideas in natural language. The tool effectively uses the nuances of the file you are working on, along with related files, ensuring its suggestions are relevant and seamlessly integrated into your text editor. This powerful capability is a result of the collaborative effort between GitHub, OpenAI, and Microsoft, utilizing an advanced generative AI model to offer real-time coding assistance that adapts perfectly to your specific coding environment.

The reliability of GitHub Copilot's suggestions is directly linked to the prevalence of a language in public repositories. For instance, languages such as JavaScript, which have extensive representation, benefit from robust support and high-quality suggestions. Conversely, lesser-known languages might not receive the same level of accuracy due to there being fewer examples in the training data. From my own experience, using JavaScript with Copilot felt seamless and intuitive, providing helpful suggestions regularly. However, when switching to a niche language, the quality of suggestions noticeably declined, highlighting the importance of the volume and diversity of training data.

Intellectual property and open source issues surrounding GitHub Copilot require careful consideration. The AI models behind Copilot are trained on public code but do not store it, which means that they are not just copying and pasting from repositories. It's crucial to understand that while Copilot uses this training data to generate code, it does so without retaining any specific source code, thereby maintaining a balance between utility and intellectual property rights.

When it comes to code completion, Copilot works diligently behind the scenes, akin to a detective piecing together clues. It analyzes the code in your editor, focusing on the lines surrounding your cursor and even other open files. All this information is fed into Copilot's model, which then generates a probabilistic prediction of what your next steps might be. This process feels almost magical as you see the tool suggesting code that fits perfectly into your current context, making development smoother and more intuitive.

In chat-based scenarios, Copilot takes on the role of a conductor, orchestrating a contextual prompt by merging a **context summary** with your submitted question. This comprehensive blend of information is processed by Copilot's model, which then predicts and suggests the most fitting response. This method turns Copilot into an interactive assistant that is capable of understanding and addressing queries with remarkable accuracy, enhancing the overall coding experience.

When you ask a question in GitHub Copilot Chat, the client automatically uses various aspects of your current context to form the question that it sends to the model. This context can include a variety of information from your workspace. Here's a breakdown:

- **The code file that is open in your active document**: This is the file that you're currently working on. The content of this file provides important context for the question.

- **Your selection (or code blocks for the current cursor position) in the document**: This is the specific part of the code that you're focused on. If you've highlighted a section of code, or if your cursor is at a particular position, this provides more specific context for the question.

- **Summaries of related documents open in your editor or from the workspace**: If you have other files open in your editor, or other files in your workspace that are related to the current file, summaries of these documents can also provide additional context.

- **Information about errors, warnings, messages, or exceptions in your error list**: If there are any errors, warnings, or other messages in your error list, this information can help the model understand what problems you might be trying to solve.

- **General workspace information, such as frameworks, languages, and dependencies**: The overall setup of your workspace, including the programming languages you're using, the frameworks you're working with, and any dependencies your project has, can also provide useful context.

- **Parts of related files in your workspace, project, or repo**: If there are other files in your workspace, project, or repo that are related to the current file or the current problem, parts of these files can also be used to provide context.

> **More information**
>
> You can use and read more about GitHub Copilot here:
>
> ```
> https://github.com/features/copilot
> ```

By using all of this information to form the question, GitHub Copilot Chat can provide more accurate and relevant suggestions. It's a way of ensuring that the model understands as much as possible about what you're trying to do, so it can provide the best possible help.

GitHub Copilot is a versatile extension available for various IDEs, including VS Code, VS, Vim, Neovim, the JetBrains IDE package, and Azure Data Studio. Its features are designed to streamline your coding workflow. Key highlights include the following:

- **Autocompletion capabilities**: GitHub Copilot can suggest not only lines of code but also entire functions and tests, significantly speeding up the coding process and reducing boilerplate code.

- **Multilingual code support**: GitHub Copilot is a polyglot, meaning that it understands and can provide assistance in a wide range of programming languages. Whether you're coding in a widely used language such as JavaScript or Python, or a less common one, GitHub Copilot has got you covered. This is made possible by the diverse range of public code repositories that it trained on.

- **Learning and adapting to coding styles**: What sets GitHub Copilot apart is its ability to learn and adapt. The more you use it, the more it learns about your coding style and preferences. Over time, it will provide suggestions that are increasingly tailored to your coding habits, making it feel like a truly personalized assistant.

> **More information**
>
> Read more about GitHub Copilot's features here:
>
> ```
> https://github.com/features/copilot
> ```

To start using GitHub Copilot, you need to set up a free trial or subscription. Once activated, you can adjust the settings in your GitHub account to customize suggestions and manage telemetry data. This adaptability ensures that GitHub Copilot remains a valuable tool that is tailored to your specific needs. For instance, *Figure 8.2* depicts how you can block or allow suggestions matching public code:

Figure 8.2: Enabling or disabling duplication detection

You have the option to control whether your prompts and suggestions are gathered and kept by GitHub, as well as whether they are processed further and shared with Microsoft, by modifying your user settings.

With the knowledge of what code assistants are, what benefits they offer, and how they differ from code generators under our belts, let's now learn how you can integrate them into your workflows.

Integrating coding assistants into your workflows

We find ourselves immersed in a dynamic technological landscape where the integration of AI-based tools stands out as an essential tool for boosting efficiency in software development. Coding assistants are powerful tools that can help developers increase their productivity, improve code quality, and reduce stress. However, to fully exploit the potential of these tools, it is important to integrate them seamlessly into your workflows.

The use of AI code assistants has a significant impact on software development. They not only speed up the development process but also help maintain code consistency and reduce the number of coding errors. By leveraging AI's ability to learn from vast amounts of data, these tools can provide insights and recommendations that would be difficult for a human to generate manually.

However, it's not all smooth sailing. There are notable challenges and limitations when incorporating AI coding assistants. These can range from navigating complex codebases to managing proprietary languages and adapting the AI to fit a developer's unique coding style. Recognizing these limitations is crucial. For instance, I've found that while AI excels in popular languages like JavaScript, it struggles with niche or less common frameworks, requiring a more hands-on approach to adaptation.

Let's delve into practicalities. Setting up and using GitHub Copilot in VS Code, for example, can greatly enhance your workflows. The step-by-step guide that follows will walk you through this process, ensuring that you can leverage all the benefits of coding assistants effectively.

Setting up GitHub Copilot in VS Code – a step-by-step guide

GitHub Copilot, integrated into VS Code, is a powerful extension that offers various functionalities. Here are some of the key features of GitHub Copilot in VS Code:

- **Real-time code suggestions**: Copilot provides real-time code suggestions as you type, helping to speed up the writing process.

- **Support for multiple programming languages**: It supports various programming languages, allowing developers to work in different environments and projects.

- **Code generation from comments**: Copilot can generate code based on the comments that you write, as it's capable of interpreting the developer's intent.

- **Refactoring assistance**: It can assist in code refactoring, offering suggestions to improve the structure and efficiency of existing code.

- **Context-sensitive and customized suggestions**: Suggestions are context-sensitive, adapting to the surrounding code to provide more relevant solutions. Additionally, Copilot learns from the developer's specific coding patterns.

- **Code documentation**: It can automatically generate comments and documentation for functions and code snippets.

- **Machine learning for coding patterns**: It utilizes machine learning to understand and suggest patterns based on common coding practices.

- **Compatibility with unit testing**: It can automatically generate code for unit tests based on existing code.

- **Efficient code review**: It facilitates the code review process by offering consistent and contextually relevant suggestions.

- **Ease in generating examples and prototypes**: It enables the quick generation of examples or code prototypes, facilitating the visualization of proposed solutions.

- **Integration with other VS Code extensions**: It works in conjunction with other extensions and tools in VS Code, extending its functionality.

- **Ease in authorization and integration with GitHub**: It provides an easy interface to authorize and integrate with GitHub accounts, simplifying project collaboration.

By following these steps, you'll be well on your way to integrating an AI coding assistant into your workflows, enhancing your productivity and code quality.

GitHub Copilot, a powerful AI-powered coding assistant, can significantly enhance your coding efficiency when integrated with VS Code. Here's an informative step-by-step guide to help you set up GitHub Copilot in your VS Code environment:

1. **Start the installation process**: Begin by navigating to the VS Code Marketplace and searching for the GitHub Copilot extension. Simply click **Install** to add the extension to your VS Code setup.

2. **Open VS Code**: Once you click **Install**, a popup will appear asking you to open VS Code. Click on **Open VS Code**. This action will take you directly to your VS Code environment.

3. **Install the extension**: Inside VS Code, you'll see the **Extension: GitHub Copilot** tab. Click on **Install** to add the extension to your IDE. This action will integrate GitHub Copilot into your VS Code, enabling it to assist you while coding.

4. **Initial sign-in to GitHub**: If this is your first time connecting VS Code with your GitHub account, you will be prompted to log in directly from VS Code. This crucial step enables GitHub Copilot to tap into your coding history, allowing it to offer more tailored coding suggestions.

5. **Seamless automatic authorization**: For those who have previously linked VS Code with GitHub, GitHub Copilot will recognize your settings and automatically authorize itself. This convenient feature eliminates the need to repeatedly authorize VS Code when you commence using GitHub Copilot.

6. **Troubleshoot a missing authorization prompt**: If the authorization prompt doesn't appear, simply click on the bell icon in the lower panel of VS Code. This will bring up the necessary authorization prompt.

7. **Grant necessary permissions**: Upon clicking the prompt, your browser will open a GitHub page requesting permissions for GitHub Copilot. Click **Authorize VS Code** to grant these permissions, ensuring that Copilot has all that it needs to assist you efficiently.

8. **Finalize authentication**: Conclude the setup process by confirming the authentication in VS Code. A dialog box will appear within VS Code, where you should click on **Open** to finalize the authentication and start enjoying the advanced features of GitHub Copilot.

With these instructions completed, you can now integrate GitHub Copilot into your development process. Embrace its support to streamline your workflows, but always apply your own critical thinking and expertise to make the final choices in your coding projects.

Prerequisites for using GitHub Copilot

Unlocking the full potential of GitHub Copilot is a straightforward process, but it requires a couple of key prerequisites:

- **Activate your GitHub Copilot subscription**: Before diving into the world of GitHub Copilot in VS Code, ensure that you have an active GitHub Copilot subscription. For detailed information on billing and subscription details, refer to the **About billing for GitHub Copilot** documentation at `https://github.com/features/copilot#pricing`.

- **-Install VS Code**: GitHub Copilot seamlessly integrates into VS Code, so it's essential to have VS Code installed on your system. If you haven't installed it yet, visit the VS Code download page for guidance on downloading and installing the latest version.

By meeting these two prerequisites, you'll be ready to harness the power of GitHub Copilot within your VS Code environment. Now, let's embark on a coding journey empowered by intelligent suggestions and enhanced productivity.

Managing coding assistants in a team environment with GitHub Copilot

Working in collaborative development environments means that managing coding assistants like GitHub Copilot effectively is essential to keep things running smoothly. It helps in maintaining consistency, streamlining workflows, and fostering better collaboration among team members. That said, navigating the complexities of using Copilot within a team can be quite challenging. Here's a practical guide to help you manage Copilot access, set appropriate policies, and handle content exclusions for your team:

Enabling and setting up Copilot Business

To start using GitHub Copilot Business, you need to set it up correctly. Here are the steps involved:

- Setting up a subscription: Ensure that your organization has a Copilot Business subscription.
- Configuring settings: Configure access, policies, and content exclusions in the Settings | Copilot section.
- Configuring network settings: If necessary, configure your network settings such as an HTTP proxy or firewall to allow Copilot on your corporate network.
- Assigning seats: Assign Copilot seats to individuals or teams via the Settings | Copilot | Access section.

By completing these steps, your organization will be ready to utilize GitHub Copilot Business effectively.

Managing Copilot Business

Proper management of Copilot Business is crucial for maintaining control and maximizing benefits. Here's what you need to do:

- **Reviewing audit logs**: Access your organization's Copilot Business audit logs to understand which actions have been taken by users, such as changes to settings or seat assignments
- **Managing access**:
  - **Enabling access for all**: Enable Copilot for all current and future members of your organization in the Settings | Copilot | Access section.

- **Enabling access for specific users**: Choose Selected members and add users individually or upload a CSV file.

- **Revoking access**: Revoke access for individuals or your entire organization via the Copilot | Access section.

- **Reviewing usage data**: View your organization's Copilot usage data, such as the number of seats assigned and the estimated cost, in the Settings | Copilot | Access section. You can also download a report or sort users list by last use.

Effective management ensures that Copilot is used appropriately and efficiently within your organization.

In *Figure 8.3*, you can see how GitHub Copilot Business access is managed, with a particular focus on the allocation of Copilot seats. This visual representation allows users to check the number of seats assigned under the Copilot Business subscription and estimate the monthly costs involved. Additionally, it provides a comprehensive view of access details, enabling administrators to effectively monitor and manage how Copilot seats are utilized within the organization.

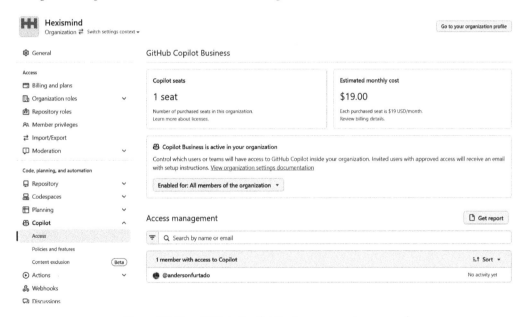

Figure 8.3: How GitHub Copilot Business access is managed

Alternative approaches

Explore different ways to view and manage Copilot seats, keeping track of their utilization and estimating the monthly costs involved. Keep an eye on how Copilot seats are assigned, making sure that they are used effectively within your team. Take a comprehensive look at GitHub Copilot Business, including details on seat allocation and related expenses.

Managing policies

To tailor GitHub Copilot to your organization's needs, you need to configure policies. Here's how:

- **Suggestion matching**: Choose Allow or Block in the Settings | Copilot | Policies section to control whether Copilot suggestions can match public code on GitHub

- **Using GitHub Copilot Chat**: Choose Allowed or Blocked in the Settings | Copilot | Policies section to enable or disable the chat feature for your organization

Configuring these policies helps you maintain control over how Copilot is used and ensures it aligns with your organization's standards.

Figure 8.4 illustrates the configuration of policies and features for GitHub Copilot Business. It showcases the options for managing suggestion-matching policies and enabling or disabling GitHub Copilot Chat within the organization. Organization owners can utilize these settings to tailor Copilot's behavior based on their requirements.

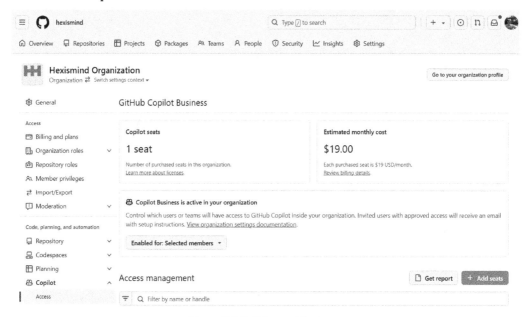

Figure 8.4: Policies and features

Alternative approaches

Set up GitHub Copilot Business policies to ensure that the tool behaves according to your organization's specific needs. Oversee policies for suggestion matching and manage the features of GitHub Copilot Chat. Adjust Copilot Business settings to match your organization's preferences and operational requirements.

Configuring content exclusions

To further customize GitHub Copilot's functionality, you can set up content exclusions. Follow these steps:

- **Configuring exclusions**: Exclude specific files or directories from being used by Copilot for code completion and suggestions

- **Configuring repository settings**: Define content exclusions that are specific to a repository in the Settings | Copilot section

- **Configuring organization settings**: Define exclusions that are applicable to any Git-based repository across `GitHub.com` or other locations

- **Configuring who is affected**: Exclusions only apply to members with Copilot seats in the same organization

  These settings ensure that sensitive or irrelevant content is not used by Copilot, providing more accurate and appropriate suggestions.

  Figure 8.5 offers a detailed look at how to set up content exclusions for GitHub Copilot within an organization. It outlines the process for repository administrators and organization owners to identify and manage files that should be excluded from code completion suggestions. This figure also illustrates the available options for setting exclusions at both the repository and organization levels, ensuring that specific files do not influence the suggestions provided by Copilot.

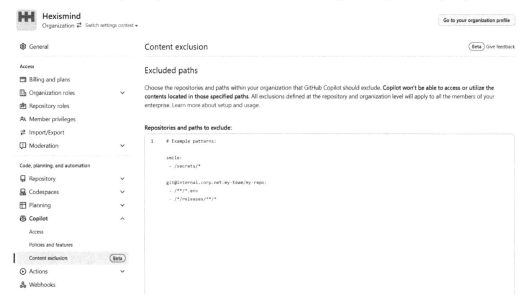

Figure 8.5: Content exclusion

> **Alternative approaches**
>
> Set up content exclusion settings to prevent certain files from being included in GitHub Copilot's code completion suggestions. Fine-tune Copilot's functionality by configuring content exclusions within your repositories or organization. Ensure that specific files do not affect Copilot's code suggestions by applying the appropriate content exclusion settings.

Propagating changes and checking effects

After making changes to your settings, you need to ensure they are applied correctly. Here's how:

- **Waiting or reloading**: Changes to content exclusions may take up to 30 minutes to be reflected in your IDE. Alternatively, manually reload the settings as explained for different IDEs.

- **Checking effect**: Open a file that is affected by exclusions and confirm that Copilot is disabled (no suggestions) and that its content isn't used for suggestions in other files.

By verifying these changes, you can ensure that your configurations are working as intended.

> **Practical tips**
>
> Use audit logs to track user activity and ensure responsible Copilot usage.
>
> Set policies based on your team's needs and security considerations.
>
> Regularly review and update content exclusions to ensure desired code coverage.
>
> Encourage team members to familiarize themselves with Copilot's features and limitations.

Effectively managing GitHub Copilot Business features requires a mix of actions. You need to audit usage, configure access, set policies, and control content exclusions. These steps help organizations get the most out of Copilot while keeping control and allowing for customization based on specific needs.

We have covered how to manage these features. This includes auditing actions, configuring access, and defining policies. With this solid foundation, we can now improve our coding practices even further.

Next, let's explore how these management strategies help us use smart code suggestions. This will boost productivity and streamline our development workflows.

Maximizing productivity with smart code suggestions

In the fast-paced world of software development, maximizing productivity is essential. One powerful method to achieve this is by utilizing smart code suggestions. Coding assistants leverage advanced algorithms to anticipate and recommend the next code snippet you might need.

The following section, *Rapid code writing*, will showcase practical applications and techniques for using these suggestions. These methods can significantly speed up coding tasks and improve efficiency in software development. We'll delve into how to seamlessly integrate these innovations into your coding environment.

Figure 8.6 illustrates how different coding assistants, such as GitHub Copilot, Kite, and Duet AI, integrate with various IDEs, including VS Code, IntelliJ IDEA, and others. This visualization aids in understanding how these tools can be incorporated into your development workflows, highlighting the interactions and compatibilities between the assistants and the IDEs.

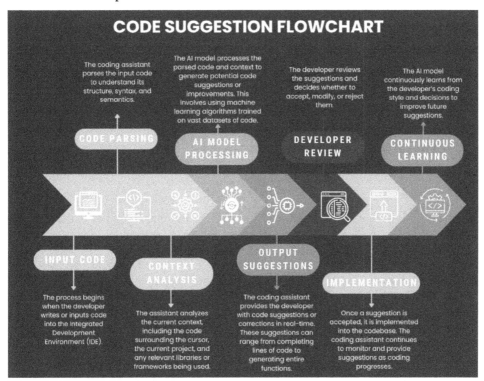

Figure 8.6: A code suggestion Flowchart

The figure illustrates how coding assistants connect with various IDEs, using lines and arrows to indicate compatibility and support. For example, GitHub Copilot's link to VS Code signifies that this assistant can be utilized within this IDE for real-time code suggestions. On the other hand, Duet AI's connections to Google Cloud products demonstrate its deep integration with Google's ecosystem. These lines represent integration paths, helping to visualize the implementation of different tools in various development environments, thereby enhancing coding efficiency and quality.

This visual representation makes it easier to understand how to leverage these tools in your development process. Each connection line highlights the potential for increased efficiency and improved code quality through the seamless integration of these assistants with the development environments.

Rapid code writing

Speed is a crucial factor in software development. With real-time code suggestions, you can accelerate the coding process. Coding assistants such as GitHub Copilot provide code suggestions that are relevant to what you're writing, allowing you to focus more on your code's logic than its syntax.

Let's take a look at a step-by-step example of text completions on VS Code using GitHub Copilot:

1. Open VS Code and navigate to the Python file that you're working on.
2. Start with a comment describing the project, such as the following:

    ```
    # This is a project to calculate the average of a list of
    numbers
    ```

3. Start typing your code. For example, if you're writing a function to calculate the average of a list of numbers, you might start typing the following:

    ```
    def calculate_average(
    ```

4. As you type, Copilot will start suggesting real-time code completions. For example, it might suggest that you complete the preceding line with `numbers):`.
5. Press *Tab* to accept a suggestion.
6. Continue writing your code. Copilot will continue to provide relevant suggestions. For example, it might suggest the body of the function to calculate the average of the list of numbers.
7. When you're done writing your code, you can use Copilot to check for better ways to optimize it.

Figure 8.7 represents an authorization request from GitHub for VS Code. This is a standard procedure when a user wants to integrate their GitHub account with VS Code. The user, in this case, is andersonfurtado, and the **GitHub for VS Code by Visual Studio Code** application is requesting access to the user's account.

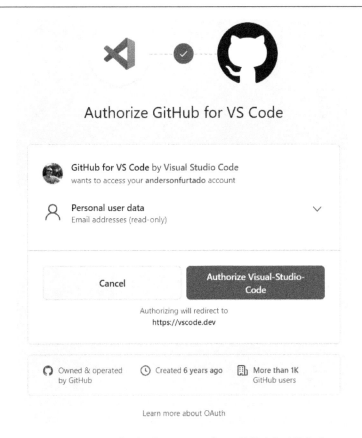

Figure 8.7: An authorization request from GitHub for VS Code

The authorization process is a security measure to ensure that the user grants explicit permission for VS Code to access their GitHub account. The access requested includes read-only access to personal user data and email addresses. Once the user authorizes this access, they will be redirected to `https://vscode.dev`. This integration allows the user to use the features of GitHub directly within VS Code, enhancing their coding workflows. It's important to note that this process should only be completed in a secure environment to protect the user's personal information.

> **Important note**
>
> Before starting the example, it's important to mention that you need to authorize GitHub for VS Code on GitHub. This can be done through your browser. In some cases, for the authorization request message on GitHub to appear, you may need to restart VS Code.

Peering into the world of VS Code, *Figure 8.8* captures a moment where the GitHub Copilot status icon comes to life. Nestled within the status bar at the bottom of the VS Code window, this icon signals that GitHub Copilot is active and on standby to assist with intelligent code suggestions.

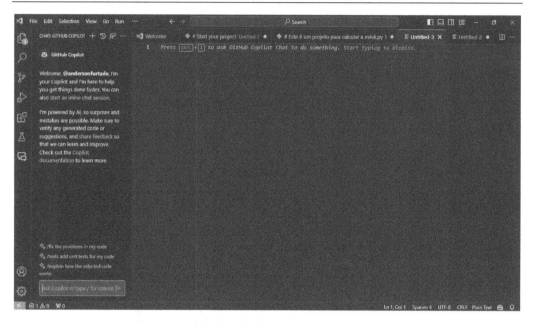

Figure 8.8: VS Code with the GitHub Copilot status icon

The GitHub Copilot status icon is more than just a symbol; it's an interactive gateway within the VS Code interface. When GitHub Copilot is active, the icon illuminates, indicating that the AI-powered code suggestions are in operation. Users can interact with this icon to delve into more options related to GitHub Copilot, such as adjusting settings or discovering the current version. This icon serves as a vital touchpoint in the user experience, offering a seamless way to navigate and engage with GitHub Copilot directly from the VS Code interface. In the new version, you can use *Ctrl + I* to ask GitHub Copilot Chat to do something or click on the icon in the bottom right corner to open Copilot Chat.

Having explored the interactive features of the GitHub Copilot status icon and its role in enhancing coding efficiency, we are now poised to delve deeper into its capabilities. With this foundation, let's explore how we can further harness the power of GitHub Copilot Chat in VS Code to elevate our coding workflows to new heights.

Harnessing the power of GitHub Copilot Chat in VS Code

GitHub Copilot Chat is a groundbreaking tool that serves as an AI programming assistant, aiding developers in navigating the world of software development with greater efficiency. It can perform a variety of tasks, making it an indispensable resource for any developer.

Figure 8.9 illustrates the use of the `task` command in GitHub Copilot Chat within VS Code. This feature allows users to request specific tasks, such as generating code, asking questions about existing code, or even creating a new Jupyter notebook.

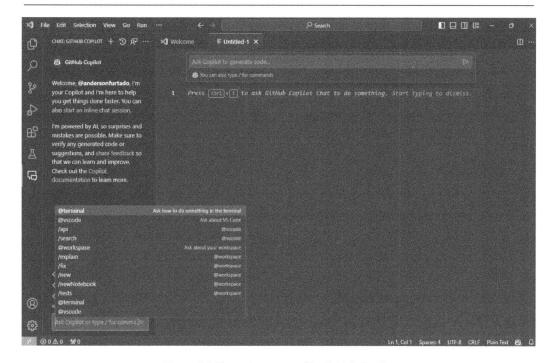

Figure 8.9: The task command in GitHub Copilot

By typing / in the chat, a list of possible tasks is displayed, providing easy and efficient interaction with GitHub Copilot. This functionality highlights the versatility of GitHub Copilot as an AI programming assistant that is capable of assisting with a wide range of software development tasks.

Here are some of the tasks you can perform by typing / in Copilot Chat:

- **Ask a question about the files in your current workspace**: GitHub Copilot can provide insights into the files in your workspace, helping you better understand existing code

- **Explain how the selected code works**: If you're struggling to understand a piece of code, GitHub Copilot can provide a detailed explanation

- **Generate unit tests for the selected code**: GitHub Copilot can generate unit tests for the selected code, helping ensure that your code works as expected

- **Propose a fix for issues in the selected code**: If GitHub Copilot detects an issue in the selected code, it can suggest a fix

- **Generate code for a new workspace**: If you're starting a new project, GitHub Copilot can generate code to help kickstart your workspace

- **Create a new Jupyter Notebook**: GitHub Copilot can create a new Jupyter Notebook for you, helping to organize and visualize your data

- **Ask questions about VS Code**: If you have questions about how to use VS Code, GitHub Copilot can provide answers

- **Generate query parameters for workspace search**: GitHub Copilot can generate query parameters to assist in searching your workspace
- **Ask about developing VS Code extensions**: If you're interested in developing your own VS Code extensions, GitHub Copilot can provide guidance
- **Ask how to do something in the terminal**: If you need help running commands in the terminal, GitHub Copilot can provide step-by-step instructions

Here's a step-by-step example of how to use GitHub Copilot Chat in VS Code:

1. **Open VS Code**: Start VS Code on your computer.
2. **Activate GitHub Copilot**: If you haven't installed the GitHub Copilot extension yet, you can find it in the VS Code extension store. Once it has been installed, the GitHub Copilot icon should appear in the status bar at the bottom of the screen.
3. **Start Copilot Chat**: There are two ways to start Copilot Chat:

   - Press *Ctrl + I* on your keyboard
   - Click on the GitHub Copilot icon in the status bar in the bottom-right corner

4. **Type your query**: Once Copilot Chat is open, you can type your query or code request. For example, you might type `Write a function to reverse a string in Python`.
5. **Use the code suggestions**: GitHub Copilot will generate a code suggestion based on your query. You can accept the suggestion by pressing *Ctrl + Enter*, or you can request alternatives.
6. **Interact with Copilot Chat**: You can continue to interact with Copilot Chat, asking additional questions or requesting more code suggestions.

Remember, while GitHub Copilot is a powerful tool for assisting with writing code, it's always important to understand the code you're writing and ensure that it meets your specific needs.

While GitHub Copilot serves as an invaluable tool, it is crucial to remain engaged and understand the code that you integrate into your projects. With this understanding, let's now explore how you can expand your coding possibilities by using the multilingual capabilities of GitHub Copilot to enhance your development workflow further.

Using multilingual capabilities

Coding assistants are powerful tools that support multiple programming languages. This is especially useful in polyglot development environments, where different parts of a project may be written in different languages.

Let's take a look at an example of web development using Copilot. Suppose that you're working on a web development project that has a frontend written in JavaScript (React) and a backend written in Python (Django); in that case, follow these steps:

1. Open VS Code and navigate to the JavaScript (React) file that you're working on for the frontend.

2. Start typing your code. Copilot will suggest JavaScript code completions.

3. If you switch to a Python (Django) file in the backend, Copilot will start suggesting Python code completions.

4. This allows you to easily switch between different programming languages without losing productivity, maintaining consistency and efficiency across both projects.

The ability of coding assistants such as GitHub Copilot to handle multiple languages is invaluable for developers working in polyglot environments. These tools offer relevant code suggestions across various programming languages, allowing developers to seamlessly switch between languages without sacrificing productivity. This feature is particularly beneficial in web development, where the frontend and backend often use different languages. As such, multilingual capabilities are crucial for boosting the efficiency and productivity of developers.

Understanding how GitHub Copilot and similar tools improve productivity through their multilingual support sets the stage for further refining our coding practices. In the next section, we'll delve into essential code optimization tips to streamline the development process and enhance code efficiency and readability.

Code optimization tips

Code suggestions go beyond speeding up the writing process; they also focus on optimizing and enhancing code efficiency. Tools such as GitHub Copilot offer valuable insights into how you can refine your code, making it more efficient and improving its overall quality. By providing these optimization tips, coding assistants help ensure that your code runs more smoothly and effectively. Here are some examples of code optimization with GitHub Copilot:

- **Using appropriate data structures**: The right data structures can significantly improve your code's efficiency. For example, if you're working with a large amount of data, Copilot might suggest using a set instead of a list to speed up search operations.

- **Avoiding unnecessary loops**: Often, operations that are performed in loops can be performed more efficiently using library functions. For example, if you're calculating the sum of a list of numbers, Copilot might suggest using the `sum()` function instead of a `for` loop.

- **Using object-oriented programming**: Object-oriented programming can make your code more modular, easier to understand, and easier to maintain. For example, if you're writing a program that deals with cars, Copilot might suggest creating a `Car` class with appropriate methods.

- **Using Copilot to check for better ways to optimize your code**: After writing your code, you can use Copilot to check for better ways to optimize your code. It might suggest refactoring that improves your code's efficiency and readability.

Mastering code autocompletion is important for any developer. With the help of smart code suggestions, you can write code more quickly, handle multiple languages with ease, and ensure that your code is optimized for better performance. This powerful tool can significantly enhance your productivity and help you become a more proficient developer. Use it wisely and watch your efficiency soar.

Having discussed the benefits of code autocompletion, let's now shift our focus to another vital aspect: **intelligent debugging**. Unlike traditional debugging, this technology not only detects errors but also offers solutions. It streamlines your development process and ensures higher code quality. By harnessing intelligent debugging, you can further enhance your coding efficiency and produce cleaner, more reliable code. Let's explore this powerful tool in more detail.

Detecting and fixing errors with intelligent debugging

Debugging is an art that requires patience, precision, and a deep understanding of the code. In the world of software development, intelligent debugging stands out as a skill. It involves the use of advanced techniques and tools to detect and fix errors efficiently. Some of these techniques include **real-time error detection**, static code analysis, step-by-step debugging, and reverse debugging. Let's take a look at a few techniques in detail.

Real-time error detection

Real-time error detection is an advanced feature that allows developers to identify and fix errors as they are introduced into the code. Tools such as GitHub Copilot can suggest corrections for code errors based on the context of the code that you are working on. However, GitHub Copilot does not make real-time corrections to your code because it does not have the ability to interact directly with your development environment.

Here's an example of how GitHub Copilot might suggest a correction for a common code error in Python.

Suppose that you have the following code with an error:

```
for i in range(10)
    print(i)
```

The error here is that a colon (:) is missing at the end of the for loop line. GitHub Copilot could suggest the following correction:

```
for i in range(10):
    print(i)
```

With a solid grasp of real-time error detection and its benefits, we can now explore another transformative feature. The next step in our journey through advanced development tools is the use of chat functionalities within IDEs such as VS Code for debugging. This innovative approach makes the debugging process not only simpler but also more effective. By leveraging conversational AI, developers can interact directly with the tool, receiving solutions and insights in a more intuitive and accessible way.

Let's dive deeper into how these chat functionalities can revolutionize your debugging process, making it smoother and more efficient. This method enhances the traditional debugging experience by providing real-time assistance and contextual understanding, ultimately leading to faster and more accurate problem resolution.

Debugging using chat and VS Code

You can also perform debugging through chat using GitHub Copilot. By submitting the problematic code and describing the unexpected behavior, Copilot can offer potential solutions or corrections. Keep in mind that GitHub Copilot cannot run or debug the code directly; it can only provide suggestions based on the information you provide. The developer is responsible for implementing and testing these suggested corrections.

Consider the following procedure for a block of Python code with an error:

1. **Provide the problematic code**: You can start by providing the code that is causing problems. For example, you might have a function that is supposed to add two numbers but is instead subtracting them:

   ```
   def add(a, b):
       return a - b
   ```

2. **Use the /fix command**: Based on your code and the problem description, you can use the /fix command to get a correction suggestion. For example, you could type /fix into the GitHub Copilot chat.

3. **Describe the problem**: Next, describe the problem. For example, The add function is subtracting the numbers instead of adding them.

4. **Get a suggestion**: Based on your code and the problem description, GitHub Copilot can suggest a possible correction. The chat will return something like the following:

    It seems like there's a logic error in your Python function. The function is supposed to add numbers, but it's subtracting them. Here's the corrected code:

    ```
    def add(a, b):
        return a + b
    ```

5. **Implement the correction**: Finally, you can implement the suggested correction in your code using VS Code. You can type the suggested correction directly into your code in VS Code.

The actual suggestions will depend on the complexity of your function and the context of your code. This is a simple example to illustrate the process.

Having explored how GitHub Copilot can assist in debugging through chat in VS Code, let's move on to another powerful feature designed to streamline the coding process. The **Fix This** feature in GitHub Copilot takes the capabilities of code suggestions further by actively proposing changes to correct specific issues in your code.

Adjusting code with the Fix This feature

GitHub Copilot is an AI tool that assists developers in writing code. It has several features, each designed to enhance a different aspect of the coding process. The **Fix This** feature, for instance, stands out for its ability to suggest corrections or improvements to existing code based on its context. This is in contrast to other features, such as **Chat** and **In-line Text Completion**. Here's a comparison:

- **Chat**: This feature allows developers to engage in a conversational interaction with the AI, asking questions or seeking advice on coding problems.

- **In-line Text Completion**: This feature, on the other hand, provides real-time suggestions as developers type their code, helping to autocomplete lines or blocks of code.

- **Fix This**: Accessible through the **Copilot** menu when right-clicking on a specific code context, this feature takes a more proactive approach. It analyzes the selected code and suggests a correction or improvement, saving developers the time and effort of manually debugging or optimizing their code.

Figure 8.10 illustrates how to access the **Fix This** feature.

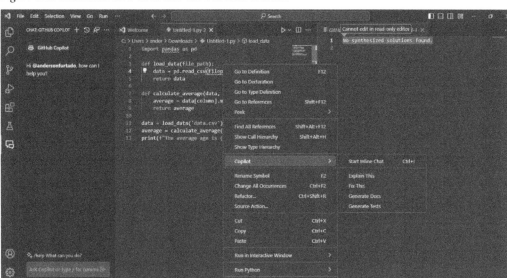

Figure 8.10: Accessing the Fix This feature

Here's a step-by-step guide to access the feature, obtain suggestions, and decide whether to accept or reject them:

1. Right-click on the code you wish to correct or improve.

2. In the menu that appears, hover over the **Copilot** option.

3. In the **Copilot** submenu, select the **Fix This** option.

4. GitHub Copilot will analyze the code context and suggest a correction or improvement.

5. You can preview the suggestion and decide whether to accept or reject it. If you accept, the suggestion will be applied to your code.

Lastly, the Fix This feature of GitHub Copilot is a valuable tool for developers' daily work. It not only helps to correct and improve code efficiently but also serves as an excellent learning tool, allowing developers to familiarize themselves with new techniques and coding best practices. This feature, along with the others offered by GitHub Copilot, makes it a comprehensive and indispensable tool for modern developers.

Now that we understand how the Fix This feature simplifies code adjustments, let's shift our focus to another powerful capability. In the following section, we'll explore how GitHub Copilot can generate unit tests. This feature facilitates thorough testing processes, ensuring your code is robust and reliable.

Generating unit tests with GitHub Copilot

To generate unit tests using GitHub Copilot, you can start by writing a comment indicating that you want to create a unit test for a specific function. GitHub Copilot will then generate a suggestion based on the context. Suppose that you have the following function:

```
def multiply(a, b):
    return a * b
```

Here's a step-by-step guide to how you can generate a unit test:

1. **Start writing a unit test**: You can start writing a unit test like this:

    ```
    def test_multiply():
        # ...
    ```

2. **Get a suggestion**: After initiating the unit test with the function definition, GitHub Copilot can generate the following complete unit test:

    ```
    def test_multiply():
        assert multiply(2, 3) == 6
        assert multiply(-1, -1) == 1
        assert multiply(0, 0) == 0
    ```

3. **Implement the suggestion**: You can implement the unit test suggestion directly in your code in VS Code.

This is a simple example, and the actual suggestions will depend on the complexity of your function and the context of your code. This example illustrates the process.

Mastering intelligent debugging techniques for error detection and resolution is an essential skill for any developer. With the help of an AI programming assistant, we can enhance this skill and make our coding process more efficient and productive. Real-time error detection, the adoption of debugging best practices, debugging using chat, and generating unit tests are key components in mastering these techniques. With these skills, we can create cleaner, more efficient, and more error-free code. Intelligent debugging is not just a skill, but a mindset that allows us to write better and more efficient code.

With a clear understanding of how GitHub Copilot can elevate our unit testing capabilities, let's move forward and explore how we can enhance collaboration and streamline our coding practices through effective code review assistance.

Streamlining collaboration through code review assistance

Effective collaboration and code quality are two fundamental pillars of software development. In this section, we will explore how GitHub Copilot in VS Code can be a powerful ally in this process.

Enhancing the code review process

In the realm of code review, the role of GitHub Copilot is transformative. Here's how:

- **Providing context-aware code suggestions during reviews**: Context-sensitive code suggestions are provided during reviews, helping to speed up the review process

- **Highlighting potential errors or style issues**: Potential errors or style issues are highlighted, allowing them to be corrected before commit

- **Automating repetitive tasks like formatting and commenting**: Repetitive tasks, such as formatting and commenting, are automated, saving valuable time

- **Integrating with code review platforms to streamline workflows**: Integration with code review platforms, such as GitHub, streamlines workflows

- **Offering suggestions for alternative approaches or improvements**: Suggestions for alternative approaches or improvements are offered, helping to improve code quality

- **Flagging code that deviates from coding standards**: Code that deviates from coding standards is flagged, ensuring code consistency

With these features, the code review process becomes more efficient and effective.

Ensuring code quality

Quality is non-negotiable in code development. Here's how GitHub Copilot ensures it:

- **Enforcing coding standards consistently**: Coding standards are consistently enforced, helping to maintain code consistency and readability

- **Tracking code quality metrics over time**: Code quality metrics are tracked over time, providing valuable insights into code quality

- **Suggesting refactoring opportunities for better maintainability**: Refactoring opportunities are suggested to improve code maintainability

- **Generating code documentation automatically**: Code documentation is automatically generated, saving time and ensuring that code is easily understood

- **Identifying potential security vulnerabilities**: Potential security vulnerabilities are identified, helping to protect code against threats

These features ensure that the code you write is of the highest possible quality.

Team collaboration features

Team collaboration is at the heart of successful software development. Here's how GitHub Copilot fosters it:

- **Sharing code snippets and suggestions easily**: Code snippets and suggestions can be easily shared, facilitating collaboration.

- **Providing feedback on code asynchronously**: Feedback on code can be provided asynchronously, enabling effective team collaboration.

- **Resolving conflicts during code merges**: Conflicts during code merges are resolved, ensuring a smooth merge process.

- **Fostering knowledge transfer and collective learning**: Knowledge transfer and collective learning are fostered, helping the team to learn and grow together.

- **Tracking team progress and contributions**: Team progress and contributions are tracked, providing valuable insights into team performance. With these features, your team can work together more effectively and efficiently.

Integrating GitHub Copilot into VS Code can significantly boost collaboration and code quality. By embedding Copilot into our workflows, we can increase team productivity and maintain continuous code improvements. To utilize these features, install the GitHub Copilot extension in VS Code and link it to your GitHub account. Once set up, Copilot can be used directly within the VS Code editor.

This concludes our look at how GitHub Copilot enhances collaboration through code review assistance. We hope that this information has been useful and insightful.

Summary

In this chapter, you were introduced to the field of coding assistants and you explored how these tools serve as secret weapons in modern development. You gained a comprehensive understanding of their functionality and benefits and learned how to apply them in your applications for enhanced productivity and code quality. You mastered the art of integrating coding assistants into your workflow, maximizing productivity with smart code suggestions, and streamlining collaboration through code review assistance.

You also became adept at handling complex state logic using coding assistants and debugging your applications effectively. By this point, you have not only understood the fundamental concepts and functions of coding assistants but also learned how to seamlessly integrate them into your development workflow. You have effectively utilized code auto-completion for increased productivity, mastered intelligent debugging techniques for error detection and resolution, and optimized collaboration through efficient code review assistance.

As we move forward to the next chapter, we will continue to reinforce the logical flow of the content.

Smarter User Interactions – Elevating User Engagement with Advanced AI

In this chapter, we will explore the realm of **advanced AI** for user interactions. We will embark on a journey to develop several exciting projects that will enhance user engagement and create a more immersive web experience. We will introduce you to our primary project, an **AI movie recommendation chatbot**. Next, we will create a simple chatbot using the **ChatterBot** library. Following this, we will explore the power of voice interactions by using the **SpeechRecognition** library to transcribe audio. We will then delve into sentiment analysis using the `TextBlob` library and **Named Entity Recognition (NER)** using **spaCy**. Additionally, we will implement database interactions using **SQLAlchemy** and build a Telegram bot to demonstrate the integration of chatbots with messaging platforms.

The main topics of this chapter are as follows:

- Unraveling advanced AI for user interactions
- Unraveling the mysteries of conversational AI
- Creating conversational experiences with chatbots
- Harnessing the power of voice recognition
- Analyzing language patterns for personalized interactions
- Generative language models and the future of content creation
- The example of an AI movie recommendation chatbot

By the end of this chapter, you will have learned how to leverage the fundamentals of advanced AI for user interactions. You will have learned how to design and integrate chatbots for conversational experiences. You will also know how to implement voice recognition for enhanced user accessibility. Additionally, you will have learned how to analyze language patterns using **Natural Language Processing (NLP)** for personalized interactions and explore the possibilities of generative language models such as ChatGPT in content creation.

Technical requirements

In this project, we will be using Python 3.7 or higher, as well as the following Python libraries:

- pandas (`https://pandas.pydata.org/`)
- NumPy (`https://numpy.org/`)
- sklearn (`https://scikit-learn.org/stable/index.html`)
- SQLAlchemy (`https://www.sqlalchemy.org/`)
- TextBlob (`https://textblob.readthedocs.io/en/dev/`)
- spaCy (`https://spacy.io/`)
- nest-asyncio (`https://github.com/erdewit/nest_asyncio`)
- python-telegram-bot (`https://python-telegram-bot.readthedocs.io/en/stable/`)

All the examples, as well as the source code, used in this chapter, are available on our GitHub repository. You can access and download the code to follow along with the projects and customize them as needed. Visit the following link to explore the code repository for this chapter:

`https://github.com/PacktPublishing/AI-Strategies-for-Web-Development/tree/main/ch9`

Unraveling advanced AI for user interactions

Advanced AI is transforming the ways in which we develop and interact with the web. It's a technology that enables machines to learn, adapt, and perform complex tasks autonomously. In web development, advanced AI can be used for a variety of applications, from content personalization to search engine optimization.

For example, implementing user behavior tracking with tools such as Google Analytics and using clustering algorithms to group similar user behaviors can significantly enhance personalization efforts. This approach helps in tailoring the user experience based on previous interactions, thus boosting engagement and retention. Additionally, employing search engine optimization techniques such as semantic search and vector space models can greatly improve search efficiency, enabling users to find what they're looking for more effectively.

This approach is also being used to improve **web accessibility**. For example, it can be used to automatically transcribe audio into text, making web content more accessible to people with hearing impairments. Additionally, it can be used to automatically translate web content into different languages, making web content more accessible to people who speak those languages. Implementing these solutions can be achieved using the `SpeechRecognition` library in Python for audio transcription and leveraging the Google Translate API for automatic translation of web content.

Furthermore, advanced AI has the potential to transform user engagement, providing more personalized, efficient, and adaptive experiences. As we delve deeper into the realm of advanced AI, our next focus will be on understanding **conversational AI**, a key component of advanced user interactions that is revolutionizing the way users interact with technology.

Unraveling the mysteries of conversational AI – a deep dive into its types, techniques, and applications

Picture a world where machines not only understand human language but also respond in a way that is indistinguishable from human responses. That's the magic of conversational AI. It's a significant leap from traditional rule-based systems, which are limited to predefined rules. Conversational AI, on the other hand, uses **Machine Learning** (**ML**) and NLP to understand and respond in a more natural and contextual manner.

There are various types of systems used to process and respond to user inputs, ranging from simple rule-based systems to more complex conversational AI systems. Rule-based systems operate by following predefined rules and patterns to generate responses. They are straightforward but often lack flexibility and adaptability. On the other hand, conversational AI systems leverage advanced techniques such as NLP and ML to understand and respond to user inputs in a more natural and context-aware manner. *Figure 9.1* compares these two types of systems, illustrating the linear and rigid nature of rule-based systems versus the dynamic and sophisticated approach of conversational AI systems.

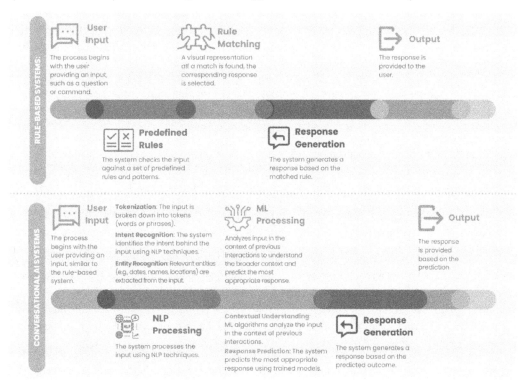

Figure 9.1: Rule-based systems versus conversational AI systems

The visual comparison between rule-based systems and conversational AI systems underscores the additional complexity and sophistication of modern AI systems. While rule-based systems follow a linear path and rely on predefined rules, conversational AI systems use NLP techniques to understand user intent and ML algorithms to analyze context and predict the best possible response.

Conversational AI comes in many forms, each with its own unique characteristics and applications. Here are a few examples:

- **Chatbots**: These digital companions simulate human conversations and are commonly used in customer service to answer frequently asked questions. For instance, a chatbot such as Amelia helps users navigate insurance services, while Eva – employed by a major bank – assists customers with banking inquiries ranging from account balances to recent transactions.

- **Virtual assistants**: Think Siri, Alexa, and Google Assistant for this type of conversational AI. They're more advanced than chatbots and can perform a variety of tasks, from answering questions to controlling smart home devices.

- **Voice agents**: These systems use voice data to interact with users. They're useful in situations where the user cannot or does not want to use a text-based interface. For example, Amazon Alexa and Google Assistant help users perform a wide range of activities, from controlling smart home devices to answering questions and playing music.

- **Dialogue systems**: These are the masterminds that can manage multi-turn conversations and are capable of maintaining context throughout the conversation. An example is IBM watsonx Assistant, which is used in customer service to handle complex inquiries and provide consistent responses based on ongoing conversations.

ML is the brain behind conversational AI. It employs algorithms that learn from data, enabling the AI to improve its responses over time. This learning process is similar to human learning, where experience leads to knowledge accumulation and skill enhancement.

Meanwhile, NLP is the heart of conversational AI. It involves the application of computational techniques to analyze and synthesize natural language and speech. This capability allows the AI to understand human language in its natural form, including synonyms, slang, and even typos.

Conversational AI shines when there is a need for natural and intuitive interaction with users. It is particularly useful in customer service applications, where it can provide quick and accurate answers to frequently asked questions, freeing up human agents to handle more complex issues.

Conversational AI is indeed a revolutionary way of interacting with technology. It's like a bridge that connects us humans with machines, enabling us to communicate with them in the same way we communicate with one another. It's a testament to how far we've come in our quest to make machines understand us, and it offers a glimpse into a future where machines can understand us even better.

In brief, conversational AI, with its use of advanced ML and NLP techniques, offers a powerful tool for enhancing user engagement and interaction. As we continue to advance in this field, we can expect to see even more sophisticated and seamless user interactions. In the next subsection, we will explore how to create conversational experiences with chatbots, delving deeper into the practical applications of conversational AI.

Creating conversational experiences with chatbots

In our digital age, we are constantly introduced to new forms of interaction. One such innovation is the chatbot, a digital ally that is transforming the way we communicate with the virtual world. Chatbots are, at their core, computer programs created to mimic human conversations in an authentic and intuitive way.

They are infiltrating all aspects of our digital lives, from customer support to education and health. However, what really makes a chatbot effective? How can they enhance our digital interactions and create richer, more engaging conversational experiences?

In this section, we will dive into the universe of chatbots. We will explore their role in user interactions, understand how they work, and discover how they can be used to create more authentic and engaging conversational experiences. We will unravel the secrets behind these digital assistants and discover how they are redefining the way we communicate in the digital world.

Mastering the art of conversational UI design for chatbots

In the context of chatbots, the cornerstone of successful interaction lies in crafting a **natural conversational flow**. This means that the chatbot should keep pace with the conversation, responding to the user's queries logically and coherently. Techniques such as intent recognition, with libraries such as **Rasa NLU**, help chatbots understand user queries. Designing conversation paths with state management and implementing feedback loops refines the chatbot's responses based on user interactions. These strategies ensure that the chatbot provides accurate and contextually relevant responses, enhancing the overall user experience.

To achieve a natural conversational flow, it's essential to understand the nuances of human language and program chatbots to respond intuitively. Here is a step-by-step guide on how to create such a flow:

1. **Understand the user's intent**: The first step in creating a natural conversational flow is to understand what the user wants to achieve during the conversation.

2. **Design the conversation path**: Once you understand the user's intent, the next step is to design a conversation path that will guide the user toward achieving their goal.

3. **Implement NLP**: NLP techniques can be used to ensure that the chatbot understands and responds to the user's queries in a natural and intuitive manner.

4. **Test and refine the conversational flow**: Finally, the conversational flow should be tested with real users and refined based on their feedback.

Another critical aspect of conversational UI design is crafting **user-friendly responses**. We believe that a chatbot should be able to communicate in a clear and friendly manner, without resorting to jargon or complex technical language. To achieve this, we strive to create responses that are informative, yet also accessible and easy to understand. Here's a step-by-step guide on how to create user-friendly responses:

1. **Understand the user's query**: The first step in crafting a user-friendly response is to understand the user's query.

2. **Craft a clear and concise response**: Once you understand the user's query, the next step is to craft a response that is clear, concise, and directly addresses the user's query.

3. **Use simple and accessible language**: The response should be written in simple and accessible language that the user can easily understand.

4. **Test and refine the response**: Finally, the response should be tested with real users and refined based on their feedback.

Therefore, the design of conversational UI for chatbots is a complex process that involves understanding human language and crafting responses that are natural and user-friendly. We are constantly seeking ways to improve and enhance our chatbots to provide the best possible experience for users.

Tips for creating engaging dialogues for chatbots

Creating engaging dialogues is an art. We believe that a good chatbot should be able to conduct conversations that are not only informative but also engaging and interesting. Here are some tips on how we can achieve this:

- **Natural flow**: The first step in creating an engaging dialogue is to ensure that the conversation flows naturally. This means that the chatbot must be able to follow the rhythm of the conversation, answering the user's questions logically and coherently.

- **Context awareness**: A good chatbot must be context-aware. This means that it must be able to understand the context of the conversation and respond accordingly. For example, if the user is talking about a movie, the chatbot should be able to recognize this and respond with relevant information about the movie.

- **Humor**: Humor can be a powerful tool for creating engaging dialogues. A chatbot that can make jokes or respond humorously to certain questions can be more enjoyable for the user to communicate with.

- **Personality**: A chatbot should have a personality. This can help make the conversation more interesting and engaging for the user. The chatbot's personality can be reflected in the way it speaks, the words it chooses, and the way it answers questions.

- **Empathy**: Finally, a good chatbot must be able to demonstrate empathy. This means that it must be able to understand the user's emotions and respond in a way that shows understanding and care.

Designing engaging dialogues for chatbots is a complex process that requires a deep understanding of human language and an ability to create responses that are natural and context-aware, as well as full of humor, personality, and empathy.

Building chatbot architectures – understanding the different types of chatbots

Once you have designed engaging dialogues, the next step is to build the chatbot architecture. There are three main types of chatbots: rule-based, retrieval-based (or AI-based), and hybrid.

When it comes to rule-based chatbots, start by defining a clear set of rules and decision trees. Imagine scripting a conversation where each user input follows a specific path, triggering predefined responses. This method is perfect for handling straightforward, repetitive tasks, ensuring consistency and predictability.

For retrieval-based chatbots, the approach shifts to utilizing ML algorithms. Here, the chatbot becomes more dynamic, classifying user inputs and fetching the most appropriate responses from a vast database. It's like having a knowledgeable assistant who can provide varied answers based on past interactions.

Hybrid chatbots are the best of both worlds. By combining the structured rules of decision trees with the flexibility of ML models, these chatbots can tackle both simple and complex interactions. It's like having a smart assistant who can follow a script but also think on its feet when necessary, offering a seamless and versatile user experience.

Each type has its own strengths, weaknesses, and basic architectures. Let's take a look at each of these types:

- **Rule-based chatbots**: These chatbots are programmed with a specific set of rules and can only respond to specific commands. They are simple to build but may struggle with complex or ambiguous queries. Rule-based chatbots are best suited for simple, straightforward tasks such as answering FAQs or guiding users through a step-by-step process. An example of a rule-based chatbot is a customer service bot on a retail website that guides users through return policies or tracks order statuses based on specific queries such as *Where is my order?* or *How do I return an item?*

- **Retrieval-based (or AI-based) chatbots**: These chatbots use ML algorithms to retrieve the best response from a predefined set of responses. They are more flexible than rule-based chatbots but still rely on a predefined set of responses. Retrieval-based chatbots are best suited for tasks that require a deeper understanding of the conversation context. An example here could be a tech support bot that uses context from past interactions to provide troubleshooting solutions for more complex queries such as *"Why isn't my device connecting to the Wi-Fi?"*

- **Hybrid chatbots**: These chatbots combine the features of rule-based and retrieval-based chatbots. They can respond to a wide range of queries and provide more natural and human-like responses. Hybrid chatbots are ideal for tasks that require both the simplicity of rule-based chatbots and the flexibility of retrieval-based chatbots. An example could be a personal assistant bot that helps with daily tasks, such as setting reminders or booking appointments, and also engages in more dynamic conversations about news topics or user preferences.

The **basic architecture of a chatbot** involves the integration of a **channel** (where the conversation will take place, for example, WhatsApp), the available **content** (what will be said and extra resources used in the interaction such as GIFs, files, and so on), and the **software** that is responsible for its creation.

Let's explore the **process of architecting a chatbot** with the following sequential steps:

1. **Requirements**: Define the target client, the strengths and weaknesses, and the benefits that the solution will provide.

2. **Specifications**: Develop the product specification, identifying the features and functionality of the bot.

3. **Conversation flow**: Build conversation flows that represent user interactions.

4. **Architecture**: Define the bot's architecture, including choosing the type of chatbot (rule-based, retrieval-based, or hybrid).

5. **Development**: Start building the bot according to the specifications.

6. **Testing**: Test the bot with real users and refine it based on their feedback.

7. **Deployment**: Deploy the bot on the chosen communication channel.

8. **Promotion**: Promote the bot to attract users.

Creating a successful chatbot involves understanding human language, designing engaging dialogues, and building the right chatbot architecture. It's a complex process that requires a deep understanding of different types of chatbots and their strengths and weaknesses. However, with the right approach, it's possible to create chatbots that provide a rich and engaging conversational experience.

As we continue our journey, our next stop will be integrating the chatbots with existing systems. In the upcoming subsection, we will explore how chatbots can be connected with backend databases, APIs, and services for continuous access to information and functionalities. This integration is crucial for chatbots to provide accurate and up-to-date responses to user queries.

Integrating chatbots with existing systems – connecting chatbots to databases, APIs, and services

One of the most crucial aspects of excellent chatbot use is the integration of chatbots with existing systems. This involves connecting chatbots to backend databases, APIs, and various services to ensure continuous access to information and functionalities. This integration allows chatbots to provide accurate, up-to-date, and contextually relevant responses to user queries, thereby enhancing the overall user experience.

Integrating chatbots with existing systems is vital for enabling seamless interactions between users and backend technologies. Here's how chatbots can be connected to enhance their functionality and user experience:

*   **Connecting with databases**: Chatbots can be linked to backend databases to access and manipulate data. This allows the chatbot to provide accurate and up-to-date responses to users. For instance, a customer service chatbot could access a customer's order history to answer questions about order status. To achieve this, you would need to establish a secure connection between your chatbot and your database, ensuring that all data transfers are encrypted and that your chatbot has the necessary permissions to access and manipulate the data.

To demonstrate this, we can use `SQLAlchemy`, a powerful **Object-Relational Mapping (ORM)** tool for Python. Here's a brief overview of how `SQLAlchemy` can be used to set up a database for a chatbot and the steps taken in the code provided:

```python
# Install the necessary libraries
!pip install sqlalchemy pandas openpyxl scikit-surprise

# Import the libraries
import pandas as pd
from sqlalchemy import create_engine, Column, Integer, String, Float
from sqlalchemy.orm import declarative_base, sessionmaker
from surprise import Dataset, Reader, SVD
import urllib.request
import zipfile
import os
# Define the SQLAlchemy models
Base = declarative_base()

class Movie(Base):
    __tablename__ = 'movies'
    movieId = Column(Integer, primary_key=True)
    title = Column(String)
    genres = Column(String)

class Rating(Base):
    __tablename__ = 'ratings'
    userId = Column(Integer, primary_key=True)
    movieId = Column(Integer, primary_key=True)
    rating = Column(Float)
    timestamp = Column(Integer, primary_key=True)

# Create the SQLite database and tables
engine = create_engine('sqlite:///movielens.db')
Base.metadata.create_all(engine)

# Create a session
Session = sessionmaker(bind=engine)
session = Session()

# Insert data into the movie table
movies_data = movies.to_dict(orient='records')
existing_movies = {
    movie.movieId
    for movie in session.query(Movie.movieId).all()
}
```

```
new_movies = [
    Movie(**data)
    for data in movies_data
    if data['movieId'] not in existing_movies
]
session.bulk_save_objects(new_movies)

# Insert data into the ratings table
ratings_data = ratings.to_dict(orient='records')
existing_ratings = {
    (rating.userId, rating.movieId, rating.timestamp)
    for rating in session.query(Rating.userId, Rating.movieId,
        Rating.timestamp
    ).all()
}
new_ratings = [
    Rating(**data)
    for data in ratings_data
    if (data['userId'], data['movieId'], data['timestamp'])
    not in existing_ratings
]
session.bulk_save_objects(new_ratings)

# Commit session
session.commit()
```

The preceding code snippet shows how to configure a SQLite database using SQLAlchemy. We start by creating an engine that connects to a SQLite database named movies.db. Next, we define the ORM classes for the Movie and Rating tables, specifying the columns and their data types. We then create the tables in the database and configure a session to interact with the database.

The example uses SQLite, which does not support encryption natively. However, in a production environment, you should use a database that supports encryption (for example, PostgreSQL or MySQL with SSL). Additionally, managing sensitive information securely is crucial. Using environment variables to store database URLs, API keys, and authentication tokens ensures that these pieces of sensitive information are not hardcoded into the source code, thereby reducing the risk of exposure. By configuring your application to access these variables at runtime, you can enhance security and maintain a higher level of data protection. This approach is particularly important when deploying applications in production environments, where security is a top priority.

For a complete implementation, including inserting data and querying the database, refer to https://github.com/PacktPublishing/AI-Strategies-for-Web-Development/tree/main/ch9/MovieLens_SQLAlchemy_Database_Creation.ipynb.

- **Integrating with APIs**: Chatbots can be integrated with various APIs to access services and functionalities. A travel chatbot, for example, could integrate with a weather forecasting API to provide updated weather information at the user's travel destination. To do this, you would need to register your chatbot with the API provider, obtain an API key, and then use this key to make requests to the API from your chatbot.

- **Connecting with services**: Chatbots can also be connected to various services to provide additional functionalities. A productivity chatbot, for example, could connect to a calendar service to help users schedule meetings and reminders. This would involve registering your chatbot with the service provider, obtaining the necessary authentication credentials, and then using those credentials to interact with the service from your chatbot.

The integration of chatbots with existing systems is a vital step in chatbot development. It not only enhances the chatbot's capabilities but also significantly improves the user experience. As we continue to explore and innovate in this field, we look forward to uncovering new ways to make our chatbots more intelligent, responsive, and user-friendly.

As we move forward on this exciting journey, our next subsection will delve into another crucial aspect of chatbot development. Here, we'll delve deeper into the practical applications of conversational AI, exploring how we can create more engaging and natural interactions with chatbots.

A step-by-step guide to building a chatbot using the Natural Language Toolkit (NLTK)

In the upcoming discussion, we'll take a hands-on approach and walk through a step-by-step guide to building a chatbot using the **Natural Language Toolkit** (**NLTK**). This guide will provide a practical understanding of how to design, implement, and fine-tune a chatbot using one of the most popular libraries in Python for processing human language data. So, stay tuned for an exciting journey into the world of chatbots!

The NLTK stands as a prominent toolkit within the Python community for processing and analyzing human language data. It offers user-friendly interfaces to a diverse array of more than 50 corpora and lexical resources, including WordNet. Additionally, NLTK encompasses a comprehensive range of text-processing libraries that support various tasks such as classification, tokenization, stemming, tagging, parsing, and semantic reasoning, making it an essential resource for developers and researchers working in the field of NLP. It wraps the efficient numerical libraries **Theano** and **TensorFlow** and allows you to define and train neural network models in just a few lines of code.

Here's a step-by-step guide on how you can use NLTK to create a simple rule-based chatbot:

1. **Import the necessary libraries**: We need to import the `NLTK` library and the `Chat` and `reflections` modules from `nltk.chat.util`:

```
import nltk
from nltk.chat.util import Chat, reflections
```

2. **Define the pairs of patterns and responses**: We need to define a list of patterns and responses. Each pattern is a regular expression that matches the user's input and the corresponding response is what the chatbot will reply with:

```
pairs = [
    [
        r"my name is (.*)",
        ["Hello %1, How are you today ?",],
    ],
    [
        r"hi|hey|hello",
        ["Hello", "Hey there",],
    ],
    [
        r"quit",
        ["Bye. It was nice talking to you. See you soon :)"]
    ],
]
```

3. **Define the chatbot function**: This function initializes the chatbot and starts the conversation:

```
def chatbot():
    print("Hi, I'm a chatbot. You can start a conversation with
        me now.")
```

4. **Create a Chat object**: We need to create a `Chat` object by passing in the pairs of patterns and responses and the reflections module:

```
chat = Chat(pairs, reflections)
```

5. **Start the conversation**: We call the `converse()` method on the `Chat` object to start the conversation:

```
chat.converse()
```

6. **Call the chatbot function**: Finally, we call the `chatbot()` function to run the chatbot:

```
if __name__ == "__main__":
    chatbot()
```

This code creates a simple rule-based chatbot using the NLTK library. The chatbot can respond to user inputs based on the defined patterns and responses. The `%1` in the response is replaced with the user's input captured by the `(.*)` group in the pattern. If the user types `quit`, the chatbot ends the conversation.

Indeed, creating a chatbot using NLTK is a fascinating process. This example demonstrates how to create a simple rule-based chatbot. However, keep in mind that creating a more advanced chatbot would require more complex patterns and responses, and possibly the use of ML techniques.

As we continue to explore the vast landscape of chatbot development, our next topic will take us into the realm of voice recognition. Harnessing the power of voice recognition can significantly enhance the capabilities of a chatbot, allowing it to interact with users in a more natural and intuitive manner.

Harnessing the power of voice recognition

We are at the forefront of a technological revolution wherein **voice recognition** is transforming the way we interact with our devices. This technology, which was once considered science fiction, is now an everyday reality that plays a crucial role in improving accessibility.

Voice recognition is more than a modern convenience; it's an empowerment tool. It allows individuals who may have difficulties with traditional UIs – whether due to physical, visual, or other types of disabilities – to control and interact with technology in a more intuitive and natural way.

Accessibility is an area where voice recognition is making a significant impact. By allowing people to control devices and access information using just their voice, we are removing barriers and opening up a world of possibilities. This is especially relevant for those who, due to various limitations, may have previously been excluded from the digital revolution.

However, despite the advances, there are still challenges to overcome. The accuracy of voice recognition and contextual understanding are areas that still need improvement. We are committed to enhancing these technologies to ensure that they are inclusive and meet the needs of all users.

In addition, as voice recognition becomes more sophisticated, new ethical and security challenges arise. One such challenge is the misuse of technology to mimic other people's voices. AI technology can now reproduce a person's voice with surprising accuracy, which opens the door to potential abuses. This includes the creation of fake voice recordings that can be used to deceive people or commit fraud.

Voice recognition is redefining human-computer interaction and playing a key role in improving accessibility. We look forward to seeing how this technology will continue to evolve and shape our digital future while tackling emerging challenges to ensure that technology is used responsibly and safely.

A practical guide for web developers – implementing voice interactions

We are at the forefront of a revolution in human-computer interaction: the era of voice. Voice-activated applications are becoming increasingly prevalent, providing an intuitive and natural interface for users. The following practical guide will walk you through the essential steps to implement voice interactions in your web applications:

- **Understanding spoken language**: The construction of voice-activated applications begins with understanding spoken language. This involves the use of NLP and ML technologies. Some popular libraries include the following:

  - **Google's Speech-to-Text API**: This API allows applications to convert audio into text, which can then be processed using NLP.

- **Microsoft's Azure AI Speech service**: This service offers a variety of features, including voice-to-text transcription and text-to-speech synthesis.

- **Mozilla's DeepSpeech**: This is an open source model for voice recognition.

- **Interpreting user intent**: After converting speech into text, the next step is to understand what the user means. This can be done using technologies such as Google's Dialogflow or Microsoft's **Language Understanding Intelligent Service** (LUIS). Both allow you to create intents and entities to capture the meaning of the user's text.

- **Providing meaningful responses**: After understanding the user's intent, the application should provide a meaningful response. This could involve performing an action (such as playing a song or setting an alarm) or providing information to the user. Here, tools such as Google's Text-to-Speech API or Microsoft's Azure Text to Speech can be useful for converting text into speech.

- **Considering privacy and security**: Privacy and security are critical considerations in the development of voice-activated applications. It's important to ensure that user interactions are secure and that their data is handled with the utmost care. This includes implementing robust security and privacy measures such as data encryption and user authentication. Additionally, it's important to consider techniques such as data anonymization and data minimization to protect user privacy.

- **Testing and iterating**: Finally, it's important to test the application with real users to ensure that it meets their needs. This can involve conducting usability tests, collecting user feedback, and iterating on the application's design and functionality based on that feedback. Tools such as Google Optimize or Microsoft Clarity can be useful for A/B testing and user behavior analysis. Google Optimize is a platform that allows you to conduct A/B, multivariate, and redirect tests on your website, while Microsoft Clarity is a user behavior analysis tool that provides insights into how users are interacting with your website.

Implementing voice interactions in web applications is an exciting challenge that offers the opportunity to significantly improve the user experience. With the right approach, web developers can lead the way in creating applications that not only understand spoken language but also respond in a meaningful and useful way.

Now that we've explored the theory and practical considerations for implementing voice interactions, let's dive into a practical example. In the next section, we'll use the `SpeechRecognition` library to transcribe audio. This will allow us to see how these concepts are applied in practice and provide a solid foundation for your own explorations in voice-activated application development.

Audio transcription with the SpeechRecognition library – a step-by-step guide for web developers

Voice-activated applications are becoming increasingly prevalent, providing an intuitive and natural interface for users. The following practical guide will walk you through the essential steps to implement voice interactions in your web applications:

1. Import the `speech_recognition` library as `sr`:

    ```
    import speech_recognition as sr
    ```

2. Create a `Recognizer` object, which is used to recognize speech:

    ```
    r = sr.Recognizer()
    ```

3. Use the microphone as the audio source. The `listen()` method is used to capture the audio from the microphone:

    ```
    with sr.Microphone() as source:
        print("Fale algo:")
        audio = r.listen(source)
    ```

4. Try to recognize the audio using Google Speech Recognition. If the audio is successfully recognized, print the transcribed text. If Google Speech Recognition does not understand the audio or if there is an issue requesting results from the service, print an appropriate error message. Consider the following code:

    ```
    try:
        print("You said: " + r.recognize_google(audio,
            language='en-EN'))
    except sr.UnknownValueError:
        print("Google Speech Recognition didn't understand the
            audio")
    except sr.RequestError as e:
        print("It was not possible to request results from the
            Google Speech Recognition service; {0}".format(e))
    ```

By following these steps, you have set up a basic system for transcribing audio using the SpeechRecognition library. This is just the beginning – there are many more features and possibilities to explore with this powerful library. As you continue to develop your voice-activated applications, remember to consider important factors such as user experience, privacy, and security.

As we move forward, our next topic of discussion will be analyzing language patterns for personalized interactions. This involves understanding how we can analyze the language patterns of users to create more personalized and effective interactions in our voice-activated applications.

Analyzing language patterns for personalized interactions

This is the time when user interactions no longer suit a one-size-fits-all approach. Personalization is the key to crafting meaningful and engaging experiences. By shaping our interactions to meet the unique needs and preferences of each user, we can elevate user satisfaction and supercharge the effectiveness of our applications.

Language analysis is the secret sauce in personalizing interactions. By deciphering a user's spoken or written language, we can unearth valuable insights into their needs, preferences, and behaviors. This treasure trove of information empowers us to mold our interactions to better serve each individual user. For instance, the AI movie recommendation chatbot project from the *AI Strategies for Web Development* book demonstrates the practical application of these techniques.

In the example, advanced techniques such as sentiment analysis and NER are leveraged to enhance user interactions. Here's a brief overview of how these are implemented:

```
from textblob import TextBlob
import spacy

# Load spaCy model
nlp = spacy.load("en_core_web_sm")

# Function for sentiment analysis
def analyze_sentiment(text):
    blob = TextBlob(text)
    return blob.sentiment

# Function for named entity recognition
def extract_entities(text):
    doc = nlp(text)
    entities = [(ent.text, ent.label_) for ent in doc.ents]
    return entities
```

Using TextBlob, the sentiment analysis function evaluates the emotional tone of user inputs, providing insights into their feelings and attitudes. This is achieved through the `analyze_sentiment` function, which returns the polarity (degree of positivity or negativity) and subjectivity (degree of personal opinion) of the text.

Using `spaCy`, the **Named Entity Recognition** (NER) function efficiently identifies and extracts essential entities such as names, locations, and dates from user inputs. The `extract_entities` function processes the text and retrieves these entities, aiding in understanding the context and customizing responses accordingly. This enhances the interaction quality by making the system more context-aware and responsive to specific user inputs.

Polarity ranges from -1 (negative) to 1 (positive). For example, a polarity of -0.5 indicates a negative sentiment. Subjectivity ranges from 0 (objective) to 1 (subjective). A subjectivity score of 1 implies that the text is purely based on personal opinion or emotion.

By integrating these techniques, the chatbot can provide more context-aware and personalized responses, enhancing the user experience significantly. For instance, if a user expresses feeling *sad*, the chatbot could recommend uplifting movies. Conversely, if the sentiment is positive, the chatbot might suggest movies that align with the user's current mood.

This combination of sentiment analysis and NER allows for a deeper understanding of user inputs, making the interactions more meaningful and tailored to individual preferences.

For a practical guide and more detailed implementation, you can refer to the example provided in the *AI Strategies for Web Development* book, which is available on GitHub:

```
https://github.com/PacktPublishing/AI-Strategies-for-Web-Development/
blob/main/ch9/Movie_Recommendation_with_Sentiment_Analysis_CLI.ipynb
```

Through the magic of language analysis, we can sketch the **user's profile**. This might reveal information such as their interests, their level of knowledge about a particular topic, and even their emotional state. These nuggets of insight can be used to add another layer of personalization to our interactions with the user. By tailoring our interactions to meet the unique needs and preferences of each user, we can enhance user satisfaction and supercharge our applications.

Here's a step-by-step guide on how you can harness the power of language analysis to personalize user interactions:

1. **Pick the right tool**: The world of language analysis is rich with libraries and tools. Some of the crowd favorites include NLTK, spaCy, TextBlob, Google Cloud Natural Language API, and Microsoft Azure Text Analytics API. Choose the tool that fits like a glove for your needs.

2. **Preprocess the data**: Before you can analyze language data, you'll need to clean it up. This might involve removing punctuation, converting all letters to lowercase, removing irrelevant words (also known as **stop words**), and lemmatizing (reducing words to their base form), among other things.

3. **Extract features**: Once your data is squeaky clean, you'll need to extract features that can be used for analysis. This might involve word frequency, the presence of certain words or phrases, syntactic complexity, and more.

4. **Sentiment analysis**: Sentiment analysis is a powerful technique that allows us to understand the emotional tone of the user's communication. By tuning into the user's sentiment, we can shape our responses to better meet their emotional need

5. **NER**: NER can be used to identify people, places, organizations, and other entities in a text. This can be useful for understanding the context of an interaction.

6. **Intent recognition**: Intent recognition can be used to understand the user's goal behind an interaction. This can be done using ML techniques to classify interactions into various intent categories.

7. **Personalizing the interaction**: Finally, based on language analysis, you can personalize the interaction with the user. This can include adapting the response based on the user's sentiment and suggesting relevant products or services based on the user's preferences, among others.

In this way, language analysis is a powerful tool for personalizing user interactions. By understanding user language patterns, we can create more personalized, meaningful, and effective experiences.

Having explored the diverse applications of language analysis for enhancing user interaction, let's delve into how these insights pave the way for more sophisticated communication strategies. As we've seen, understanding and leveraging language patterns can significantly elevate the personalization of user experiences. Now, let us shift our focus to the emerging potential of generative language models and their transformative role in content creation, further expanding our toolbox for engaging with users in meaningful ways.

Generative language models and the future of content creation

Generative language models, including Transformer-based models such as GPT and BERT, are revolutionizing the field of NLP. These models are trained on large volumes of text, enabling them to learn the syntactic and semantic structure of human language. The choice of the best language model depends on the specific needs of the project. Factors such as the complexity of the task, the amount of training data available, and the computational capacity should be considered.

Generative language models have a wide range of applications in content creation. They can be used to automatically generate article summaries, draft blog posts, create video scripts, and much more. OpenAI, for instance, used a generative language model to generate blog posts that were published on their website. These posts were automatically generated by the model and reviewed by human editors before publication.

In the domain of web development, automated content generation is an invaluable tool. There are several libraries, such as `NLTK`, `spaCy`, and `StanfordNLP` that facilitate the integration of generative language models into development workflows.

When choosing between different models such as GPT-3 and BERT, it's essential to consider their respective strengths and limitations. GPT-3, with its large capacity and ability to generate coherent and contextually relevant text, is excellent for tasks requiring creative content generation. However, its size and computational requirements can be a limitation. On the other hand, BERT excels at understanding the context and meaning of text, making it suitable for tasks such as text classification and question-answering. Fine-tuning these models for specific tasks can be achieved using frameworks such as Hugging Face's Transformers library, which provides tools and pre-trained models to streamline the process.

By discussing the trade-offs between these models and providing practical examples of how to fine-tune them using Hugging Face's Transformers library, developers can better understand how to leverage these powerful tools to meet their project's specific needs.

A step-by-step guide to integrating a generative language model into your development workflow

To integrate a generative language model into your development workflow, you can follow these steps:

1. Choose the generative language model that best suits your needs.

2. Use an NLP library to load and use the model.

3. Develop an API to expose the functionality of the model. This may involve defining endpoint routes, implementing request-handling functions, and setting up authentication and authorization.

4. Integrate the API into your development workflow. This may involve adding API calls to your code, setting up triggers to invoke the API, and implementing logic to handle API responses.

The generative language models are shaping the future of content creation. They offer a powerful and efficient approach to creating high-quality content that is personalized for each user. As this technology continues to evolve, we look forward to seeing how it will continue to drive innovation in content creation. In the next section, we'll use the GPT-2 Simple library to generate text, further exploring the capabilities of these models.

Exploring text generation with GPT-2 Simple

In this section, we will delve into the practical application of generative language models for text generation. Specifically, we'll be using the **GPT-2 Simple** library, a powerful tool that simplifies the process of leveraging the GPT-2 model developed by OpenAI. This library provides an accessible and efficient way to generate text, making it an excellent resource for both beginners and experienced practitioners in the field of NLP. To do this, follow these steps:

1. Import the `gpt_2_simple` library as `gpt2`:

```
import gpt_2_simple as gpt2
```

2. Download the GPT-2 model. The `"124M"` model is one of the smaller models and is a good starting point:

```
gpt2.download_gpt2(model_name="124M")
```

3. Start a TensorFlow session and load the GPT-2 model:

```
sess = gpt2.start_tf_sess()
gpt2.load_gpt2(sess, model_name="124M")
```

4. Generate text using the GPT-2 model. The generated text starts with the prefix `"The future of AI is"` and has a length of 100 tokens:

```
text = gpt2.generate(
    sess,
```

```
        model_name="124M",
        prefix=" The future of AI is",
        length=100,
        return_as_list=True
) [0]
```

5. Print the generated text:

    ```
    print(text)
    ```

Indeed, the GPT-2 Simple library provides a powerful and accessible way to generate diverse and creative text, opening new avenues for content creation and language-based applications. As we harness the capabilities of generative language models, we're not only enhancing our understanding of these models but also discovering innovative ways to apply them.

As we move forward, we'll continue to delve deeper into more advanced techniques and libraries that allow us to further leverage the capabilities of generative language models. This exploration will be particularly relevant as we embark on our next project: an AI movie recommendation chatbot.

The example of an AI movie recommendation chatbot

In this project, we will develop a movie recommendation chatbot using the **MovieLens** dataset. The chatbot will understand user preferences and recommend suitable movies based on the similarity of user ratings.

Project overview

The workflow of this project includes the following steps:

1. **Telegram token**: Generate a token for the Telegram bot (see the *Detailed steps to configure the bot* subsection).

2. **Data preprocessing**: Load and prepare the data for further processing.

3. **ML model training**: Use the preprocessed data to train our ML model.

4. **Chatbot implementation**: Use the trained model to implement the chatbot functionality.

5. **Chatbot testing and evaluation**: Test the chatbot and evaluate its performance.

Key features

Here are the key features of the chatbot:

- **Movie recommendation**: The chatbot provides movie recommendations based on a given movie title.

- **User-friendly chat interface**: It's interactive and easy to use with Telegram.

Data description

We will use the MovieLens dataset, a widely used dataset for movie recommendations. This dataset includes information about users, their ratings, and the movies they rated. You can access and download the dataset at `https://files.grouplens.org/datasets/movielens/ml-latest-small.zip`.

Step-by-step Python code

Let's dive into the step-by-step Python code to build our chatbot using the MovieLens dataset:

1. **Install the necessary libraries**: First, we need to install the required libraries for our project:

   ```
   !pip install sqlalchemy pandas scikit-surprise textblob spacy
   python-telegram-bot nest-asyncio
   !python -m spacy download en_core_web_sm
   ```

2. **Import the required libraries**: Next, we must import the necessary libraries for data handling, model training, and chatbot implementation:

   ```
   import threading
   import asyncio
   import pandas as pd
   from surprise import Dataset, Reader, SVD
   import urllib.request
   import zipfile
   import os
   from sqlalchemy import create_engine, Column, Integer, String,
   Float
   from sqlalchemy.orm import declarative_base, sessionmakerfrom
   textblob import TextBlob
   import spacy
   from telegram import Update
   from telegram.ext import Application, CommandHandler,
   MessageHandler, filters, CallbackContext
   import nest_asyncio
   from google.colab import userdata
   ```

3. **Load the spaCy model**: Load the `spaCy model` for NER:

   ```
   # Load spaCy model
   nlp = spacy.load("en_core_web_sm")
   ```

4. **Apply the patch to allow the use of asyncio in Jupyter Notebook**: We apply a patch to enable asyncio operations within Jupyter Notebook:

   ```
   nest_asyncio.apply()
   ```

5. **Download and unzip the MovieLens dataset**: We need to download and extract the MovieLens dataset:

```
url = 'https://files.grouplens.org/datasets/movielens/ml-latest-
small.zip'
urllib.request.urlretrieve(url, 'ml-latest-small.zip')

with zipfile.ZipFile('ml-latest-small.zip', 'r') as zip_ref:
    zip_ref.extractall()

movies_file = os.path.join('ml-latest-small', 'movies.csv')
ratings_file = os.path.join('ml-latest-small', 'ratings.csv')
```

6. **Load the data**: We must load the movies and ratings data into `pandas` DataFrames:

```
movies = pd.read_csv(movies_file)
ratings = pd.read_csv(ratings_file)
```

7. **Insert the data into the database**: We need to configure the SQLite database and insert the data:

```
# Configure the SQLite database
DATABASE_URL = 'sqlite:///movies.db'
engine = create_engine(DATABASE_URL)
Base = declarative_base()

# Define the ORM classes
class Movie(Base):
    __tablename__ = 'movies'
    movieId = Column(Integer, primary_key=True)
    title = Column(String)
    genres = Column(String)

class Rating(Base):
    __tablename__ = 'ratings'
    id = Column(Integer, primary_key=True, autoincrement=True)
    userId = Column(Integer, index=True)
    movieId = Column(Integer, index=True)
    rating = Column(Float)
    timestamp = Column(Integer)

# Create the tables in the database
Base.metadata.create_all(engine)

# Configure the session
Session = sessionmaker(bind=engine)
session = Session()

# Download and unzip the MovieLens dataset
```

```
url = 'https://files.grouplens.org/datasets/movielens/ml-latest-
small.zip'
urllib.request.urlretrieve(url, 'ml-latest-small.zip')

with zipfile.ZipFile('ml-latest-small.zip', 'r') as zip_ref:
    zip_ref.extractall()

# Full path to the files
movies_file = os.path.join('ml-latest-small', 'movies.csv')
ratings_file = os.path.join('ml-latest-small', 'ratings.csv')

# Load the data
movies = pd.read_csv(movies_file)
ratings = pd.read_csv(ratings_file)

# Insert the data into the database
movies.to_sql(
    'movies',
    engine,
    if_exists='replace',
    index=False
)
ratings.to_sql(
    'ratings',
    engine,
    if_exists='replace',
    index=False
)
```

8. **Prepare the data for the Surprise library**: We prepare the ratings data for use with the Surprise library:

```
# Prepare the data for the Surprise library
reader = Reader(rating_scale=(0.5, 5.0))
data = Dataset.load_from_df(
    ratings[['userId', 'movieId', 'rating']],
    reader
)

# Split the data into training and test sets
trainset = data.build_full_trainset()
```

9. **Train the Singular Value Decomposition (SVD) model**: We must then train the SVD model on the training data:

```
# Train the SVD model
algo = SVD()
algo.fit(trainset)
```

10. **Define the Movie Recommendation function**: We will now define a function to recommend movies based on a given movie title:

```
# Function to get movie recommendations from the database
def get_movie_recommendations_from_db(
        movie_id, num_recommendations=5):

    users_who_rated_movie = session.query(Rating.userId).filter(
        Rating.movieId == movie_id
).distinct().all()

users_who_rated_movie = [u[0] for u in users_who_rated_movie]

other_movie_ids = session.query(Rating.movieId).filter(
    Rating.userId.in_(users_who_rated_movie)
).distinct().all()

other_movie_ids = [m[0] for m in other_movie_ids]

predicted_ratings = []
for mid in other_movie_ids:
    if mid != movie_id:
        predicted_ratings.append(
            (mid, algo.predict(uid=0, iid=mid).est)
        )

predicted_ratings.sort(key=lambda x: x[1], reverse=True)
top_n_movies = [movie_id for movie_id, rating
                in predicted_ratings[:num_recommendations]]

recommended_movies = session.query(Movie.title).filter(
    Movie.movieId.in_(top_n_movies)
).all()

return [m[0] for m in recommended_movies]

# Function to check if a movie title exists
def check_movie_title(title, session):
    result = session.query(Movie).filter(
        Movie.title.ilike(f'%{title}%')
    ).all()
    return result

# Function for sentiment analysis
def analyze_sentiment(text):
    blob = TextBlob(text)
```

```
            return blob.sentiment

    # Function for named entity recognition
    def extract_entities(text):
        doc = nlp(text)
        entities = [(ent.text, ent.label_) for ent in doc.ents]
        return entities
```

11. **Set up the Telegram bot**: We will then set up a Telegram bot to interact with users and provide movie recommendations:

```
    # Token for your bot (Using 'secrets' functionality in
      Google Colab)
    TOKEN = userdata.get('YOUR_TELEGRAM_BOT_TOKEN')

    # Function to start the bot
    async def start(update: Update, context: CallbackContext) -> None:
        await update.message.reply_text(
            "Welcome to the Movie Recommendation CLI!\n"
            "Enter a movie title or a message (or <exit> to quit):"
        )

    # Function for handling text messages
    async def handle_message(update: Update, context: CallbackContext)
    -> None:
        user_input = update.message.text.strip()
        if user_input.lower() == 'exit':
            await update.message.reply_text("Goodbye!")
            return

    # Sentiment analysis
    sentiment = analyze_sentiment(user_input)
    await update.message.reply_text(
        f"Sentiment Analysis: Polarity = {sentiment.polarity}, "
        f"Subjectivity = {sentiment.subjectivity}"
    )

    # Recognition of named entities
    entities = extract_entities(user_input)
    await update.message.reply_text(
        f"Named Entities: {entities}"
    )

    # Movie search
    found_movies = check_movie_title(user_input, session)

    if found_movies:
```

```
            context.user_data['found_movies'] = found_movies
            movie_list = '\n'.join(
                f"{idx+1}. {movie.title} (ID: {movie.movieId})"
                for idx, movie in enumerate(found_movies)
            )
            await update.message.reply_text(
                f"Found {len(found_movies)} movie(s):\n{movie_list}\n\n"
                "Please enter the number of the movie for recommendations:"
            )
        else:
            await update.message.reply_text(
                f"No movies found with title '{user_input}'. Please try "
                f"again"
            )


# Function to recommend movies
async def recommend_movies(
    update: Update,
    context: CallbackContext
) -> None:
    try:
        idx = int(update.message.text.strip()) - 1
        found_movies = context.user_data.get('found_movies', [])

        if 0 <= idx < len(found_movies):
            movie = found_movies[idx]
            recommendations = get_movie_recommendations_from_db(
                movie.movieId
            )

            if recommendations:
                rec_message = '\n'.join(
                    f"{i+1}. {rec}" for i, rec in
                    enumerate(recommendations)
                )
                await update.message.reply_text(
                    f"Recommendations for '{movie.title}':\n"
                    f"{rec_message}"
                )
            else:
                await update.message.reply_text(
                    f"No recommendations found for '{movie."
                    f"title}'."
                )
        else:
```

```
            await update.message.reply_text(
                "Invalid selection. Please enter a valid number."
            )
    except (ValueError, IndexError):
        await update.message.reply_text(
            "Invalid selection. Please enter a valid number."
        )

    await update.message.reply_text(
        "Enter a movie title or a message (or 'exit' to quit):"
    )
```

12. **Configure and run the bot**: We must then configure the bot to use the defined functions and start polling for updates:

```
# Function to run the bot
def run_bot():
    asyncio.set_event_loop(asyncio.new_event_loop())
    application = Application.builder().token(TOKEN).build()
    application.add_handler(CommandHandler("start", start))
    application.add_handler(
        MessageHandler(
            filters.Regex(r'^\d+$'),
            recommend_movies
        )
    )
    application.add_handler(
        MessageHandler(
            filters.TEXT & ~filters.COMMAND,
            handle_message
        )
    )
    asyncio.get_event_loop().run_until_complete(
        application.run_polling(stop_signals=None)
    )

# Bot configuration
def main():
    thread = threading.Thread(target=run_bot)
    thread.start()

if __name__ == '__main__':
    main()
```

With these steps, we've set up a functional Telegram bot that is capable of recommending movies based on user input. This bot leverages the MovieLens dataset and the Surprise library to train an SVD model for collaborative filtering.

Detailed steps to configure the bot

This section provides a step-by-step guide to configure a Telegram bot using BotFather and the python-telegram-bot library. Follow these instructions to set up your bot and integrate it into your application.

1. **Create a new bot**:

    I.   **Access BotFather**: Open the Telegram app and search for *BotFather*.

    II.   **Start a chat**: Begin a conversation with BotFather.

    III.   **Create a new bot**: Use the `/newbot` command.

    IV.   **Choose a name**: Follow the instructions to select a name for your bot.

    V.   **Choose a username**: Select a username for your bot, which must end with `Bot` (e.g., `MovieRecBot`).

    VI.   **Copy the token**: After creating the bot, BotFather will provide you with a token. Copy this token for later use.

2. **Install the python-telegram-bot library**:

    I.   Open your terminal or command prompt.

    II.   Run the following command to install the necessary library:

    ```
    pip install python-telegram-bot
    ```

3. **Configure the bot in Python code**:

    I.   Open your Python development environment (e.g., Google Colab, Jupyter Notebook, VSCode, or PyCharm).

    II.   Paste the following code, replacing `'YOUR_TELEGRAM_BOT_TOKEN'` with the token you copied from BotFather:

    ```
    # Token for your bot
    TOKEN = userdata.get('YOUR_TELEGRAM_BOT_TOKEN')
    ```

> **Note for Google Colab users utilizing secret functionality**
>
> This notebook is designed to be run on Google Colab. If you are using Google Colab, you will need to include the token in the `secrets` functionality:
>
> **Name**: YOUR_TELEGRAM_BOT_TOKEN
>
> **Value**: Insert the token generated by the reader on Telegram as instructed in the preceding subsection
>
> If you are using environments other than Google Colab, you will need to adapt the code to include the token.

For users working in environments other than Google Colab, an adjustment to the code will be necessary.

> **Note for users not using Google Colab Secret**
>
> If you are using environments other than Google Colab, you will need to adapt the code to include the token directly:
>
> # Token for your bot (replace `'YOUR_TELEGRAM_BOT_TOKEN'` with your actual token)
> `TOKEN = 'YOUR_TELEGRAM_BOT_TOKEN'`.

With these steps, we've set up a functional Telegram bot that is capable of recommending movies based on user input. This bot leverages the MovieLens dataset and the `Surprise` library to train an SVD model for collaborative filtering.

Testing the chatbot

To test the chatbot, follow these steps:

1. Ensure that you have installed the necessary libraries.
2. Run the provided code to start the bot.
3. Open Telegram and search for your bot using the bot token.
4. Start a conversation with the bot by typing `/start`.
5. Send the bot the title of a movie from the dataset, such as `Toy Story (1995)`.
6. The bot should respond with a list of recommended movies based on your input.

The chatbot will be able to recommend movies based on the user's preferences. It can be further improved by adding more features, such as recommendations based on rating.

This project demonstrated how to create an AI-powered movie recommendation chatbot using the MovieLens dataset and the `Surprise` library. While this example provided a basic implementation, there are several limitations to consider for real-world applications. The model needs to handle contextual understanding and error paths, as well as integrate with existing movie databases. Additionally, employing generative AI can enhance human-like interactions and make recommendations feel more natural and personalized. Using ML models such as collaborative filtering for personalized content recommendations is just the beginning; further refinements are necessary to create a fully functional and user-friendly chatbot.

You can download the complete project on GitHub at: `https://github.com/PacktPublishing/AI-Strategies-for-Web-Development/blob/main/ch9/Movie_Recommender_with_Telegram_Bot.ipynb`

Summary

In this chapter, we delved into the realm of advanced AI for user interactions. We embarked on a journey to develop several exciting projects that enhanced user engagement and created a more immersive web experience. We introduced you to our project, an AI movie recommendation chatbot, and created a simple chatbot using the `ChatterBot` library.

We explored the power of voice interactions by using the `SpeechRecognition` library to transcribe audio and delved into sentiment analysis using the `TextBlob` library. We ventured into the world of generative AI by using the GPT-2 Simple library to generate text.

In the next chapter, we will delve into smart testing strategies and learn how to fortify web applications with AI insights. Stay tuned!

10

Smart Testing Strategies – Fortifying Web Applications with AI Insights

Following the practices of test automation, we delve into the realm of testing strategies that leverage AI to enhance the security, performance, and reliability of web applications. In this chapter, we will explore how cutting-edge AI technologies can revolutionize the testing phase, providing valuable insights and uncovering potential issues that traditional methods might overlook.

The first section will introduce you to the concept of smart testing with AI. Next, we will learn to use AI tools to optimize and automate performance testing. We will gain proficiency in leveraging AI for comprehensive security testing and learn to integrate AI-driven bias detection into web application testing. Finally, we will understand and apply AI-based techniques for reliability and validity testing.

In this chapter, we will cover the following main topics:

- Introduction to Smart Testing with AI
- AI-Enhanced Performance Testing
- Intelligent Security Testing Protocols
- AI-Driven Bias Detection and Mitigation
- Reliability and Validity Assurance through AI

By the end of this chapter, you will have understood the concepts and principles of smart testing with AI and how to use AI tools to optimize and automate performance testing. You will also know how to set up support for comprehensive security testing using AI and integrate AI-driven bias detection into web application testing. Finally, you will understand and apply AI-based techniques for reliability and validity testing.

Introduction to Smart Testing with AI

In the evolving landscape of web application testing, we find ourselves at the crossroads where traditional methods intersect with the innovative capabilities of AI. This juncture, known as smart testing, is transforming the way we approach the security, performance, and reliability of web applications.

The journey of this chapter begins with an exploration of the principles and concepts underpinning smart testing with AI. We delve into the transformative role of AI in testing, its potential to automate tasks, identify patterns, predict risk areas, and optimize test execution. The tangible benefits of smart testing, such as cost reduction, improved security, and increased speed of the testing process, are also brought to the forefront.

Benefits of smart testing One of the areas most impacted by this revolution is the field of **software testing**. In this section, we will delve deeply into the concepts and principles of smart testing with AI.

Smart testing with AI is an approach that uses AI to automate and optimize the software testing process. It is based on the idea that AI can learn and improve from experience, and can be used to learn about the software being tested and make predictions about where bugs might occur. Let's explore the benefits of intelligent testing with AI, an approach that is redefining the boundaries of what is possible.

- One of the most tangible benefits of intelligent testing with AI is *cost reduction*. AI, with its ability to automate tasks and increase efficiency, has the potential to transform the economic landscape of software testing. With AI, we can carry out more tests in less time, optimizing the use of resources and, consequently, reducing costs.

- AI also plays a crucial role in *improving software security*. It can help identify vulnerabilities that may go undetected by manual testing. In a world where cyber security is a growing concern, AI's ability to identify and fix these vulnerabilities is an invaluable asset. With AI, we can ensure that our software is not only functional, but also secure and reliable.

- Another benefit of intelligent testing with AI is *increased speed*. AI can speed up the testing process, allowing developers to release applications more quickly. In a world where speed to market can be a competitive differentiator, the agility provided by AI is a valuable asset.

With a clear understanding of the significant advantages that smart testing with AI offers, such as cost reduction, enhanced security, and increased speed, we are well-equipped to appreciate its impact on the software development lifecycle. Now, let's delve into the key concepts behind smart testing with AI and explore how these can be practically implemented to transform your testing strategy.

Key concepts and implementation

AI is becoming increasingly prevalent in our daily lives, and the software that powers it needs to be tested effectively. Smart testing with AI allows companies to ensure the quality of their software, reduce time to market, and save operational costs.

There are several key concepts that are fundamental to smart testing with AI:

- **Machine Learning**: Smart testing with AI uses machine learning algorithms to learn about the software and predict where bugs might occur.

- **Test Automation**: AI is capable of automating many of the manual tasks involved in software testing, increasing the efficiency and accuracy of tests.

- **Data Analysis**: AI can analyze large volumes of test data to identify patterns and trends that might indicate software quality issues.

- **Adaptation and Continuous Learning**: AI has the ability to learn and improve with experience. This means that the more tests are carried out, the more effective the AI becomes at predicting and identifying bugs.

Implementing smart testing with AI involves several steps:

- **Define Testing Goals**: Before you start testing, it's important to clearly define what you hope to achieve with your tests.

- **Collect Test Data**: Test data is the foundation of smart testing with AI. The more data you have, the more effective your testing will be.

- **Train AI Models**: Use your test data to train AI models that can predict where bugs might occur.

- **Implement Automated Tests**: Use your AI models to automate your tests and identify bugs more efficiently.

- **Analyze Test Results**: Analyze the results of your tests to identify patterns and trends and improve your future testing efforts.

There are many examples of companies that are using smart testing with AI to improve the quality of their software. For example, Microsoft uses AI to test Windows 10, allowing them to identify and fix bugs more quickly than ever before.

To wrap it up, smart testing with AI represents a new frontier in the field of software testing. By understanding the underlying concepts and principles, we can begin to explore the full potential of this innovative approach. So, let's dive into the world of smart testing with AI and discover what it has to offer.

AI-Enhanced Performance Testing

AI has revolutionized the field of performance testing by enabling us to optimize and automate the process. By harnessing the power of artificial intelligence, we can now identify trends, failure patterns, and critical areas for improvements with unparalleled accuracy and efficiency.

Gone are the days of manually sifting through heaps of data to find insights. With AI, we can analyze vast amounts of information in a fraction of the time. This allows us to quickly pinpoint performance bottlenecks, detect anomalies, and identify areas that require further investigation.

One of the key advantages of AI-enhanced performance testing is its ability to *uncover hidden patterns and correlations*. By leveraging advanced machine learning algorithms, we can identify the underlying causes of performance issues and develop targeted solutions. This not only saves time and resources but also ensures that the improvements we make are tailored to the specific needs of our system.

Moreover, AI can adapt and learn from past performance testing results, continuously improving its ability to predict and prevent future issues. This proactive approach allows us to stay one step ahead, mitigating potential problems before they impact our system's performance.

Another benefit of AI in performance testing is its ability to provide real-time insights. By monitoring system performance in real-time, AI algorithms can detect anomalies as they occur, alerting us to potential issues before they escalate. This proactive monitoring ensures that our system operates at its optimal level, minimizing downtime and maximizing user satisfaction.

It is possible to identify several AI algorithms that can be useful for smart testing. Here are some detailed examples:

- **Decision Trees**: Decision trees are machine learning models that use a tree structure to represent a series of possible decision paths and their final outcomes. In the context of smart testing, decision trees can be used to understand the relationships between different variables in the software. For example, they can help identify which combinations of inputs lead to software failures.

- **Neural Networks**: Neural networks are computing systems inspired by the human brain that are excellent at identifying complex patterns in data. In smart testing, neural networks can be used to analyze test data and predict where bugs might occur. For example, a neural network can be trained on past test data and used to predict the likelihood of failure for new test cases.

- **Clustering Algorithms**: Clustering algorithms, like K-means, are unsupervised learning techniques that group similar data. In the context of smart testing, these algorithms can be used to group similar test cases, which can help identify problematic areas in the software. For example, if a large number of failing test cases are in the same cluster, this could indicate an area of the software that needs special attention.

- **Reinforcement Learning**: Reinforcement learning is a type of machine learning where agents learn optimal behaviors through trial and error, interacting directly with their environment. This method is particularly useful in the realm of smart testing, as it allows a software testing agent to discover efficient strategies and make informed decisions on its own. By continuously adjusting its actions based on the feedback received from the outcomes of tests, the agent can optimize the testing process, enhancing effectiveness and efficiency. The agent can learn which actions (e.g., test inputs) lead to rewards (e.g., detecting a bug) and adjust its behavior accordingly.

Each of these algorithms has its own advantages and disadvantages, and the choice of the right algorithm depends on the specific needs of your testing project. By understanding how these algorithms work and how they can be applied to testing, you will be better equipped to implement smart testing with AI.

Python Libraries for Performance Testing

Performance testing is a critical aspect of software development. It helps ensure that applications run smoothly under their expected workload. Python, known for its simplicity and readability, offers a variety of libraries that can aid in the performance testing process.

In this section, we will explore some of these libraries and how they can be utilized to enhance performance testing.

- **timeit**: The timeit module in Python is designed to help developers measure the execution time of small code snippets accurately. It is equipped with both a command-line interface and a callable interface, making it versatile for various testing scenarios. The design of timeit helps avoid several common pitfalls associated with timing functions, ensuring that the measurements are both reliable and repeatable. This tool is essential for optimizing code by pinpointing performance bottlenecks.

- **cProfile**: The cProfile module is an integral part of Python, designed specifically for profiling Python applications. This module generates a profile, which comprises statistics detailing the frequency and duration of execution for different segments of the program. Utilizing cProfile, developers can gain insights into the performance characteristics of their applications, helping to identify areas where optimization is needed to enhance efficiency.

- **Py-Spy**: It isa powerful sampling profiler for Python applications. This tool provides a clear visualization of where a Python program is allocating its time, all without the need for restarting the program or making any alterations to its code. Py-Spy operates discreetly in the background, offering developers a detailed overview of performance bottlenecks and runtime efficiency, which is invaluable for optimizing and streamlining application performance.

- **Yappi**: Yappi (**Yet Another Python Profiler**) is a profiler that tracks thread and greenlet activity. It allows you to profile multi-threaded Python programs.

- **memory-profiler**: Memory-profiler is a module designed for Python that allows for meticulous tracking of a program's memory usage. This tool is particularly useful as it provides both an overall assessment of a process's memory consumption and detailed, line-by-line analysis. By employing memory-profiler, developers can pinpoint where their Python programs are most memory-intensive, facilitating targeted optimizations to enhance efficiency and performance.

- **Multi-Mechanize**: Multi-Mechanize is a freely available framework used for conducting performance and load tests on websites and web services. This tool enables users to execute multiple Python scripts concurrently to simulate traffic and interactions, effectively testing how well a site or service performs under stress. By using Multi-Mechanize, developers can identify potential bottlenecks and ensure their application can handle expected user loads gracefully.

- **Locust**: Locust is an accessible, distributed load testing tool designed to assess the capacity of websites and other systems to handle concurrent users. Its user-friendly interface allows developers to simulate traffic and test system performance under various load conditions. This tool is invaluable for determining the maximum number of simultaneous users a system can support before performance begins to degrade.

The choice of library depends on the specific needs of your project and the system you are testing. Therefore, it's crucial to research and experiment with different options to find the best solution for you. Always ensure that any library you choose is up-to-date and maintained, as outdated libraries can introduce performance issues.

By leveraging these libraries, developers can automate their tasks, identify performance bottlenecks more efficiently, and optimize their code for better performance. As we continue to advance in the field of software development, these tools will undoubtedly play a crucial role in shaping efficient and high-performing applications.

Enhancing Performance Testing with Machine Learning

As AI experts, we are always looking for ways to optimize and automate our processes. One of these ways is through the use of AI tools to enhance our performance testing.

Consider a scenario where we are testing the performance of an e-commerce website, in particular. We can use machine learning algorithms to analyze the test data and identify critical scenarios, such as increased traffic during a flash sale.

```
from sklearn.ensemble import IsolationForest

# Train the machine learning model
model = IsolationForest(contamination=0.01)
model.fit(test_data)

# Identify critical scenarios
critical_scenarios = model.predict(test_data)
```

To illustrate, we are using the `IsolationForest` algorithm from the `sklearn` library to identify critical scenarios. This algorithm is particularly useful for anomaly detection, which allows us to identify scenarios that are significantly different from the norm.

Furthermore, we can use machine learning algorithms to automatically adjust the test loads based on the system conditions. This means we can ensure that our tests are always reflecting the real conditions that our systems will face, allowing us to identify and fix issues before they affect end users.

```
from sklearn.linear_model import LinearRegression

# Train the machine learning model
```

```
model = LinearRegression()
model.fit(load_data, performance_data)

# Adjust the test load
predicted_performance = model.predict(new_load_data)
```

In this example, we are using the `LinearRegression` algorithm to predict the system performance based on the test load. This allows us to adjust the test load to ensure we are always testing our system under the most relevant conditions.

So, the application of machine learning algorithms allows us to optimize our performance testing, saving time and resources, while ensuring that our systems are always performing at their best. By adopting these tools and techniques, we can ensure that we are always one step ahead, ready to face the challenges of the future.

Having established the importance and benefits of AI in performance testing, let's now turn our attention to another critical aspect of system development - security.

In the next section, we will delve into the realm of Intelligent Security Testing Protocols, exploring how we can leverage AI to fortify our systems against potential threats and vulnerabilities.

Intelligent Security Testing Protocols

In today's digital landscape, where cyber threats are becoming increasingly sophisticated, it is crucial for organizations to integrate security testing solutions that employ AI. These intelligent protocols are designed to identify vulnerabilities, detect potential threats, and fortify defenses against cyber attacks. In this section, we will explore the significance of leveraging AI for comprehensive security testing and provide insights into best practices and techniques.

One of the key advantages of intelligent security testing protocols is their ability to analyze vast amounts of data in real-time. By utilizing AI algorithms, these protocols can quickly identify patterns and anomalies that may indicate potential vulnerabilities or threats. For example, AI-powered security testing tools can analyze network traffic to detect any suspicious activities or behavior that may suggest an ongoing attack.

Another benefit of leveraging AI for security testing is the ability to automate the process and reduce the reliance on manual efforts. Traditional security testing methods often require significant human resources and time, which can be costly and inefficient. With intelligent protocols, organizations can automate the testing process, allowing for continuous monitoring and faster identification of vulnerabilities. This not only saves time and resources but also ensures that security measures are up to date and effective against emerging threats.

To gain proficiency in leveraging AI for comprehensive security testing, organizations should consider the following best practices:

- **Understand the capabilities and limitations**: It is essential to have a clear understanding of what AI can and cannot do in the context of security testing. While AI algorithms can be powerful in identifying patterns and anomalies, they may not be foolproof and can still miss certain types of threats.

- **Implement a layered security approach**: Intelligent security testing protocols should be integrated into a larger security framework that includes multiple layers of protection. This can include firewalls, intrusion detection systems, encryption, and user access controls. By combining different security measures, organizations can create a robust defense system that can withstand various types of attacks.

- **Stay updated with the latest AI advancements**: AI technology is continuously evolving, and new algorithms and techniques are being developed to enhance security testing capabilities. It is crucial for organizations to stay updated with the latest advancements and incorporate them into their testing protocols. This can involve attending conferences, participating in training programs, and collaborating with AI experts.

Intelligent security testing protocols that leverage AI are essential in today's digital landscape. By integrating these protocols, organizations can enhance their ability to identify vulnerabilities, detect threats, and fortify their defenses against cyber attacks. By following best practices and staying updated with the latest advancements, organizations can gain proficiency in leveraging AI for comprehensive security testing and ensure the protection of their digital assets.

Python Libraries for Enhanced Security Testing

In the rapidly evolving landscape of cybersecurity, the need for robust and efficient security testing tools has never been more critical. Python offers a plethora of libraries specifically designed for security testing. These libraries, backed by a vibrant community of developers and cybersecurity professionals, provide a comprehensive toolkit to tackle various security testing tasks.

In this section, we delve into some of these libraries, shedding light on their functionalities and how they can be harnessed to fortify cybersecurity defenses.

- **OWASP ZAP**: The **Zed Attack Proxy** (**ZAP**) is a globally recognized free security tool. It is designed to automatically discover security vulnerabilities in web applications during the development and testing phases.

- **Scapy**: It is a powerful tool created with Python for interactive packet manipulation. It allows users to craft or decode packets across numerous protocols, send them across networks, capture them, and even facilitate interactions between requests and replies among other features. This flexibility makes Scapy an invaluable resource in network testing and security assessments.

- **PyCryptodome**: `PyCryptodome` is a standalone Python package of low-level cryptographic primitives. It supports a broad range of encryption and hashing algorithms.

- **Metasploit Framework**: Although not a Python library itself, the Metasploit Framework is a formidable penetration testing tool that has Python bindings available. It enables the creation of custom exploits and the automation of penetration testing activities.

- **hashlib**: `hashlib` is a Python standard library that provides a set of hash functions, including MD5, SHA1, and SHA256, among others. It's instrumental in verifying data integrity.

- **Burp Suite**: Similar to Metasploit, Burp Suite is not a Python library itself, but it is a tool that can be used alongside Python for security testing. It is a graphical tool for testing Web application security.

- **PyOD**: `PyOD` is a versatile Python library dedicated to identifying outliers in complex, multivariate datasets, an area commonly known as outlier or anomaly detection. This toolkit offers a wide array of methods for effectively spotting unusual data points which can be pivotal for robust data analysis.

- **Snyk**: Snyk is a developer-first security tool that assists organizations in using open source securely. It is designed to be used in the Software Development Life Cycle (SDLC) and can be seamlessly integrated into existing security tooling.

The choice of library depends on the specific needs of your project and the system you are testing. Therefore, it's crucial to research and experiment with different options to find the best solution for you. Always ensure that any library you choose is up-to-date and maintained, as outdated libraries can introduce security vulnerabilities.

Python, with its wide range of dedicated libraries, serves as a robust language for security testing. By leveraging these libraries, security professionals can automate their tasks, identify vulnerabilities more efficiently, and fortify defenses against cyber threats. As we continue to advance in the field of cybersecurity, these tools will undoubtedly play a crucial role in shaping a secure digital landscape. Remember, security is not a one-time task but an ongoing process that requires continuous learning and adaptation.

Python Code Examples for Intelligent Security Testing

In this section, we will explore several Python code examples that demonstrate different techniques and libraries used for conducting security testing with AI.

OWASP ZAP to perform a penetration test

Let's consider a practical example of how we can use AI for security testing. In this example, we will use the Python library OWASP ZAP to perform a penetration test on a website.

```
# Importing the necessary library
from zapv2 import ZAPv2
import time

# Defining the target of our test
target = 'http://yourwebsite.com'

# Creating an instance of ZAP
zap = ZAPv2()

# Starting the scanner
zap.urlopen(target)
scanid = zap.spider.scan(target)

# Checking the progress of the scanner
while (int(zap.spider.status(scanid)) < 100):
    print('Spider progress %: ' + zap.spider.status(scanid))
    time.sleep(2)

print('Spider completed')

# Starting the active scanner
scanid = zap.ascan.scan(target)
while (int(zap.ascan.status(scanid)) < 100):
    print('Active scanner progress %: ' + zap.ascan.status(scanid))
    time.sleep(2)

print('Active scanner completed')

# Printing the results
print('Vulnerabilities found:')
print(zap.core.alerts())
```

This code performs a penetration test on the specified website, identifying potential vulnerabilities. First, it starts a *Spider*, which crawls the website to gather information. Then, it starts an active scanner, which uses the information gathered by the Spider to test for potential vulnerabilities. Finally, it prints all the found vulnerabilities.

Anomaly Detection with PyOD:

PyOD is a Python library for anomaly detection. It provides various techniques to identify anomalies in a dataset.

```
from pyod.models.knn import KNN
from pyod.utils.data import generate_data

# Generating a sample dataset
X_train, y_train, X_test, y_test = generate_data(n_train=200, n_
test=100, n_features=2)

# Creating a KNN model
clf = KNN()

# Training the model
clf.fit(X_train)

# Getting the predictions
y_train_pred = clf.labels_
y_train_scores = clf.decision_scores_
```

Having explored how PyOD can be effectively utilized for anomaly detection, let's shift our focus to applying machine learning to enhance security measures. In the next section, we will dive into how Scikit-learn can be employed for classifying security logs, further empowering your data analysis capabilities within diverse workflows.

Security Log Classification with Scikit-learn:

Scikit-learn is a Python library for machine learning. It provides various techniques for classifying security logs.

```
from sklearn.feature_extraction.text import TfidfVectorizer
from sklearn.naive_bayes import MultinomialNB
from sklearn.pipeline import make_pipeline

# Creating a pipeline model
model = make_pipeline(TfidfVectorizer(), MultinomialNB())

# Training the model
model.fit(train_logs, train_labels)

# Predicting the categories of the test logs
labels = model.predict(test_logs)
```

In this example, we utilize Scikit-learn, a versatile machine learning library for Python, to classify security logs effectively. Here's a breakdown of the steps and components in the code:

- **TfidfVectorizer**: This component converts a collection of raw documents into a matrix of TF-IDF features. It's particularly useful in text mining and helps in emphasizing words that are more interesting, i.e., frequent in a document but not across documents.

- **MultinomialNB**: This stands for Multinomial Naive Bayes, an algorithm well-suited for text classification tasks that involve multiple categories. It's based on the Bayesian probability theory.

- **make_pipeline**: This function simplifies the steps of processing the data and applying the classifier. By using a pipeline, the vectorization and the application of the Naive Bayes algorithm are linked together. This ensures that all steps in the processing and classification are conducted within the pipeline, maintaining consistency in data handling.

`Training the model:` `model.fit(train_logs, train_labels)` trains the machine learning model using the `train_logs` as input data and `train_labels` as the target outcomes.

`Predicting the categories:` After the model is trained, it can predict the categories of new, unseen data. `model.predict(test_logs)` applies the trained model to `test_logs` to predict their categories.

This method is efficient for processing and classifying large volumes of text data, such as security logs, where it can help identify patterns and categorize entries based on their content.

Tips and Best Practices

-Always validate input and output data when working with AI.

-Stay up-to-date with the latest security vulnerabilities and patches.

-Use a defense-in-depth approach, do not rely on a single technique or tool.

-Regularly test your systems and fix any found vulnerabilities as soon as possible.

-Remember that security is an ongoing process and requires constant monitoring and regular updates.

There are many other libraries and techniques you can use to conduct security testing with AI. Some alternatives include TensorFlow for deep neural networks, Keras for high-level neural networks, and Pandas for data manipulation. The choice of library or technique depends on your specific needs and the system you are testing. Therefore, it's important to research and experiment with different options to find the best solution for you.

To sum up, these examples demonstrate how Python and AI can be leveraged to enhance security testing protocols. By integrating AI into our security testing, we can identify vulnerabilities, detect potential threats, and fortify defenses against cyber attacks more effectively and efficiently. As we continue to gain proficiency in leveraging AI for comprehensive security testing, we are not only keeping our systems secure but also staying ahead in the race against cybercriminals.

AI-Driven Bias Detection and Mitigation

In today's rapidly evolving technological landscape, it is crucial for web applications to integrate AI-driven bias detection into their testing processes. This ensures that potential biases present in the application's algorithms are identified and mitigated, guaranteeing fair and unbiased outcomes for all users.

Understanding bias, its detection and integration

Biases can be introduced into web applications in various ways, including:

- **Developer bias**: Developers can introduce bias into their web applications unconsciously, reflecting their own prejudices.

- **Biased training data**: The data used to train AI models may be biased, which can lead to biased models.

- **Biased test environments**: Test environments can be biased, which can lead to biased test results.

Bias detection involves identifying and analyzing biases that might exist within AI algorithms and models. By implementing AI-driven bias detection into web application testing, we can ensure that the systems we develop are fair, unbiased, and inclusive. This process involves examining the data used for training the AI models, identifying any biases or skewed representations, and taking corrective measures.

AI can be used to detect bias in web applications in a number of ways, including:

- **Data analysis**: AI can be used to analyze web application usage data to identify patterns that may indicate bias.

- **Code analysis**: AI can be used to analyze web application source code to identify patterns that may indicate bias.

- **Usability testing**: AI can be used to carry out automated usability tests to identify usability problems that may lead to biases.

To integrate AI-driven bias detection into web application testing, several steps can be followed:

- **Data collection and preprocessing**: Gather a diverse and representative dataset to train the AI models. Ensure that the data is unbiased and does not perpetuate any stereotypes or discriminatory practices. Preprocess the data to remove any biases or imbalances that might exist.

- **Bias detection algorithms**: Implement AI algorithms that can detect biases within the trained models. These algorithms analyze the output of the AI system and identify any discrepancies or unfair outcomes. They can detect biases related to gender, race, age, or any other protected characteristics.

- **Mitigation strategies**: Once biases are detected, it is crucial to develop mitigation strategies to address them. This can involve retraining the AI models with additional data to reduce bias, adjusting the decision-making process to ensure fairness, or implementing post-processing techniques to mitigate biases in the system's output.

- **Continuous monitoring and improvement**: Bias detection and mitigation should be an ongoing process. Regularly monitor the AI system's performance, collect feedback from users, and make necessary adjustments to reduce biases further. Continuous improvement is essential to ensure that the system remains fair and unbiased over time.

In addition to these steps, we are also employing several techniques to detect bias in AI:

- **Algorithm Bias**: This type of bias refers to a property of the AI algorithm itself. In the context of machine learning, bias, along with variance, describes a property of the algorithm that influences prediction performance.

- **Sensitivity Analysis**: This technique involves changing the input data and observing changes in the results. If small changes in the input data lead to large changes in the results, this could indicate the presence of bias.

- **Fairness Testing**: These are designed to detect whether a system is unfairly discriminating against certain groups. For example, a fairness test might check whether a movie recommendation system is equally recommending movies directed by men and women.

- **Model Auditing**: This technique involves inspecting the machine learning model itself to identify the presence of bias. This could involve analyzing the weights assigned to different features or analyzing the structure of the model.

- **Explainable AI (XAI)**: XAI is a research area that focuses on making machine learning models more interpretable. This can help identify bias by making it easier to understand how the model is making its decisions.

- **Statistical Adjustment**: Statistical adjustment is crucial in observational studies to address potential detection biases. It involves examining potential biases that could skew results and applying methods to adjust or stratify these biases to accurately interpret the relationships being studied. This approach helps in refining the associations observed and ensures that the findings are more reliable and reflective of true effects, rather than being distorted by external variables.

- **Statistical Process Control Charts**: Thiis technique involves applying statistical process control charts to detect when the mean of the bias becomes different from zero. Specifically, it suggests using CUSUM (Cumulative Sum Control Chart) and EWMA (Exponentially Weighted Moving Average Chart) charts. These advanced control charts provide a more effective means of identifying subtle process deviations, enabling quicker and more precise corrective actions.

By integrating AI-driven bias detection into web application testing, we can create more inclusive and equitable systems. It helps prevent discriminatory practices and ensures that AI technologies are used responsibly. By following the steps mentioned above and implementing best practices, we can mitigate biases and build AI systems that promote fairness and equality.

Let's build on one of our previous examples of a web application that makes movie recommendations to users. If we find that the application is primarily recommending movies directed by men, we might suspect there is a bias in the system. Using the bias detection techniques we've learned, we can investigate the issue, identify the source of the bias, and take steps to correct it. This might involve reevaluating our training data, reviewing our algorithms, or soliciting feedback from users to better understand their experiences.

The integration of AI-driven bias detection and mitigation into web application testing is crucial for ensuring fair and unbiased outcomes. By employing machine learning techniques, leveraging diverse datasets, and continuously updating algorithms, potential biases can be detected and addressed. Following a step-by-step approach and involving diverse stakeholders will further enhance the effectiveness of bias detection and mitigation efforts. Together, these practices contribute to the development of web applications that prioritize fairness and equality for all users.

AI Bias Detection Libraries

Bias detection in AI is an important area of research and several libraries have been developed to help researchers and developers identify and mitigate bias in their machine learning models.

Here are some of the most popular libraries, all available in Python:

- **Fairlearn**: This is an open source library that can be used to evaluate, understand and mitigate bias in machine learning models.

- **Aequitas**: An open source library that provides a set of tools for auditing the fairness of machine learning models.

- **AI Fairness 360 (AIF360)**: AI Fairness 360 (AIF360) is an innovative open-source tool created by IBM, designed to enhance the fairness of algorithms and datasets. It equips users with a robust suite of metrics to assess biases within datasets and models, along with detailed explanations of these metrics. Furthermore, AIF360 offers a variety of algorithms specifically tailored to reduce bias in both datasets and models, supporting efforts to build more equitable and just AI systems.

- **What-If Tool (WIT)**: Developed by Google, this tool allows you to visualize the impact of different variables on model performance, making it easier to identify bias.

- **SHAP (SHapley Additive exPlanations)**: This is an open source library for explaining the outputs of any machine learning model. It connects game theory with local fairness, consistency and accuracy.

- **Local Interpretable Model-Agnostic Explanations (Lime)**: This open-source library can be used to explain the predictions of any classifier or regressor in a faithful and interpretable way.

Each of these libraries has its own strengths and limitations, and choosing the right one depends on the specific context and requirements of your project. It's important to note that bias detection is an ongoing process that requires constant vigilance.

> **Tips**
> **Catalogue of Bias (CoB)**: Developed by the Oxford **Center for Evidence-Based Medicine (CEBM)**, this catalog guides researchers, health professionals, students, managers, among others, on the existence of different types of bias.

Reliability and Validity Assurance through AI

In today's fast-paced technological landscape, ensuring the *reliability and validity* of software applications is of utmost importance. To achieve this, understanding and applying AI-based techniques for reliability and validity testing have become essential.

AI presents a powerful toolset for proactive monitoring and predicting potential issues before they negatively impact the application in production. By harnessing the capabilities of AI, we can enhance the overall quality and performance of our software applications.

Testing and best practices

Reliability testing involves assessing the ability of an application to consistently perform its intended functions without failure. AI can play a crucial role in automating this process by analyzing vast amounts of data and identifying patterns that indicate potential reliability issues. With AI-powered reliability testing, we can detect and address vulnerabilities before they cause disruptions or compromise user experience.

On the other hand, **validity testing** focuses on ensuring that the application produces accurate and valid results. AI can assist in this aspect by analyzing data inputs and outputs, comparing them with expected outcomes, and identifying any discrepancies. By leveraging AI for validity testing, we can uncover hidden errors or biases that might affect the reliability and trustworthiness of our applications.

To implement AI-based reliability and validity assurance, there are several best practices to consider. First and foremost, it is crucial to establish a *comprehensive testing strategy* that integrates AI techniques seamlessly. This strategy should include defining relevant key performance indicators (KPIs) and metrics, as well as designing appropriate test scenarios and datasets.

Moreover, it is essential to *collect and curate high-quality data* that accurately represents the real-world usage and conditions of the application. This data will serve as the foundation for training AI models and validating their effectiveness in testing.

In addition to data, AI algorithms and models also need to be *continuously monitored and updated* to keep up with evolving software environments. Regular maintenance and refinement of AI systems will ensure their reliability and effectiveness in identifying potential issues.

To summarize, applying AI-based techniques for reliability and validity testing is a game-changer in the software development industry. By leveraging its power, we can proactively monitor and predict potential issues, enhance the reliability and validity of our applications, and ultimately deliver a seamless user experience.

Python Libraries for Reliability and Validity Testing

When it comes to data validation, having the right tools is crucial. There are several libraries available that offer a wide range of features to ensure the reliability and validity of your data. In this section, we will explore some popular libraries and discuss their strengths and best use cases.

- **Reliability** is a powerful Python library specifically designed for reliability engineering and survival analysis. It extends the functionality of `scipy.stats` and includes specialized tools that are typically only found in proprietary software. With Reliability, you can estimate probability distribution functions, perform survival analysis, conduct reliability analysis, run hypothesis tests, and even simulate reliability scenarios. This library is a must-have for reliability engineers and data analysts working with system and component reliability evaluation.

- **Pandas-dq** is the ultimate data quality tool for pandas dataframes. It offers a comprehensive set of tools for assessing data quality and identifying potential issues within datasets. With Pandas-dq, you can detect missing values, identify inconsistent data, spot outliers, find duplicate entries, and get an overall summary of data quality. This library is indispensable for any data analyst working with pandas dataframes.

- **Validator Collection** is a versatile Python library that provides over 60 functions for validating the type and content of input values. Whether you need to validate data types, check for valid values, set minimum and maximum lengths, or enforce specific format rules, Validator Collection has got you covered. This library is valuable for validating a wide range of data.

- **Datatest** is a library specifically designed to validate and document data behavior during testing. With Datatest, you can validate data, generate test data, and document your tests effectively. This library is particularly useful for software engineers who need to ensure the quality of their application's data.

- **Cerberus** is a lightweight and extensible data validation library that is based on regular expressions. It provides a simple syntax for defining validation rules. Cerberus is an excellent choice for applications that require efficient and flexible data validation.

- **Colander** is a library used to validate and deserialize data obtained from XML, JSON, or HTML form posts. It offers a convenient solution for validating structured data formats. If your application deals with structured formats, Colander is a great choice for data validation.

- **Jsonschema** is a Python implementation of JSON Schema. It allows you to validate JSON data against a JSON schema. If your application requires JSON data validation, Jsonschema is a solid choice.

- **Schema** is a library for validating Python data structures. It provides a simple syntax for defining validation rules. Schema is a good choice for applications that need Python data validation.

- **Schematics** is another library used for data structure validation. It offers a simple syntax for defining validation rules. If you need flexible data validation, Schematics is worth considering.

- **Valideer** is a lightweight and extensible library for data validation and adaptation. It provides a simple syntax for defining validation rules and adapting data to meet those rules.

When selecting a data validation library, there are a few factors to consider. First, consider the type of data you will be working with. Some libraries specialize in specific data types, while others offer more versatility. Efficiency is also important, especially if you're working with large amounts of data. Flexibility is crucial if you need to define complex validation rules. Finally, make sure to check the documentation of each library to ensure it meets your needs and provides clear guidance on how to use it effectively.

To put it briefly, the choice of a data validation library depends on your specific requirements. Each library discussed here offers unique features and strengths. By carefully considering the type of data you're working with, efficiency, flexibility, and documentation, you can select the right library to ensure the reliability and validity of your data.

Summary

In the previous chapter, we explored strategies that leveraged AI to enhance the security, performance, and reliability of web applications. We explored how cutting-edge AI technologies could revolutionize the testing phase, providing valuable insights and uncovering potential issues that traditional methods might overlook.

We started with an introduction to the concept of smart testing with AI. This was followed by learning to use AI tools to optimize and automate performance testing. We then gained proficiency in leveraging AI for comprehensive security testing and learned to integrate AI-driven bias detection into web application testing. The chapter concluded with understanding and applying AI-based techniques for reliability and validity testing.

Concluding the chapter, you have a good understanding of the concepts and principles of smart testing with AI. You learned to use AI tools to optimize and automate performance testing along with setting up support for comprehensive security testing using AI. You learned to integrate AI-driven bias detection into web application testing. Finally, you understood and applied AI-based techniques for reliability and validity testing.

In the next chapter, we will start learning about future-proof web development: advanced AI strategies.

Part 3:
Future-Proofing
Web Development – Advanced
AI Strategies

In this part, we explore advanced strategies to future-proof your web development projects by incorporating AI. We'll discuss the impact of AI on web development jobs, the rise of machine users, and how to navigate this new landscape. Additionally, you'll learn about AI-augmented development and how to turn innovative ideas into reality with intelligent web applications. We also cover the crucial aspects of navigating trust, risk, and ethics in AI development.

This part includes the following chapters:

- *Chapter 11, Augmented Workforce – AI's Impact on Web Development Jobs*
- *Chapter 12, Machine Users Unveiled – Navigating the Intersection of Human and Machine*
- *Chapter 13, AI-Augmented Development – Shaping Tomorrow's Digital Landscape*
- *Chapter 14, From Idea to Reality – Crafting Intelligent Web Applications*
- *Chapter 15, Guardians of the Digital Realm – Navigating Trust, Risk, and Ethics in AI*

11

Augmented Workforce – AI's Impact on Web Development Jobs

As the digital landscape evolves, so do the roles and responsibilities within the realm of web development. In this chapter, we delve into the transformative impact of AI on web development jobs, exploring strategies to optimize the value delivered by human staff through the establishment of a connective tissue that leverages intelligent technology, workforce analytics, and skill augmentation. The focus is on accelerating and scaling talent building in the context of an augmented connected workforce.

In this chapter, we will cover the following main topics:

- Conceptualizing an augmented workforce
- Navigating the AI revolution in web development jobs
- Accelerating digital skills and reducing time to competency
- Getting started – practical steps for implementation

By the end of this chapter, you will understand the concepts around the augmented workforce, have developed an adaptive mindset to navigate the changing landscape of web development jobs, and be able to implement a connective tissue strategy that optimizes the use of intelligent technology and analytics in web development roles. Furthermore, you will be able to recognize and adapt to the forces driving the trend of accelerating digital skills and reducing time to competency and execute practical steps to initiate augmented connected workforce initiatives, focusing on key outcomes and workforce segments.

Conceptualizing an augmented workforce

The rapid advancement of technology has brought about a fundamental shift in the way organizations operate. As we navigate the era of digital transformation, the concept of an **augmented workforce** has emerged as a key strategy for organizations to enhance their competitive advantage. By leveraging intelligent technologies, organizations can augment the skills and capabilities of their workforce, leading to improved efficiency, productivity, and innovation. Gartner predicts that by 2027, 25% of CIOs will use augmented connected workforce initiatives to reduce time to competency by 50% for key roles (available at `https://emt.gartnerweb.com/ngw/globalassets/en/publications/documents/2024-gartner-top-strategic-technology-trends-ebook.pdf?_gl=1*gbpyoj*_ga*NDA3OTY3NTczLjE3MDIwODkwMDQ.*_ga_R1W5CE5FEV*MTcwMjIxNTg5My4zLjEuMTcwMjIxNjQ5MC41NC4wLjA`).

The concept of an augmented workforce involves developing human talent using intelligent technologies that enhance the skills of workers, allowing them to perform more complex, creative, and strategic tasks, while technologies take over the more routine, repetitive, and dangerous tasks. In addition, the concept of an augmented workforce combines the digital and the physical, creating hybrid and integrated work environments, where workers can interact with machines, data, and information in a natural and intuitive way.

Finally, the concept of an augmented workforce emphasizes the delivery of value by both humans and the intelligent technology, in a complementary and synergistic way, seeking to optimize the results and impacts on the organization, customers, and society.

To understand and apply the concept of an augmented workforce, it is necessary to consider the different dimensions of focus that contribute to the integration of technology and human resources within an organization, that is, the strategic, technological, and organizational aspects.

Figure 11.1 highlights the main elements that contribute to the smooth integration of technology and human resources within an organization. These pillars range from seamless technological integration and the creation of synergistic partnerships between humans and machines to insightful knowledge management and improved workforce engagement.

Figure 11.1: Pillars of technological and human resources integration in organizations

These seven pillars provide a solid foundation for organizations looking to digitally transform their operations and culture. *Figure 11.1* serves as a strategic visual guide for business leaders who want to leverage technology to improve workforce performance and achieve their strategic objectives. We will explain each of them here:

- **Seamless tech integration**: Technological integration is the process of connecting and harmonizing the different intelligent technologies that make up the augmented workforce, using standards, protocols, and interfaces that ensure their interoperability, compatibility, and security. Technological integration allows intelligent technologies to communicate, synchronize, and complement each other, creating a cohesive and efficient system that enhances the performance and value of the augmented workforce.

- **Synergistic human-machine partnerships**: Human-machine collaboration is the process of interacting and cooperating with the intelligent technologies that are part of the augmented workforce, using methods, tools, and practices that favor trust, transparency, and synergy between humans and machines. Human-machine collaboration allows humans and machines to support, complement, and improve each other, creating a partnership and mutual learning relationship that enriches the experience and outcome of the augmented workforce.

- **Insightful knowledge management**: Knowledge management is the process of selecting, organizing, and presenting relevant and reliable information to workers, using intelligent technologies such as analytics, AI, and **Machine Learning** (**ML**). These technologies allow for filtering, analyzing, and synthesizing large volumes of data, transforming it into insights and recommendations that help workers in decision-making, problem-solving, and innovation. Knowledge management also involves creating interfaces and platforms that facilitate access, sharing and updating information, and collaboration between workers and machines.

- **Enhanced workforce engagement**: People management is the process of attracting, retaining, developing, and engaging workers, using intelligent technologies such as applications, mobile devices, and wearables that allow continuous communication, collaboration, and feedback. These technologies also enable monitoring and evaluating the performance, productivity, and well-being of workers, providing data and indicators that guide recognition, reward, and improvement actions. People management also implies creating a culture and organizational climate that encourages trust, autonomy, diversity, and inclusion of workers, as well as their adaptation to changes and technologies.

- **Dynamic skill development**: Skill development is the process of empowering workers to acquire new skills and competencies, using intelligent technologies that provide an immersive, personalized, and fun learning experience. These technologies allow the simulation and practice of real and complex scenarios, as well as real-time feedback and guidance. Skill development is divided into two sub-processes: lifelong learning and social and emotional skills assessment:

  - **Lifelong learning**: Lifelong learning is the sub-process of promoting the constant updating and evolution of workers, using intelligent technologies such as augmented reality, mixed reality, and gamification, which provide a fun, motivating, and adaptive learning experience. These technologies allow workers to learn autonomously, flexibly, and in a personalized way, according to their needs, preferences, and goals. Lifelong learning also involves creating a culture and a learning environment that encourages curiosity, experimentation, and reflection of workers, as well as recognition and appreciation of their learning.

  - **Social and emotional skills assessment**: Social and emotional skills assessment is the sub-process of measuring and improving the social and emotional skills of workers, using intelligent technologies such as chatbots, virtual assistants, virtual reality, and AI, which provide a realistic, immersive, and empathic interaction. These technologies allow workers to practice and receive feedback on their social and emotional skills, such as communication, collaboration, leadership, negotiation, and empathy, among others. Social and emotional skills assessment also involves creating a culture and a work environment that encourages the development and application of these skills, as well as the support and guidance of leaders and peers.

- **Innovative organizational design**: Organizational design is the process of defining the structure, culture, and work processes of the organization, using intelligent technologies such as workflow, automation, and robotics, which enable greater efficiency, flexibility, and innovation. These technologies allow the integration and coordination of activities and interactions between humans and machines, as well as the optimization of resources and costs. Organizational design also involves defining the roles, responsibilities, and competencies of workers and leaders, as well as aligning them with the strategy, mission, and vision of the organization.

- **Culture of innovation and experimentation**: An organizational culture of innovation and experimentation means creating and maintaining an environment and a mindset that encourages the generation and validation of new ideas, products, and services, using intelligent technologies that integrate the augmented workforce as sources of inspiration, information, and feedback. An organizational culture of innovation and experimentation allows humans and machines to be more creative, agile, and adaptable, creating innovative and disruptive solutions that add value and differentiation to the augmented workforce.

The concept of an augmented workforce represents an opportunity and a challenge for organizations and workers, who will need to prepare for the future of work that is increasingly hybrid, integrated, and intelligent. Thus, it is necessary to understand and apply the concept of an augmented workforce in its various dimensions, which involve strategic, technological, and organizational aspects, that aim to optimize the performance and potential of the human workforce in partnership with intelligent technologies.

The augmented workforce also requires a change in the mindset and behavior of workers and leaders, who need to adapt, learn, collaborate, and trust each other and machines, as well as redefine their roles, skills, and work processes. Building an augmented workforce is therefore a way of developing human talent using intelligent technologies, which expand their capabilities and possibilities, creating a more efficient, productive, qualified, and satisfied workforce. However, this transformation also brings challenges and opportunities for professionals working in the field of web development, who need to prepare for the impact of AI on their careers. In the next section, we'll explore how to navigate the AI revolution in web development jobs, presenting strategies, trends, and tips for standing out in this ever-changing landscape.

Navigating the AI revolution in web development jobs

In the ever-evolving landscape of web development jobs, the rise of AI and the augmented workforce has brought about significant changes. As professionals in this field, it is crucial to develop an adaptive mindset that enables us to navigate this revolution successfully.

The first step in navigating the AI revolution is to comprehend the changes happening in web development jobs. AI technologies, such as ML and natural language processing, have revolutionized the way websites and applications are developed. With the help of an augmented workforce, which combines human expertise with AI capabilities, tasks that were once time-consuming can now be automated, allowing developers to focus on more complex and creative aspects of their work.

To thrive in this new era, it is essential to develop an adaptive mindset. This means investing time in learning new programming languages, exploring AI frameworks, and keeping an eye on emerging trends in the industry. By adopting a proactive approach to learning, we can stay ahead of the curve and remain relevant in the changing job market.

In addition to continuous learning, flexibility and agility are crucial traits for navigating the AI revolution in web development jobs. With the introduction of AI technologies, the roles and responsibilities of web developers are evolving. It is no longer enough to focus solely on coding and technical skills. Developers must also possess strong problem-solving abilities, adaptability, and the willingness to collaborate with AI systems. Being flexible and agile allows us to embrace new opportunities and adapt to the changing demands of the industry.

As AI becomes an integral part of web development, collaboration between humans and machines becomes paramount. Rather than perceiving AI as a threat to job security, we should view it as a tool that enhances our capabilities. By leveraging the strengths of AI systems, such as automating repetitive tasks and analyzing vast amounts of data, we can streamline our workflows and deliver more efficient and effective solutions to clients. Embracing this collaboration paves the way for innovation and growth in the field of web development.

In essence, navigating the AI revolution in web development jobs requires an adaptive mindset. By understanding the changes happening in the industry, embracing continuous learning, being flexible and agile, and collaborating with AI systems, we can position ourselves for success.

Strategic implementation of an augmented workforce in web development

Nowadays, web development plays a crucial role in the success of businesses. To keep up with the increasing demand for innovative and user-friendly websites, companies need to optimize their workforce. Now, we will explore the implementation of a connective tissue strategy for an augmented workforce in web development, which aims to maximize the use of intelligent technology and analytics.

To stay competitive in the web development industry, it is essential to embrace intelligent technology. By integrating AI and ML algorithms into our workflows, we can automate time-consuming tasks, improve efficiency, and enhance the overall quality of our work. Using AI-powered tools, we can streamline processes such as code generation, bug detection, and performance optimization.

Data analytics is a powerful tool that can provide valuable insights into the performance of websites and the behavior of users. By leveraging analytics, we can gather quantitative and qualitative data to make informed decisions and drive continuous improvement. Through the analysis of user behavior, we can identify pain points, optimize user experience, and ultimately increase conversion rates. Additionally, analytics can help us track the performance of our development team, identify bottlenecks, and allocate resources effectively.

To fully optimize the use of intelligent technology and analytics, it is crucial to implement a **connective tissue strategy**. This strategy involves fostering collaboration and communication between different stakeholders in web development, including developers, designers, data analysts, and project managers. By dismantling departmental barriers and encouraging collaboration among interdisciplinary teams, we can ensure that everyone is aligned toward the same goal of delivering high-quality websites.

The following are tips for implementing a connective tissue strategy:

- Collaborate with other web developers who use intelligent technology. You can share your experiences, challenges, solutions, and ideas with other web developers who use intelligent technology, creating a network of learning and innovation.

- Keep up to date with the trends and advances of intelligent technology. You should be aware of the new tools, features, functionalities, and applications of intelligent technology, which can further improve your work and your added value.

- Respect the ethical and legal principles of using intelligent technology. You should use intelligent technology in a responsible, transparent, fair, and safe way, respecting the rights, privacy, and dignity of the people involved in your work.

To implement a connective tissue strategy that optimizes the use of smart technology and analytics in web development roles, we suggest the following:

- Identify the tasks that can be automated or supported by smart technology. For example, you can use low-code or no-code tools to create user interfaces, use virtual assistants to answer frequently asked questions from clients, use cloud platforms to host and manage your projects or use automated testing tools to ensure the quality of your code.

- Choose the smart technology tools best suited to your needs. You should consider factors such as cost, ease of use, compatibility, security, reliability, and scalability. You should also evaluate the impact of smart technology on your productivity, satisfaction, motivation, and well-being.

- Train and adapt to smart technology tools. You must learn how to use smart technology tools effectively and efficiently, taking advantage of their features and functionalities. You should also be prepared to adapt to changes and updates to the tools, as well as the feedback and suggestions they can provide.

- Foster collaboration. Encourage open communication and collaboration between different teams to share knowledge and best practices.

- Implement AI-powered tools. Integrate AI-powered tools and platforms into the development process to automate repetitive tasks and improve productivity.

- Establish data-driven decision-making. Implement a data-driven approach by leveraging analytics to guide decision-making and continuously monitor and optimize website performance.

- Monitor and evaluate the performance of your augmented workforce. You should use analysis tools to measure and track the results of your augmented workforce, such as quality, speed, accuracy, innovation, and customer satisfaction. You should also use analysis tools to identify areas for improvement, learning opportunities, and best practices.

Implementing a connective tissue strategy for the augmented web development workforce is essential to staying competitive in the digital age. By harnessing the power of smart technology and analytics, companies can optimize their web development processes, improve the user experience, and drive business growth. By following the step-by-step implementation process described, companies can ensure a smooth transition to a more efficient and effective web development workflow.

What's more, the web developer who gets ahead and adopts this strategy won't be caught by surprise by market changes and challenges and will be future-proofed. They will have a competitive advantage over their competitors and will be able to adapt quickly to new demands and opportunities.

In the next chapter, we'll look at the emerging forces that are accelerating digital skills and reducing web developers' time to competence.

As we continue to explore the transformative impact of AI in web development, it is crucial to understand the dynamics that are not only enhancing but also accelerating the acquisition of digital skills. The upcoming section delves into the emerging forces that are streamlining the path to greater competency among web developers. Let's explore how these forces are shaping the future of web development and what it means for professionals in the field.

Accelerating digital skills and reducing time to competency

The demand for web developers with expertise in AI and other augmentation technologies is on the rise. These technologies are becoming increasingly essential and indispensable for web development, leading to the emergence of new roles and specializations in the field. Additionally, the skills and competencies required for web developers are evolving, encompassing not only technical abilities but also social, emotional, and creative skills. Moreover, organizations are transforming their culture and values to foster innovation and experimentation, leveraging augmentation technologies as sources of inspiration, information, and feedback.

As these technologies become integral to web development, developers with expertise in AI will be sought after to create innovative, intelligent solutions. By leveraging AI, web developers can build advanced functionalities, optimize user experiences, and deliver personalized content. Their ability to integrate AI into web development processes will be crucial for organizations aiming to stay competitive in the digital era.

With the increasing complexity of web development, AI-based platforms and services are emerging to provide developers with enhanced ease, agility, and quality. These platforms leverage AI algorithms to automate repetitive tasks, streamline workflows, and facilitate collaboration among developers. By utilizing AI-powered tools and frameworks, web developers can expedite the development process and focus more on crafting unique, user-centric experiences. The rise of AI-based platforms and services is revolutionizing the way web developers work, enabling them to create sophisticated web applications with greater efficiency.

In this dynamic scenario, the skill of adaptability emerges as crucial. Web developers will not only need to continually update their skill sets but also keep up to date with the latest technological trends and innovations in order to excel in these new roles. Adaptability not only empowers developers to navigate rapid technological change but also positions them to seize new opportunities and face challenges in the competitive web development environment. This ability to adapt quickly to new tools and technologies is therefore indispensable for continued success and relevance in the field of web development. Specializations such as AI-driven web development, augmented reality web design, and data-driven user experience/user interface development are emerging to address the demand for specialized expertise. Web developers will need to continuously update their skill sets and stay abreast of the latest trends to excel in these new roles.

In addition to the crucial adaptability already highlighted, other skills, such as collaboration, communication, and problem-solving, are becoming indispensable for web developers. These skills are fundamental for working effectively in multidisciplinary teams and managing complex projects. In addition, creativity and a deep understanding of human-centered design principles are essential for creating engaging and intuitive web experiences.

As the digital landscape evolves, web developers need to be flexible to the accelerating demand for digital skills and reduced time to competency. The integration of AI and augmentation technologies presents both challenges and opportunities for web developers. By acquiring expertise in these areas and developing a diverse skill set, web developers can position themselves at the forefront of innovation and drive the future of web development. Embracing the changing landscape and continuously updating skills will be key to staying relevant and competitive in the dynamic world of web development.

In the next section, we'll provide concrete steps to not just adapt to these changes but to thrive. Let's dive into actionable strategies that will empower you to continuously evolve and maintain your competitive edge in this dynamic field.

Getting started – practical steps for implementation

You know that your job involves creating and maintaining websites and web applications, using different languages, frameworks, and tools. But you also know that your work is constantly evolving, due to new technologies, trends, and market demands.

To stay up to date and competitive, you need to develop and improve your digital skills, which are the set of knowledge, attitudes, and behaviors needed to use digital tools effectively. In addition, you need to reduce competency time, which is the period needed to acquire and demonstrate the digital skills required by your professional and personal context.

But how can you do this quickly and efficiently, without compromising the quality of your learning and performance? How do you start a connected and augmented workforce initiative that aims to improve your productivity, quality, innovation, and job satisfaction? *Figure 11.2* visually represents the key stages involved in effectively integrating intelligent technologies into the workforce. This step-by-step guide is designed to help organizations systematically enhance their workforce capabilities, ensuring a smooth transition to an augmented workforce model. By following these steps, organizations can achieve improved productivity, efficiency, and innovation.

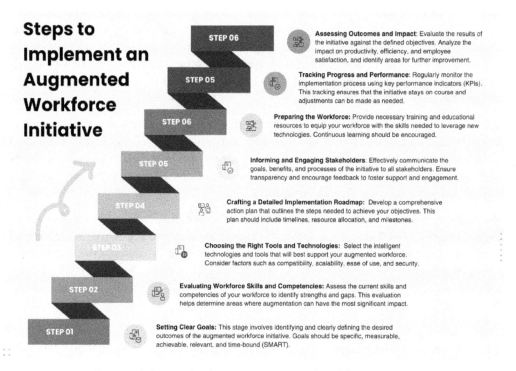

Figure 11.2: Steps to implement an augmented workforce initiative

By visualizing the implementation process, *Figure 11.2* serves as a practical roadmap for organizations aiming to optimize their workforce with intelligent technologies. Here, we provide a comprehensive guide on how to get started with this transformative process:

1. **Define your objectives**: The first step in implementing augmented connected workforce initiatives is to clearly define your objectives. Identify the desired outcomes you wish to achieve, whether it's improving collaboration, optimizing efficiency, or enhancing employee satisfaction. By establishing these goals, you can effectively align your efforts and measure the success of your initiatives.

2. **Assess current workforce capabilities**: Before diving into implementation, it is crucial to assess your current workforce capabilities. Evaluate the skills and competencies of your employees, identify any gaps that need to be addressed, and determine the areas where augmented connectivity can bring the most significant impact. This assessment will help you tailor your initiatives to the unique needs of your workforce.

3. **Choose the technologies and tools**: Choose the technologies and tools that will be used to connect and increase your workforce, taking into account the availability, accessibility, compatibility, and security of the resources.

4. **Develop a roadmap**: With your objectives established and an understanding of your current capabilities, it's time to develop a roadmap for implementation. Break down your initiatives into manageable phases, setting realistic timelines and milestones. Consider the resources required, potential challenges, and the necessary support from stakeholders to ensure a smooth and successful implementation process.

5. **Communicate and educate**: Communication and education are key to garnering support and enthusiasm for augmented connected workforce initiatives. Clearly communicate the benefits of these initiatives to all stakeholders, including employees, managers, and executives. Provide training and educational resources to ensure everyone is equipped with the knowledge and skills needed to embrace and leverage augmented connectivity.

6. **Monitor and evaluate**: Once your initiatives are underway, it is crucial to regularly monitor and evaluate their progress. Establish **Key Performance Indicators** (**KPIs**) that align with your objectives and continuously track them. Solicit feedback from employees and stakeholders to identify areas for improvement and make necessary adjustments. This iterative process ensures that your initiatives remain effective and adaptive to changing needs.

By following these practical steps, you can successfully implement augmented connected workforce initiatives. Remember to define your objectives, assess your current capabilities, develop a roadmap, communicate, educate, and continuously monitor and evaluate your initiatives. With a strategic and human-centered approach, you can unlock the full potential of an augmented connected workforce, driving innovation, collaboration, and success.

Summary

In this chapter, you were introduced to the concept of an augmented workforce, a strategy to optimize human workers' value using intelligent technology, workforce analytics, and skill augmentation. You also learned how to navigate the AI revolution in web development Jobs, which is changing how websites and web applications are created and maintained.

You learned how to implement a connective tissue strategy, a set of practices and tools to integrate and align the people, processes, and technologies involved in web development. You learned how to recognize and adapt to the emerging forces and the factors that drive the trend of accelerating digital skills and reducing time to competency, which is essential to stay updated and competitive in the digital age. You learned how to initiate an augmented connected workforce initiative, following practical steps to plan, execute, and evaluate your initiative, focusing on the outcomes and the segments of the workforce.

In the next chapter, we will explore how machine users are reshaping the digital landscape, making many human-readable digital storefronts obsolete.

12

Machine Users Unveiled – Navigating the Intersection of Human and Machine

In this chapter, we will explore the phenomenon of machine users, which are software agents that interact with digital interfaces on behalf of humans or other machines. We will understand how they are transforming the digital landscape, making many of the online stores designed for humans obsolete. We will also learn how to adapt the web development paradigm to meet the needs and expectations of these new customers.

In this chapter, we will cover the following main topics:

- Decoding machine customers – understanding the future of consumerism market opportunities and scenarios
- Case study – gas station service for autonomous cars
- Impact on purchases and commerce
- Preparing for the future with machine customers

By the end of this chapter, you will have developed skills to understand and profile the machine user, discern their preferences and behaviors, create strategic scenarios that explore market opportunities and impacts, gain expertise in architecting data sources and API platforms specifically designed for the machine user, evaluate the market opportunities presented by Internet-of-Things-enabled products and machine users, and hone the skill of thinking strategically about the future and positioning your businesses to thrive in the age of the machine user.

Decoding machine customers – understanding the future of consumerism

In this section, we will introduce the concept of the **Machine Customer** (**MC**) and explore its differences from the human user. With the rise of technology, companies have now gained the ability to create their own customers, a trend identified by Gartner in their article *Gartner Top 10 Strategic Technology Trends for 2024* (you can find a link to the article here: `https://www.gartner.com/en/articles/gartner-top-10-strategic-technology-trends-for-2024`). The arrival of MCs is set to revolutionize the digital commerce landscape, making it imperative for businesses to understand and adapt to this new phenomenon.

Businesses can harness the power of AI and machine learning to develop and manage MCs through various advanced techniques and tools. **Natural Language Processing** (**NLP**) enables the creation of virtual assistants capable of understanding and engaging in human-like conversations, facilitating effective customer interactions. Reinforcement learning algorithms play a crucial role in optimizing decision-making by learning from past interactions and continuously improving performance. Machine learning models used in predictive analytics can forecast customer needs and preferences, enabling the delivery of personalized recommendations. Essential tools such as TensorFlow, PyTorch, and scikit-learn provide the necessary frameworks for building, training, and deploying these sophisticated models. Moreover, AI-driven chatbots and virtual assistants can significantly enhance customer support by offering real-time, customized responses, ensuring a smooth and efficient user experience.

The MC represents a new breed of consumer, one that is not bound by human limitations. Unlike their human counterparts, MCs operate on a rational and logical basis, driven by algorithms, objective data, logic, and patterns. They are devoid of emotions, personal experiences, and subjective interpretations. This fundamental distinction brings about a paradigm shift in how companies interact with their customers and underscores the need for businesses to develop skills in understanding and profiling machine users, discerning their preferences, and behaviors.

While human users are influenced by emotions, experiences, and subjectivity, MCs rely solely on logic and patterns. This divergence in decision-making processes has profound implications for businesses seeking to cater to both types of consumers. Companies must adapt their strategies to accommodate the unique traits of these MCs, who operate in a data-driven and objective manner.

MCs excel at *processing information* based on measurable and objective data. They are capable of analyzing vast amounts of information in a fraction of the time it would take a human user. In contrast, human users consider nuances, subjectivity, and personal interpretations when processing information.

The rise of MCs presents several challenges for businesses. Adapting to this new consumer landscape requires companies to develop new skills, including understanding and profiling machine users. Moreover, businesses must architect the necessary data sources and API platforms to serve MCs, ensuring their digital storefronts remain relevant in the face of this transition. Gartner predicts that by 2028, MCs will render 20% of human-readable digital storefronts obsolete.

As we delve deeper into the practical applications of AI and machine learning, it becomes evident how these technologies can transform everyday household appliances. The integration of advanced algorithms and data structures not only enhances convenience but also promotes sustainability and efficiency in managing daily tasks. To illustrate this, let's explore a specific use case where smart refrigerators are seamlessly connected with local supermarkets, showcasing the potential of AI-driven innovation in a real-world setting.

Use case – smart refrigerators connected to local supermarkets

In a bustling urban environment, smart refrigerators equipped with AI and machine learning capabilities are revolutionizing the way households manage their groceries. These advanced appliances use sensors and algorithms to monitor the stock of food items, track expiration dates, and even suggest recipes based on available ingredients.

In a city such as San Francisco, a family uses a smart refrigerator connected to a network of local supermarkets. The fridge, equipped with AI and machine learning capabilities, monitors the milk and eggs, notifying them when stocks are low. On a busy weekday, the fridge detects that the milk is about to run out and automatically places an order with a nearby supermarket. The AI system at the supermarket confirms the order, prepares the delivery, and the items are delivered to the family's doorstep within a few hours. This seamless integration, powered by AI and machine learning, saves time, reduces waste, and ensures the family always has fresh groceries on hand.

Figure 12.1 illustrates the concepts discussed about integrating MCs into a smart kitchen. It demonstrates how the application of AI and advanced algorithms can transform household management, from stock monitoring to efficient product delivery.

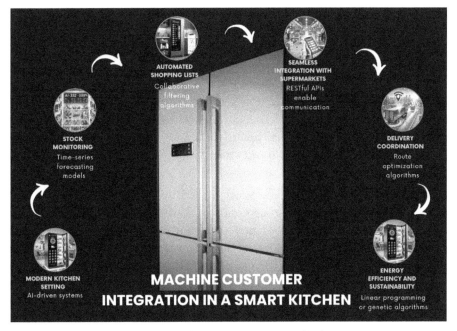

Figure 12.1: MC integration in a smart kitchen

The implementation of smart refrigerators connected with local supermarkets involves several key technological components:

- **Stock monitoring and notifications**: Smart refrigerators leverage advanced AI-driven sensors to monitor the quantity and freshness of food items, utilizing machine learning algorithms such as time-series forecasting and regression models to analyze usage patterns and predict when items will run out. Time-series forecasting models such as **AutoRegressive Integrated Moving Average** (**ARIMA**) and **Long Short-Term Memory** (**LSTM**) networks analyze historical consumption data to predict future stock levels, while regression models, including linear regression and more complex techniques such as Random Forest Regressor, predict the depletion rate of items based on usage patterns. Databases store historical usage data, and data arrays or tensors represent current stock levels for real-time analysis. These models are trained on historical consumption data to learn patterns of usage over time, and validation is performed using a separate dataset to ensure accuracy in predicting stock depletion.

- **Automated shopping lists**: Based on consumption patterns and current stock levels, machine learning algorithms generate an automated shopping list that is personalized according to household preferences and dietary needs, allowing for manual adjustments by the user. Collaborative filtering algorithms, such as matrix factorization or **K-Nearest Neighbors** (**KNN**), recommend items based on the preferences and behaviors of similar users, while classification algorithms like decision trees or logistic regression classify items as necessary or optional based on historical consumption data. Preference matrices and user profiles maintained in databases store and update shopping lists. These algorithms are trained using datasets of past purchases and user preferences, with validation conducted by comparing the algorithm's recommendations with actual user preferences and adjustments.

- **Seamless integration with supermarkets**: The smart refrigerator connects to local supermarkets via an integrated app to replenish items when necessary, with the AI system automatically placing orders with the preferred supermarket. The homeowner can choose to approve the order before it is finalized or let the system handle it autonomously. RESTful APIs facilitate communication between the refrigerator and supermarket systems, while AI algorithms recommend the best supermarket based on factors such as price, proximity, and past user preferences. JSON objects and API endpoints handle the data exchange between the refrigerator and supermarket systems. Machine learning models are trained on transactional data to optimize supermarket selection and order placement, with API calls tested and validated to ensure accurate and secure data transmission.

- **Delivery coordination**: Once the order is placed, the supermarket prepares the groceries for delivery using its AI systems. Homeowners can track the delivery status in real-time and receive notifications about the expected arrival time. Delivery systems use route optimization algorithms, such as Dijkstra's or A* search, to optimize delivery routes, while GPS data processed using stream processing frameworks provides real-time updates. Graph data structures represent delivery routes, and streams of real-time data are handled using event-driven architectures. Models for route optimization are trained using historical delivery data, and real-time tracking systems are validated through testing with live data to ensure accuracy and reliability.

- **Energy efficiency and sustainability**: By optimizing grocery purchases and reducing food waste, smart refrigerators with AI and machine learning contribute to more sustainable living, ensuring that only necessary items are purchased and consumed in a timely manner. This promotes better resource management. Optimization algorithms such as linear programming or genetic algorithms optimize purchase schedules and quantities to minimize waste, while AI models predict the environmental impact of purchases and suggest alternatives to reduce carbon footprints. Optimization problems are represented using matrices, and sustainability metrics are stored in databases. Optimization models are trained using data on food consumption and waste patterns, with sustainability models validated using real-world data to ensure accurate predictions and recommendations for reducing waste.

Understanding the differences then between MCs and human users is essential for companies to thrive in the digital age. However, in order to take advantage of the market opportunities that MCs offer, it is also necessary to create strategic scenarios that explore the possible demands, challenges, and impacts of this new type of consumer. This is what we'll see in the next section.

Market opportunities and scenarios

The emergence of MCs is a groundbreaking trend that is set to revolutionize the market. As companies gain the ability to create their own customers, the potential impact is immense. According to Gartner, by 2028, there will be 15 billion connected products behaving as customers, with trillions of dollars in purchases influenced by these machines by 2030 (`https://www.gartner.com/en/articles/gartner-top-10-strategic-technology-trends-for-2024`).

To support the vast connectivity of 15 billion connected products, a robust and scalable technical infrastructure is essential. This infrastructure relies on cloud computing, edge computing, and IoT platforms, each playing a crucial role in managing the data and communication needs of such an extensive network.

The transition from traditional locked-in customers to free and ultimately creative customers is underpinned by advanced machine learning models and AI techniques. Each stage of this transition leverages specific AI technologies to enhance customer experience, personalization, and engagement.

There are three phases in the evolution of MCs, according to the degree of autonomy and complexity of their purchasing decisions (`https://www.gartner.com/en/articles/machine-customers-will-decide-who-gets-their-trillion-dollar-business-is-it-you`).

The emerging trend of MCs represents a significant shift in how businesses approach market opportunities. As detailed in a Gartner article, the evolution of MCs unfolds in three distinct phases based on their autonomy and complexity in making purchasing decisions:

1. **Tied Customers**: These machines act as co-customers alongside their owners, performing limited functions and operating under pre-established rules.

2. **Free Customers**: Machines in this phase can autonomously choose between different suppliers and services, making decisions based on cost-benefit analyses.

3. **Creative Customers**: The most advanced category, these machines can create new demands and solutions autonomously, leveraging learning algorithms and artificial intelligence.

For tied customers, the technical infrastructure relies heavily on cloud computing and centralized data storage. Cloud platforms such as AWS, Google Cloud, and Azure provide the necessary computing power and storage capabilities to handle large datasets and perform complex calculations. Machine learning models such as recommendation systems are pivotal in this phase. Collaborative filtering and content-based filtering are implemented using algorithms such as matrix factorization and nearest-neighbors, supported by cloud-based machine learning services. Supervised learning models for predicting customer behavior and segmenting customers are trained and deployed using cloud resources, ensuring scalability and availability.

As customers evolve into free customers, the infrastructure must support more dynamic and real-time interactions. This is achieved through a combination of cloud computing and edge computing. Cloud platforms continue to handle heavy processing tasks, while edge devices perform local computations to reduce latency and improve response times. NLP powers chatbots and virtual assistants, requiring real-time processing capabilities. Sentiment analysis tools run on both cloud and edge environments to quickly process customer feedback. Reinforcement learning models, which adapt recommendations based on ongoing interactions, leverage edge computing for real-time decision-making, while the cloud supports model training and updates. Multi-armed bandit algorithms balance exploration and exploitation by running experiments at the edge, with the cloud aggregating results for broader insights. Unsupervised learning models, such as clustering and anomaly detection, use a hybrid approach to process data both locally and centrally, ensuring timely and relevant insights.

In the creative customer phase, the infrastructure must facilitate high levels of interaction and content generation. This phase heavily relies on a hybrid cloud and edge computing architecture. Generative models, such as **Generative Adversarial Networks (GANs)** and **Variational Autoencoders (VAEs)**, require substantial computational power provided by GPUs in cloud environments. These models generate new content and personalize experiences, necessitating a scalable cloud infrastructure for training and deployment. Advanced NLP techniques, such as text generation with models such as GPT-3, operate on cloud platforms to handle the intensive processing demands. Semantic search capabilities, which enhance user query understanding, utilize distributed databases and search engines optimized for both cloud and edge environments. Human-AI collaboration tools, supporting co-creation and interactive feedback, depend on real-time data processing enabled by edge computing, while the cloud aggregates and refines the AI models. Deep learning models, including **Convolutional Neural Networks (CNNs)** for image and video content creation and **Recurrent Neural Networks (RNNs)** for sequence generation, leverage the computational power of cloud-based AI services, with edge devices providing immediate processing capabilities for interactive applications.

These technologies transform the customer experience, turning users from passive recipients to active participants in the digital commerce landscape. To capitalize on this emerging trend of MCs, businesses need to be proactive in identifying and leveraging the market *opportunities* presented by MCs. Here are some key opportunities to consider:

- **Customization**: Tailoring products and services to cater to machine-driven preferences. As machines become more sophisticated, businesses can create personalized experiences that align with their specific needs and preferences.

  Recommendation systems and personalization algorithms play a critical role in achieving such customization. These systems analyze vast amounts of data to understand user behavior and preferences, allowing businesses to offer tailored recommendations and experiences. For instance, streaming services such as Netflix use collaborative filtering algorithms to suggest movies and shows based on users' viewing history and preferences. Similarly, e-commerce platforms such as Amazon utilize content-based filtering to recommend products that match the user's past purchases and browsing behavior. The data pipelines for these systems involve collecting user data, processing and analyzing it using machine learning models and continuously updating the recommendations based on new data. Techniques such as matrix factorization, deep learning, and natural language processing are commonly used to enhance the accuracy and relevance of these recommendations. By leveraging these advanced algorithms, businesses can create highly personalized and engaging experiences for their machine and human customers alike.

- **Algorithmic marketing**: Utilizing data-driven insights to develop targeted and effective marketing strategies. By analyzing machine-generated data, businesses can gain valuable insights into customer behavior and preferences, enabling them to deliver highly relevant and personalized marketing messages.

- **Predictive analytics**: Leveraging machine-generated data to forecast market trends. By analyzing patterns and trends in machine data, businesses can make informed predictions about future market trends, enabling them to stay ahead of the competition.

- **AI integration**: Opportunities for businesses providing AI solutions for machine interactions. As machines become more prevalent in customer interactions, businesses can develop AI solutions that enhance the customer experience and optimize performance.

With a clear understanding of how MCs can revolutionize market dynamics and the strategic opportunities they present, let's delve deeper into the practical considerations businesses must address to successfully integrate these technologies into their operations.

Considerations

The rise of MCs also presents various scenarios that businesses need to consider. These scenarios include the following:

- **Increased efficiency**: Machines can contribute to faster and more precise decision-making, leading to increased efficiency in various industries. Businesses can leverage machine-driven insights to streamline operations and make more informed decisions.

  To integrate machine-driven insights into business operations, companies use advanced data analytics platforms and real-time processing frameworks. These technologies enable efficient handling and analysis of large datasets for actionable insights. Platforms such as Apache Hadoop and Spark support batch processing and real-time analytics, allowing timely data processing and decision-making. Real-time processing frameworks such as Apache Kafka and Flink facilitate continuous data collection and analysis, enabling instant reactions to changes and trends. By incorporating these technologies, businesses enhance operational efficiency and strategic decision-making.

- **New revenue streams**: Exploring monetization opportunities through machine-driven transactions. As MCs become more prevalent, businesses can develop innovative business models and revenue streams to capitalize on this emerging market.

- **Challenges in human interaction**: Adapting to scenarios where machines dominate certain market segments. Businesses need to adapt their strategies and processes to ensure effective interaction and collaboration between humans and machines.

- **Ethical considerations**: Addressing concerns related to data privacy and algorithmic biases. As machines become more integrated into customer interactions, businesses must prioritize ethical practices to ensure the protection of customer data and minimize algorithmic biases.

The integration of MCs into business models brings about significant transformations and considerations. These range from boosting operational efficiency and creating innovative revenue streams to addressing the unique challenges of human-machine interactions and ethical concerns. Businesses must strategically navigate these scenarios to harness the full potential of machine-driven transactions and interactions, ensuring they maintain a balance between technological advancement and ethical responsibility.

Industry-specific opportunities

Different industries will be impacted differently by the rise of MCs. Here are some industry-specific opportunities to consider:

- **Finance**: Automated financial advisory services for MCs. By leveraging AI and machine learning, businesses can provide personalized financial advice and investment strategies to MCs.

In automated financial advisory services, machine learning models such as linear regression, decision trees, and neural networks are widely used for predictive analytics and risk assessment. Linear regression predicts financial trends from historical data, while decision trees aid in investment decisions by evaluating different scenarios. Neural networks handle vast data to offer personalized financial advice and identify complex market patterns.

Predictive analytics utilizes these models to forecast market trends, stock prices, and investment returns. For risk assessment, logistic regression and support vector machines assess financial risks and potential losses by analyzing market volatility, economic indicators, and individual investment behaviors.

- **Retail**: Customized shopping experiences based on machine preferences. By analyzing machine data, businesses can create personalized shopping experiences that align with the preferences and needs of MCs.

- **Healthcare**: AI-driven diagnostics and personalized treatment plans. Machines can analyze vast amounts of health data, enabling businesses to provide accurate diagnoses and personalized treatment plans.

- **Technology**: Development of advanced AI solutions catering to machine interactions. As machines become more prevalent, businesses specializing in AI solutions can develop advanced technologies that optimize machine interactions and enhance the overall customer experience.

These developments promise to redefine how businesses operate across different industries, delivering more precise and efficient services tailored to the capabilities and needs of MCs.

Thriving in a competitive market

In this rapidly evolving landscape, businesses need to stay competitive by adopting innovative strategies and collaborating with AI-driven enterprises. The competitive landscape for MCs includes the following:

- **Innovative products**: Companies that are creating cutting-edge solutions specifically designed for machine-driven markets. These companies are at the forefront of innovation and are shaping the future of MC interactions.

- **Adaptation strategies**: Established businesses that are adapting their strategies to embrace the rise of MCs. These businesses are proactively integrating machines into their operations and leveraging the opportunities presented by this trend.

- **Collaborations and partnerships**: Opportunities for collaboration between traditional businesses and AI-driven enterprises. By collaborating with AI-driven companies, traditional businesses can leverage their expertise and resources to enhance their MC offerings.

These alliances allow traditional businesses to tap into advanced AI expertise and resources, enhancing their offerings and positioning themselves strongly in the MC market.

Understanding regulations and trends

As the prevalence of MCs increases, businesses need to navigate the regulatory environment to ensure compliance and ethical practices. Key considerations in the regulatory environment include the following:

- **Data protection**: Compliance with regulations ensuring the privacy and security of machine-generated data. Businesses must implement robust data protection measures to safeguard customer information and maintain trust.

  To ensure data protection in AI systems, businesses employ strategies such as encryption, access control, and compliance with regulations including GDPR and CCPA. Encryption techniques such as AES secure data in transit and at rest, making it unreadable without proper keys. Access control mechanisms, such as **role-based access control** (**RBAC**) and **multi-factor authentication** (**MFA**), restrict data access to authorized users.

  Compliance frameworks mandate transparent data handling, user consent, and rights to data access, modification, or deletion. Regular audits and **data protection impact assessments** (**DPIAs**) ensure ongoing compliance. Monitoring involves using advanced security tools such as SIEM systems for continuous network activity surveillance and automated threat alerts, ensuring swift incident responses. These measures protect machine-generated data, ensure regulatory compliance, and maintain customer trust, which is crucial for the success of AI systems.

- **Ethical AI practices**: Industry standards for the ethical use of AI in MC scenarios. Businesses must prioritize ethical considerations when developing and deploying AI solutions to ensure fairness, transparency, and accountability.

While ethics play a big role in retaining the opportunities we already have, trends help us create new ones. The future of MCs holds several exciting trends that businesses should anticipate. Keeping up with trends is essential to staying relevant.

These *trends* include the following:

- **Expansion of AI applications**: Anticipating the growth of AI in diverse market sectors. AI is expected to play a more significant role in various industries, driving innovation and transforming customer experiences.

- **Consumer adoption**: Tracking the speed at which consumers are adopting machine-driven services. As consumers become more accustomed to interacting with machines, businesses need to align their strategies with evolving consumer preferences.

- **Emergence of new industries**: Identifying sectors that might evolve due to the prevalence of MCs. As MCs become more prevalent, new industries and business models may emerge, presenting opportunities for innovative businesses.

The rise of MCs presents both significant market opportunities and unique scenarios for businesses. By embracing customization, algorithmic marketing, predictive analytics, and AI integration, businesses can position themselves at the forefront of this emerging trend. Additionally, businesses need to navigate challenges in human interaction and address ethical considerations to ensure responsible and sustainable growth in this new era. By capitalizing on industry-specific opportunities and staying competitive in the evolving landscape, businesses can thrive in the era of MCs.

Case study – gas station service for autonomous cars

AI is transforming various industries and sectors, creating new opportunities and challenges for businesses and customers. One of the emerging applications of AI is the integration of AI solutions with MCs, i.e., devices or systems that can autonomously purchase goods or services on behalf of human owners or users. This type of AI integration requires careful consideration of the design and implementation aspects, as well as the ethical and social implications of the AI-enabled transactions.

This makes designing systems and architectures to seamlessly integrate AI for interactions with MCs crucial in today's business landscape. It involves creating a framework that allows businesses to effectively leverage AI capabilities in order to meet the needs and expectations of their machine-driven customer base.

In this section, we will present a case study of architecting for AI integration for a gas station service for autonomous cars. We will use the **Architect Your AI (AYAI) Canvas** as a framework to guide our analysis and discussion. The AYAI Canvas provides a comprehensive overview of the key components and considerations in designing and implementing AI solutions. It encompasses various aspects, dividing them into essential categories:

- **Requirements**: The target audience includes autonomous vehicle owners and operators. The primary objectives are to automate refueling services, reduce waiting times, and optimize fuel distribution. The problem to be resolved is ensuring efficient and timely refueling for autonomous cars, addressing predictive analytics and optimization challenges. This problem involves handling large volumes of data from various sensors and historical records to provide real-time solutions.

- **Operational management**: Scalability is crucial as the system needs to handle a growing number of autonomous vehicles and gas stations. Computational efficiency can be achieved by using cloud-based platforms such as AWS or Azure for data processing and storage, and edge computing devices for real-time decision-making at gas stations. Maintenance and upgrading involve regular updates to the machine learning models and data processing pipelines, utilizing version control systems. Testing and evaluation require continuous monitoring of model performance using metrics including accuracy, **Mean Absolute Error** (**MAE**), and throughput. Security and privacy are maintained through encryption (e.g., AES), access control mechanisms (e.g., RBAC), and compliance with regulations such as GDPR and CCPA. Ethical considerations include ensuring data transparency and user consent for data collection.

- **Essential components**: The model includes regression models for predicting fuel demand, clustering algorithms for optimizing station layouts, and reinforcement learning for routing autonomous cars. The platform involves cloud services for scalable data processing and storage, and edge computing devices for real-time analytics. Tools and frameworks include Apache Spark for data processing, TensorFlow for model training, Docker for containerization, and Kubernetes for orchestration.

- **Data flow**: Input interfaces involve vehicle sensors, gas station sensors, and APIs for data collection. Data sources include real-time sensor data, historical refueling patterns, and transaction records. Data collection methods involve IoT devices and APIs, while data preparation includes cleaning, normalization, and transformation. Data storage solutions involve cloud-based databases such as PostgreSQL and NoSQL options such as MongoDB. Data delivery mechanisms include real-time dashboards for monitoring and APIs to provide refueling instructions to autonomous vehicles.

- **Architecture design**: The architecture involves sensors for data collection, cloud infrastructure for scalable processing and storage, and edge computing devices for real-time analytics. Typical use cases include predicting fuel demand to avoid shortages, optimizing gas station layouts to minimize wait times, and routing vehicles to the nearest available station. Learning and improvement mechanisms involve continuous model training with updated data, feedback loops from real-time data to improve predictions, and regular performance evaluations.

The AYAI Canvas, as presented in *Chapter 5*, serves as a holistic guide, ensuring a thorough understanding of AI solution requirements and facilitating effective communication among stakeholders involved in the development process.

In the upcoming sections, we look at all these categories in detail.

Requirements

The first category of the AYAI Canvas is the requirements, which define the scope and purpose of the AI solution. In our case study, the requirements are as follows:

- **Target audience**: The intended users or stakeholders of the AI solution are the gas station owners, the autonomous car owners or users, and the car manufacturers or service providers. The gas station owners want to offer a convenient and efficient service for autonomous cars, increasing their customer base and revenue. Autonomous car owners or users want to ensure that their cars are refueled when needed, without having to intervene manually or worry about the cost and quality of the gas. The car manufacturers or service providers want to enhance the functionality and performance of their cars, providing a seamless and satisfying experience for their customers.

- **Solution objectives**: The specific goals the AI solution aims to achieve are to enable autonomous cars to automatically detect the need for refueling, locate the nearest and most suitable gas station, negotiate the best price and payment method, and complete the refueling process safely and securely. The AI solution should also provide feedback and reports to the stakeholders, allowing them to monitor and evaluate the service quality and customer satisfaction.

- **Problem to be resolved**: The issue the AI solution will address is the lack of a standardized and reliable service for refueling autonomous cars, which may result in inconvenience, inefficiency, or safety risks for the stakeholders. The current solutions rely on human intervention, manual input, or predefined rules, which may not be optimal or adaptable to the dynamic and complex scenarios of the real world.

- **Type of problem**: The problem can be considered in multiple ways:

  - It can be classified as a multi-objective optimization problem, where the AI solution has to balance multiple and potentially conflicting criteria, such as cost, time, distance, quality, safety, and preference

  - The problem can also be seen as a multi-agent problem, where the AI solution has to interact and coordinate with multiple and potentially competing agents, such as other autonomous cars, gas stations, or human drivers

  - The problem can also be viewed as a reinforcement learning problem, where the AI solution has to learn from its own actions and outcomes, as well as from the feedback and behavior of the other agents

With a comprehensive understanding of the requirements for our AI solution, we have defined the target audience, solution objectives, the problem to be resolved, and the nature of this problem. This foundational knowledge is crucial as it sets the stage for the effective development and deployment of the AI solution, ensuring that it meets the needs and expectations of all stakeholders involved. Now, let's explore the next essential phase of our AI solution: operational management.

Operational management

The second category of the AYAI Canvas is operational management, which assesses the feasibility and sustainability of the AI solution. In our case study, the operational management aspects are as follows:

- **Scalability**:

  - The AI solution should be able to handle increased workload and demand, as the number of autonomous cars and gas stations grows.

  - The AI solution should also be able to adapt to different environments and conditions, such as traffic, weather, or regulations.

  - The AI solution should also use scalable and distributed architectures, such as cloud computing, edge computing, or peer-to-peer networks, to ensure high availability, reliability, and performance.

- **Computational efficiency:**

  - The AI solution should be able to process large and complex data, as well as perform sophisticated and dynamic computations, in a timely and accurate manner.

  - The AI solution should also be able to optimize the use of computational resources, such as memory, bandwidth, or energy, to reduce the cost and environmental impact.

  - The AI solution should use efficient and robust algorithms, such as deep learning, evolutionary algorithms, or swarm intelligence, to achieve high accuracy, speed, and flexibility.

- **Maintenance and upgrading:**

  - The AI solution should be able to maintain and upgrade its functionality and performance, as the requirements and expectations of the stakeholders change.

  - The AI solution should also be able to detect and correct errors, bugs, or anomalies, as well as prevent or recover from failures, attacks, or disasters.

  - The AI solution should use automated and continuous processes, such as DevOps, testing, or monitoring, to ensure high quality, security, and resilience.

- **Testing and evaluation:**

  - The AI solution should be able to test and evaluate its functionality and performance, as well as the satisfaction and trust of the stakeholders, using various methods and metrics.

  - The AI solution should also be able to compare and benchmark its results and outcomes, as well as the costs and benefits, with other alternatives or competitors.

  - The AI solution should use rigorous and transparent methods, such as experiments, simulations, or surveys, to ensure high validity, reliability, and accountability.

- **Security and privacy:**

  - The AI solution should be able to protect the data and transactions of the stakeholders, as well as the integrity and confidentiality of the AI system, from unauthorized or malicious access, use, or modification.

  - The AI solution should also be able to comply with the legal and ethical standards and regulations, as well as the preferences and consent of the stakeholders, regarding the collection, storage, and processing of the data and transactions.

  - The AI solution should use advanced and secure techniques, such as encryption, authentication, or blockchain, to ensure high privacy, trust, and compliance.

- **Ethical considerations**:

  - The AI solution should be able to integrate ethical considerations into its design and implementation, as well as its actions and outcomes, respecting the values and principles of the stakeholders and the society.

  - The AI solution should also be able to explain and justify its decisions and behaviors, as well as the risks and uncertainties, to the stakeholders and the regulators, ensuring high transparency, fairness, and accountability.

  - The AI solution should use ethical and human-centered approaches, such as value-sensitive design, ethical frameworks, or explainable AI, to ensure high responsibility, morality, and acceptability.

Having thoroughly examined the operational management facets of our AI solution, we can now ensure that it meets the demands of scalability, computational efficiency, maintenance, testing, security, privacy, and ethical considerations. These crucial elements form the backbone of an effective, sustainable, and trustworthy AI system. Moving forward, let's explore the essential components that will enable us to meet these operational objectives and deliver a robust and reliable AI solution.

Essential components

The third category of the AYAI Canvas is essential components, which specify the technical elements and choices of the AI solution. In our case study, the essential components are as follows:

- **Model**: The AI model or algorithm to be used for the AI solution is a hybrid model that combines multiple techniques and paradigms, such as deep neural networks, genetic algorithms, and multi-agent systems. The hybrid model can leverage the strengths and overcome the limitations of each technique and paradigm, achieving high performance and adaptability. It can also enable the integration and coordination of multiple AI models or agents, achieving high functionality and diversity.

- **Platform**: The infrastructure where the AI model will run is a hybrid platform that combines multiple architectures and technologies, such as cloud computing, edge computing, and peer-to-peer networks. The hybrid platform can provide high availability, reliability, and scalability, as well as low latency, cost, and energy consumption. It can also enable the distribution and collaboration of multiple AI models or agents, achieving high efficiency and robustness.

- **Tools**: The tools necessary for development, training, and deployment of the AI solution are a hybrid set of tools that combines multiple frameworks and libraries, such as TensorFlow, PyTorch, and OpenAI. The hybrid set of tools can provide high functionality, flexibility, and compatibility, as well as low complexity, time, and effort. They can also enable the use and reuse of multiple AI models or agents, achieving high productivity and innovation.

- **Frameworks**: The AI frameworks that align with the solution's requirements are a hybrid set of frameworks that combines multiple standards and guidelines, such as IEEE, ISO, and AI HLEG. This hybrid set of frameworks can provide high quality, security, and compliance, as well as low risk and uncertainty, and can also enable the alignment and coordination of multiple AI models or agents, achieving high transparency, fairness, and accountability. Having established the critical technical elements necessary for our AI solution, including the model, platform, tools, and frameworks, we now have a robust foundation for its development and deployment. These essential components are pivotal in ensuring that the AI solution performs optimally, remains adaptable, and adheres to high standards of quality, security, and compliance. Next, let us delve into the data flow aspects of our AI solution, which are crucial for its operational success and effectiveness.

Having established the critical technical elements, let us now delve into the data flow aspects of our AI solution. It encompasses how data is collected, processed, stored, and delivered, which are crucial steps for leveraging data-driven insights and making informed decisions.

Data flow

The fourth category of the AYAI Canvas is data flow, which identifies the data sources and processes of the AI solution. In our case study, the data flow is as follows:

- **Input interfaces**: The input interfaces are the ways how data enters the system, such as sensors, cameras, GPS, or voice. The input interfaces must be able to capture and transmit relevant and accurate data, such as the location, speed, fuel level, or destination of the car, as well as the availability, price, and quality of the gas station. Input interfaces in an AI system capture and transmit data using various formats and protocols. Sensors use formats such as JSON or XML and transmit via MQTT or HTTP. Cameras capture images or videos in formats such as JPEG or MP4, using RTSP for transmission. GPS data, often in NMEA format, is transmitted via HTTP or HTTPS. Voice data is captured in WAV or MP3 formats and processed through REST APIs. Integration involves IoT gateways that unify these formats and protocols, ensuring consistent and accurate data transfer to the AI system for analysis. For example, sensors send JSON data via MQTT, cameras use RTSP for JPEG images, GPS transmits NMEA data over HTTP, and voice commands are processed through REST APIs.

- **Data sources**: The data sources are the origins of the data for the AI model, such as Google Maps, Google Drive, or the gas station's database. Data sources must provide relevant and reliable data, such as the location, price, or quality of the gas station, as well as the preferences and history of the autonomous car. These data sources should use standardized and compatible protocols and formats, such as JSON, XML, or CSV, to facilitate data integration and processing.

- **Data collection**: Data collection are the strategies for gathering the relevant data for the AI model, such as web scraping, web service, or sensing. Data collection must be able to obtain and transmit data efficiently and accurately, taking into account aspects such as the frequency, volume or quality of the data. For data collection we must use appropriate and reliable techniques and tools, such as Beautiful Soup, RESTful API, or MQTT, to ensure data availability and reliability.

- **Data preparation**: Data preparation is the process of preparing the data for the AI model, such as cleaning, transforming or analyzing the data. With data preparation we must be able to improve and optimize the quality and usefulness of the data, considering aspects such as the consistency, completeness, or relevance of the data. We could use effective and robust methods and libraries, such as pandas, NumPy, or scikit-learn, to ensure the quality and usefulness of the data.

- **Data storage**: Data storage is the solution for storing data, such as Google Cloud Storage, MongoDB, or SQLite. The solution must be able to store and manage data in a secure and scalable way, taking into account aspects such as the size, type, or structure of the data. The data warehouse must use appropriate and secure systems and technologies, such as SQL, NoSQL, or blockchain, to guarantee data integrity and privacy.

- **Data delivery**: Data delivery is the way in which results or predictions are delivered, such as Google Assistant, Telegram, or email. The data delivery system we choose must be able to deliver and present the data in a convenient and understandable way, considering aspects such as the format, content, or feedback of the data. It should use appropriate and interactive interfaces and channels, such as chatbots, dashboards, or reports, to ensure data satisfaction and trust.

With a comprehensive understanding of the data flow processes, we have established a clear pathway for how data will be captured, processed, and utilized within our AI solution. This ensures that our system can efficiently and effectively handle data from various sources, maintain high-quality data standards, and deliver meaningful insights to stakeholders. Now, let's move on to the architecture design of our AI solution, which will integrate these data flow components into a cohesive and robust system.

Architecture design

The fifth AYAI Canvas category is architecture design, which explores the types, use cases, and learning and improvement mechanisms of the AI solution. In our case study, the architecture design is as follows:

- **Architecture types**: Architecture types are the ways in which the components and processes of the AI solution are organized and connected, such as layered architecture, service-oriented architecture, or event-based architecture. Architecture types must be able to meet the requirements and objectives of the AI solution, considering aspects such as the modularity, flexibility, or interoperability of the solution. They should use appropriate and consistent patterns and models, such as MVC, SOA, or EDA, to ensure the clarity and coherence of the solution.

- **Using the solution**: Use cases are the practical application scenarios of the AI solution, such as route planning, price negotiation, or fuel supply. The use cases should be able to demonstrate and validate the functionality and performance of the AI solution, considering aspects such as the effectiveness, efficiency, or safety of the solution. The use cases should also use realistic and relevant examples and simulations, such as Google Maps, Google Pay, or Google Car, to ensure the applicability and reliability of the solution.

- **Learning and improvement**: Learning and improvement mechanisms are the ways in which the AI solution learns and improves itself, such as supervised learning, unsupervised learning, or reinforcement learning. Learning and improvement mechanisms must be able to adapt and optimize the AI solution, taking into account aspects such as the accuracy, speed, or complexity of the solution. The learning and improvement mechanisms must also use appropriate and advanced techniques and algorithms, such as deep learning, genetic algorithm, or Q-learning, to guarantee the intelligence and evolution of the solution.

The AYAI Canvas serves as a holistic guide, ensuring a complete understanding of the requirements and considerations of the AI solution and facilitating effective communication between those involved in the development process.

Architecting for AI integration for MCs requires careful consideration of data infrastructure, machine learning models, real-time processing, microservices, APIs, and scalability. By embracing these components and gaining expertise in the field, businesses can effectively leverage AI capabilities and deliver exceptional experiences to their machine-driven customer base. In addition, they need to analyze the impacts that these solutions can have on shopping and commerce, both from the point of view of consumers and suppliers. In the next section, we'll discuss how the integration of AI with MCs can affect purchasing patterns, preferences, and behaviors, as well as strategies, offers, and business models.

Impact on purchases and commerce

The impact of MCs on purchases and commerce cannot be ignored. As we evaluate market opportunities presented by this emerging trend, it is important to understand the implications and potential benefits that MCs bring to businesses and consumers alike.

The rise of MCs, which refers to the use of AI and machine learning in consumer interactions, has revolutionized the way businesses operate. These intelligent systems have the ability to analyze vast amounts of data, predict consumer behavior, and provide personalized recommendations, ultimately enhancing the overall shopping experience.

Machine learning models such as collaborative filtering and content-based filtering are key in predicting consumer behavior and providing personalized recommendations. Collaborative filtering uses user interactions (e.g., ratings, purchase history) to suggest products based on similar users' preferences, with algorithms such as k-NN playing a major role. Content-based filtering recommends items by analyzing product attributes aligned with a user's past interactions, utilizing techniques such as TF-IDF and cosine similarity.

One of the key advantages of MCs is the ability to deliver *personalized recommendations* tailored to each individual's preferences. By analyzing past purchases, browsing history, and other relevant data, these systems can offer personalized product suggestions that align with the customer's interests. This level of personalization not only saves time for consumers but also increases customer satisfaction by delivering a more relevant and enjoyable shopping experience.

MCs also bring significant benefits to businesses, particularly in terms of *efficiency and cost reduction*. By automating various aspects of the purchasing process, such as inventory management and order fulfillment, businesses can streamline their operations and allocate resources more effectively. This not only eliminates human error but also reduces labor and operational costs, ultimately improving the bottom line.

The presence of MCs opens up new market opportunities for businesses. With AI-powered systems capable of analyzing market trends and consumer behavior in real-time, businesses can *identify untapped customer segments* and tailor their marketing strategies accordingly. This targeted approach allows businesses to better understand their customers' needs and preferences, resulting in increased sales and a stronger market position.

While the benefits of MCs are evident, it is important to address ethical considerations and maintain a balance between automation and human interaction. Although AI-powered systems can provide personalized recommendations, some customers may still prefer human assistance and the human touch in their shopping experience. Therefore, businesses need to strike a balance between automation and maintaining the option for human interaction, ensuring that the customer's preferences are respected.

The impact of MCs on purchases and commerce is undeniable. These intelligent systems have the potential to revolutionize the way businesses operate, providing enhanced personalization, efficiency, and cost reduction. By embracing this emerging trend and leveraging the power of AI, businesses can tap into new market opportunities and deliver a seamless shopping experience. However, it is crucial to strike a balance between automation and human interaction, ensuring that the customer's preferences are met.

Preparing for the future with MCs

As we navigate the ever-evolving technological landscape, it is imperative that we hone our skills to think strategically about the future. In this age of machine users, businesses must position themselves to thrive in this new paradigm. By embracing the potential of MCs, we can unlock endless possibilities for growth and success.

To work effectively with MCs, professionals should develop specific technical skills and knowledge areas, including data science, AI model training, API development, and cybersecurity. Data science expertise is crucial for analyzing and interpreting large datasets to derive actionable insights. AI model training involves understanding and applying machine learning algorithms to build and refine intelligent systems. Proficiency in API development is essential for creating and integrating interfaces that allow different software systems to communicate effectively. Cybersecurity knowledge is vital to protect data and systems from threats and ensure privacy and compliance.

Tips for strategies when engaging with MCs in business

-**Identify potential MCs in your sector and segment**: Which machines could benefit from your product or service? What are their characteristics, capabilities, and limitations? What are their objectives, motivations, and challenges?

-**Analyze future trends and scenarios that could impact MCs**: What are the external forces that could influence the behavior and demands of MCs? What opportunities and threats might arise? What are the most likely and most desirable scenarios?

-**Create a unique and differentiated value proposition for MCs**: How can your product or service meet the needs and expectations of MCs? How can your product or service stand out from the competition and create a competitive advantage? How can your product or service adapt to changes and evolve with MCs?

-**Establish a relationship of trust and collaboration with MCs**: How can you communicate your value and generate engagement with MCs? How can you collect and use MC data and feedback to improve your product or service? How can you establish a relationship of trust and collaboration with MCs, while respecting their autonomy and privacy?

In order to prepare for the future with MCs, we must first develop a strategic mindset. This means thinking beyond the present and envisioning the potential scenarios that may arise as technology continues to advance. By actively seeking opportunities to innovate and adapt, we can position our businesses at the forefront of this digital revolution.

To effectively cater to MCs, it is crucial to have a deep understanding of their needs and preferences. By analyzing data and leveraging artificial intelligence, we can gain valuable insights into their behaviors and expectations. This knowledge will enable us to tailor our products and services to meet their demands, ensuring a seamless and personalized experience.

While machines may be the customers of the future, it is essential to remember that they are ultimately designed and programmed by humans. Therefore, it is crucial to maintain a human touch in our interactions with MCs. By fostering trust, authenticity, and empathy, we can create meaningful connections with these digital entities, ensuring long-term loyalty and satisfaction.

Collaboration is key in the age of MCs. By forging strategic partnerships with tech companies and experts in the field, we can leverage their knowledge and expertise to propel our businesses forward. These partnerships can provide access to cutting-edge technologies, facilitate innovation, and open up new avenues for growth.

In this rapidly changing landscape, it is crucial to embrace a culture of continuous learning and adaptation. By staying abreast of the latest technological advancements and industry trends, we can proactively identify opportunities for growth and evolution. This mindset will enable us to stay ahead of the curve and ensure our readiness for any challenges that may arise.

Preparing for the future with MCs requires a strategic mindset, a deep understanding of their needs, and a commitment to continuous learning and adaptation. By embracing these principles, we can position our businesses to thrive in this age of technology. Let us embrace the potential of MCs and unlock a future filled with endless possibilities.

Summary

In this chapter, we explored the phenomenon of machine users and how they are transforming the digital landscape. We learned to adapt the web development paradigm to cater to these new customers and covered topics such as decoding the machine user, market opportunities and scenarios, and architecting for AI integration.

We developed skills to understand and profile the machine user, create strategic scenarios, architect data sources and API platforms for the machine user, and evaluate market opportunities presented by Internet-of-Things-enabled products. Finally, we honed the skill of thinking strategically about the future and positioning businesses to thrive in the age of the machine user.

In the next chapter, we will embark on a journey into the future of software engineering with AI-augmented development.

13

AI-Augmented Development – Shaping Tomorrow's Digital Landscape

In this chapter, we will explore software development with the help of **artificial intelligence** (**AI**), a trend that is shaping the future of the digital landscape. AI can improve the productivity, creativity, and quality of software developers by offering tools that automate, optimize, and innovate the development process. We'll introduce **Gemini Code Assist** (formerly known as AI Duet), an integrated platform that combines three essential components of AI development: design tools for code (platforms such as Sketch2Code and Figma with AI plugins), coding assistants (tools such as Tabnine and GitHub Copilot) and AI-enhanced testing tools (including DeepCode), in this chapter. We'll also discuss how generative AI and **Machine Learning** (**ML**) can be used to create personalized and adaptive software solutions. Finally, we'll look at the impact of AI on the field of software engineering and the opportunities and challenges it brings.

In this chapter, we will cover the following main topics:

- The impact of AI-augmented development on software engineering
- Understanding the AI-augmented development components
- Enhancing the software development life cycle with Gemini Code Assist (formerly AI Duet)
- Practical strategies for leveraging AI in software development
- How to integrate AI into software development teams

By the end of this chapter, you will have learned to recognize the benefits and challenges of AI development for software engineering. You will have understood and applied AI technologies to revolutionize the software development process, embracing the future of the industry.

The impact of AI-augmented development on software engineering

At the forefront of web development, we are witnessing the transformative power of AI-augmented development in the field of software engineering. The integration of AI into the development process is revolutionizing how we create and optimize web applications. In this section, we will explore the profound impact of AI on software engineering, highlighting its benefits and implications for developers and businesses alike.

One of the key aspects of modern web development is the implementation of design systems with **design-to-code capabilities**. This innovative approach allows us to seamlessly translate design concepts into functional code, reducing development time and effort. With AI-augmented development, these capabilities are further enhanced, enabling us to create robust and visually appealing web applications with greater efficiency and accuracy.

By harnessing the power of AI, we can leverage ML algorithms to analyze and interpret design patterns, automatically generating code snippets that adhere to the established design system. This eliminates the need for manual coding and reduces the chances of human error. As a result, developers can focus on more complex tasks, such as optimizing performance and enhancing **user experience (UX)**.

AI-augmented development also fosters improved collaboration and communication among developers, designers, and stakeholders. With AI-powered tools, we can create real-time collaboration platforms that facilitate seamless interaction and exchange of ideas. These platforms leverage **Natural Language Processing (NLP)** and ML algorithms to provide intelligent suggestions and feedback, enhancing the overall development process.

Furthermore, AI can assist in automating repetitive tasks, freeing up developers' time to engage in more meaningful discussions and creative problem solving. By reducing the burden of mundane tasks, AI allows us to focus on the human aspect of development, fostering a more collaborative and innovative environment.

With AI-augmented development, we can significantly enhance the quality and reliability of web applications. AI algorithms can analyze vast amounts of data to identify potential bugs, vulnerabilities, and performance issues, allowing developers to proactively address them. This not only improves the overall UX but also helps businesses ensure the security and stability of their web applications.

To achieve enhanced quality and reliability in web applications, integrating AI tools and techniques into the software development life cycle is crucial. Here are some of the most effective AI-driven solutions for quality assurance and reliability testing in web applications:

- **AI-driven performance monitoring**:
  - **New Relic AI**: This utilizes ML to automatically detect performance anomalies in real time, identifying trends and patterns in application performance data to help developers address issues quickly

- **Dynatrace**: This employs AI to provide deep insights into performance, predicting and identifying performance degradation, conducting root cause analysis, and optimizing application performance across various environments

- **Anomaly detection systems**:

  - **Splunk**: This features an ML toolkit that includes anomaly detection capabilities to identify unusual patterns or outliers in log data, which is essential for the early detection of security breaches or system failures

  - **Amazon CloudWatch Anomaly Detection**: This uses ML to continuously monitor and analyze metrics for anomalies, helping to detect unexpected changes in application performance or usage patterns

- **Automated testing tools**:

  - **Testim**: This utilizes AI to create, execute, and maintain automated tests, adapting to UI changes to make the testing process more resilient and reducing maintenance overhead

  - **Applitools**: This applies AI for visual UI testing, automatically detecting visual bugs by comparing screenshots across different versions to ensure the application looks and functions correctly on all devices and browsers

- **Static code analysis**:

  - **DeepCode**: An AI-powered code review tool that analyzes code repositories to identify potential bugs and vulnerabilities, using ML models trained on a vast amount of open-source code to provide recommendations for code improvements

  - **SonarQube with SonarLint**: This offers static code analysis with AI enhancements, providing continuous feedback on code quality and highlighting potential issues such as security vulnerabilities and code smells

- **Security vulnerability scanning**:

  - **Snyk**: This integrates with the development environment to automatically find and fix vulnerabilities in open-source dependencies, using AI to prioritize vulnerabilities based on severity and potential impact

  - **Veracode**: This provides an AI-driven approach to application security testing, scanning for vulnerabilities in the code and offering remediation suggestions to help developers secure their applications from the start

By incorporating these AI tools and techniques, developers can ensure their web applications are functional, user-friendly, secure, and robust. This proactive approach to quality assurance and reliability testing facilitates the delivery of high-quality software that meets user expectations and business requirements.

Moreover, AI-powered testing frameworks can automate the testing process, identifying bugs and providing detailed reports on application behavior. This accelerates the testing phase, allowing for faster deployment and more reliable software releases.

Consider Testim, an AI-powered automated testing tool. When integrated into the development workflow, Testim starts by creating automated tests based on user interactions and changes in the UI. As development progresses, Testim adapts to these changes, ensuring tests remain relevant and up to date.

During the testing phase, Testim's AI algorithms analyze application behavior to detect anomalies or bugs. For instance, if a previously functional feature suddenly fails, Testim flags the issue and provides detailed information about the failure, including the steps leading to the bug and its exact location in the code.

Upon completing the tests, Testim generates comprehensive reports summarizing the test results. These reports detail the number of tests passed and failed, the severity of detected bugs, and suggestions for fixing the issues. Presented in a user-friendly format, these reports help developers understand problems and take corrective actions.

By incorporating these AI tools and techniques, developers can ensure their web applications are not only functional and user friendly but also secure and robust. This proactive approach to quality assurance and reliability testing facilitates the delivery of high-quality software that meets user expectations and business requirements.

The impact of AI-augmented development on software engineering is undeniable. By leveraging AI-powered tools and techniques, developers can streamline the development process, enhance collaboration, and improve software quality. As we continue to embrace the possibilities of AI, the future of web development looks promising, paving the way for innovative and efficient solutions in the digital landscape. In the next section, we'll explore the main components of AI-enhanced development, such as code assistants, automated testing, and intelligent debugging.

Understanding the AI-augmented development components

In recent years, the field of software engineering has witnessed a significant transformation with the emergence of AI-augmented development. This innovative approach harnesses the power of AI technologies, such as generative AI and ML, to assist software engineers in creating, testing, and delivering applications. With the integration of AI-augmented development tools, developers can enhance their productivity and address the growing demand for software solutions. In this section, we will explore the three key components of AI-augmented development and discuss why it is currently trending in the software engineering industry.

Let's look at the three key components first:

- **AI-powered design-to-code tools**: These tools have revolutionized the software development process. They enable engineers to seamlessly translate design prototypes into functional code, eliminating the need for manual coding. By automating this tedious task, software engineers can focus more on higher-level activities, such as designing and composing compelling business applications. This component of AI-augmented development streamlines the development process and enhances overall efficiency.

- **AI coding assistants**: Imagine having an AI-powered assistant by your side, helping you write code faster and more accurately. AI coding assistants have become an invaluable resource for software engineers. By analyzing existing code bases and leveraging ML algorithms, these assistants can suggest code snippets, detect errors, and even generate code automatically. As a result, developers can significantly reduce the time spent on writing code and increase their productivity. According to Gartner, by 2028, it is predicted that 75% of enterprise software engineers will be utilizing AI coding assistants, up from less than 10% in early 2023 (`https://www.gartner.com/en/articles/gartner-top-10-strategic-technology-trends-for-2024`).

- **AI-augmented testing tools**: Ensuring the quality and reliability of software applications is paramount in the development process. AI-augmented testing tools leverage AI technologies to enhance the testing capabilities of software engineers. These tools can automatically generate test cases, detect bugs, and even predict potential issues before they occur. By automating these testing processes, developers can save time and resources while delivering high-quality applications to end users.

The rise of AI-augmented development can be attributed to several factors. Firstly, previously mentioned tools seamlessly integrate with a developer's environment, providing them with enhanced code generation capabilities, design-to-code transformation, and improved application testing. Secondly, AI-assisted software engineering significantly improves developer productivity, enabling development teams to keep up with the increasing demand for software solutions. Lastly, by reducing the time spent on writing code, engineers can focus on more critical tasks, such as designing innovative and impactful business applications.

AI-augmented development has revolutionized the field of software engineering by leveraging the power of AI technologies. With its three essential components – design-to-code tools, AI coding assistants, and AI-augmented testing tools – developers can streamline their workflows, increase productivity, and deliver high-quality applications. As the industry continues to embrace AI-augmented development, we can expect to see a significant rise in the adoption of these tools by software engineers in the coming years.

To illustrate how AI-augmented development can be applied in practice, we will present a step-by-step guide on how to use Gemini Code Assist (formerly AI Duet), a tool that integrates the three essential components of AI-augmented development into a single platform.

Enhancing the software development life cycle with Gemini Code Assist

In today's fast-paced world, software development must continually adapt to new challenges. AI-augmented development is instrumental in this adaptation, offering not only speed and efficiency but also enhanced decision-making capabilities. By integrating AI, developers can predict potential issues before they become problematic, tailor solutions more precisely to user needs, and even innovate in UX design. This proactive approach transforms how software is conceived and delivered, aligning development processes more closely with dynamic market demands and user expectations.

DevOps, when integrated with the software development life cycle, is formed by two essential cycles: development and operation. The **development cycle** covers the conception, creation, and coding of the software, while the **operation cycle** focuses on the deployment, monitoring, and maintenance of the software in a production environment.

With tools such as Google Cloud's Gemini Code Assist leading the charge, developers have access to unprecedented capabilities that streamline and enhance every phase of the development life cycle. This guide will explore how Gemini Code Assist transforms the conventional stages of software creation, from design and coding to testing and deployment, demonstrating AI's transformative impact on the software industry. From the initial design phase to the final impact assessment, we will show you how AI is reshaping the world of software development. Let's begin:

1. **Design together**: In this stage, the team collaborates to create an effective design. With Google's AI assistance, developers can quickly respond to feature requests, conduct effective brainstorming sessions, and clean up architecture diagrams. Additionally, they can use Bard to ask questions about the architecture and identify potential risks in the proposed implementation. The conversation with Bard can be exported to Google Docs to start the design document. The *Help me write* feature of Google Docs can be used to generate an outline, allowing developers to focus on more complex design questions.

2. **Code with help**: Once the design document is approved and the frontend page is ready to start testing, developers can begin coding. At this stage, Google's AI assistance can be used to help developers write and submit code more efficiently. Generative AI can assist in automatically generating parts of the code, saving developers time and effort. In addition, AI can help identify and fix security vulnerabilities in the code, as well as suggest improvements to increase the resilience of the application.

3. **Operate with confidence**: Once the code for the new feature is reviewed and merged into the main branch, it's deployed to the production environment. As the on-call app developer, finding service logs is crucial, facilitated by the Gemini Code Assist console's chat within the Cloud Run console. Collaboration with the **site reliability engineering** (**SRE**) team leads to the creation of service-level objectives for the inventory service. For detailed service health analysis, Gemini Code Assist's features assist in crafting complex queries within Cloud Monitoring. Additionally, a security oversight from the previous week, where a teammate retained an overly permissive **Identity and Access Management** (**IAM**) role, is identified and addressed using insights from the Security Command Center, aided by AI-generated summaries to expedite comprehension and resolution.

4. **Share the impact**: A week goes by, and the product lead has asked you to present a few slides at the upcoming all hands. Work is done with a business analyst colleague to prepare. The goal is to understand the impact of creating a new product showcase – did those new products sell better after being featured on their own dedicated page? The process starts by creating a to-do list in Google Sheets, using the help me organize feature. Then, diving into the sales data, using Gemini Code Assist in Spanner's SQL code completion feature to query the raw transaction data from the last few weeks. More data is gathered from the sales rollup tables in BigQuery. As the business analyst writes SQL queries with expert ease, Duet's code explanation feature is used to better understand the data being gathered. From there, jump to Google Slides and use Gemini Code Assist's *Help me visualize* tool to generate supporting imagery for the impact report.

In summary, generative AI plays a crucial role in all stages of the software development life cycle, from idea generation to application optimization for end users. It's a powerful tool that can enhance the efficiency and effectiveness of software developers. This AI-augmented development process is not only efficient but also ensures high-quality output, making it a valuable approach in modern software development.

Gemini Code Assist – an AI-augmented development tool

Gemini Code Assist introduces a new paradigm in software development by leveraging advanced AI to augment the development process. This analysis explores its capabilities, highlighting how it integrates with existing development workflows to enhance productivity, creativity, and code quality:

1. **Enhancing productivity**: Gemini Code Assist automates repetitive and labor-intensive tasks, thus increasing productivity. Its AI-based code generators can interpret natural language descriptions to produce code snippets. This functionality allows developers to quickly generate boilerplate code, enabling them to focus on more complex aspects of their projects. Additionally, the tool offers intelligent debugging systems that identify and suggest fixes for potential bugs, reducing the time spent on troubleshooting and improving overall efficiency.

2. **Facilitating creativity**: The platform supports creative development through real-time coding assistance. It uses a **large language model** (**LLM**) to predict and suggest code completions, alternative solutions, and answers to complex queries. This continuous assistance helps developers concentrate on innovative problem solving rather than routine coding tasks. By providing relevant suggestions and solutions, Gemini Code Assist encourages developers to explore new approaches and methodologies in their work.

3. **Improving code quality**: Gemini Code Assist includes AI-enhanced testing tools that play a crucial role in maintaining high code quality. These tools can automatically generate and execute test cases, analyze results, and provide detailed performance reports. This automated testing process helps in the early detection of issues, ensuring that the final product is robust and reliable. The tool's ability to identify code vulnerabilities and offer remediation suggestions further contributes to producing high-quality software.

4. **Seamless integration with development environments**: The tool is designed to integrate seamlessly with popular **integrated development environments** (**IDEs**) and repositories. As developers write or modify code, Gemini Code Assist actively monitors these changes and provides real-time suggestions and corrections. This integration ensures that the assistance provided is contextually relevant and timely, allowing developers to maintain their workflow without interruptions.

5. **Leveraging AI for personalized and adaptive solutions**: Gemini Code Assist employs generative AI and ML to create personalized and adaptive software solutions. By analyzing user behavior and preferences, the tool tailors functionalities to meet specific needs, enhancing UX and making software more intuitive. This adaptability is particularly useful in developing applications that require customization based on user interaction patterns.

6. **Addressing ethical and practical challenges**: The introduction of AI tools such as Gemini Code Assist also brings certain challenges. Ethical considerations, such as bias in AI algorithms and the potential for misuse, must be addressed. Developers need to ensure that the AI models used are trained on diverse and representative datasets to mitigate biases. Additionally, the rapid pace of AI advancements necessitates continuous learning and adaptation by developers to keep up with new technologies and methodologies.

Figure 13.1 details how a developer interacts with the IDE or repository, and how Gemini Code Assist (formerly known as AI Duet) enhances the software development process with AI-powered design tools and testing tools.

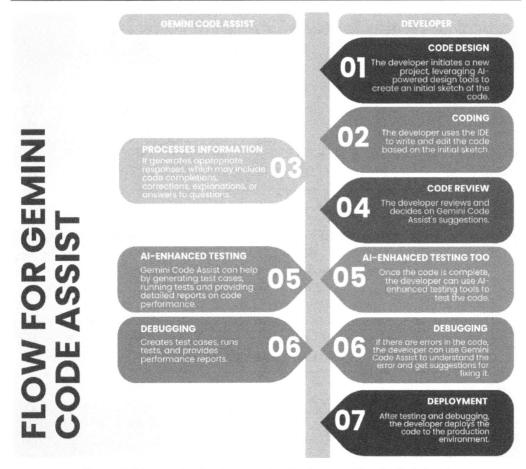

Figure 13.1: Interaction flow between the developer and Gemini Code Assist

The interaction flow detailed in the preceding figure demonstrates how Gemini Code Assist integrates seamlessly into the development process, enhancing productivity, creativity, and code quality through various stages from initial design to deployment. By leveraging AI-powered tools, developers can optimize their workflow, reduce errors, and create more robust and adaptive software solutions.

With an understanding of how Gemini Code Assist can transform your development process, let's delve into practical strategies for leveraging AI in software development. These strategies will guide you on how to integrate AI effectively into your workflow, ensuring you maximize its benefits and stay ahead in the fast-evolving tech landscape.

Practical strategies for leveraging AI in software development

In today's fast-paced world, software development is a crucial aspect of business success. As technology continues to advance, so does the need for more efficient and effective software development processes. Thankfully, the advent of AI has brought about new possibilities in this field. According to a recent study by Gartner (`https://www.gartner.com/en/articles/set-up-now-for-ai-to-augment-software-development`), AI has the potential to automate mundane software development tasks and assist engineers in producing code more quickly. In this section, we will explore five ways in which software engineers can leverage AI throughout the software development life cycle and provide guidance for software engineering leaders to integrate AI seamlessly into their teams:

- **Empower code generation with generative AI**: Generative AI tools, such as GitHub Copilot, Amazon CodeWhisperer, and Google Codey, offer an excellent choice for enterprises seeking AI-enabled code generation. By utilizing these tools, software engineers can automate the process of writing and understanding software code, significantly increasing productivity. Additionally, plug-in coding assistants powered by ML can offer predictions on future code fragments, aiding in the speedy build of software applications. To help readers choose the right AI-powered code generation tools for their specific needs, the following comparison table (*Figure 13.2*) highlights key features, strengths, and weaknesses of GitHub Copilot, Amazon CodeWhisperer, and Google Codey.

Comparison of AI-Powered Code Generation Tools

Tool	Key Features	Strengths	Weaknesses
GitHub Copilot	AI code generation, real-time code suggestions	High productivity, seamless integration with GitHub	May require subscription, potential for over-reliance
Amazon CodeWhisperer	Code generation, real-time code suggestions	Seamless integration with AWS, boosts productivity	Best used within AWS ecosystem
Google Codey	AI code generation, machine learning code predictions	Strong AI capabilities, predictive coding assistance	Limited availability outside Google ecosystem

Figure 13.2: Comparison of AI-powered code generation tools

By examining the preceding table, developers can make informed decisions on which AI-powered code generation tool best fits their development needs.

- **App modernization made easy**: OpenAI's ChatGPT chatbot has proven to be a valuable asset for translating software code from one language to another, simplifying the app modernization process. However, caution must be exercised when using generative AI tools, as inaccuracies and factual errors may occur. Despite this, it is projected that by 2027, 70% of professional developers will be utilizing AI-powered coding tools to enhance their productivity.

- **Managing technical debt with generative AI**: Technical debt, originating from software application architecture, design, and development, can be effectively managed with the help of generative AI. By leveraging AI, software engineers can detect and measure sources of technical debt, providing a clear understanding of its implications, risks, and the effort required for remediation. However, it is important to note that generative AI should not be used for remediation or tracking technical debt, as it may yield inaccurate results.

- **Meeting user expectations with AI-powered products**: Generative AI has set new UX standards, increasing users' expectations of AI-driven products and services. To ensure user satisfaction, software developers should incorporate conversational prompt-based interfaces into their software products. Neglecting this feature may lead to unhappy users and a decline in the popularity of the software.

- **Enhancing software testing with AI**: AI is transforming the field of software testing by improving test efficacy and reducing delivery cycle times. By leveraging AI, software engineers can benefit from enhanced test planning and prioritization, streamlined test creation and maintenance, efficient test data generation, accurate visual testing, and comprehensive test and defect analysis. These advancements in software testing contribute to overall product quality and user satisfaction. AI can significantly enhance test planning and prioritization by analyzing vast amounts of historical test data to identify high-risk areas that require more rigorous testing. For example, AI algorithms can analyze past defect patterns and predict which parts of the software are most likely to fail, allowing testers to prioritize these areas.

AI has the potential to revolutionize software development by automating mundane tasks, accelerating code production, and enhancing UX. By leveraging generative AI tools, software engineers can streamline their processes, manage technical debt effectively, and revolutionize software testing. For software engineering leaders, embracing an AI-first mentality and investing in dedicated AI solutions are key to staying ahead in this rapidly evolving field. The future of software development lies in the harmonious partnership between humans and AI.

Now, with a firm grasp of the potential and power of AI-augmented development, let's turn our focus to practical implementation. The next section will guide software engineering leaders on effectively incorporating AI technologies into their workflows.

How to integrate AI into software development teams

AI is a technology that can transform the way we create and use software applications. It can help us solve complex problems, optimize processes, improve UX, and generate value for businesses. However, for us to fully leverage the potential of AI, it needs to be effectively integrated into software development teams. In this section, we will present some actions that software engineering leaders should consider so that they can achieve this goal, based on Gartner's recommendations (`https://www.gartner.com/en/articles/set-up-now-for-ai-to-augment-software-development`).

Let's start:

- **Adopt an AI mindset from the start**: The first action is to adopt an AI mindset from the start of the project, encouraging the exploration of AI techniques to improve application development. This means that developers should be open to learning about the possibilities and challenges of AI and seek innovative solutions that use this technology. In addition, leaders should set clear and measurable goals for the use of AI and align expectations with project stakeholders. So, encourage teams to explore AI by initiating projects that directly involve AI technologies. For instance, a development team could be tasked with creating a chatbot to streamline customer service interactions, encouraging them to learn and apply NLP techniques.

- **Provide a framework to identify AI opportunities**: The second action is to provide a framework to identify when and where AI can yield better results. This involves analyzing the needs and requirements of the project, and assessing whether AI can offer benefits in terms of quality, efficiency, scalability, security, or other aspects. It is also important to consider the costs and risks associated with implementing AI and compare them with available alternatives. The framework should guide developers in choosing the most suitable AI techniques for each case, such as ML, NLP, and computer vision. Develop a decision matrix to help identify opportunities for AI integration that can enhance project outcomes. This matrix could evaluate factors such as potential improvements in efficiency and quality against the costs and complexity of implementing AI solutions, helping to pinpoint where tools such as ML could be most beneficial.

- **Invest in dedicated AI solutions**: The third action is to invest in dedicated AI solutions to support various roles and tasks in software engineering. These solutions can be tools, platforms, services, or libraries that use AI to facilitate or automate activities such as design, coding, testing, debugging, integration, deployment, and monitoring. These solutions can increase the productivity, quality, and creativity of developers, as well as reduce errors and rework. Some examples of AI solutions for software engineering are intelligent assistants, code generators, code analyzers, and automatic testers. For example, implementing platforms such as TensorFlow or PyTorch for ML projects can aid in tasks ranging from predictive analytics to automated testing, thus boosting productivity and reducing the likelihood of errors.

- **Expand the data engineering pipeline**: The fourth action is to expand the data engineering pipeline to leverage AI enrichment and enable intelligent applications. This means that developers should collect, store, process, analyze, and visualize data efficiently and securely, using AI to extract insights and value from data. In addition, developers should integrate the data with AI models, and use these models to provide intelligent features to applications, such as recommendations, customizations, predictions, and detections. Intelligent applications can improve performance, usability, and end-user satisfaction. By integrating comprehensive data management tools such as Apache Kafka for real-time data streaming and processing, teams can enhance their applications with features such as real-time analytics and dynamic UX customization.

- **Foster collaboration between development and model-building teams**: The fifth action is to foster collaboration between development teams and model-building teams to avoid overlapping responsibilities and ensure smooth deployment. This involves creating a culture of collaboration and communication, where both teams understand their roles and responsibilities, and work together to implement AI solutions. This can help avoid conflicts, reduce delays, and ensure that the AI models are correctly integrated into the software applications. Establish regular sync-up meetings between software developers and AI model builders to ensure alignment and seamless integration of AI capabilities into applications. These meetings can help clarify responsibilities, share insights, and quicken the pace of development.

- **Continuously train and upskill the team**: The sixth action is to continuously train and upskill the team in AI technologies. This involves providing regular training sessions, workshops, and resources to help developers learn about the latest AI techniques and tools. It also involves creating a learning culture, where developers are encouraged to learn and share their knowledge with others. This can help to build a team of skilled AI practitioners, who can effectively use AI to improve software development. Create ongoing educational programs and provide access to courses from platforms such as Coursera or Udemy that cover advanced AI topics. Encouraging participation in hackathons or internal projects focused on AI can also foster practical experience and innovation.

Effectively integrating AI into software development teams is a complex task that requires a strategic and diligent approach. It's not just about adopting new tools or technologies but transforming the mindset, processes, skills, and culture of the team. To navigate this transformation successfully, a structured checklist can serve as a valuable guide, ensuring that every critical aspect is addressed systematically:

1. **Assessment and planning**:

   - **Identify objectives**: Define clear objectives for integrating AI into your development processes. Determine what problems you aim to solve or what improvements you want to achieve.

   - **Evaluate readiness**: Assess your team's current capabilities, infrastructure, and tools to determine readiness for AI integration.

   - **Stakeholder alignment**: Ensure all stakeholders understand the benefits and implications of AI integration. Secure their support and alignment with the project goals.

2. **Data collection and management**:

    -   **Identify data sources**: Determine the types of data that will be valuable for AI-driven insights (e.g., source code data, user interaction data, performance data).

    -   **Set up data pipelines**: Implement data pipelines using tools such as Apache Kafka for real-time data collection and streaming.

    -   **Ensure data quality**: Establish processes for data cleaning, normalization, and validation to maintain high data quality.

3. **Infrastructure and tools**:

    -   **Select AI tools**: Choose appropriate AI-powered tools for different stages of the development process, such as GitHub Copilot for code generation, Testim for automated testing, and Dynatrace for performance monitoring.

    -   **Scalable storage solutions**: Implement scalable storage solutions such as Amazon S3 or Google Cloud Storage to handle large volumes of data.

    -   **Processing frameworks**: Utilize data processing frameworks such as Apache Spark or Flink for efficient data processing.

4. **Model development and integration**:

    -   **Build AI models**: Use ML frameworks such as TensorFlow, PyTorch, and scikit-learn to develop AI models that can analyze data and generate insights.

    -   **Integrate AI models**: Integrate AI models into your development environment to provide intelligent features such as code suggestions, anomaly detection, and predictive analytics.

5. **Testing and validation**:

    -   **Automated testing tools**: Implement AI-powered automated testing tools such as Testim to create and maintain test cases, ensuring the software remains robust and error-free.

    -   **Continuous integration**: Set up **continuous integration** (**CI**) pipelines to automatically run tests and validate code changes.

    -   **Performance monitoring**: Use tools such as New Relic AI and Dynatrace to monitor application performance and detect issues in real time.

6. **Security and compliance**:

    -   **Vulnerability scanning**: Use AI-powered security tools such as Snyk and Veracode to identify and fix vulnerabilities in the code.

    -   **Compliance checks**: Ensure that AI models and data processing adhere to relevant regulations and standards, such as **General Data Protection Regulation** (**GDPR**).

7. **Deployment and maintenance**:

- **Automated deployment**: Set up automated deployment pipelines to streamline the release process.

- **Real-time monitoring**: Continuously monitor the application in production using tools such as Amazon CloudWatch and Splunk for anomaly detection.

- **Feedback loop**: Establish a feedback loop to collect user feedback and performance data, using this information to continuously improve the AI models and development processes.

By following these actions, software engineering leaders can effectively integrate AI into their teams and leverage its potential to create innovative, high-quality, and intelligent software applications. This can lead to significant improvements in productivity, quality, creativity, and user satisfaction, as well as provide a competitive edge in today's increasingly digital and data-driven market.

However, it's important to remember that AI is just a tool that can help solve problems and generate value. The ultimate success of the project depends on the team's ability to understand user needs, create effective and innovative solutions, and deliver high-quality software. Therefore, AI should be integrated in a way that supports and enhances these goals, rather than replacing them.

Summary

In this chapter, you explored software development with the help of AI, a trend that is shaping the future of the digital landscape. You learned how AI can improve the productivity, creativity, and quality of software developers by offering tools that automate, optimize, and innovate the development process.

You were introduced to Gemini Code Assist, an integrated platform that combines three essential components of AI development: design tools for code, coding assistants, and AI-enhanced testing tools. You also discussed how generative AI and ML can be used to create personalized and adaptive software solutions. Finally, you looked at the impact of AI on the field of software engineering and the opportunities and challenges it brings.

The lessons and skills covered in this chapter are crucial for modern software development. They provide developers with the tools and knowledge to leverage AI effectively, transforming their workflow and improving productivity. Understanding the impact of AI-augmented development allows businesses to stay competitive in an increasingly digital world, ensuring they can create innovative, high-quality, and user-centric software solutions. By integrating AI into the development process, teams can achieve greater efficiency, reduce errors, and enhance collaboration, ultimately leading to more successful and impactful software projects.

In the next chapter, we'll explore the crucial role of AI in creating intelligent web applications.

Further reading

- Gartner. (2024). *Top 10 Strategic Technology Trends for 2024*. Retrieved from `https://www.gartner.com/en/articles/gartner-top-10-strategic-technology-trends-for-2024`

- Gartner. (2023). *Set Up Now for AI to Augment Software Development*. Retrieved from `https://www.gartner.com/en/articles/set-up-now-for-ai-to-augment-software-development`.

- Google Cloud. (2023). *How AI-driven software creation tools speed up your development*. Retrieved from `https://cloud.google.com/blog/products/application-development/how-ai-driven-software-creation-tools-speed-up-your-development`

14

From Idea to Reality – Crafting Intelligent Web Applications

As we transition into an era dominated by intelligent technologies, this chapter explores the pivotal role of **artificial intelligence** (**AI**) in crafting intelligent web applications. From foundational capabilities to broad-ranging use cases, readers will uncover how intelligent applications, augmented with AI and connected data, are reshaping consumer and business interactions.

In this chapter, we will delve into advanced AI principles relevant to user interactions and how to automate repetitive tasks through AI. The first section will introduce you to the principles of decoupled architecture for independent application entities. Next, we will acquire skills to bridge the gap between AI algorithms and diverse datasets. Finally, we will create data-infused business insights and understand how AI contributes to business analytics for insightful decision-making.

In this chapter, we will cover the following main topics:

- Intelligent applications – revolutionizing the future of technology
- Building an intelligent chatbot for e-commerce – laying the groundwork
- Data and design – creating an intelligent chatbot for e-commerce
- Deployment and user engagement – utilizing AI for business analytics and web application
- Evolution through learning – unlock the potential of AI for business analytics

By the end of this chapter, you will have gained a deep understanding of advanced AI principles relevant to user interactions. You will have mastered the principles of automating repetitive tasks through AI. You will also know how to set up support for decoupled architecture for independent application entities. You will also have acquired skills to bridge the gap between AI algorithms and diverse datasets. You will also understand how AI contributes to business analytics for insightful decision making.

Intelligent applications – revolutionizing the future of technology

In the era of digital transformation, intelligent applications are becoming a cornerstone of technological advancement, as highlighted by a Gartner report. According to Gartner, by 2026, 30% of new applications will incorporate AI to drive personalized and adaptive user interfaces, marking a significant increase from the current rate of under 5%. This indicates a substantial shift towards more dynamic and responsive applications. You can read more about this trend on the Gartner website (`https://emt.gartnerweb.com/ngw/globalassets/en/publications/documents/2024-gartner-top-strategic-technology-trends-ebook.pdf?_gl=1*gbpyoj*_ga*NDA3OTY3NTczLjE3MDIwODkwMDQ.*_ga_R1W5CE5FEV*MTcwMjIxNTg5My4zLjEuMTcwMjIxNjQ5MC41NC4wLjA`).

Intelligent applications possess the ability to automate and enhance various tasks across a wide range of use cases. With their advanced capabilities, these applications can independently perform tasks either on their own or in collaboration with other applications, taking productivity to new heights.

So, why are intelligent applications currently trending? The answer lies in the transformative power of generative AI. By harnessing the potential of AI, these applications can provide a truly intelligent experience for customers, users, product owners, architects, and developers alike. This translates into improved outcomes and data-driven decision-making by tailoring the app experience to the individual user.

Moreover, intelligent applications are infused with valuable data from transactions and external sources. By incorporating this data, these applications can provide valuable insights to business users within the app itself. This eliminates the need for separate business intelligence tools, streamlining the assessment and understanding of the state of their business.

To embark on the journey toward intelligent applications, it is crucial to establish a center of excellence or a dedicated team to capture, explain, catalog, map, and monitor the breadth and depth of intelligence as a capability for your apps. This will ensure that you have a clear understanding of how intelligent applications can transform the scope, purpose, and functionality of your enterprise apps.

Furthermore, it is important to foster a shared understanding of intelligent applications and their potential use cases throughout your organization. By doing so, you can harness the full potential of these applications and leverage them to their maximum capacity.

It is also essential to evaluate the impact on your wider portfolio of apps and services as you expand the range and scope of intelligent applications in the medium to long term. By incorporating intelligent applications into your overall strategy, you can stay ahead of the curve and reap the benefits of this groundbreaking technology.

According to Gartner, by 2026, 30% of new apps will utilize AI to drive personalized adaptive user interfaces, a significant increase from the current rate of under 5%. This statistic highlights the growing importance and relevance of intelligent applications in shaping the future of technology.

Briefly, intelligent applications have the potential to revolutionize the way we interact with technology. By infusing AI and connected data into our apps, we can unlock a whole new level of intelligence and efficiency. Organizations must embrace this transformative trend and harness the power of intelligent applications to stay ahead in the competitive landscape of tomorrow.

Building an intelligent chatbot for e-commerce – laying the groundwork

In this section, we will cover the initial stages of developing an intelligent web application for e-commerce. Our goal is to create a chatbot that can interact with customers, provide product recommendations, and process orders. Inspired by the real-life example of Etsy, a platform that sells handmade and creative products, our chatbot will simulate a conversation with a customer browsing the website.

To provide a clearer understanding of the initial stages of developing our intelligent chatbot for e-commerce, here is *Figure 14.1*.

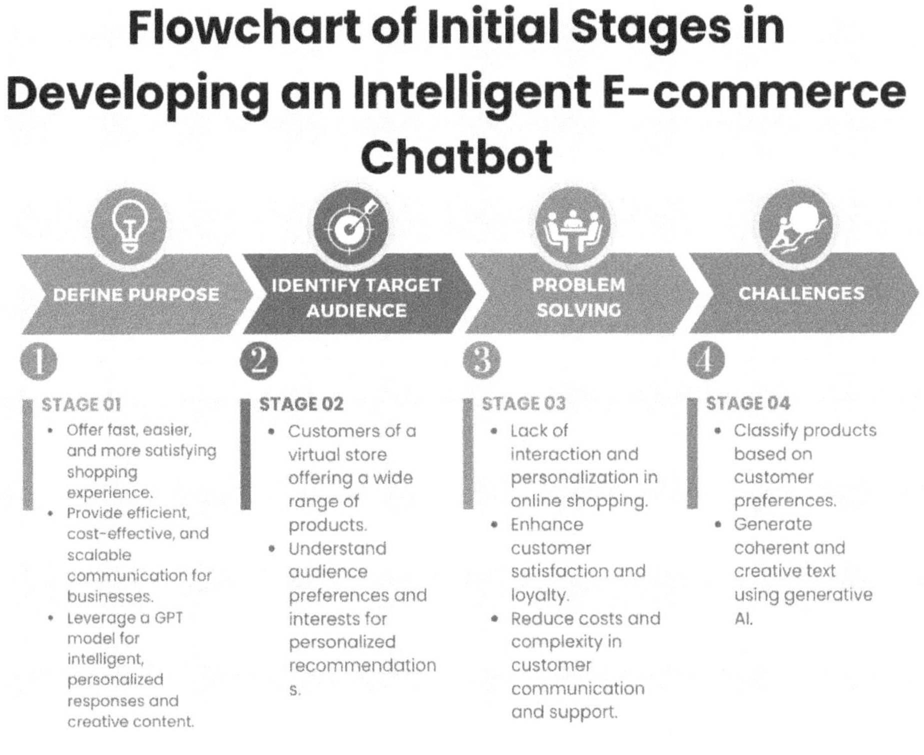

Flowchart of Initial Stages in Developing an Intelligent E-commerce Chatbot

DEFINE PURPOSE | **IDENTIFY TARGET AUDIENCE** | **PROBLEM SOLVING** | **CHALLENGES**

STAGE 01
- Offer fast, easier, and more satisfying shopping experience.
- Provide efficient, cost-effective, and scalable communication for businesses.
- Leverage a GPT model for intelligent, personalized responses and creative content.

STAGE 02
- Customers of a virtual store offering a wide range of products.
- Understand audience preferences and interests for personalized recommendations.

STAGE 03
- Lack of interaction and personalization in online shopping.
- Enhance customer satisfaction and loyalty.
- Reduce costs and complexity in customer communication and support.

STAGE 04
- Classify products based on customer preferences.
- Generate coherent and creative text using generative AI.

Figure 14.1: Flowchart of the initial stages of developing an intelligent e-commerce chatbot

To begin the conversation, let's create a basic flowchart of how a chatbot comes into play:

1. To start, we need to define the *purpose* of our chatbot. We aim to offer customers a faster, easier, and more satisfying shopping experience. Additionally, we want to provide businesses with an efficient, cost-effective, and scalable communication solution. By leveraging the powerful GPT model from OpenAI, our chatbot will be able to generate intelligent and personalized responses, as well as creative content such as poems, stories, and music. Here are the specific functionalities the chatbot will provide to achieve these aims: answering FAQs, handling order processing, offering product recommendations, providing customer support, personalized interaction, handling promotions and discounts, multi-channel support, and collecting feedback.

2. Next, we must identify our *target audience*. Our chatbot is designed for customers of a virtual store that offers a wide range of products across various categories, including art, jewelry, clothing, home decor, toys, electronics, sports, books, music, and health. By understanding our audience's preferences and interests, our chatbot will be able to search, recommend, and display relevant and personalized products.

3. The *problem* we aim to solve is the lack of interaction and personalization in online shopping. This can lead to low customer satisfaction and loyalty, as well as high costs and complexity in customer communication and support. By providing a chatbot that can understand and cater to individual preferences, we can enhance the overall shopping experience and build stronger customer relationships.

Our chatbot will face two main types of problems:

*   Firstly, it will need to classify products based on customer preferences. This involves analyzing customer data and identifying relevant categories and criteria.

*   Secondly, our chatbot will need to generate coherent and creative text based on prompts. This requires the utilization of the GPT-3 model's natural language processing capabilities.

To ensure scalability, we will use **Firebase** as our cloud service. Firebase offers various solutions for web and mobile app development and operation, including database management, authentication, storage, hosting, and analytics. With Firebase, our chatbot can automatically scale to handle increased demand and data volume without compromising performance.

Before delving into the specific capabilities and features of our chatbot, let's outline some key aspects that will be essential for its development and operation:

*   **Computational capabilities**: Efficient computational capabilities are essential for our chatbot. By utilizing the GPT-3 model, which is based on deep neural networks, we can achieve rapid and accurate task execution while minimizing resource usage. These neural networks learn and adapt from vast amounts of data, enabling them to produce high-quality results.

- **Maintenance and updates**: Maintenance and updates are crucial for the continuous improvement of our chatbot. By using GitHub as our versioning and collaboration platform, we can manage and share the chatbot's source code, track changes and contributions, and facilitate continuous integration and delivery. This allows us to quickly correct errors, enhance functionality, and incorporate new features.

- **Testing and evaluation**: To ensure the chatbot meets the requirements and functions correctly, rigorous testing and evaluation are necessary. Streamlit, a Python-based tool for creating interactive web applications, will be employed for this purpose. Streamlit provides a graphical interface to test and evaluate the chatbot, displaying results and metrics in real time.

- **Data security and privacy**: Data security and privacy are paramount concerns. Firebase will be used to protect product, order, and user data through encryption, authentication, and security rules. This ensures that the chatbot can reliably safeguard sensitive information from unauthorized access, improper modifications, and accidental losses.

- **Ethical considerations**: Lastly, ethical considerations will be integrated into our solution. Following the ethical principles for AI, our chatbot will respect autonomy, prevent harm, promote well-being, uphold fairness, ensure explainability, take responsibility, and prioritize privacy. These principles guide the development and use of AI in a beneficial, fair, and humane manner.

By laying the groundwork for our intelligent chatbot, we can create a powerful tool that revolutionizes e-commerce by providing personalized and engaging customer experiences. With a focus on user interaction and advanced AI principles, our chatbot will transform the way customers shop online.

Now that we've established the foundational components for our intelligent chatbot, let's delve into the next critical phase: data and design. In this section, we'll explore how to harness data effectively and design a chatbot that is not only intelligent but also intuitive and user friendly for e-commerce environments.

Data and design – creating an intelligent chatbot for e-commerce

In this section, we will delve into the data collection, analysis, and architectural design aspects of our project, showcasing how we are building an intelligent chatbot for an e-commerce platform. Our goal is to provide a unique and personalized shopping experience for our customers, powered by AI.

To achieve this, we have chosen to utilize the **GPT model** from OpenAI. This state-of-the-art natural language processing model is known for its ability to generate coherent and creative text based on prompts. Built on deep neural networks, GPT can learn and adapt from vast amounts of data, ensuring high-quality results.

For our web application platform, we have selected **Flask** and **Node.js/Express** as our frameworks. Flask allows us to create web applications quickly and easily with Python, offering simplicity, flexibility, and support for numerous extensions. Node.js and Express provide a robust framework for creating efficient and reliable backend functionality, handling high-concurrency operations, managing asynchronous tasks, and facilitating real-time communication. Additionally, we are utilizing **Firebase** as our cloud service platform, which provides a range of solutions for web and mobile app development, including database services, authentication, storage, hosting, and analytics.

By using both Flask and Node.js/Express together, we leverage the strengths of each framework. Flask will handle the core web application logic, while Node.js/Express will manage the high-performance backend operations. This combination ensures a well-rounded, efficient, and scalable solution for our intelligent chatbot.

To implement the functionalities of our chatbot, we are utilizing various tools and libraries. **Python** serves as our programming language, while **LangChain** facilitates integration with the OpenAI API. In addition, we are leveraging several Python libraries such as Flask for web application development, requests for HTTP requests, `pandas` and `numpy` for data manipulation, `nltk` for natural language processing, and `firebase_admin` for connecting and interacting with Firebase.

Our chatbot interacts with customers through a chat interface on the e-commerce platform. Customers can input their questions, requests, and commands, and the chatbot responds with answers, recommendations, and confirmations. The data source for our chatbot is an online database of over 40,000 e-commerce products. This database contains information such as product names, prices, categories, descriptions, and images.

We opted for a NoSQL database because of its superior scalability, seamless integration capabilities, and robust performance. NoSQL databases excel at managing large datasets and can scale out horizontally, which is ideal for the dynamic and vast product information our chatbot needs to handle. Moreover, the flexible data models offered by NoSQL databases allow them to easily adapt to the varied and changing data structures common in e-commerce environments. This adaptability supports quick development and iteration, ensuring our chatbot can deliver real-time responses and maintain high performance even as the data volume increases.

Data collection is performed by downloading the e-commerce product database. Additionally, the chatbot collects customer order data through the chat interface. We then prepare the collected data by cleaning and transforming it for use by the chatbot. This includes removing incomplete product information, converting prices to the local currency, categorizing products based on their descriptions, and vectorizing product descriptions for product recommendations.

Firebase serves as our *storage solution* for both product and customer order data. It provides real-time database services for data storage and synchronization in web and mobile applications, as well as cloud storage for file storage and delivery, including product images.

The chatbot delivers responses, recommendations, and confirmations through the chat interface, allowing customers to interact and view the results. Additionally, it provides notifications to customers when necessary.

In terms of architecture, our chatbot follows a typical client-server architecture for the web application. The client is the chat interface on the e-commerce platform, while the server is the web application that implements the chatbot. We also utilize a microservices architecture for integration with the OpenAI API and Firebase. Each microservice represents a specific function or method, such as product search, recommendation generation, order processing, response generation, and data storage.

Customers utilize our chatbot to inquire about products, check availability, and inquire about prices and shipping options. They can also receive personalized product recommendations based on their preferences and interests, as well as place orders for products. The chatbot continuously learns and improves its recommendations and responses based on customer interactions, including feedback, ratings, comments, and customer data such as search and purchase history. It also stays up to date with industry trends and technological advancements to provide the latest product offerings and features.

By developing this intelligent chatbot for e-commerce, we aim to revolutionize the online shopping experience, providing customers with personalized assistance, relevant recommendations, and seamless order processing. Through the power of AI, we are creating a transformative platform that enhances customer satisfaction and engagement.

As we continue to advance our intelligent chatbot project, the next vital phase involves the meticulous integration of AI building blocks. The next section will guide us through the integration of intelligent features essential for crafting a smart e-commerce chatbot.

Building blocks of AI integration – integrating intelligent features for a smart e-commerce chatbot

As we embark on the journey of creating an intelligent chatbot for e-commerce, we are faced with the task of integrating various building blocks of AI. Our goal is to create a chatbot that can effectively interact with customers, answer their questions, recommend products, and process orders. To achieve this, we will address both backend and frontend development, as well as the integration of intelligent features such as recommendation systems. Additionally, we will emphasize the importance of thorough testing to ensure optimal functionality and performance.

Let's start the journey:

- To begin, we need to understand the principles of decoupled architecture for independent application entities. By decoupling different components of our chatbot, we can ensure flexibility and scalability in future updates and improvements.

- For server-side logic and database integration, we will utilize both Flask and Node.js/Express. Flask will handle the core web application logic, while Node.js and Express will manage high-performance backend operations. This combination provides a robust framework for creating efficient and reliable backend functionality. With their help, we can seamlessly integrate our chatbot with the necessary databases and ensure smooth data retrieval and storage.

- To leverage the capabilities of the OpenAI API for intelligent features, we will use LangChain. This powerful tool allows us to tap into the potential of natural language processing and generate intelligent responses based on the context of the conversation and product data. By incorporating this technology, our chatbot can provide personalized and relevant information to customers, enhancing their overall experience.

  LangChain is particularly useful for this integration because it streamlines the process of connecting with the OpenAI API. Its modular design allows for flexible and efficient implementation of various AI functionalities. Additionally, LangChain supports prompt engineering, which is essential for creating tailored responses that are accurate and relevant to specific contexts.

  For example, if a customer asks, "Can you recommend a gift for a tech enthusiast?" LangChain helps the chatbot understand the query, utilize the GPT model, and generate a personalized response. The chatbot might suggest options such as the latest smart speaker, smartwatch, or wireless earbuds, providing a helpful and engaging interaction.

- Testing is a crucial aspect of developing a high-quality chatbot. We will employ Jest and Cypress to conduct comprehensive unit integration and end-to-end testing for our web application. These testing frameworks ensure that our chatbot functions as intended, delivering accurate responses and seamless interactions with customers.

This section provides you with the necessary knowledge and tools to build a smart e-commerce chatbot. By integrating AI features, such as recommendation systems, and thoroughly testing our application, we can create a chatbot that effectively engages with customers, enhances their shopping experience, and efficiently processes their orders. Let's embark on this journey of creating an intelligent chatbot for e-commerce together.

As we've explored the foundational elements of constructing an intelligent chatbot for e-commerce, it's essential to move forward with implementing our system into a live environment and engaging real users. The next section will guide us through the final stages of launching our chatbot and utilizing AI to enhance business analytics and web application management.

Deployment and user engagement – utilizing AI for business analytics and web application

The integration of AI has become increasingly crucial for insightful decision making through effective business analytics. By harnessing the power of AI algorithms and diverse datasets, we can unlock valuable insights that can drive our organizations forward. In this section, we will explore the best practices for deploying your web application and engaging users to maximize its potential.

Let's begin:

- **Deploying your web application with Netlify**: To ensure a seamless user experience, it is essential to choose a reliable platform for deploying your web application. Netlify offers a comprehensive suite of features that simplify the deployment process, allowing you to focus on delivering a high-quality product. With Netlify, you can effortlessly deploy your web application and benefit from its robust performance and scalability.

  Additionally, while there are several alternative deployment options such as AWS, Heroku, Google Cloud Platform, and Microsoft Azure, we chose Netlify due to its simplicity, integrated features, strong performance, scalability, and cost-effectiveness. Netlify's user-friendly interface and seamless integration with Git repositories make it an ideal choice for developers looking to deploy and manage web applications efficiently.

- **Tracking and improving performance with Google Analytics and Firebase Performance Monitoring**: Once your web application is deployed, it is crucial to monitor its performance and user behavior to identify areas for improvement. Google Analytics offers powerful tracking capabilities, providing valuable insights into user engagement, traffic sources, and conversion rates. Additionally, Firebase Performance Monitoring allows you to measure key performance metrics, such as app startup time and network latency, enabling you to optimize your web application's performance.

- **Advertising and promoting your web application through social media and search engine optimization (SEO) techniques**: To reach a wider audience and maximize user engagement, it is essential to leverage social media and SEO techniques. Utilize platforms such as Facebook, Twitter, and Instagram to advertise your web application and engage with your target audience. Additionally, implementing effective SEO strategies, such as *keyword optimization* and *link building*, can significantly improve your web application's visibility in search engine results.

By following the best practices mentioned previously – utilizing platforms such as Netlify for deployment, employing Google Analytics and Firebase Performance Monitoring for tracking, and leveraging social media and SEO techniques for promotion – you can ensure a seamless user experience. These strategies are instrumental in driving the success of your web application, allowing your organization to thrive in today's competitive landscape by making insightful decisions based on AI-driven data analysis.

With a solid foundation of best practices for web application deployment and user engagement established, let us now explore the next crucial phase: harnessing the power of AI for business analytics. As we delve into this section, we'll examine how to continuously learn and adapt by leveraging AI to enhance decision-making processes.

Evolution through learning – unlock the potential of AI for business analytics

As the technological landscape evolves at an unprecedented pace, businesses face a critical need to adapt and harness the transformative capabilities of AI in their analytics endeavors. A profound comprehension of AI's role in business analytics empowers us to make informed decisions, steer growth, and ensure success. Within this section, we delve into optimal strategies for continuous learning processes, encompassing the tracking of performance metrics, gathering user feedback, conducting A/B tests, and iteratively retraining AI models as required.

Let's learn a bit more about the strategies:

- To effectively track the performance metrics of your AI models, we recommend utilizing LangChain and OpenAI Playground. These tools provide a comprehensive framework to define and monitor crucial metrics such as accuracy, precision, recall, and F1 score. By keeping a close eye on these metrics, you can assess the effectiveness of your AI models and identify areas for improvement in real-time.

- User feedback is a valuable resource that can help you refine and enhance your AI models. Firebase Feedback and Google Forms are excellent tools for collecting and analyzing user feedback. By actively seeking input from your users, you can gain valuable insights into their experiences and identify any pain points or areas that require optimization. This user-centric approach ensures that your AI models align with the needs and expectations of your target audience.

- Conducting A/B tests is an essential practice in AI model development. Platforms like VWO, Adobe Target, and AB Tasty provide powerful tools for comparing different versions of your AI models. By testing multiple variations simultaneously, you can gather data on the performance of each version and make data-driven decisions on which model performs best. A/B testing allows you to iterate and refine your models based on real-world results, ensuring continuous improvement and optimal performance.

    Let's look at an example. You have two versions of your product recommendation algorithm: Model A (current) and Model B (new version). To determine which model performs better, you can set up an A/B test. Half of your users interact with Model A and the other half with Model B. You would monitor metrics such as click-through rates, conversion rates, and user engagement times. If Model B shows higher click-through and conversion rates, you might decide to adopt it as the new standard. By iterating based on these real-world results, you ensure your AI models continuously improve and align with user needs.

- Finally, it is fundamental to embrace the concept of continuous learning and evolution in AI model development. Utilize LangChain and OpenAI Playground to retrain and update your AI models as needed. By incorporating user feedback and test results, you can fine-tune your models to deliver optimal performance. This iterative process ensures that your AI models remain relevant and effective in an ever-changing business landscape.

Understanding how AI contributes to business analytics is essential for making insightful decisions that drive growth and success. By following the best practices outlined in this section, you can unlock the full potential of AI in your business analytics endeavors. Embrace continuous learning and evolution and watch as your AI models propel your business forward.

Before we delve into the detailed aspects of deploying and utilizing AI for business analytics and web application management, let's recap the critical points covered so far in building our intelligent chatbot for e-commerce. We've explored the essential components and strategies necessary for integrating AI capabilities into our chatbot.

Summary

In this chapter, we embarked on a journey through the realm of crafting intelligent web applications amidst the burgeoning era of AI dominance. Exploring foundational principles and diverse applications, we uncovered the transformative impact of AI-driven solutions on both consumer experiences and business operations.

We commenced by delving into advanced AI principles pertinent to enhancing user interactions and streamlining operational workflows through automation. Beginning with an introduction to decoupled architecture for fostering independent application entities, we navigated through the intricacies of integrating AI algorithms with diverse datasets to unleash the full potential of intelligent applications.

Our exploration culminated in the creation of data-enriched business insights and the pivotal role of AI in facilitating informed decision making through robust business analytics. From revolutionizing technology futures to deploying intelligent chatbots for e-commerce and harnessing AI for user engagement and analytics, we traversed a spectrum of topics aimed at empowering you with actionable insights and practical skills.

As we conclude this chapter, equipped with a deep understanding of advanced AI principles and their application in crafting intelligent web solutions, we now prepare to embark on the next phase of our journey. In the next chapter, we will delve into the ethical dimensions and risk management strategies inherent in the adoption of AI technologies, ensuring our ventures into the digital landscape are guided by principles of trust and responsibility.

## 15

Guardians of the Digital Realm – Navigating Trust, Risk, and Ethics in AI

Discussing ethics, trust, and risk factors in AI, as is done in this chapter, is vital as they directly influence how AI technologies are developed, deployed, and controlled. As AI becomes more integral to our daily lives and global infrastructure, ethical considerations surrounding its use become paramount. This chapter underscores the importance of embedding ethical considerations into AI systems to prevent biases, protect human rights, and ensure that the deployment of AI technologies aligns with societal values and legal standards. We will cover everything from the fundamental principles of *AI ethics* to practical strategies for *AI model governance*, using the innovative AI TRiSM framework.

AI TRiSM stands for **Trust, Risk, and Security Management in AI**. It focuses on ensuring AI systems are trustworthy, secure, and ethically aligned by promoting transparency, managing risks, and implementing robust security measures.

In this chapter, we will delve into the crucial role of AI professionals in web development and the creation of business value through the AI TRiSM framework. AI professionals play a pivotal role in integrating and advancing AI technologies within web development. Their expertise is critical for leveraging AI to enhance user experiences, optimize backend operations, and ensure ethical AI implementations.

Furthermore, we will explore how the AI TRiSM framework can be applied to create substantial business value. This framework helps organizations align AI strategies with business objectives, focusing on trust, risk, and security to drive growth, innovation, and competitive advantage. We'll discuss practical strategies for embedding AI TRiSM principles into everyday business processes and decision-making, demonstrating how it fosters a robust governance model that enhances AI reliability and effectiveness.

The main topics of this chapter include the following:

- Fundamental principles of AI ethics
- Structuring and implementing governance frameworks for AI models
- Understanding and applying the AI TRiSM framework
- Creating business value through TRiSM

By the end of this chapter, you will have a solid understanding of how to navigate ethical and governance challenges in AI and how to apply the concepts learned in this chapter to the development of reliable and responsible AI technologies.

Fundamental principles of AI ethics

The AI revolution has brought with it a series of ethical challenges that shape our world in profound and complex ways. Issues such as data privacy, algorithmic bias, and the potential for AI to perpetuate or even exacerbate social inequalities are at the forefront of these challenges.

Algorithmic bias refers to systematic errors in AI systems that lead to unfair outcomes, often disadvantaging certain groups. For example, a hiring algorithm that consistently rejects candidates from a particular demographic group demonstrates algorithmic bias.

Social inequalities involve disparities in access to resources and opportunities among different social groups, which AI can inadvertently amplify if not carefully managed. For instance, AI systems used in loan approvals might deny loans disproportionately to certain racial groups if trained on biased historical data.

This chapter embarks on an essential journey to understand how AI ethics is not only shaping our present but also molding our future. This chapter is an essential journey into understanding how AI ethics is shaping our present and future. We'll cover everything from fundamental principles of AI ethics to practical strategies for the governance of AI models, using the innovative AI TRiSM framework.

At the heart of ethics in AI are ethical dilemmas that arise as AI systems become more sophisticated and pervasive. These dilemmas are intricate and multifaceted, often challenging traditional notions of ethics and morality. Key issues include the following:

- **Transparency of algorithmic decisions**: Ensuring that decisions made by AI systems are understandable and explainable to humans. Lack of transparency can lead to mistrust and misuse of AI.
- **Accountability for AI actions**: Determining who is responsible when an AI system makes a mistake or causes harm. This includes creators, operators, and users of the AI system.

- **Ensuring fairness and avoiding bias**: Preventing AI systems from perpetuating or amplifying existing biases in society. AI systems should be designed to treat all individuals fairly, regardless of their background.

- **Privacy and security of data**: Protecting vast amounts of data used by AI systems from unauthorized access and misuse. This includes safeguarding personal information and ensuring data integrity.

To successfully navigate the AI era, it is imperative that we understand these dilemmas and are prepared to face them. In the following sections, we will identify and analyze each of these dilemmas in detail, exploring their implications and discussing potential solutions.

Ethics in AI involves weighing up complex issues such as data privacy, algorithmic bias, and the impact of AI on society. In a world where algorithms make decisions that affect human lives, it is crucial to identify and analyze these ethical dilemmas carefully.

The principles we discuss here underpin the responsible development and deployment of AI technologies, ensuring they serve society beneficially while mitigating risks. By grasping the significance of transparency, accountability, fairness, and privacy, we lay the groundwork for more ethical AI systems. Let's continue our exploration by examining key ethical principles in AI development, which are crucial for building technologies that truly enhance our lives without compromising our values.

Key ethical principles in AI development

Ethical considerations in AI are foundational to building systems that not only enhance technological capabilities but also safeguard human interests and societal norms. The principles we're about to explore ensure that AI systems operate in a way that respects human autonomy, promotes fairness, and prevents harm. This framework not only enhances the trustworthiness of AI systems but also aligns their functionality with human values and ethical standards. Here's a look at key ethical principles that must be integrated into AI development:

- **Respect for human autonomy**: This is one of the fundamental principles of AI ethics. AI must respect the ability of human beings to freely make their own informed decisions without manipulation, coercion, or deception. This means that AI must guarantee the consent of users and ensure transparency.

- **Transparency**: When developing an AI-powered e-commerce platform, it is crucial for developers to ensure transparency regarding the use of customer data. Customers must be clearly informed about how their information will be utilized for personalization and product recommendations. Furthermore, it is essential to provide customers with the option to actively decide if and how their data is used, thereby reinforcing their control over their personal information. This approach not only builds trust but also aligns with best practices for user privacy and data protection in the development of intelligent systems.

- **Prevention of harm**: This is another essential principle. AI must avoid or minimize risks and negative impacts on the health, safety, dignity, rights, and well-being of human beings and the environment. AI models must be developed, implemented, and used responsibly, ethically, and legally, following the principles of precaution, proportionality, and accountability. AI must also be robust, reliable, secure, and resilient, avoiding errors, failures, attacks, or misuse.

  The prevention of harm principle urges developers to proceed with caution, conducting extensive testing and risk assessments to preempt and mitigate potential harm. This proactive approach ensures that AI systems do not inadvertently cause harm to users or the environment.

- **Proportionality** demands that the benefits of AI systems outweigh their risks. This principle ensures that measures implemented are appropriate to the level of risk involved, balancing innovation with necessary safety and ethical safeguards.

- **Accountability** is crucial for maintaining trust and integrity in AI systems. It ensures that all AI outputs are traceable and that there are mechanisms in place to hold developers and operators accountable. This includes maintaining thorough documentation, enabling audits, and providing means to address any errors or biases that arise.

- **Justice and fairness**: Crucial principles in AI ethics, justice, and fairness ensure that AI systems operate without bias and discrimination. These principles promote equity by demanding that AI systems treat all users fairly, regardless of background or demographic. Implementing these principles involves designing algorithms that are transparent, auditable, and adjustable to prevent and correct biases, thereby fostering greater inclusivity and equity. This commitment helps build trust in AI applications and supports ethical compliance across varied contexts.

- **Privacy and security**: Protecting personal data and ensuring compliance with privacy laws is essential. This includes safeguarding data from unauthorized access and misuse, maintaining data integrity, and ensuring that users have control over their information.

Developers must carry out rigorous security tests to ensure that the AI model is not susceptible to cyber-attacks that could compromise the privacy of customer data.

In addition, justice and fairness are crucial principles in AI ethics. AI must be fair, impartial, and non-discriminatory, respecting equality, diversity, and the non-violation of human rights. It must be transparent, auditable, and verifiable, allowing for the detection and correction of biases, errors, or injustices. AI must be inclusive, accessible, and democratic, guaranteeing the participation, representation, and voice of all those affected or interested.

Furthermore, AI must be adjusted according to user feedback, taking into account different demographic groups to avoid discrimination and bias in personalization results.

Examples of precautionary measures in AI projects

To ensure the ethical and responsible deployment of AI technologies, it is crucial to implement precautionary measures that address potential risks and challenges. These measures help mitigate negative impacts and enhance the trustworthiness and reliability of AI systems. Next are some examples of how various industries have successfully implemented precautionary measures in their AI projects:

- **Extensive testing and simulation**: Before deploying AI systems in critical applications such as healthcare or autonomous driving, extensive testing and simulation are conducted to identify and mitigate potential risks. For instance, self-driving car companies perform millions of miles of simulations to ensure their algorithms can handle a wide range of scenarios safely.

- **Bias audits**: Regular audits of AI algorithms are conducted to detect and correct biases. For example, some companies use fairness-aware algorithms to audit hiring tools to ensure they do not discriminate against any demographic group.

- **Explainability tools**: Implementing tools that make AI decisions transparent and explainable. In finance, for instance, AI systems used for credit scoring must provide clear reasons for their decisions, ensuring that customers understand why they were approved or denied credit.

- **User control mechanisms**: Providing users with control over how their data is used and offering opt-out options. Social media platforms, for example, allow users to manage their privacy settings and control the type of data that is collected and how it is used.

By incorporating these precautionary measures, organizations can better navigate the ethical complexities of AI deployment. These practices foster greater trust and acceptance of AI technologies, paving the way for their successful integration into various aspects of our lives.

In conclusion, ethical considerations are at the heart of responsible AI development. Understanding and applying key ethical principles in AI development is crucial to ensure that AI systems respect human autonomy, prevent harm, and uphold justice and fairness. Throughout the Integrated AI loops framework, which was detailed in *Integrated AI loops: Streamlining AI Development for Web Applications* subsection of *Chapter 3*, from the initial stages of problem definition to continuous learning and improvement, it is imperative to integrate these ethical concepts into every decision-making process. Respecting user consent, safeguarding data privacy, ensuring system robustness, and promoting fairness are not only ethical imperatives but also essential for building trustworthy and reliable AI systems. By adhering to these principles, AI professionals and developers can contribute to the responsible advancement of AI technologies, ultimately benefiting society as a whole.

We have delved into critical ethical principles essential for responsible AI development. Next, we will explore how these ethical concepts can be practically applied in the development of AI systems. This includes translating abstract ethical standards into actionable guidelines that shape the design, implementation, and operation of AI.

Applying ethical concepts in AI development

Applying ethical concepts to AI development is a vital aspect of building responsible and reliable AI systems. This involves translating abstract ethical principles into concrete guidelines that guide the creation and implementation of AI models.

AI professionals must be equipped to make ethical decisions throughout the entire life cycle of an AI project, from conception to deployment and ongoing maintenance. This requires a thorough understanding of the ethical implications of every decision made during the development process.

In the previous sections, we explored fundamental principles of AI ethics, emphasizing the importance of transparency, accountability, fairness, and privacy. These principles are not just theoretical but serve as practical guidelines that shape the responsible development and deployment of AI technologies. To enhance understanding and retention, we present *Figure 15.1*, which offers a visual representation of how these ethical principles are integrated throughout the AI development life cycle using the Integrated AI Loops framework:

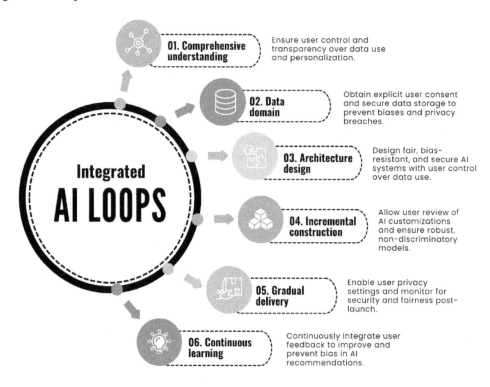

Figure 15.1: Ethical considerations in the Integrated AI Loops framework

By visually mapping ethical considerations within the Integrated AI Loops **framework**, we can better understand how to implement these principles effectively. This approach ensures that AI systems are developed and deployed in a manner that aligns with societal values and ethical standards.

Loop – Comprehensive understanding

While defining the problem and scope of the AI-powered e-commerce platform, it is important to ensure that users have control over their choices and decisions, including the personalization and recommendation of products.

When establishing quality criteria and success metrics, consideration should be given to how to avoid risks to the privacy and security of customer data from the outset.

When identifying the target audience and customer segments, avoid discrimination and bias by ensuring that all groups are treated fairly and equally.

Here are the loop's best practices:

- **Transparency**: Clearly inform users about how their data will be used and for what purposes
- **Informed consent**: Obtain explicit consent from users for data collection and usage
- **User engagement**: Allow users to have control over their preferences and decisions
- **Automated responses**: Ensure automated responses are transparent and allow user feedback to refine the AI's interaction approach

Loop – Data domain

When collecting data, obtain explicit consent from users when necessary and provide transparency about how this data will be used.

Make sure that data collected is stored securely to avoid privacy breaches and information leaks.

Be careful to avoid including data that could introduce bias and discrimination into AI models.

Here are the loop's best practices:

- **Explicit consent**: Always obtain explicit consent from users before collecting data
- **Transparency in data use**: Provide clear information about how and why data is being collected and used
- **Data security**: Use encryption and other security measures to protect collected data
- **Bias prevention**: Conduct regular audits to identify and remove biased data
- **Automated data handling**: Implement automated data processing techniques to ensure consistent application of data security and privacy measures

Loop – Architecture design

During architecture design, ensure that users have control over how their information is used and personalized.

Choose AI techniques that minimize risks and guarantee data security, such as fair and secure recommendation systems—for example, privacy-preserving algorithms. These are specific methods or algorithms applied within AI systems to protect user data. They ensure that the data used in processes such as **Machine Learning (ML)** does not expose personal information, thus maintaining privacy.

Evaluate AI techniques for possible algorithmic biases and select the most effective and equitable ones. Techniques such as auditing algorithms for bias, implementing fairness constraints, or using algorithms designed for equity, such as those that adjust recommendations to prevent reinforcing existing biases, are critical to ensuring AI systems operate justly.

Here are the loop's best practices:

- **User control**: Ensure users can decide how their information is used and personalized
- **Security in architecture**: Incorporate privacy-preserving and secure algorithms from the start
- **Bias evaluation**: Use audit tools to identify and mitigate potential biases in algorithms
- **Automated security checks**: Integrate automated security checks within the system architecture to continuously monitor and address vulnerabilities

Loop – Incremental construction

When implementing the AI model, give users the option of reviewing and adjusting customizations and recommendations made by the system.

Carry out rigorous security tests to identify and correct any vulnerabilities that could threaten the privacy or security of customer data.

Ensure that the AI model does not discriminate against or violate the rights of specific customer groups.

Here are the loop's best practices:

- **User review**: Allow users to review and adjust customizations and recommendations made by the system
- **Security testing**: Conduct rigorous tests to identify and correct vulnerabilities
- **Non-discrimination**: Ensure the AI model does not discriminate against specific customer groups
- **Automated updates**: Use automated processes to update AI models and algorithms regularly, ensuring they remain robust and fair

Loop – Gradual delivery

At launch, allow users to control their privacy and personalization settings.

Monitor the system closely after launch to detect any security or privacy issues and respond to them promptly.

Check that the system does not discriminate against or unfairly disadvantage any group of users.

Here are the loop's best practices:

- **Privacy settings**: Enable users to control their privacy and personalization settings upon launch
- **Continuous monitoring**: Monitor the system continuously after launch to detect and promptly address any security or privacy issues
- **Fairness verification**: Ensure the system does not unfairly disadvantage any group of users
- **Automated alerts**: Implement automated alert systems to notify developers of any detected biases or security breaches in real time

Loop – Continuous learning

Maintain users' ability to adjust their preferences and settings as their interests change.

Use information collected through user feedback and performance data to continuously improve the system and avoid privacy and security risks.

Respond to changes in user behavior, ensuring that the system does not introduce bias or unfairness into its recommendations.

Here are the loop's best practices:

- **Feedback integration**: Use user feedback to continuously improve the system and avoid privacy and security risks
- **Adaptability**: Maintain the ability for users to adjust their preferences and settings as their interests change
- **Bias detection**: Ensure the system adapts without introducing biases or unfairness into its recommendations
- **Automated learning**: Implement automated learning mechanisms to integrate user feedback seamlessly and update AI models accordingly

In previous discussions (*Chapter 3*), we introduced the concept of the Integrated AI Loops framework. This framework is crucial for the structured and effective development and deployment of AI models in web applications, ensuring that they meet both user needs and business objectives efficiently. These are some ethical aspects to consider in each phase of the Integrated AI Loops framework, ensuring that AI is developed and implemented ethically and responsibly.

Having outlined the critical phases of the Integrated AI Loops framework, we now turn our attention to a fundamental component necessary for the ethical application of these technologies: structuring and implementing governance frameworks for AI models. This next section will delve into how organizations can establish robust governance structures that not only comply with regulatory standards but also embody ethical practices throughout the life cycle of AI development and deployment.

Structuring and implementing governance frameworks for AI models

In an era where AI is becoming increasingly central to our lives, the need for robust governance of AI models has never been more critical. **Governance** in AI refers to a set of policies, procedures, and practices that ensure the responsible development and use of AI. This section explores how to effectively structure and implement governance frameworks for AI models, ensuring they are fair, trustworthy, secure, and, above all, beneficial to society.

Understanding the importance of governance

Governance in AI models is essential for mitigating risks, including those related to bias, privacy, security, and reliability. Effective governance ensures that AI models are developed and used in an ethical, transparent, and responsible manner, fostering public trust and the adoption of AI. Furthermore, robust governance is crucial for the long-term sustainability of AI projects, ensuring they can adapt to changes in laws, regulations, and societal expectations.

Governance frameworks provide a structure for decision-making and management of AI models. They include guidelines for the following:

- **Ethical impact assessment**: Evaluating the potential impacts of AI models on individuals and society

- **Transparency and explainability**: Ensuring decisions made by AI models are understandable and justifiable

- **Privacy and data protection**: Protecting personal information and ensuring compliance with privacy laws

- **Security**: Implementing security measures to protect AI models from manipulation and attacks

- **Continuous monitoring and evaluation**: Establishing processes to monitor the performance of AI models and continually assess their impacts

To guide organizations in ethical, transparent, and responsible AI development and usage, several key governance frameworks have been developed by leading global organizations:

- **Ethics Guidelines for Trustworthy AI (European Commission)**: Developed by the European Commission, this framework emphasizes the need for trustworthy AI, focusing on seven essential requirements: human oversight, robustness and safety, privacy and data governance, transparency, diversity, non-discrimination and fairness, societal and environmental well-being, and accountability.

- **AI Principles (Organisation for Economic Co-operation and Development – OECD):** The OECD's principles highlight the promotion of AI that is innovative and trustworthy and respects human rights and democratic values. These principles focus on transparency, robustness, security, fairness, and accountability as foundations for AI development and use.

- **Montréal Declaration for a Responsible Development of Artificial Intelligence:** The Montréal Declaration outlines 10 principles for responsible AI development, including well-being, respect for autonomy, privacy and intimacy protection, solidarity, democratic participation, equity, inclusive diversity, prudence, responsibility, and sustainable development.

- **Institute of Electrical and Electronics Engineers (IEEE) Ethically Aligned Design:** Developed by the IEEE, this set of recommendations aims to ensure AI and robotics systems are developed with ethics at the forefront. The document addresses human rights, well-being, data transparency, and accountability to encourage responsible innovation in technology.

In closing, the exploration of specific governance frameworks, such as the Ethics Guidelines for Trustworthy AI by the European Commission, the OECD's AI Principles, the Montréal Declaration for a Responsible Development of Artificial Intelligence, and the IEEE's Ethically Aligned Design, underscores the global commitment to fostering ethical, transparent, and responsible development and use of AI. These frameworks collectively embody a comprehensive approach to AI governance, emphasizing the importance of human oversight, ethical integrity, inclusivity, and environmental consideration.

The diversity of these frameworks reflects the multifaceted nature of AI and the broad spectrum of considerations that must be addressed to harness its potential responsibly. From ensuring robustness and safety to advocating for non-discrimination, fairness, and democratic participation, the principles laid out guide organizations toward creating AI systems that not only advance technological innovation but also uphold and promote societal values and human rights.

As AI continues to evolve and permeate various sectors of society, the implementation of these governance frameworks becomes increasingly critical. They serve not only as a blueprint for ethical AI development but also as a call to action for organizations, developers, policymakers, and stakeholders to collaborate and commit to the responsible stewardship of AI technologies. By adhering to these guidelines, the AI community can navigate the complex ethical landscape, mitigate risks, and ensure that AI serves as a force for good, contributing positively to societal progress and the well-being of all.

The journey toward responsible AI is ongoing and requires continuous effort, dialogue, and adaptation. The frameworks discussed provide a solid foundation, but the ultimate success in achieving ethical, transparent, and responsible AI will depend on a collective commitment to these principles and a willingness to evolve governance practices as technology and societal needs change. As we move forward, let us embrace these frameworks as guiding lights on the path to a future where AI not only pushes the boundaries of what is technologically possible but also aligns with our deepest values and aspirations for a just and equitable world.

Considerations for implementing governance frameworks

The effective implementation of a governance framework requires a holistic approach involving multiple stakeholders, including AI developers, end users, regulators, and broader society. Key steps include the following:

- **Policy definition**: Establishing clear policies that reflect ethical values and organizational goals

- **Procedure development**: Creating detailed procedures for applying policies, including methods for ethical impact assessment and security review processes

- **Training and awareness**: Ensuring all those involved in creating and managing AI models are aware of governance principles and know how to apply them

- **Feedback mechanisms**: Implementing mechanisms to collect feedback from users and other stakeholders, allowing for the continuous improvement of AI models

The essence of establishing robust and effective AI governance lies in a holistic and inclusive approach. This process necessitates the active participation of a diverse group of stakeholders, including AI developers, end users, regulators, and society at large. By defining clear policies, developing precise procedures, fostering an environment of continuous education and awareness, and setting up channels for open feedback, organizations can create a governance framework that not only aligns with ethical values and organizational goals but also adapts to the evolving landscape of AI technology and its impact on society.

The journey toward responsible AI governance is ongoing and requires a commitment to these foundational steps. As we move forward, the collective effort to implement these frameworks with diligence and foresight will be pivotal in shaping the future of AI—a future where technology operates within the bounds of ethical responsibility, transparency, and accountability, ensuring the well-being of all stakeholders involved.

As we conclude the discussion on the implementation of governance frameworks, it's evident that the path is laden with challenges, such as the swift advancement of AI technology, the vast array of AI applications, and variances in global laws and regulations; however, these obstacles are not insurmountable. The key to navigating this complex landscape lies in fostering international collaboration, establishing global standards for AI governance, and dedicating resources to research that deepens our understanding of AI's societal impacts. This proactive approach not only aids in overcoming hurdles but also sets a foundation for responsible and ethical AI development and use.

The transition toward responsible AI governance is both a journey and a commitment. It involves the adoption and adaptation of significant AI governance frameworks, enabling organizations to cultivate trust, fairness, security, and sustainability within their AI endeavors. This strategic focus not only enhances the societal benefits of AI but also mitigates inherent risks and challenges associated with its deployment.

Moving forward, the next critical step in this journey is understanding and applying the AI TRiSM framework. This framework represents a pivotal tool in the arsenal of AI governance, offering a structured approach to navigating trust, risk, and security in AI models. By integrating the principles and strategies outlined in the AI TRiSM framework, organizations can further solidify their commitment to developing AI technologies that are not only innovative but also aligned with ethical standards and societal values. The upcoming section will delve into the intricacies of the AI TRiSM framework, providing insights into its application and the tangible benefits it brings to the realm of AI governance.

Understanding and applying the AI TRiSM framework

In an era where AI is woven into every facet of our lives, from personal assistants to sophisticated decision-making systems, addressing trust, risk, and security is not just necessary; it's a strategic imperative. Gartner's AI TRiSM framework presents a *comprehensive guideline that underscores the importance of governance, reliability, impartiality, security, robustness, effectiveness, and privacy in AI systems*. This framework not only facilitates the interpretation and explainability of models but also enhances privacy, model operations, and resilience against adversarial attacks. By integrating these principles (as proposed by Gartner), this section will explore how AI TRiSM acts as a guiding light for navigating the complex and often challenging domain of AI governance, ensuring that AI systems are both trustworthy and beneficial for users and businesses alike (`https://www.gartner.com/en/articles/what-it-takes-to-make-ai-safe-and-effective`).

The core of AI TRiSM

The AI TRiSM framework embodies a critical aspiration in the realm of AI: creating a world where AI decisions are not only clear and fair but also steadfastly secure. This framework was developed by Gartner and is dedicated to building a robust digital environment that instills a deep sense of trust in AI technologies.

This framework is actively being implemented and is recognized as a cutting-edge technological trend poised to transform businesses in the near future. Companies adopting this framework have reported up to a 50% increase in adoption rates, attributed primarily to improvements in model accuracy, as Gartner has noted (`https://www.gartner.com/en/articles/what-it-takes-to-make-ai-safe-and-effective`).

That's the vision behind AI TRiSM: to foster a digital environment where we can fully trust AI-driven decisions. It stands on three foundational pillars:

- **Trust**: Developing reliable AI systems that stakeholders can depend on, emphasizing fairness, transparency, and accountability
- **Risk**: Proactively identifying and mitigating potential adverse impacts of AI technologies on individuals and society
- **Security**: Ensuring the robustness of AI systems against threats, thus protecting data integrity and system functionality

This foundation ensures that as we advance further into the digital age, our reliance on AI is underpinned by systems that are transparent, fair, and secure. Ultimately, AI TRiSM empowers us to harness the full potential of AI in a manner that fosters trust among users, protects individuals and society from harm, and secures the digital ecosystem against emerging threats. Through this, we can truly realize the benefits of AI, ensuring it works for the betterment of humanity.

Implementation and responsibilities within AI TRiSM

The implementation of AI TRiSM is more than a technical task; it is a shared responsibility that requires a nuanced approach. *Builders and owners* of AI systems are tasked with ensuring the explainability, management, and security of the models. This includes creating transparent AI systems where decisions can be easily understood and justified, ensuring that models are continuously monitored and updated to reflect the latest data and ethical standards, and implementing robust security measures to protect against attacks and vulnerabilities.

For *AI system users*, the focus shifts to anomaly detection, data protection, and application security. This means users must be equipped to identify unexpected or unusual patterns in AI outputs, safeguard personal and sensitive data, and secure the application layer of AI systems against potential threats. It underscores the necessity of a comprehensive understanding of AI systems' inner workings and external factors that may influence their performance and integrity.

The *true* effectiveness of AI TRiSM transcends technical controls, embracing organizational governance. This involves establishing a culture of privacy, fairness, and bias control that mirrors societal values. It requires the establishment of measurable workflows and policies that not only comply with legal standards but also advance ethical AI use. **Organizational governance** in the context of AI TRiSM means creating an ecosystem where AI's ethical implications are continuously evaluated against evolving societal standards, ensuring that AI technologies are developed and utilized in a manner that is ethical, responsible, and aligned with societal values.

The movement toward AI TRiSM is gaining momentum, promising to enhance the value of AI projects by improving model precision, consistency, and, importantly, fairness across AI-driven applications. It's a testament to the growing recognition of the need for an integrated approach to trust, risk, and security management in AI, one that goes beyond mere compliance to foster genuine trust between humans and AI systems. As AI becomes more embedded in our daily lives, the principles of AI TRiSM serve as critical guideposts for ensuring that these technologies are leveraged responsibly.

Embarking on the AI TRiSM journey

Embarking on the AI TRiSM journey begins with establishing a dedicated task force focused on AI TRiSM efforts, promoting cross-departmental collaboration to manage a comprehensive set of tools as part of AI TRiSM. Organizations should define clear policies for acceptable use and establish systems for recording and approving access to AI models. This initial step is crucial for laying the groundwork for successful AI TRiSM implementation that honors ethics, accountability, and human values at the heart of AI.

Having laid the foundational steps for embarking on the AI TRiSM journey, we now understand the critical importance of structured collaboration and clear governance to align AI practices with organizational values and ethics. This strategic setup not only ensures that AI systems operate within ethical boundaries but also facilitates smoother integration across different organizational departments.

As we move forward, it is vital to translate these structured practices into tangible business value. The next section will delve into how these TRiSM principles can be leveraged to enhance business operations, drive innovation, and maintain a competitive edge in the marketplace.

Creating business value through TRiSM

In the dynamic world of AI, the principles of TRiSM serve not only as a safeguard but as a cornerstone for unlocking unparalleled business value. Next, we delve into how organizations can apply TRiSM to achieve operational excellence, ensure ethical compliance, and drive innovation.

Leveraging TRiSM to enhance decision-making processes is pivotal in harnessing the full potential of AI within organizations. This strategic approach ensures that AI systems are not only reliable but also that they operate within a framework that does not compromise on accuracy or integrity. A critical component of this process involves the application of Gartner's identified four key pillars within the AI TRiSM framework, which collectively contribute to the refinement of decision-making capabilities by managing risks effectively:

- **Explainability/model monitoring**: At the core of trustworthy AI systems is the principle of explainability. By making AI models understandable and their operations transparent, organizations empower stakeholders to trust the insights generated by AI. This trust is crucial for leveraging AI in critical decision-making processes. Ongoing model monitoring ensures that this trust is maintained over time, as stakeholders can see that the models continue to operate as intended, retaining their integrity and relevance.

- **ModelOps**: ModelOps, short for Model Operations, is a critical practice in the management of AI models. It involves the integration of ML models into production environments through continuous integration, delivery, and monitoring. This approach ensures that AI-driven decisions remain accurate and effective over time. By adopting ModelOps, organizations can maintain and enhance the quality of AI-driven decisions. The integration of ModelOps represents a proactive stance toward sustaining high-quality AI functionality. It enables rapid detection and response to any anomalies in AI models, ensuring that decision-making processes are based on the most current and accurate information. This minimizes the risk associated with decisions made on outdated or incorrect data, thereby enhancing operational reliability and efficiency. Furthermore, this proactive stance on anomaly detection and model management reduces downtime and ensures AI systems operate at peak efficiency.

- **AI application security**: Strengthening AI applications against adversarial attacks is paramount in preserving the integrity of decision-making processes. Secure AI applications are less likely to be compromised, ensuring that data and insights driving organizational decisions are accurate and untampered. This security aspect of TRiSM directly contributes to the reliability of AI systems, a critical factor when decisions have significant implications for the organization.

- **Privacy**: Implementing robust privacy measures is essential in maintaining stakeholder trust, particularly when decisions are made based on personal or sensitive information. By safeguarding this information, organizations demonstrate a commitment to ethical considerations, further enhancing the trustworthiness of AI-driven decision-making processes. Privacy measures ensure that the organization respects and protects individual rights, which is increasingly becoming a decisive factor for stakeholders when trusting AI systems.

The interconnection between TRiSM's four pillars and enhanced decision-making processes is evident. By ensuring AI models are explainable, continuously monitored for anomalies, resistant to adversarial attacks, and respectful of privacy, organizations can significantly improve the trustworthiness and reliability of AI systems. This, in turn, enhances the organization's ability to make informed, accurate, and ethical decisions based on AI insights. Adopting a comprehensive TRiSM approach not only mitigates risks associated with AI deployment but also unlocks the potential for AI to drive significant business value through improved decision-making capabilities.

Implementing TRiSM for creating business value

To effectively harness TRiSM for creating business value, organizations should consider the following strategic steps:

- **Integrate TRiSM into corporate strategy**: Align TRiSM initiatives with broader business objectives to ensure AI deployments contribute to strategic goals.

- **Establish a TRiSM governance framework**: Create a structured governance model that defines roles, responsibilities, and processes for TRiSM in AI development and deployment.

- **Develop and enforce policies for ethical AI use**: Craft clear policies that guide ethical AI development, focusing on fairness, privacy, and transparency. Ensure these policies are actively enforced and adhered to across the organization.

- **Conduct regular risk assessments and security audits**: Schedule periodic evaluations of AI systems to identify potential risks and vulnerabilities, applying corrective measures promptly.

- **Implement continuous model monitoring and management**: Utilize ModelOps to regularly update, test, and monitor AI models, ensuring their performance aligns with ethical and business standards.

- **Foster a culture of continuous improvement**: Encourage an organizational culture that embraces TRiSM principles for ongoing learning, adaptation, and enhancement of AI systems.

- **Stakeholder engagement**: Engage with customers, employees, regulators, and partners to gather insights and feedback, ensuring TRiSM initiatives are well rounded and address broader societal concerns.

Incorporating the principles of TRiSM into AI strategies transcends mere risk management—it embodies a commitment to leveraging trust, risk, and security as foundational pillars for fostering innovation, achieving operational excellence, and enhancing strategic decision-making. This comprehensive approach empowers organizations to adeptly navigate the intricacies of the digital era, unlocking unparalleled opportunities for growth, differentiation, and enduring success.

When TRiSM is applied to the realm of web development, the role of AI professionals becomes increasingly crucial. These experts are tasked with integrating TRiSM principles into the fabric of web development projects, ensuring that AI-driven features and functionalities not only adhere to the highest standards of trustworthiness and security but also actively contribute to the overall value proposition of the website or application.

By embedding TRiSM at the core of AI-enhanced web development, professionals can create more secure, reliable, and ethically aligned web applications. This strategic integration not only addresses immediate challenges of the digital landscape but also positions web platforms for sustained competitive advantage and innovation, reflecting a broader organizational commitment to excellence and ethical responsibility in the use of AI technologies.

The crucial role of AI professionals in web development

The integration of TRiSM principles into the domain of web development marks a pivotal shift in how organizations approach the creation and enhancement of digital platforms. As AI continues to redefine the capabilities and functionalities of web applications, the role of AI professionals in this landscape becomes increasingly critical. Their expertise is not just a technical necessity but a strategic asset in implementing TRiSM, ensuring that web applications are not only innovative and user-centric but also secure, trustworthy, and ethically aligned.

Now, let's explore the role of AI professionals in the strategic implementation of TRiSM in web development:

- **Embedding trust at the core**: AI professionals play a key role in embedding trust into the web development process. This involves designing AI systems that are transparent and explainable, ensuring that users can understand and trust AI-driven elements of web applications. By prioritizing trust, AI experts help build a foundation for user confidence, essential for the long-term success and adoption of web platforms.

- **Proactive risk management**: The digital landscape is fraught with potential risks, from data breaches to ethical dilemmas. AI professionals in web development are tasked with identifying these risks early in the development process and integrating robust risk management strategies. This includes conducting ethical impact assessments and employing ModelOps for continuous monitoring and improvement of AI models, ensuring that web applications remain aligned with both organizational values and user expectations.

- **Ensuring security across all fronts**: Security is a non-negotiable aspect of TRiSM, and AI professionals contribute significantly to safeguarding web applications against adversarial attacks and vulnerabilities. This entails developing AI systems with built-in resistance to cyber threats and implementing comprehensive data protection measures to safeguard user information. Security measures put in place by AI experts not only protect the integrity of web applications but also reinforce user trust.

- **Advocating for privacy and ethical AI use**: AI professionals are at the forefront of advocating for privacy and ethical AI use in web development. They ensure that AI-driven features comply with global privacy regulations and ethical standards, addressing concerns such as data misuse and algorithmic bias. This advocacy is crucial in navigating the ethical complexities of AI, fostering a culture of responsibility and transparency within the web development community.

The contribution of AI professionals extends beyond the technical implementation of TRiSM principles. They serve as catalysts for organizational change, driving the adoption of ethical AI practices and fostering a culture of innovation that is conscious of trust, risk, and security considerations. By integrating TRiSM into web development, AI professionals not only enhance the functional and ethical quality of web applications but also position organizations to thrive in an increasingly competitive and digitally driven market.

With a deeper understanding of the crucial role that AI professionals play in implementing TRiSM within web development, it's evident how integral their expertise is to the broader context of digital innovation and security.

As we continue to navigate through the complexities of integrating AI in web environments, it becomes paramount to align these efforts with global standards and guidelines. Next, we will delve into **International Organization for Standardization (ISO)** standards for TRiSM implementation, which provide a structured framework to guide organizations in effectively embedding trust, managing risks, and ensuring security within their AI-infused web applications. These standards serve as a roadmap for organizations aiming to harness the full potential of AI while upholding the highest levels of integrity and ethical responsibility.

ISO standards and guidelines for TRiSM implementation

The role of AI professionals in this domain extends to a deep understanding of various standards, guidelines, and frameworks essential for implementing TRiSM effectively. These include a range of international standards, such as those from **International Organization for Standardization (ISO)**, guides, and frameworks specifically designed to navigate the complexities of trust, risk, and security in AI-enhanced web applications.

AI professionals must be familiar with several key ISO standards that provide a foundation for TRiSM in web development:

- **ISO/IEC 27001**: This standard outlines best practices for an **information security management system (ISMS)**, offering a systematic approach to managing sensitive company information so that it remains secure

- **ISO/IEC 27701**: Extending *ISO/IEC 27001*, this standard focuses on privacy information management, providing guidance on protecting personal data along with broader information security risks

- **ISO/IEC 30500**: Specifically designed for AI systems, this standard provides guidelines for establishing, implementing, maintaining, and continually improving an AI ethics management system

For AI trust, risk, and security management in web development, relevant ISO standards might include the following:

- **ISO/IEC 27001**: ISMSs

- **ISO/IEC 27701**: Privacy information management

- **ISO/IEC 27018**: Code of practice for protecting personal data in the cloud

- **ISO/IEC 27017**: Cloud services security

When it comes to AI specifically, professionals might look toward guidelines and frameworks such as the following:

- **ISO/IEC TR 24028:2020**: Information technology — Artificial intelligence - Overview of trustworthiness in artificial intelligence

- **ISO/IEC TR 24027:2021**: Information technology — Artificial intelligence - Bias in AI systems and AI-aided decision making

- **ISO/IEC 22989:2022**: Information technology — Artificial intelligence - Artificial intelligence concepts and terminology

- **ISO/IEC 23894:2023**: Information technology — Artificial intelligence - Guidance on risk management

- **ISO/IEC 38507:2022**: Information technology — Governance of IT - Governance implications of the use of artificial intelligence by organizations

- **ISO/IEC TR 24368:2022**: Information technology — Artificial intelligence - Overview of ethical and societal concerns

- **ISO/IEC 42001:2023**: Information technology — Artificial intelligence - Management system

- **ISO/IEC 8183:2023**: Information technology — Artificial intelligence - Data life cycle framework

- **ISO/IEC 5338:2023**: Information technology — Artificial intelligence - AI system life cycle processes

- **ISO/IEC 5339:2024**: Information technology — Artificial intelligence - Guidance for AI applications

- **ISO/IEC TR 5469:2024**: Artificial intelligence — Functional safety and AI systems

In addition to ISO standards, AI professionals in web development should be versed in several critical frameworks and guides that further support the integration of TRiSM:

- **NIST AI Risk Management Framework (RMF)**: Developed by the **National Institute of Standards and Technology** (**NIST**), the AI RMF offers a structured approach to managing risks in AI systems, focusing on trustworthiness and public engagement.

One notable example of effective AI risk management can be seen in a leading European bank's approach to call center optimization and customer-credit decisions. According to the report *Confronting the risks of artificial intelligence* (`https://www.mckinsey.com/capabilities/quantumblack/our-insights/confronting-the-risks-of-artificial-intelligence/`) by McKinsey & Company, the bank applied advanced analytics and AI capabilities while adhering to rigorous risk management principles. The bank implemented a robust set of business principles detailing how and where machines could be used to make decisions affecting a customer's financial health, ensuring human oversight in critical decision-making processes. This structured risk identification and mitigation framework allowed the bank to prioritize risks, enforce proper controls, and ensure transparency, fairness, and accountability in their AI-driven initiatives. This approach exemplifies how financial institutions can effectively manage AI risks while leveraging the benefits of AI technologies.

- **Ethics Guidelines for Trustworthy AI (European Union)**: These guidelines emphasize the need for AI systems to be lawful, ethical, and robust, offering insights into realizing trustworthy AI through ethical impact assessments and continuous ethical monitoring.

- **IEEE Ethically Aligned Design**: This set of recommendations from the IEEE provides a comprehensive roadmap for prioritizing human rights and well-being in AI systems, including detailed guidance on transparency and accountability.

The integration of TRiSM principles, guided by a comprehensive understanding of relevant ISO standards, ethical guidelines, and risk management frameworks, is essential for AI professionals tasked with web development. This holistic approach not only enhances the security and reliability of web applications but also ensures they are aligned with global ethical standards, paving the way for sustainable growth and long-term success in the digital arena.

Summary

This chapter provided a comprehensive exploration of ethical considerations, governance models, and the critical AI TRiSM framework in the realm of AI. We navigated through essential ethics in AI, unraveling the intricate layers of governance required for AI models and the pivotal role of the AI TRiSM framework in enhancing the trustworthiness and safety of AI systems.

The insights gained in this chapter are essential for anyone who wishes to successfully navigate the field of AI, ensuring that their applications are fair, safe, and beneficial to society.

Moving forward to our next chapter, we will embark on an exploration of cutting-edge development environments and the latest advancements that are driving the evolution of AI technologies. This next chapter promises to equip you with insights into the dynamic and ever-evolving landscape of AI, preparing you for technological trends that are defining our future.

Part 4:
The Road Ahead –
Anticipating Trends in AI
and Web Development

In the final part of this book, we look ahead to the future of AI and web development. This section covers emerging development environments and cutting-edge AI technologies, the convergence of new realities and interfaces with web development, and the evolving regulatory landscape. By understanding these trends, including the G^3 AI Framework, the EU AI Act, and the ISO/IEC 42001 standards, you'll be equipped to stay at the forefront of AI and web development. The G^3 AI framework is crucial as it integrates governance, management, and strategy guidance for AI applications, ensuring responsible and transparent AI practices. This knowledge will ensure your projects are both innovative and compliant with new standards while emphasizing the shared responsibility of developers and organizational leaders in maintaining ethical AI practices and mitigating risks.

This part includes the following chapters:

- *Chapter 16, Next-Gen Development Environments and Advancements in AI Technologies*

- *Chapter 17, Emerging Realities and Interfaces*

- *Chapter 18, AI Regulation and Governance – Compliance with the EU's AI Act and ISO/IEC 42001 Standards*

16

Next-Gen Development Environments and Advancements in AI Technologies

Technology is perpetually evolving, reshaping how we live, work, and interact. At the forefront of this transformation are advancements in development environments and **artificial intelligence (AI)** technologies, redefining the boundaries of the possible. This chapter embarks on a journey through the latest innovations shaping the future of software development. We will explore the revolution of GitOps, the rise of cloud development environments, collaborative practices driving innovation, and emerging AI technologies such as neuro-symbolic AI, **federated machine learning (FML)**, and WebAssembly. This chapter aims to provide a comprehensive understanding of these critical areas, highlighting their importance in today's technological landscape.

The main topics of this chapter include the following:

- The GitOps revolution and implementing GitOps principles for streamlined workflows
- Embracing the cloud for enhanced development and leveraging cloud tools and resources
- Collaboration best practices in next-gen development
- Avant-garde AI technologies – exploring neuro-symbolic AI, FML, and WebAssembly

As the field of technology continues to evolve, staying updated with the latest trends and tools is not just beneficial; it's essential to any developer or organization aspiring to innovate and lead in their sector.

The GitOps revolution and implementing GitOps principles for streamlined workflows

GitOps, an operations strategy applying software development practices such as version control and **continuous integration/continuous deployment** (**CI/CD**) to infrastructure automation, is revolutionizing how we manage and operate software systems. By treating infrastructure configuration with the same rigor as application code, GitOps promotes significant improvements in automation, predictability, and security.

Traditional infrastructure management relies heavily on manual processes for configuring and deploying systems, which can lead to inconsistencies and human errors. This manual approach often results in environments that vary between development, testing, and production, making it difficult to ensure reliability and predictability. Additionally, changes in traditional setups are rarely version-controlled, meaning there's no straightforward way to track modifications or revert to previous states if an issue arises. Recovery from failures is often slow and cumbersome, requiring significant manual intervention.

In contrast, *GitOps revolutionizes infrastructure management* by applying software development practices such as version control and CI/CD to infrastructure operations. With GitOps, all infrastructure configurations are treated as code and stored in Git repositories, providing a clear history of changes and the ability to roll back to known good states easily. This approach ensures consistency across all environments, as the same code that defines the infrastructure is used for development, testing, and production. Automated deployment processes reduce manual errors and enhance efficiency, while built-in security features of version control systems such as Git enhance overall security. GitOps enables faster recovery from failures through automated rollback capabilities, making it a more reliable and efficient method for managing modern software systems.

Embracing GitOps offers several compelling advantages:

- **Automation and efficiency**: Automated deployments and operations reduce manual errors and increase efficiency. An example of a tool that facilitates automation in GitOps is Argo CD. This tool continuously checks Git repositories for updates and automatically aligns the application state to match the desired configurations defined in Git. This process ensures that deployments are consistent and repeatable, significantly minimizing the chance of manual errors and enhancing overall operational efficiency.

- **Improved reliability**: By treating infrastructure as code, GitOps ensures that environments are reproducible, version-controlled, and easily rollbackable to a known good state.

- **Enhanced security**: Using Git for infrastructure management leverages built-in security features such as access control, change tracking, and audit trails.

- **Faster recovery**: The ability to quickly revert to a previous state improves recovery times in the event of a failure. Consider a scenario during an e-commerce site's major sales event, such as Black Friday. The team deployed a new update to enhance the user experience, but the update contained a critical bug that disrupted the checkout process, causing potential loss of revenue and customer dissatisfaction. With Argo CD's rollback capability, the team swiftly reverted to the last stable version of the application. This quick recovery restored the checkout functionality, minimized downtime, and ensured the continuation of sales, highlighting the vital role of rollback features in maintaining service reliability during crucial times.

At its core, GitOps is more than a mere methodology; it's a paradigm shift that champions the use of Git as the single source of truth for both infrastructure and application deployment. This approach harnesses the power of version control, enabling developers to manage infrastructure with the same precision and accountability as application code. The essence of GitOps lies in its ability to automate deployment processes, ensuring consistency across environments, enhancing security through meticulous change tracking, and significantly improving recovery times with straightforward rollback capabilities.

The GitOps revolution heralds a new era where traditional operational models are replaced with a more streamlined, developer-centric framework. This revolution is characterized by its emphasis on automation, immutability, and CD, integrating development and operations into a cohesive, agile process. The shift toward GitOps is driven by the industry's demand for faster, more reliable software delivery mechanisms that can adeptly navigate the complexities of modern systems and dynamic cloud environments.

The revolution builds on several key principles that form the foundation of GitOps:

- **Infrastructure as code** (IaC): This principle advocates for the management and provisioning of infrastructure through code, stored in Git, enabling automated setup and teardown of environments

- **Immutable infrastructure**: Once deployed, infrastructure components are not modified directly; instead, changes are made in Git and redeployed, promoting stability and reliability

- **Continuous deployment**: Changes in Git trigger automated deployment processes, ensuring that the production environment always reflects the state defined in the repository

- **Developer-centric operations**: GitOps empowers developers by allowing them to use familiar tools and processes for operational tasks, bridging the gap between code development and deployment

These principles are essential for accelerating development cycles and improving system reliability. By leveraging the immutability of infrastructure and comprehensive automation, GitOps ensures that the desired state is consistently maintained, thus providing a robust framework for modern software development.

In the following subsections, we will delve deeper into the specific principles of GitOps, such as IaC and immutable infrastructure, and examine how CD and developer-centric operations contribute to creating streamlined workflows and enhancing operational efficiency.

Implementing GitOps for streamlined workflows

The adoption of GitOps principles marks the beginning of a journey toward more efficient, secure, and resilient software development practices. The implementation process involves a deep understanding of GitOps workflows, the selection of compatible tools, and embracing a culture that values automation and continuous improvement.

Let's dive into the key components and considerations for successfully adopting GitOps:

- **Navigating GitOps workflows**: Effective GitOps workflows are the linchpin of this approach, ensuring that every change, from code commit to deployment, is automated and traceable. This automation extends beyond deployment to encompass testing, security checks, and even rollback procedures, facilitating a seamless, error-minimized pathway from development to production.

- **The arsenal of GitOps tools**: Choosing the right set of tools is crucial to the successful implementation of GitOps. Tools such as Terraform for IaC, Kubernetes for container orchestration, and Argo CD or Flux for continuous delivery, are instrumental in building a robust GitOps pipeline. These tools not only automate deployments but also enforce the principles of immutability and CD that are central to the GitOps philosophy.

- **GitOps security**: Security in GitOps is paramount. Practices such as encrypting secrets, using **Secure Shell** (**SSH**), which is a cryptographic network protocol used for secure communication between devices over an unsecured network, keys for authentication, and enforcing role-based access controls ensure that infrastructure management is both secure and efficient. Specific tools and frameworks that help implement these security practices include HashiCorp Vault and Kubernetes **RBAC** (**role-based access control**). HashiCorp Vault is used for securely storing and accessing secrets, ensuring that sensitive data such as passwords and API keys are encrypted and only accessible to authorized services. Kubernetes RBAC manages permissions within a Kubernetes cluster, allowing administrators to define who can perform specific actions on various resources. By utilizing these tools, organizations can enforce stringent security measures, protecting their infrastructure from unauthorized access and potential threats.

- **Cultivating a GitOps culture**: The transition to GitOps also necessitates a cultural shift within organizations. A GitOps culture emphasizes collaboration, transparency, experimentation, and continuous learning. It encourages teams to share knowledge openly, experiment with new ideas, and view failures as opportunities for growth, thereby fostering an environment of innovation and continuous improvement.

- **Overcoming challenges**: While the shift to GitOps promises numerous benefits, it also presents challenges such as mastering new tools, adhering to rigorous security practices, and managing the initial complexity of setup. Overcoming these challenges requires commitment, continuous learning, and adaptability, underpinned by a clear understanding of the goals and benefits of GitOps.

Practical implementation of GitOps can be exemplified by the use of **Google Kubernetes Engine** (**GKE**), which enables developers to efficiently and securely orchestrate containers. By integrating

Git repositories as the single source of truth for infrastructure configuration, teams can automate the deployment of applications and services, significantly reducing the chance of human error and increasing delivery speed.

Best practices in GitOps

Successfully implementing GitOps requires more than just using the right tools; it involves following established best practices to ensure a smooth, secure, and efficient workflow. These practices are crucial for maximizing the benefits of GitOps and maintaining a high standard of operational excellence.

Implementing GitOps successfully requires adherence to *best practices* such as the following:

- Ensuring all changes are made through pull requests for accountability and review
- Automating all aspects of the deployment process to minimize human error
- Establishing robust monitoring and alerting to detect and respond to issues in real time

Beyond improving operational efficiency, GitOps offers significant benefits in terms of security and compliance. By versioning the entire infrastructure state and applying code review practices, organizations can enhance the auditing, traceability, and governance of their IT operations. This model fosters a culture of transparency and collaboration, essential to agile development and the maintenance of complex systems.

As we delve into the efficiencies gained through GitOps, it's natural to extend this streamlined approach to the broader spectrum of cloud development environments, where the principles of automation, scalability, and flexibility further amplify the benefits of modern software development practices.

Embracing the cloud for enhanced development and leveraging cloud tools and resources

In the contemporary era of software development, the cloud has emerged not merely as a tool but as a transformative force, reshaping the landscape of development practices and methodologies. The journey into **cloud computing** is a pivotal evolution from traditional infrastructure to a more dynamic, scalable, and efficient model, empowering developers to innovate at an unprecedented pace. This section delves into the core aspects of embracing cloud computing for enhanced development, highlighting the pivotal role of cloud tools and resources.

The adoption of cloud computing marks a significant shift in software development. This evolution is characterized by the transition from on-premises, rigid infrastructures to flexible, cloud-native environments. The essence of cloud development lies in its agility, enabling teams to deploy applications swiftly, scale resources on demand, and reduce both operational costs and complexity. This agility fosters an environment where innovation thrives, allowing developers to experiment with new ideas without the prohibitive costs and logistical barriers associated with traditional IT infrastructure.

Cloud development offers several distinct advantages that are transforming the software development landscape. Here are the key points to consider:

- The *advantages of cloud development* are manifold. Scalability stands at the forefront, offering the ability to effortlessly scale computing resources to meet demand. This is complemented by cost-effectiveness, with cloud providers offering pay-as-you-go models that eliminate large upfront investments and reduce ongoing operational expenses. Accessibility is another hallmark of cloud development, with cloud-based tools and platforms enabling developers to work collaboratively from any location, thus enhancing productivity and facilitating remote work. Moreover, the cloud serves as a catalyst for innovation, providing access to cutting-edge technologies and services that enable developers to explore new horizons without significant risk or investment.

- Selecting the right *cloud platform and tools* is critical to harnessing the full potential of cloud development. Major platforms such as **Amazon Web Services** (**AWS**), Microsoft Azure, and **Google Cloud Platform** (**GCP**) offer a broad spectrum of services that cater to various aspects of development, from compute and storage to AI and machine learning. Within these ecosystems, developers have access to a plethora of tools designed to streamline the development process. IaC tools such as Terraform and AWS CloudFormation simplify the provisioning and management of infrastructure, while serverless computing and containerization services foster a more efficient deployment model. Furthermore, CI/CD pipelines facilitate automated testing and deployment, ensuring that applications are delivered quickly and reliably.

- To fully benefit from cloud development, it's imperative to adhere to *best practices* that ensure security, optimize performance, and manage costs effectively. Here are some key areas to focus on:

  - **Security and compliance**: Implement encryption for data at rest and in transit to protect sensitive information. Utilize access control policies, including **multi-factor authentication** (**MFA**), to ensure only authorized personnel can access critical systems. Conduct regular security audits and vulnerability assessments to identify and mitigate potential risks. Ensure compliance with regulations such as GDPR, HIPAA, or CCPA by implementing necessary controls and processes.

  - **Performance optimization**: Use monitoring tools such as AWS CloudWatch, Azure Monitor, and Google Cloud Operations Suite (formerly Stackdriver) to monitor and observe cloud resources and applications. Implement auto-scaling to dynamically adjust resources based on demand, ensuring optimal performance without over-provisioning. Regularly review and optimize application code and database queries to improve efficiency and reduce latency.

  - **Cost management**: Leverage cost management tools such as AWS Cost Explorer, Azure Cost Management and Billing, and Google Cloud Billing to monitor and control expenditures. Implement budgeting and alerting mechanisms to track spending and receive notifications of potential cost overruns. Regularly review resource utilization and rightsizing instances to ensure that only necessary resources are being used.

- **Disaster recovery**: Utilize services such as AWS Backup, Azure Site Recovery, and Google Cloud Backup and DR to automate data backup and recovery processes. Regularly test disaster recovery plans to ensure they are effective and can be executed quickly in the event of an outage. Ensure data redundancy across multiple geographic locations to protect against regional failures.

- **Managing cloud services**: Utilize managed services provided by cloud platforms, such as AWS Managed Services, Azure Managed Services, and Google Cloud Managed Services, to offer operational support, infrastructure management, and automation capabilities. Invest in comprehensive training programs such as AWS Training and Certification, Microsoft Learn for Azure, and Google Cloud Training to equip teams with the necessary skills and knowledge. Adopt industry-standard security frameworks such as the NIST Cybersecurity Framework or ISO/IEC 27001 to manage security risks. Employ security tools such as AWS Shield for **Distributed Denial of Service (DDoS)** protection, Azure Security Center for threat management, and Google Cloud Armor for application security. Conduct regular security training and awareness programs to ensure all team members understand and adhere to security protocols.

Implementing disaster recovery plans is crucial to ensure business continuity, leveraging the cloud's inherent scalability and data replication capabilities. AWS Backup centralizes and automates data backup across AWS services, Azure Site Recovery provides business continuity by keeping applications running during outages, and Google Cloud Backup and DR manages backup and disaster recovery for applications and databases running on Google Cloud.

- Despite its benefits, the transition to cloud development can present *challenges*, including the complexity of managing cloud services, the need to upskill teams, and ensuring robust security in a multi-tenant environment. Overcoming these challenges requires a strategic approach, emphasizing education, the use of managed services, and a focus on security best practices:

  - To tackle the complexity of managing cloud services, organizations can utilize managed services provided by cloud platforms. These services, such as AWS Managed Services, Azure Managed Services, and Google Cloud Managed Services, offer operational support, infrastructure management, and automation capabilities. This allows businesses to concentrate on their core activities while ensuring their cloud environments are efficiently managed.

  - Upskilling teams is crucial for a successful transition to cloud development. Investing in comprehensive training programs can equip teams with the necessary skills and knowledge. Resources such as AWS Training and Certification, Microsoft Learn for Azure, and Google Cloud Training offer a wide range of courses and certifications covering various aspects of cloud computing. These programs help team members stay current with the latest technologies and best practices, ensuring they are well-prepared to manage and utilize cloud services effectively.

- Ensuring robust security in a multi-tenant environment requires adopting industry-standard security frameworks and best practices. Implementing frameworks such as the NIST Cybersecurity

Framework or ISO/IEC 27001 provides a structured approach to managing security risks. Additionally, employing security tools such as AWS Shield for DDoS protection, Azure Security Center for threat management, and Google Cloud Armor for application security can enhance the overall security posture. Regular security training and awareness programs can further ensure that all team members understand and adhere to security protocols.

- As we embrace cloud development, it's clear that the journey doesn't end here. The *future* promises further advancements, with trends such as edge computing, hybrid and multi-cloud strategies, and serverless architectures shaping the next wave of innovation. These developments will continue to expand the capabilities of cloud computing, offering new opportunities for developers to push the boundaries of what's possible.

The exploration of cloud computing for enhanced software development not only opens up a realm of possibilities but also paves the way for a collaborative revolution in how we build and deploy software. As we transition from the individualistic confines of traditional development environments to the vast, interconnected expanse of the cloud, the necessity for effective collaboration among developers becomes increasingly evident. The next section will focus on the critical strategies and methodologies that enable developers to harness the collective power of cloud-based tools and platforms.

Collaboration best practices in next-gen development

In today's rapidly evolving software development landscape, effective collaboration has become a cornerstone of success. As technologies advance and projects grow in complexity, the need for cohesive teamwork and streamlined communication is more critical than ever. This section delves into the best practices for fostering effective collaboration in next-gen development environments.

Collaboration in software development isn't a new concept, but its importance has surged with the advent of agile methodologies and DevOps practices. Effective collaboration leads to greater efficiency, improved code quality, and a more harmonious work environment. However, it's not just about having the right tools; it involves cultivating the right culture, establishing efficient processes, and ensuring that every team member is aligned with the project's goals. This can be particularly challenging in large and distributed teams, but it is essential for project success.

So, let's embark on this journey and discover how we can transform the way we collaborate in next-gen development:

- **Collaboration tools**: Collaboration tools are vital to facilitating communication and coordination among team members. Let's explore some of the most popular and effective tools used in next-gen software development:

  - Version control systems such as Git, along with platforms such as GitHub and GitLab, are foundational. They enable team members to share code, conduct reviews, and manage changes efficiently. These systems support collaborative coding, ensuring that everyone works with the latest version of the code base.

- Communication platforms such as Slack and Microsoft Teams are indispensable for real-time interaction. These tools allow for instant messaging, video calls, and file sharing, which help teams stay connected, regardless of their geographical location.

- Project management tools such as Jira and Trello help teams organize tasks, track progress, and manage workflows. These tools support agile practices, providing features such as Kanban boards and sprint planning to keep projects on track.

- Many collaboration tools now integrate advanced features such as CI/CD, issue tracking, and automated testing. These features help maintain high code quality and enable faster, more reliable software delivery. However, it's crucial to select tools that fit the specific needs of the team and the project.

- Cultural practices such as regular stand-ups, where team members share updates and address issues, and code reviews, where peers review each other's code for quality and improvement, are essential. These practices not only ensure alignment but also promote continuous learning and collaboration.

- **Agile practices**: Agile practices, such as Scrum and Kanban, emphasize collaboration, communication, and adaptability. They encourage teams to work together to solve problems rather than do so in silos. This approach leads to greater efficiency, more innovative solutions, a faster development cycle, fewer errors, and a higher-quality end product. Here are key points to consider when implementing agile and DevOps practices:

  - Implementing agile and DevOps practices can be challenging. It requires a cultural shift and the adoption of new tools and processes. Teams must embrace iterative development, continuous feedback, and flexible responses to change. The benefits, however, can be substantial, transforming the way teams collaborate and deliver value.

  - Scrum involves working in short, iterative cycles called sprints, with regular reviews and retrospectives to improve processes continuously. Kanban focuses on visualizing work, limiting work in progress, and optimizing flow. Both frameworks support continuous improvement and foster a collaborative environment.

- **Collaboration culture**: Creating a collaborative culture is fundamental to leveraging the benefits of next-gen development. This culture encourages open communication, idea exchange, and teamwork, leading to greater innovation and more effective problem-solving. A positive work environment fosters job satisfaction, higher employee retention, and ultimately, a higher-quality end product. To build and maintain such a culture, consider the following key aspects:

  - Building such a culture requires strong leadership, mutual trust, and respect. Leaders must model collaborative behavior, encourage diverse viewpoints, and create a safe space for team members to share ideas and feedback. It's about fostering an environment where every team member feels valued and empowered to contribute.

- Challenges in building a collaborative culture include overcoming resistance to change, bridging communication gaps, and managing conflicts constructively. However, the effort pays off by creating a more cohesive, motivated, and high-performing team.

In this section, you learned about the best practices for collaboration in next-gen development. With the right tools, agile and DevOps practices, and a strong collaboration culture, development teams can work together more effectively and efficiently, leading to high-quality software products.

In the upcoming section, we will delve into the cutting-edge advancements in the field of AI. We will explore the intricacies of neuro-symbolic AI, a new approach that combines the strengths of both neural networks and symbolic AI. We will also discuss FML, a technique that allows for machine learning models to be trained across multiple devices or servers while maintaining data privacy. Lastly, we will touch upon WebAssembly, a binary instruction format that allows code to run at near-native speed in the web browser.

Exploring neuro-symbolic AI, FML, and WebAssembly

This section serves as your gateway to understanding the intricate blend of neural networks and symbolic AI known as neuro-symbolic AI, the privacy-preserving technique of FML, and the high-performance capabilities of WebAssembly in the browser environment.

Our exploration will be comprehensive, current, and accessible, irrespective of your prior familiarity with these technologies. Real-world examples and case studies will be our companions, bringing these concepts to life.

Neuro-symbolic AI

Neuro-symbolic AI is an innovative approach that merges two significant branches of AI: neural networks and symbolic AI. This fusion aims to leverage the strengths of both branches to create AI systems that can learn from data and reason with the learned knowledge, providing a more comprehensive and robust AI solution.

Neural networks, a subset of machine learning, are excellent at handling raw data and learning from it. They excel in tasks involving perception, such as image recognition or natural language processing. However, they often struggle with tasks that require explicit reasoning or when the data is sparse or absent. This is a problem that many AI researchers and practitioners are actively trying to solve.

On the other hand, **symbolic AI**, also known as classical AI, excels at reasoning with explicit knowledge. It uses symbols and rules to represent knowledge and applies logical reasoning to solve problems. However, symbolic AI systems usually require manual knowledge engineering and often struggle to handle raw data. This is another challenge that the AI community is working to overcome.

The integration of these two branches in neuro-symbolic AI aims to overcome the limitations of each while leveraging their strengths. The goal is to create AI systems that can both learn from raw data and reason with the learned knowledge. This is a current trend in AI research and development, and many believe it could be the key to creating more intelligent and versatile AI systems.

However, implementing neuro-symbolic AI is not without its challenges. One of the main difficulties lies in the integration of symbolic reasoning with neural learning. This requires developing novel architectures and learning algorithms that can effectively combine these two fundamentally different approaches. Researchers are actively exploring different strategies to address this problem.

Despite these challenges, neuro-symbolic AI holds great promise. It is being explored for use in various fields, including healthcare, finance, and more. Its ability to learn from data and reason with the learned knowledge makes it a powerful tool for tackling complex problems that require both perception and reasoning.

In the context of web development, neuro-symbolic AI could potentially be used to create more intelligent and adaptive web applications. For instance, it could be used to develop recommendation systems that not only learn from user behavior but also reason about user preferences and needs. This could lead to more personalized and effective recommendations, enhancing the user experience.

In conclusion, neuro-symbolic AI represents a significant advancement in the field of AI. By combining the strengths of neural networks and symbolic AI, it offers a more robust and comprehensive AI solution. As research in this area continues, we can expect to see more innovative applications of neuro-symbolic AI in the future.

With a solid understanding of neuro-symbolic AI and its potential applications, let's delve into another exciting advancement in AI technology. Next, we will explore FML, a new paradigm that offers promising solutions for data privacy and security while enabling collaborative learning across decentralized data sources.

FML – a new paradigm

FML is an innovative approach to machine learning that decentralizes the training process, allowing AI models to be trained directly on user devices. This approach is characterized by three key components:

- **Distributed machine learning**: FML breaks away from the traditional model of centralizing all data on a single server for AI model training. Instead, it distributes the training process across multiple devices, each training a local model using its own data.

- **Local model training**: In FML, AI models are trained directly on user devices, leveraging local computational power. This means raw data never needs to leave the device, enhancing data privacy.

- **Model update sharing, not raw data**: After local training, each device sends only model updates to the central server. The server then aggregates these updates to improve the global model, ensuring raw data is never shared and user privacy is maintained.

By understanding the benefits, applications, and future directions of FML, we can appreciate its potential to transform various industries. This approach paves the way for more collaborative and efficient machine learning practices.

Benefits of FML

FML is a groundbreaking approach to machine learning that offers significant benefits in terms of data privacy and network efficiency. By decentralizing the training process and allowing AI models to be trained directly on user devices, FML opens up new possibilities for creating powerful and efficient AI solutions that respect user privacy.

One of the primary benefits of FML is *data privacy*. As raw data never leaves the user's device, powerful AI models can be trained without compromising user privacy. This is particularly important in sectors where data privacy is a significant concern, such as healthcare and finance.

FML also offers benefits in terms of *network efficiency*. By training models locally and sharing only model updates, FML reduces the amount of data that needs to be transferred across the network. This can result in significant bandwidth savings and improve overall system efficiency.

The benefits of FML are profound and have the potential to transform the way we approach machine learning. By safeguarding data privacy and improving network efficiency, FML represents a significant step toward a future where machine learning can be carried out more securely and efficiently. As we continue to explore and develop this technology, we are likely to see even more benefits and applications of FML in the future.

Challenges in FML

Despite its benefits, FML also presents several challenges:

- **Data heterogeneity**: In a federated environment, data is distributed across many different devices. This data can vary significantly in terms of quality and quantity, which can make model training more complex.

- **Synchronization**: Coordinating model updates across many different devices can be challenging. It's crucial to ensure all updates are correctly aggregated to improve the global model.

- **Security**: While FML protects data privacy by ensuring raw data is never shared, it's still necessary to secure model updates during transmission. This requires robust security solutions to ensure model updates are not intercepted or tampered with.

While FML presents a promising solution to the challenges of data privacy and network efficiency in machine learning, it also introduces its own set of challenges. These include dealing with data heterogeneity, ensuring synchronization of model updates across devices, and securing model updates during transmission. Overcoming these challenges requires innovative solutions and ongoing research.

As we continue to explore this new paradigm, we are likely to develop more robust and efficient methods to address these challenges, paving the way for the wider adoption of FML in various fields. The journey toward fully realizing the potential of FML is filled with challenges, but each challenge overcome brings us one step closer to a future where machine learning can be more secure, private, and efficient. The future of machine learning is not without its challenges, but with FML, we are well-equipped to face them.

Applications of FML

FML has a wide range of potential applications:

- **Mobile devices**: FML can be used to enhance personalization on mobile devices without compromising user privacy. For instance, it can be used to train personalized recommendation models directly on a user's device.

- **Internet of Things** (**IoT**): In IoT devices, FML can be used to leverage local computational power. This can enable IoT devices to make real-time intelligent decisions without the need for constant communication with a central server.

- **Healthcare**: In the healthcare sector, FML can be used to train models on sensitive data without the need to share this data. This can enable the development of personalized and effective AI solutions while maintaining patient privacy.

- **Web development**: In web development, FML can be used to enhance the user experience, allowing real-time personalization without compromising users' data privacy.

Indeed, as FML continues to evolve and mature, we are likely to see an increasing number of applications in various fields. This paradigm shift in machine learning, with its significant benefits and challenges, is part of a broader trend of rapid technological advancement.

One such advancement that is gaining traction in the field of web development is WebAssembly. In the next section, we will delve into the world of WebAssembly, exploring its capabilities, benefits, and potential impact on the future of web development.

WebAssembly

In the ever-evolving landscape of web development, a new player has emerged that promises to revolutionize the way we build web applications. This player is **WebAssembly**, often abbreviated as **Wasm**, a low-level language designed to run alongside JavaScript in web browsers.

Wasm is a compact, binary instruction format designed for a stack-based virtual machine. It serves as a portable compilation target for high-level programming languages such as C, C++, and Rust, enabling their execution on web platforms for both client-side and server-side applications. This format allows developers to write code in multiple languages and run it efficiently in web browsers, enhancing the performance and capabilities of web applications.

As we delve deeper into the world of WebAssembly, we'll explore its benefits, challenges, and potential applications, particularly in the realm of web development.

Benefits

WebAssembly offers a range of benefits that make it a valuable addition to the web development toolkit. Let's delve into these benefits in detail:

- This language is designed with a focus on *performance*. It provides near-native execution speed by using a compact binary format that allows for faster parsing compared to JavaScript. This leads to quicker page loads, enhancing the user experience on web applications.

- WebAssembly is language-agnostic, meaning it can support multiple programming languages. This allows developers to work in the language they are most comfortable with, while still targeting the web platform. Furthermore, WebAssembly code is designed to run on any browser and on any operating system, providing a truly *portable* solution.

- It executes within a sandboxed environment for added *security*. This means that WebAssembly applications run in a confined environment separate from the system, reducing the risk of malicious activities.

The benefits of WebAssembly, including superior performance, portability, and security, make it an attractive choice for web developers. These benefits have the potential to significantly enhance user experience and development efficiency. As we transition from the benefits, it's important to note that while WebAssembly offers significant advantages, it also presents its own set of challenges.

Challenges

Like any emerging technology, WebAssembly presents its own set of challenges. These challenges need to be understood and addressed for web developers to fully leverage the potential of WebAssembly.

While WebAssembly is designed to work alongside JavaScript and web APIs, seamless interaction between these different components (*interoperability*) can be challenging. Developers need to ensure that their WebAssembly modules can communicate effectively with the JavaScript context and the various web APIs available.

As a relatively new technology, WebAssembly requires robust tooling and libraries for developers to fully leverage its capabilities. The need for more comprehensive resources and learning materials can be a barrier to widespread *adoption*.

While WebAssembly presents challenges such as interoperability and adoption, the developer community is actively working to overcome them. As more tools and resources become available, these challenges are likely to be mitigated. Despite these challenges, the potential applications of WebAssembly across various domains are vast and exciting.

Applications

WebAssembly offers a wide range of potential applications, from web games to scientific computing, and is shaping the future of web development:

- In *web games*, WebAssembly allows for the creation of complex, high-performance web games. By executing code at near-native speed, it enables games to have more intricate graphics, smoother gameplay, and overall better performance. This advancement opens up new possibilities for web-based gaming, allowing for a richer and more engaging user experience.

- With regard to *web applications*, WebAssembly can significantly enhance the performance of heavy web applications. Tasks that require intensive computation can be offloaded to WebAssembly, providing a smoother user experience. This is particularly beneficial to applications that handle large amounts of data or perform complex calculations.

- In the realm of *scientific computing*, WebAssembly enables heavy calculations to be performed directly in the browser. This opens up possibilities for web-based applications in fields such as data visualization, machine learning, and physics simulations. Scientists and researchers can now perform complex computations without leaving their web browsers.

- WebAssembly is revolutionizing *web development* by allowing developers to create efficient, performant, and secure web applications. As the technology continues to mature, we can expect to see an increasing number of web applications leveraging WebAssembly.

To conclude, WebAssembly is a game-changer for web development. It offers significant benefits in terms of performance, portability, and security. However, like any technology, it also presents its own set of challenges. As we continue to explore and understand this technology, we can look forward to a future where web applications are more powerful, more efficient, and more secure. The future of web development is here, and it is being shaped by technologies such as WebAssembly.

Summary

In this chapter, we went on an exploration into the future of development environments and the impact of AI technologies. We delved into the concept of FML, discussing its definition, benefits, challenges, and applications, particularly in the realm of web development. We also explored WebAssembly, a low-level language for the web that runs code faster than JavaScript, and its potential applications in web development.

We discussed the benefits of these technologies, including improved performance, portability, and security, as well as the challenges they present, such as interoperability and adoption. We also looked at their potential applications, from web games to scientific computing, and how they can enhance user experience and development efficiency.

Through this chapter, we gained a deeper understanding of these next-generation technologies and their transformative potential in the field of web development.

In the next chapter, we will embark on a captivating exploration of the future as we delve into the convergence of emerging realities and interfaces with web development. From the immersive landscapes of virtual and augmented reality (VR/AR) to the evolution of **conversational user interfaces** (**CUIs**) and the omnipresence of ubiquitous computing, you will gain profound insights into the transformative impact on web development practices. Stay tuned for an in-depth look at these exciting technologies.

17

Emerging Realities and Interfaces

This chapter delves into the innovative landscape of emerging realities and interfaces and their transformative role in web development. Initially, we'll explore how to integrate cutting-edge technologies such as **virtual reality** (**VR**) and **augmented reality** (**AR**) into web platforms. These technologies not only enhance user interaction through immersive experiences but also open up new possibilities for user engagement and interface design.

Next, we will discuss the development and impact of **conversational user interfaces** (**CUIs**) in web development. Here, we'll focus on how **Natural Language Processing** (**NLP**) and ML are used to create interfaces that offer seamless, intuitive user interactions, effectively mimicking human conversation.

Lastly, we'll cover ubiquitous computing and its implementation in web development, emphasizing how this technology powers personal assistants and broadens the functionality of web applications through pervasive computing environments.

The following topics will be covered in this chapter:

- VR/AR and web development
- Exploring CUIs and web development
- Ubiquitous computing and web development

By the end of this chapter, you'll have acquired essential skills that are crucial for any modern web developer. You'll know how to integrate VR and AR technologies into web development, enhancing user engagement through immersive experiences. Additionally, you'll have mastered the art of crafting conversational interfaces that facilitate seamless user interactions, making digital communication feel as natural as a face-to-face conversation. Furthermore, you will have developed the ability to create seamless user experiences by applying ubiquitous computing technologies, ensuring that your web applications are as pervasive and user-friendly as possible.

VR/AR and web development

VR and AR are transformative technologies that are reshaping the digital landscape. Both technologies hold immense potential for enhancing the way we interact with the web.

VR is an immersive experience where the user is transported into a three-dimensional computer-generated environment. This is typically achieved through the use of a VR headset that tracks the user's head movement, allowing them to look around the virtual environment as if they were truly there. VR has the power to transport us to new worlds, from exploring the depths of the ocean to walking on the surface of Mars.

AR, on the other hand, is a technology that overlays digital information into the real world. This can be achieved through the use of a smartphone or tablet, or more specialized devices such as AR glasses. AR enhances our perception of the real world by adding digital elements or *augmentations*, such as directions on a map, player stats in a sports game, or even virtual furniture in a room.

While both technologies offer immersive experiences, they are used in different ways and have different implications for web development.

AR hardware requirements and compatibility

Creating AR experiences involves different hardware requirements, primarily focusing on integrating digital information with the physical world.

Most AR applications are accessible via *mobile devices* (smartphones and tablets) equipped with cameras and sensors. These devices must support AR frameworks such as ARKit for iOS or ARCore for Android to ensure compatibility and performance.

Specialized **AR glasses**, such as Microsoft HoloLens or Magic Leap, provide more immersive AR experiences. These devices need to be compatible with the software and applications being developed, ensuring they can accurately overlay digital information onto the real world.

Emerging AR technologies include *wearables* such as AR contact lenses or headsets that integrate seamlessly into daily life. Ensuring compatibility with existing AR platforms and software is essential for developing effective AR applications.

VR headsets, such as the Oculus Rift, HTC Vive, and PlayStation VR, are essential for creating immersive experiences. These headsets need to be compatible with high-performance PCs or gaming consoles capable of rendering complex 3D environments smoothly.

Motion controllers or gloves are necessary for users to interact with the VR environment. These devices must be compatible with the chosen VR headset and capable of precise tracking to provide a seamless interaction experience.

Tracking systems, including sensors or cameras, are vital for tracking head and body movements. Compatibility between the tracking system and the VR headset is crucial to ensure accurate and responsive interactions within the VR space.

High-performance **computing power** is required to handle the intensive graphics and processing demands of VR applications. This typically involves PCs or consoles with powerful GPUs and ample RAM to render immersive environments without lag.

In summary, the development of effective AR and VR applications requires carefully considering hardware compatibility and performance requirements. Ensuring that devices can support the necessary software frameworks and provide smooth, immersive experiences is crucial. As we look beyond these technical considerations, it is also important to address the broader challenges and limitations that VR and AR technologies face. Understanding these obstacles and seeking innovative solutions will be key to unlocking the full potential of these transformative technologies.

Challenges and limitations

Despite their potential, VR and AR technologies face several challenges and limitations that must be addressed for widespread adoption and effective implementation.

One of the primary barriers to adopting VR and AR technologies is the high cost of equipment. VR headsets, AR glasses, and the necessary computing power can be expensive, limiting accessibility for many users and developers. Additionally, developing high-quality VR and AR experiences often requires significant investment in specialized software and hardware, further increasing costs.

The data collection capabilities of VR and AR devices raise significant privacy concerns. These technologies can capture extensive information about user behavior, environment, and interactions, potentially leading to unauthorized data usage or breaches. Ensuring robust data protection and user consent mechanisms is crucial to addressing these concerns.

The immersive nature of VR and AR can lead to ethical issues, particularly concerning content creation and consumption. Realistic depictions of harmful activities, user addiction, and the impact on mental health are areas of concern. Developers must establish ethical guidelines and consider the societal implications of their VR and AR applications.

Developing VR and AR experiences involves overcoming several technical challenges, including ensuring smooth performance, minimizing latency, and achieving accurate tracking. These challenges require advanced technical knowledge and resources to address effectively.

Potential solutions

Addressing the challenges and limitations of VR and AR technologies involves several strategies:

- **Cost reduction**: Technological advancements and increased competition in the market are likely to drive down the cost of VR and AR hardware. Additionally, utilizing open source software and tools can reduce development costs and foster a collaborative community.

- **Enhancing privacy**: Implementing strong encryption and data protection protocols can help secure user data. Transparency in how data is collected, used, and stored is essential to build user trust and ensure informed consent.

- **Ethical development**: Establishing industry-wide ethical guidelines for VR and AR content creation can help mitigate potential risks. Prioritizing accessibility and ensuring diverse representation in VR and AR experiences can create more equitable and engaging digital environments. VR and AR are reshaping the digital landscape, offering immersive and augmented experiences that significantly enhance how we interact with digital content.

By understanding the hardware requirements, addressing the challenges, and implementing best practices, developers can create innovative and ethical VR and AR applications that enhance user experiences and drive technological progress.

VR/AR in web development

The integration of VR/AR into web development is a rapidly growing area. With the advent of web-based VR/AR libraries and frameworks such as A-Frame and React 360, developers now have the tools they need to create VR/AR experiences on the web.

A-Frame is a web-based VR development framework that allows developers to create VR experiences using HTML. This makes VR more accessible to web developers who are already familiar with HTML, CSS, and JavaScript. It provides a declarative, extensible, and composable structure that can handle the complexity of VR on the web.

React 360, on the other hand, is a framework for creating VR and AR experiences on the web using React. This allows developers to create complex user interfaces in VR/AR using the same component model they would use to create web applications with React. It provides a powerful way to create immersive 3D experiences that can run on both VR headsets and in the browser.

Both frameworks offer a range of features to help developers create VR/AR experiences on the web, including support for controller input, text rendering, 360 video support, and more.

Crafting immersive digital experiences

Creating immersive digital experiences with VR/AR involves more than just the technology itself. It also requires an understanding of the design principles for VR/AR, careful consideration of user interaction, and a conscious approach to accessibility.

Design principles for VR/AR differ from those for traditional web design. For instance, in VR/AR, space is a key consideration. Developers need to think about how users move and interact within the virtual environment. Additionally, the user interface in VR/AR is often three-dimensional, requiring a different approach to user interface design.

User interaction in VR/AR also differs from user interaction on the traditional web. Instead of clicking and scrolling, users in VR/AR might point, grab, and even walk. This requires developers to think carefully about how users interact with the user interface and how to facilitate these interactions.

Accessibility is another important consideration when creating immersive digital experiences. It's important to ensure that VR/AR experiences are accessible to all users, including those with disabilities. This might include offering alternative control options, ensuring text is readable, and considering issues such as motion sickness.

Real-world applications of VR/AR in web development

The applications of VR/AR in web development are vast and varied. Here, we'll delve into some of the most innovative and impactful applications that are transforming industries and redefining user experiences:

- **Virtual retail stores**: VR is revolutionizing the retail industry by creating virtual retail stores. This allows users to *walk* through a store and *see* products as if they were actually there. This immersive shopping experience can increase user engagement and provide a unique selling proposition for businesses. For instance, imagine a VR setup like the one used by IKEA, where users can virtually navigate a meticulously designed store layout and interact with furniture by checking details or visualizing different colors and configurations in a room setting.

- **Immersive real estate tours**: AR is being used to create immersive real estate tours that allow users to "visit" a property without leaving their home. This not only saves time but also allows users to see the property from angles that wouldn't be possible in a traditional visit. Consider a real estate application such as Zillow, which uses AR to offer virtual open house tours.

- **Interactive education**: VR/AR is transforming education by creating interactive learning experiences. From virtual field trips to interactive textbooks, these technologies are enhancing student engagement and improving learning outcomes. An educational platform, such as Google Expeditions, enables students to embark on virtual field trips across the globe – from coral reefs under the sea to the surface of Mars.

- **Healthcare training**: VR/AR is being used to train healthcare professionals by providing them with realistic simulations. This allows them to practice procedures and make mistakes in a safe environment before performing them on real patients. Applications such as Osso VR provide surgical training through highly detailed virtual simulations. Surgeons can practice complex procedures in a risk-free environment, enhancing their skills without the ethical concerns and pressures of practicing on real patients.

- **Product prototyping**: AR is being used in product design and prototyping, allowing designers to visualize and interact with 3D models of their designs in the real world. This can speed up the design process and facilitate collaboration. Autodesk's VRED technology allows automotive designers to create and interact with 3D models of new vehicle designs. Engineers and designers can evaluate aesthetics and functionality, performing virtual wind tunnel tests or simulating the manufacturing process directly within the AR environment.

- **Virtual workspaces**: With the rise of remote work, VR is being used to create virtual workspaces. These allow remote teams to collaborate in a shared virtual environment, improving communication and teamwork. Tools such as Microsoft Mesh enable teams to meet in virtual spaces, where they can collaborate, share, and interact with 3D content as if they were physically together. This technology bridges the gap between remote team members, fostering a collaborative environment that mimics real office interactions.

- **Cultural preservation**: VR/AR is being used to preserve and share cultural heritage. From virtual tours of historical sites to interactive exhibits in museums, these technologies are making culture more accessible to people around the world. Projects such as CyArk are utilizing VR to digitally capture and archive the world's cultural heritage sites. This allows global access to endangered sites and detailed exploration of historical contexts, which can be invaluable for education and preservation efforts.

Looking to the future, it's clear that VR/AR will play an increasingly important role in web development. As technology continues to evolve and become more accessible, we can expect to see even more innovative applications of VR/AR in web development. By staying abreast of these trends, web developers can leverage these powerful technologies to create immersive and engaging web experiences.

Now that we've explored the transformative potential of VR/AR in web development, it's important to recognize the depth of engagement and innovation these technologies bring to various sectors. From virtual retail environments to immersive educational tools, VR/AR not only enhances user experience but also opens new avenues for creative and effective solutions in web development.

The next section will delve into how CUIs are redefining the way users interact with web applications, offering more intuitive and human-like communication.

Exploring CUIs and web development

In the journey to improve interaction with users on web platforms, we as developers face the constant challenge of making interfaces more intuitive and responsive. The CUI is emerging as a promising solution, employing advanced NLP techniques to create more natural and engaging experiences, the development of intuitive conversational flows, the incorporation of appropriate personality and tone into the interface, the implementation of context-aware responses, and continuous testing and iteration.

One notable example of a successful CUI is *Google Assistant*, which uses sophisticated NLP algorithms to provide context-aware, personalized responses that enhance user engagement and satisfaction.

Utilizing NLP techniques

In our endeavor to enhance human-computer interaction through CUIs, the application of advanced NLP techniques is pivotal. We are committed to understanding and implementing state-of-the-art NLP practices to ensure our interfaces are not only functional but engagingly interactive.

Let's explore the critical steps that lay the foundation for building sophisticated conversational systems:

1. **Understanding user intent**: The accurate comprehension of user intent through semantic analysis is our foundational step. We employ language models trained on extensive datasets, enabling them to grasp the nuances of human language. These models form the basis for crafting responses that meet user expectations and enrich the conversation. For example, when a user asks, *What's the weather like in Paris today?*, the model discerns the intent as a request for weather information rather than geographical details about Paris.

2. **Tokenization and parsing**: We utilize tokenization and syntactic parsing to break down text inputs into smaller components, making it easier to interpret user requests. This process allows us to identify and extract key entities and relationships within sentences, which is essential for providing relevant and precise responses. For instance, in the sentence *Book a flight to New York on Friday*, tokenization helps separate *New York* as the destination and *Friday* as the travel date.

3. **Word sense disambiguation**: Tackling the challenge of words with multiple meanings, we apply disambiguation algorithms to correctly interpret user intent based on context. This is crucial in complex conversations where context shifts rapidly. An example would be distinguishing between the word *bank* in *I need to visit the bank* and *I sat by the river bank*.

4. **Implementing attention mechanisms and recurrent neural networks**: To maintain context throughout an interaction session, we use attention mechanisms and recurrent neural networks. These models ensure that our system doesn't merely respond to isolated inputs but considers the entire conversation flow, adapting its responses based on the interaction dynamics. This approach allows the system to remember earlier parts of the conversation, such as recalling a user's preference expressed early in the dialog when making recommendations.

The following are some concrete examples that illustrate how these advanced technologies are being integrated into different sectors to enhance user engagement and efficiency, thereby transforming everyday interactions into seamless digital experiences.

- **E-commerce**: In an online shopping context, our NLP-driven CUI can assist customers by answering questions about products, processing returns, or recommending items based on previous interactions

- **Customer support**: NLP techniques enable our CUIs to provide timely and context-aware solutions to customer inquiries, significantly reducing response times and improving customer satisfaction

- **Healthcare**: For telehealth platforms, our CUI can interpret patient symptoms described in natural language and offer preliminary advice or direct the conversation to appropriate medical personnel

Through these advanced NLP techniques, we continuously enhance our interfaces' ability to understand and communicate effectively, making user interactions as natural as a conversation between humans. This not only improves the user experience but also sets new standards for conversational interface development on the web.

Having explored how advanced NLP techniques significantly improve the capacity of interfaces to communicate naturally and effectively, we recognize the transformative impact on web development. In the next section, we'll uncover how to structure dialogue to naturally guide users through their interactions, ensuring a seamless and enjoyable experience.

Designing intuitive conversation flows

When building CUIs, creating intuitive conversation flows is essential to ensure that the interaction is not only effective but also enjoyable for the user. We strive to develop flows that guide the user logically and naturally through their interactions, ensuring a smooth and coherent experience.

One of the first steps in the design of conversational flows involves the *detailed mapping of possible user journeys*. By understanding the purpose of the interaction and the user's needs, we can structure dialogs that anticipate and respond to these needs efficiently.

Figure 17.1 illustrates an example conversation flow in a CUI. This conversation flow represents a typical interaction scenario between a user and an automated system, such as a virtual assistant. The flowchart details the key steps involved in guiding the user intuitively and efficiently to achieve their goal, whether it's booking a flight, checking flight status, or canceling a booking. The structure includes identifying the conversation's goal, mapping out user inputs, outlining system responses, highlighting decision points, handling errors, and confirming actions. Additionally, it emphasizes the importance of collecting user feedback and iteratively improving the system based on that feedback:

CONVERSATIONAL USER INTERFACE

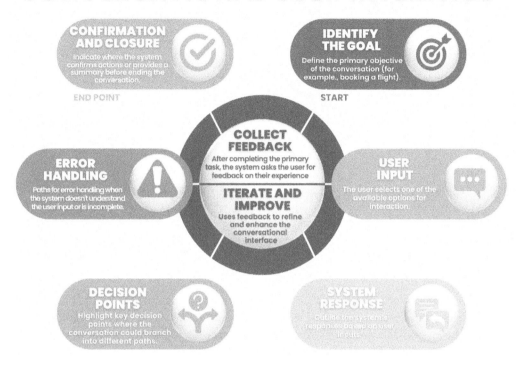

Figure 17.1: CUI flow

The visualization of the conversation flow in a CUI presented in this figure highlights the critical elements of a well-structured interaction. By defining clear goals, mapping potential user inputs, and outlining system responses, the CUI can provide a natural and effective user experience. The inclusion of feedback collection and iterative improvement processes ensures that the interface continually evolves to meet user needs better. For example, for a flight booking service, our conversation flows are designed to collect information about destinations, dates, and travel preferences sequentially and logically, making it easy for the user to carry out this task without redundancy or confusion.

We also implement systems that allow users to take initiative within the conversation:

- **Entry points**: We design flexible entry points that let users input commands or change the conversation topic without losing the previous context. This approach is crucial for keeping the conversation natural and adaptive, respecting user autonomy.

- **Error recovery mechanisms**: Including error recovery mechanisms in conversation flows is essential. This means that when misunderstandings occur – whether from ambiguous user inputs or speech recognition failures – our system is equipped to politely and efficiently request clarification, guiding the user back to the desired conversation path without frustration.

Moreover, constantly iterating and testing conversation flows with real users are integral parts of our design process:

- **Collect feedback**: We gather detailed feedback to identify friction points and opportunities for improvement

- **Iterate and improve**: Based on this feedback, we refine our flows to ensure each interaction is more tuned and tailored to user expectations

By designing intuitive conversational flows, we not only simplify user-computer interaction but also enrich the user experience, making technology more accessible and enjoyable to use. Our goal is always to create CUIs that behave less like machines and more like intelligent, understanding partners.

Incorporating personality and tone into the interface

In developing CUIs, one of our primary concerns is ensuring that the interaction is not only functional but also emotionally resonant with the user. This can be achieved by embedding appropriate personality and tone into the interface, a strategy that transforms basic digital experiences into rich and engaging interactions.

First, we identify the target audience and the context in which the interface will be used to define a congruent tone of voice. For example, a CUI designed for customer service in a retail setting might be crafted to be friendly and welcoming, whereas an interface for an online banking service might adopt a more formal and trustworthy tone.

We delve into an example to illustrate these principles in practice shortly.

When comparing the conversational styles of Siri and Alexa, noticeable distinctions emerge in their design and user engagement. Apple's Siri is designed to appeal to a wide demographic of iPhone, iPad, and Mac users, which includes a diverse range of ages and professional backgrounds. Siri employs a tone that is friendly, casual, and personable, often incorporating humor and informal language to create a relaxed and approachable interaction. This style helps users feel comfortable when performing various tasks such as setting reminders, sending messages, providing directions, and answering trivia questions. Siri's tone remains consistently friendly across different contexts, ensuring an inviting user experience.

In contrast, Amazon's Alexa is geared toward users of Amazon Echo and other Alexa-enabled devices, with a significant focus on smart home enthusiasts and frequent Amazon service users. Alexa's tone is professional yet warm, aiming to be helpful and efficient. This tone is slightly more formal than Siri's, highlighting reliability and competence. Alexa excels in managing smart home functionalities, such as controlling lights and thermostats, and performing tasks related to shopping, providing information, and playing music. The tone is practical and direct, aligning well with the context of home and entertainment system management.

Overall, Siri favors a friendly and humorous tone, making interactions feel like conversations with a companion, while Alexa adopts a more formal and professional tone, prioritizing efficiency and dependability. Both assistants adjust their tone based on the specific task, but Siri engages users through personality and wit, whereas Alexa focuses on delivering clear and actionable responses. Understanding these nuances allows developers to better tailor their CUIs to suit the target audience and context, ensuring that interactions are both effective and engaging.

Implementing a consistent personality in the CUI involves several elements:

- **Word choice**: We carefully select words that reflect the desired personality, ensuring that each message conveys the appropriate tone. This includes the use of expressions and phrases that are identifiable and create a sense of familiarity and trust.

- **Response style**: The style of responses is tailored to mirror the brand's personality. For instance, a young and dynamic brand might use a more casual and direct language style.

- **Emotional feedback**: We empower our CUIs to recognize and respond to users' emotional cues, adjusting the interaction based on the perceived emotional state. This may involve using empathy in situations where the user is frustrated or enthusiasm when the user expresses satisfaction.

Additionally, consistency is key to maintaining the integrity of the interface's personality throughout the interaction. This means every part of the conversation should reinforce the same brand image, from the initial greeting to the end of the interaction. Consistency in tone and personality helps build a stronger and more trustworthy relationship with the user.

Finally, personality and tone are not just about what the interface says, but how it says it. Including variations in speech speed, intonation, and volume can help make the CUI's voice sound more natural and personal. These nuances significantly contribute to a richer and more satisfying user experience.

By effectively incorporating personality and tone, we transform CUIs from mere communication tools into virtual representatives that reflect and strengthen brand identity, significantly enhancing user interaction.

As we delve deeper into refining CUIs, it becomes imperative to focus on incorporating context-aware responses. This approach significantly enhances the interaction by making it more relevant and personalized, ensuring that users feel genuinely understood. Now, let's move forward to the next section, where we'll discuss how to implement context-aware responses in CUIs.

Implementing context-aware responses

In the evolution of CUIs, the ability to provide context-aware responses marks a significant advancement in how we interact with users. Understanding and responding according to the conversation's context not only enhances the effectiveness of the interaction but also enriches the user experience by making it more personalized and relevant.

To implement context-aware responses, we must follow a detailed approach:

1. **Context analysis**: We start by analyzing the context in which the user is engaged. This includes understanding the conversation history, the user's environment, and even the time and location, if applicable. For example, a restaurant reservation system might suggest places close to the user or consider the current time to recommend breakfast or dinner options.

2. **Context modeling**: We use AI models that can maintain and update the context state throughout the conversation. These models are trained to detect significant changes in the dialog and adjust responses based on these insights. For instance, if a user mentions being in a hurry during an interaction, the system might choose to simplify options and expedite the response process.

3. **Dynamic responses**: Responses are generated not just based on what the user has said but also taking into account the accumulated context. This allows the CUI to offer solutions that seem intuitively tailored to the user's needs and current situation.

4. **Feedback and continuous learning**: The system is continually fed with user feedback to improve the accuracy and relevance of contextual responses. This involves real-time data analysis and machine-learning-based adjustments to refine context modeling and response generation.

Moreover, it is crucial to ensure that the system can handle ambiguities and interpretation errors effectively. In situations where the context is uncertain or the user's input is ambiguous, the system is designed to request clarifications intelligently and respectfully, ensuring that the conversation proceeds smoothly and coherently.

By implementing context-aware responses, we not only enhance the utility of our CUIs but also create a user experience that feels genuinely understood and valued. This strengthens user trust and loyalty, which are essential for the long-term success of any digital platform.

As we delve into the nuances of implementing context-aware responses, it's essential to reflect on the insights gained and the strides made toward creating CUIs that truly resonate with users. Now, let's transition to exploring the critical steps of testing and iterating these interfaces. This next phase is crucial in ensuring that our CUIs not only function correctly under various scenarios but also continue to evolve and improve based on user interactions and feedback.

Testing and iterating the conversational interface for an optimal user experience

In the journey to refine CUIs, continuous testing and iteration play crucial roles. Our goal is not only to create functional interfaces but also to provide an exceptionally rich and intuitive user experience. For this purpose, we must adopt a rigorous and meticulous process of testing and iteration:

1. **Defining success metrics**: Before beginning testing, we establish clear success metrics, including task completion rate, user satisfaction, and response effectiveness. These metrics help us to accurately assess the CUI's performance in real usage scenarios.

2. **Usability testing**: We conduct usability tests with real participants, representative of our target audience. During these tests, we observe users interacting with the CUI across a variety of scenarios to identify usability issues and areas of friction. Direct observation allows us to adjust elements such as conversation fluidity, response comprehension, and conversational navigation efficiency.

3. **Feedback analysis**: After each testing session, we collect detailed feedback from users. This includes both their quantitative and qualitative impressions. Feedback is analyzed to identify patterns and trends that suggest where the interface can be improved.

4. **Rapid iteration**: Based on the insights gained, we rapidly iterate on the CUI's design and functionalities. We make continuous adjustments and refinements, which are then tested again to verify whether they result in tangible improvements. This cycle of feedback and iteration is essential for evolving our interface so that it increasingly meets user expectations and needs.

5. **A/B and multivariate testing**: To validate changes, we frequently implement A/B and multivariate testing. This allows us to compare different versions of the CUI to determine which changes produce the best outcomes in terms of user engagement and interface effectiveness.

6. **Continuous monitoring**: Even after deployment, we continue to monitor the CUI's performance. We use advanced analytics tools to track how users interact with the interface over time, allowing us to make proactive adjustments as new challenges and opportunities arise.

By embracing an iterative approach in CUI development, we ensure that our technology not only meets but exceeds user expectations. This process of continuous testing and enhancement is fundamental to keeping our CUIs at the forefront of technology and usability.

Reflecting on the meticulous process of refining our CUIs through continuous testing and iteration highlights the importance of adaptability and responsiveness in technology development. Next, we'll turn our attention to the concept of ubiquitous computing in web development. This innovative field extends the power of computation beyond conventional devices, integrating it into the very fabric of everyday life.

Ubiquitous computing and web development

Ubiquitous computing, or *ubicomp*, involves integrating computation into everyday environments. Our goal in leveraging this technology is to create seamless interactions between humans and digital information. By embedding computing processes in the background of daily activities, we enhance the natural engagement of users with their digital devices, making technology an intuitive extension of their actions.

In smart homes, ubiquitous computing allows homeowners to interact with their living environment seamlessly and intuitively. Devices such as smart thermostats, lighting systems, and security cameras can be controlled remotely via smartphones or voice commands. For instance, a smart thermostat learns a user's daily routine and adjusts the temperature accordingly, providing comfort while saving energy. Smart lighting systems can be programmed to turn on and off based on occupancy or time of day, enhancing convenience and energy efficiency.

In urban settings, ubiquitous computing plays a crucial role in enhancing the efficiency and livability of cities. Smart traffic management systems, for example, use sensors and cameras to monitor traffic conditions in real time. This data is analyzed to optimize traffic light timings, reduce congestion, and improve safety. Another application is in smart parking systems, where sensors detect available parking spaces and direct drivers to them via mobile apps, reducing the time spent searching for parking and decreasing traffic congestion.

By integrating these technologies, ubiquitous computing transforms everyday interactions with digital devices, making technology an inherent part of our daily lives. The seamless integration of computation into our environments enhances user engagement and interaction, making digital experiences more intuitive and effective. These advancements not only illustrate the practical applications of ubiquitous computing but also highlight its potential to improve efficiency and quality of life in both personal and public domains.

Key technologies

The backbone of ubiquitous computing involves several sophisticated technologies, each contributing to the seamless nature of these systems. Let's take a look at these technologies:

- **Sensors and IoT devices**: These devices collect a vast array of data from their environment, from temperature to user interactions, enabling real-time responses and adjustments. The challenge lies in sensor data fusion and interpretation, ensuring accurate and context-aware responses from systems.

- **Cloud computing**: Essential for handling extensive data loads and complex processing tasks, cloud computing offers scalable resources that support the extensive computation needs of IoT devices. This includes the deployment of containerized applications and the use of microservices architectures to enhance scalability and manageability.

- **Edge computing**: By processing data at or near the source of data generation, edge computing drastically reduces latency and bandwidth use, which is crucial for applications that require immediate processing. Techniques such as fog computing extend this concept by decentralizing the computing resources and logic from a centralized cloud to the edges of the network.

- **AI and ML**: The integration of AI and ML allows systems to learn from data, predict user needs, and make autonomous decisions. This involves complex algorithms ranging from neural networks for pattern recognition to reinforcement learning for adaptive system responses based on user interaction patterns.

Now, let's shift our focus to how these technologies are applied specifically in the realm of web development.

Applications in web development

Ubiquitous computing significantly impacts web development, enabling sophisticated applications that include the following:

- **Personal assistants**: Leveraging NLP and predictive analytics, these AI-driven interfaces can understand context, anticipate user needs, and offer personalized suggestions. These systems integrate deep learning models that process user input and environmental data to provide responses that are not only reactive but also proactive. For example, consider a personal assistant such as Siri or Google Assistant. Google Assistant integrates with a wide range of services, including calendars, emails, maps, and smart home devices, to provide personalized recommendations. It can suggest departure times for meetings based on real-time traffic data and user habits, recommend nearby restaurants based on previous dining preferences, and even provide reminders for tasks mentioned in emails. This seamless integration across various services enables Google Assistant to offer tailored advice that fits into the user's daily routine and personal preferences.

- **Smart homes and offices**: Automated systems in homes and offices adjust environmental parameters such as lighting and temperature in real time based on user preferences and learned behaviors. The challenge involves creating algorithms capable of interpreting diverse data types and making real-time decisions that optimize environmental conditions for comfort and energy efficiency. A practical example is the Nest thermostat, which adjusts the temperature based on user behavior patterns and preferences learned over time. It can sense occupancy and adjust the heating or cooling to save energy when no one is home and prepare the environment when it anticipates the return of the residents.

- **Wearable technology**: These devices continuously collect health and activity data, providing insights and real-time feedback to users. The development focus here is on creating efficient data processing algorithms that operate within the limited computing resources of wearable devices while ensuring user privacy and data security. The Apple Watch is a prime example. It collects a wide range of health data, such as heart rate, blood oxygen levels, and physical activity. This data not only helps users monitor their health in real time but also allows the device to provide personalized feedback, such as reminding the user to stand up after long periods of sitting or providing monthly summaries of health trends.

The societal impact of ubiquitous computing is immense, enhancing daily life and work efficiency through more intuitive and less obtrusive technology interactions. Our ongoing research and development are aimed at pushing the boundaries of what these technologies can achieve, focusing on advanced algorithms, system integration, and user-centric design. This continuous advancement is essential to realizing the full potential of ubiquitous computing in web development and beyond.

Summary

In this chapter, we explored the exciting frontier of ubiquitous computing and its integral role in web development, particularly through the lenses of personal assistants, AR/VR integration, and smart city technologies. We delved into how these technologies are shaping more interactive, personalized, and efficient environments, preparing you to harness their full potential in your projects. As we close this discussion on ubiquitous computing, we have laid a strong foundation for understanding how these pervasive technologies integrate seamlessly into everyday digital interactions. This knowledge is crucial as we continue to innovate and adapt web development practices to meet modern demands.

Next, we will shift our focus toward the critical aspects of regulation, governance, and management in AI. Understanding how to protect and manage data within AI-driven systems is essential for ensuring that these innovations not only enhance user experience but also safeguard user privacy and comply with regulatory standards.

18

AI Regulation and Governance – Compliance with the EU's AI Act and ISO/IEC 42001 Standards

In this era of AI, understanding and adhering to emerging regulations such as the EU AI Act (`https://www.europarl.europa.eu/doceo/document/TA-9-2024-0138_EN.html`) and ISO/IEC 42001 standards (`https://www.iso.org/obp/ui/en/#iso:std:iso-iec:42001:ed-1:v1:en`) is essential. These regulations are critical in guiding the secure and ethical development of AI technologies and ensuring compliance with international norms. As AI permeates various sectors, a structured approach to regulation is crucial for its responsible and ethical application.

This chapter will guide you through effectively navigating and implementing AI regulations within the context of web development. We'll start with an overview of the AI regulatory environment, followed by detailed steps for planning and implementing an AI governance system that aligns with these standards.

The following topics will be covered in this chapter:

- Overview of AI regulations
- Overview of the G³AI framework
- AI governance
- AI management

By the end of this chapter, you will have acquired the necessary skills to interpret and apply the **European Union's (EU's)** AI Act, ensuring AI systems are developed and utilized within legal frameworks. You will also know how to design and implement effective AI governance and management systems that align with both organizational goals and regulatory requirements.

Additionally, you will be able to manage AI operations efficiently while ensuring compliance with regulations, conduct comprehensive AI risk assessments, develop strategies to mitigate risks, and employ continuous improvement strategies in AI projects to keep them at the forefront of technological and regulatory advancements.

Overview of AI regulations

In the context of the growing integration of AI in various sectors, effective regulation is becoming indispensable to ensure that its development and use are safe, ethical, and in line with social needs. This section explores two of the main regulatory frameworks: the EU's AI Act and the ISO/IEC 42001 standard.

The EU's AI Act

In this section, we'll explore the direct impact of the EU's AI Act on the development and implementation of AI systems on the web. As AI continues to evolve and become more deeply integrated into web development ecosystems, understanding these regulations becomes crucial to ensuring that applications not only comply with legal standards but also promote ethical and safe practices.

The purpose of the AI Act

The **AI Act** establishes a legal framework for AI within the EU, aiming to harmonize regulations across member states. The intention is to create an environment that facilitates the safe and ethical development of AI while promoting innovation and competitiveness within the market.

One significant challenge is the variation in legal and administrative processes across member states. Each country has regulatory bodies and procedures, which can lead to discrepancies in how the AI Act is enforced. For developers and companies operating in multiple countries, this means navigating a patchwork of regulatory interpretations and compliance requirements. Additionally, the resources and expertise available to enforce these regulations may vary significantly between countries, potentially leading to inconsistent application of the rules.

Another challenge is the dynamic nature of AI technology itself. AI systems are continually evolving, and the regulatory framework must be adaptable to keep pace with these advancements. Ensuring that regulations are flexible enough to accommodate new developments while maintaining rigorous standards for safety and ethics is a delicate balance. Regular updates to the regulatory framework and continuous training for enforcement personnel are necessary to address this issue.

Monitoring compliance is also a complex task. Effective oversight requires robust mechanisms for auditing AI systems, which can be resource-intensive. Implementing these mechanisms uniformly across all member states is essential but challenging. Developing standardized tools and processes for compliance checks can help mitigate these difficulties, but it requires significant coordination and collaboration at the EU level.

Despite these challenges, the harmonization of AI regulations through the AI Act offers numerous benefits. A unified regulatory framework can foster greater innovation by providing clear guidelines and reducing the legal uncertainties that can deter investment. It also promotes trust among users and the public by ensuring that AI systems meet high standards of safety and ethics across the EU.

While the AI Act provides a crucial framework for the ethical and safe development of AI in the EU, addressing the practical challenges of implementation and monitoring compliance across different jurisdictions is vital. By tackling these issues, the EU can ensure that the benefits of AI are realized in a way that is consistent, fair, and conducive to innovation.

By clearly defining legal and ethical obligations, the AI Act directly influences how AI systems are integrated into web platforms, from the design phase to implementation and maintenance. Developers must be aware of these regulations to avoid legal violations and ensure that their applications are responsible and transparent.

Risk classification under the AI Act

AI systems are examined and classified based on the level of risk they present. This classification is crucial for determining the intensity of the compliance measures that must be applied.

The EU's AI regulation (AI Act) classifies risk levels as follows:

- **Unacceptable risk**: Prohibits AI systems that use subliminal, manipulative, or deceptive techniques to distort behavior and impair informed decision-making. It also includes biometric categorization systems that infer sensitive attributes.

- **High risk**: Regulates high-risk AI systems, such as biometric technologies and other critical systems. Providers of these systems have specific obligations.

- **Limited risk**: This applies to AI systems with limited risks, such as chatbots and deepfakes. There are lighter transparency obligations here.

- **Minimal risk**: Minimal risk AI systems are not regulated and include most AI applications currently available in the EU single market.

By understanding these obligations, developers can ensure that their AI systems are compliant with the AI Act, promoting safe, ethical, and innovative applications. In the next section, we will provide a detailed exploration of the practical challenges and strategies for implementing these compliance measures effectively.

Figure 18.1 (`http://g3ai.global/library`) illustrates risk classification under the AI Act, highlighting the different levels of risk and corresponding compliance measures. This visual representation provides a clear overview of how AI systems are categorized and the implications for their design and operation:

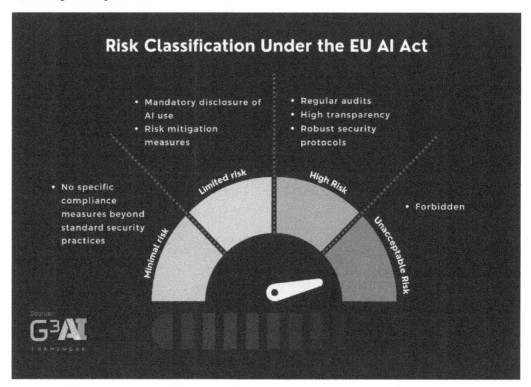

Figure 18.1 – Risk classification under the EU AI Act (this image is from G³ AI Global)

Developers need to understand how their AI systems are classified to implement the appropriate security measures. Systems considered high risk will require regular audits, greater transparency, and robust security protocols, directly affecting the architecture and design of the system. For example, an AI system used in healthcare diagnostics would be classified as high risk due to the potential impact on patient health and safety. This classification necessitates stringent security measures, comprehensive logging, and regular compliance audits, thereby influencing the overall system architecture to ensure data integrity, privacy, and robustness.

Understanding the technical implications of each risk classification on system architecture is essential for developers to design compliant and secure AI systems. *Figure 18.2* outlines layers of system architecture, categorized by different levels of risk, and details the specific technical implications for each level. This structured approach helps developers implement necessary measures effectively to ensure safety, compliance, and efficiency in AI applications:

Layer / Risk Level	Unacceptable Risk	High Risk	Limited Risk	Minimal Risk
Presentation Layer	Not applicable	• Robust user interfaces with rigorous input validation. • Clear error messages and user feedback. • Transparency about AI interaction.	• Mandatory transparency about AI interaction. • User-friendly interfaces with basic input validation	• Basic user interfaces with minimal input validation
Application Layer	Not applicable	• Auditable AI algorithms. • Decision-making modules with regular audits. • Risk assessment and mitigation components. • Secure fallback mechanisms.	• Auditable algorithms. • Decision-making modules with basic risk mitigation. • Fallback functionalities for common errors.	• Basic decision-making modules with no frequent audits required.
Data Layer	Not applicable	• Encrypted data storage. • Data anonymization services. • Secure data ingestion pipelines. • Strict data retention policies.	• Data storage with standard security. • Data anonymization as needed. • Data ingestion pipelines with moderate security.	• Data storage with basic security. • Data ingestion without stringent security requirements.
Security Layer	Not applicable	• Multi-factor authentication. • Advanced authorization. • Secure data transmission (TLS/SSL). • Intrusion detection systems. • Continuous security monitoring.	• Basic authentication and authorization. • Secure data transmission (TLS/SSL). • Basic security monitoring. • Standard access controls.	• Basic authentication. • Secure data transmission. • Minimal security aligned with best practices.
Compliance and Logging Layer	Not applicable	• Detailed audit trails. • Extensive logging services. • Continuous compliance monitoring tools. • Regular compliance reports.	• Basic logging of main events. • Sporadic compliance monitoring. • Periodic activity reports.	• Simple event logging. • Periodic compliance reviews. • Basic activity reports.
Monitoring and Maintenance Layer	Not applicable	• Real-time monitoring dashboards. • Automated alert systems. • Regular audits. • Proactive maintenance plans. • Frequent updates and patches.	• Basic monitoring dashboards. • Automated alerts for critical events. • Periodic maintenance reviews. • Regular updates.	• Basic monitoring tools. • Sporadic scheduled maintenance. • Updates as needed.

Figure 18.2 – Layers, risk levels, and technical implications in AI system architecture

Figure 18.2 provides a clear overview of the technical implications for AI system architecture across different risk levels:

- **Presentation layer**: This involves user interfaces and interaction mechanisms, where input validation and transparency about AI interaction vary according to the risk level

- **Application layer**: This includes AI algorithms and decision-making modules, with stringent auditing and risk mitigation requirements for high-risk systems, and simpler functionalities for minimal-risk systems

- **Data layer**: This layer covers data storage and management, which requires encryption and rigorous anonymization for high-risk systems, while minimal-risk systems follow standard security practices

- **Security layer**: This encompasses authentication, authorization, and data security, ranging from advanced measures such as multi-factor authentication for high-risk systems to basic security for minimal-risk systems

- **Compliance and logging layer**: This involves auditing and logging system activities, with detailed audit trails and continuous monitoring for high-risk systems, compared to basic logging for minimal-risk systems

- **Monitoring and maintenance layer**: This layer focuses on continuous monitoring and system upkeep and features real-time dashboards, proactive maintenance for high-risk systems, and basic monitoring tools for minimal-risk systems

By understanding and implementing these architectural considerations, developers can ensure that their AI systems are designed to meet appropriate regulatory requirements, enhancing security and compliance across different risk levels. For instance, systems classified as high risk will require regular audits, greater transparency, and robust security protocols, which means the architecture must support extensive logging, secure data transmission, and rigorous access controls. Additionally, the design must accommodate regular updates and monitoring to comply with ongoing regulatory requirements. By ensuring these elements are integrated from the outset, developers can create AI systems that are not only compliant but also secure and trustworthy.

Main points of the agreement

As we explore the EU's AI Act and its implications, it becomes clear that strict adherence to these standards is not just a legal obligation but a lever for fostering trust and responsible innovation. In this context, we'll highlight four fundamental pillars that every developer should integrate into their process of creating and managing AI systems. These pillars serve as a roadmap for ensuring that AI technologies are developed ethically and are compliant with international norms. The following are the key principles developers need to consider:

- **Transparency and compliance**: In the world of AI development, clarity is king. Transparency in AI models is an unavoidable requirement that includes strict compliance with EU copyright laws and full disclosure of the content used in training. This practice not only strengthens the trust of end users but also ensures that AI applications remain within legal parameters, avoiding infringements that can result in severe sanctions.

- **Risk management**: The dynamics of AI development require constant vigilance of the associated risks. Developers must institute and follow rigorous risk assessment protocols, adequately preparing for any security incident. Continuous compliance with the AI Act implies frequent monitoring and adaptation of risk mitigation strategies, ensuring that AI systems are robust and defensible against emerging threats.

- **Biometric surveillance and categorization**: As technology advances, so do privacy and ethical concerns. Strict restrictions are imposed on the use of biometric surveillance and biometric categorization systems, reflecting the need to balance innovation and privacy. Developers face the challenge of incorporating functionalities that fully respect users' identity and personal data, without compromising the effectiveness of AI solutions.

- **Implications of indiscriminate scraping**: In a world where data is the new gold, integrity in its collection is indispensable. The ban on the untargeted collection of facial images reinforces the barrier against the misuse of sensitive data. This aspect of the regulations profoundly affects the way data is collected and used to train AI systems, requiring developers to adopt more conscientious and ethical methods of data acquisition.

Each of these aspects guides AI and web developers in how their innovations can be built on foundations of trust, security, and ethics. By integrating these principles, developers not only adhere to regulations but also pave the way for the acceptance and success of their technological solutions on the global market.

With a firm understanding of the EU's AI Act and the essential principles of transparency, risk management, biometric surveillance, and data collection integrity, you are now equipped with the foundational knowledge necessary for ethical and compliant AI development. This knowledge underscores the importance of aligning AI innovations with regulatory frameworks, thereby fostering a culture of responsible technology use and enhancing public trust.

Building on this regulatory foundation, we'll turn our attention to ISO/IEC 42001, a comprehensive international standard that provides a framework for the governance and management of AI systems. The next section will delve into how ISO/IEC 42001 complements the EU's AI Act, offering structured guidelines for establishing, implementing, maintaining, and continually improving an AI management system.

Understanding ISO/IEC 42001

In today's scenario of technological innovation, the implementation of AI systems requires technical competence and a strong adherence to ethical principles and regulatory standards.

The ISO/IEC 42001 standard has emerged as a compass for organizations seeking to direct their AI efforts responsibly and effectively. This global standard was developed to unify AI management practices, involving contributions from world leaders in technology, governance, and research.

In this section, we'll unravel the objectives, challenges, target audience, and benefits of this fundamental standard.

What is ISO/IEC 42001?

The **ISO/IEC 42001 standard** establishes an international framework for AI management systems. It represents a global consensus on best practices for developing, implementing, and managing AI technology responsibly. Born out of collaboration between governments, academics, and industry, this standard is designed to help organizations navigate the complex regulatory and ethical environment of AI.

Objectives of the standard

ISO/IEC 42001 establishes clear objectives to ensure that all AI systems are developed, implemented, and managed with transparency, security, and accountability:

- Promote transparent and ethical management practices
- Guarantee the security and privacy of data handled by AI systems
- Facilitate ongoing compliance with current laws and regulations

With this understanding of the standard's goals, let's delve into the specific challenges AI presents in the implementation and daily operation phases, and explore effective strategies to address these complexities.

AI challenges

Implementing AI in the web environment presents unique challenges, all of which ISO/IEC 42001 helps to address:

- **Ethics and transparency**: It ensures that AI is used fairly and that its operations are understandable to end users
- **Data security**: It establishes robust protocols to protect sensitive information from unauthorized access and leakage
- **Dynamic compliance**: It adapts to changes in global laws and market practices to maintain regulatory compliance

With a firm grasp of the hurdles faced by organizations implementing AI, we can now explore who exactly stands to benefit the most from adhering to the ISO/IEC 42001 standards. This will help us understand how diverse entities, from start-ups to multinational corporations, can implement these practices effectively within their specific operational frameworks.

Target audience

From innovative start-ups to global conglomerates, ISO/IEC 42001 is relevant to any organization that uses AI:

- **Technology start-ups**: It is required to correctly structure AI practices from the outset
- **Multinational companies**: It is required to manage complex AI systems operating in several jurisdictions

With this understanding of who needs these guidelines, let's turn our attention to the tangible benefits of implementation. This will illustrate how adherence to these standards not only bolsters operational integrity but also enhances competitive edge in the market.

Benefits of its implementation

Adopting ISO/IEC 42001 brings tangible and intangible benefits:

- **Strengthening trust**: Compliance with the standard increases the trust of customers and business partners
- **Optimizing operational efficiency**: It promotes management practices that improve the overall performance of AI systems
- **Market positioning**: It highlights the company as an entity committed to responsible innovation

Having explored the significant benefits of adopting ISO/IEC 42001 – such as strengthening trust, optimizing operational efficiency, and enhancing market positioning – we can see how these advantages foster a competitive and ethical operational environment. These benefits are essential for any organization aiming to leverage AI technology responsibly and effectively.

Now that we understand the value of implementing these standards, let's move forward to the practical aspects of how an organization can plan and implement the AI governance and management system through the G³AI framework.

Overview of the G³AI framework

The **G³AI framework** represents a commitment to providing a unified, global approach to the governance and management of AI. This framework is not just a tool but a pact with operational excellence and integrity in the AI universe. It is designed to ensure that the development and use of AI systems take place within internationally recognized ethical and legal standards while addressing the challenges of integrating diverse global regulations and standards.

At the heart of the G³AI framework is the conviction that technology should serve humanity fairly and responsibly. We have therefore defined guidelines that help organizations deploy AI technologies that not only meet performance and innovation expectations but also respect fundamental ethical principles. The framework is designed to be robust, ensuring that all AI systems are created with an awareness of their vast social and legal implications.

The integration of regulations, such as the EU's AI Act, ISO 42.001, UNESCO's recommendations on the Ethics of AI, the OECD's AI classification, and the World Economic Forum's guidelines, poses a significant challenge. Each of these standards addresses different aspects of AI, from transparency and data privacy to liability and the safety of AI systems. The complexity arises in harmonizing these regulations, which often have different focuses and requirements.

Purpose of the G³AI framework

The G³AI framework was developed to provide a robust structure for the governance and management of AI systems on a global scale. The framework intends to ensure that the adoption and implementation of AI are done ethically, safely, and effectively, respecting international standards and adapting to diverse regulatory and cultural contexts. It promotes responsible innovation, improves governance, minimizes risks, and enhances operational effectiveness, thus benefiting all stakeholders involved.

G³AI is versatile and applicable in a wide range of sectors, including health, finance, education, and industry. It is designed to be flexible, allowing specific adjustments to meet the needs of each sector and context, ensuring effective application in a global scenario.

Structure of the G³AI framework

The G³AI framework is structured to guide executives and organizational leaders, AI specialists, and web developers in the effective application of AI governance and management practices. This section delves into the framework's dimensions, components, and metamodels, focusing on how these structures can be implemented in a technical and detailed way.

Figure 18.3 presents the G³AI framework (`http://g3ai.global/library`), a visual representation meticulously designed to elucidate the structure and fundamental components of this innovative model:

Figure 18.3: G³ AI framework (this image is from G³ AI Global)

In the complex field of AI, the need for structured governance and management is critical to ensure that AI implementations are ethical, accountable, and effective. The G³AI framework, which is designed to guide organizations in the use of AI, is based on three main dimensions: **AI strategy**, **AI governance**, and **AI management**.

AI strategy

Developing a robust AI strategy is essential for aligning an organization's technological capabilities with its strategic and regulatory objectives. This involves identifying stakeholder expectations through consultations, aligning identified benefits with strategic goals, and planning the necessary resources, including technology, human skills, and budget.

Integration with existing processes ensures compatibility and optimization while assessing organizational impact helps identify efficiency gains and training needs. Robust governance structures are crucial for continuous policy updates and risk management while following standards such as ISO/IEC 42001. Effective AI portfolio management involves creating business cases and identifying opportunities, ensuring measurable and aligned benefits. Managing strategic AI risks includes continuous risk analysis and mitigation strategies. Promoting innovation within ethical and regulatory boundaries and applying continuous improvement practices ensures the strategy evolves responsibly.

A detailed implementation plan and stakeholder management are key for successful transformation, with ongoing benefit management to monitor success and sustainability. This comprehensive approach ensures the organization can adapt and thrive with technological advancements, providing significant and sustainable value.

AI governance

This dimension focuses on the development and implementation of policies and standards that guide the ethical and responsible use of AI. **AI governance** involves defining accountability frameworks, creating privacy and data security policies, and implementing ethical practices that ensure respect for human rights and fairness. The aim is to create a regulatory environment that not only promotes the safe development of AI but also fosters public and stakeholder confidence in the technology.

Essentially, it works as a mechanism that translates the needs and expectations of stakeholders – which can include anything from employees and customers to regulators and society at large – into clear, enforceable guidelines. These guidelines are key to shaping organizational behavior concerning AI technology and establishing the parameters within which all AI projects must operate.

In addition to setting standards, AI governance plays a crucial role in assessing management's progress in meeting these guidelines. This includes continuously monitoring and evaluating the effectiveness of organizational policies and strategies in promoting safe and ethical AI practices. The guidelines, often expressed through detailed organizational policies and comprehensive strategies, are designed not only to guide day-to-day operations but also to ensure that the implementation of AI aligns with the organization's broader ethical values and strategic objectives.

AI management

This dimension deals with the practical application of AI strategies within organizations, ensuring that AI operations are carried out efficiently and in line with the organization's strategic objectives.

AI management includes everything from the planning and development of AI systems to their implementation and ongoing monitoring. Effective AI management ensures that the technologies implemented are not only technically feasible but also optimized to deliver sustainable and strategic value to the organization.

The ISO/IEC 42001 standard provides a framework for AI management systems, helping organizations establish and maintain effective AI practices. This standard emphasizes the importance of integrating AI strategies with broader business goals and ensuring continuous improvement through structured processes. One of the core methodologies underpinning effective AI management, as highlighted by ISO/IEC 42001, is the **Plan-Do-Check-Act** (**PDCA**) cycle. This cycle is fundamental to continuous improvement in the field of AI:

1. **Plan**: This phase involves establishing the objectives and processes needed to deliver results in line with the expected outcomes and the organization's AI policies. During planning, AI strategies are defined, the necessary resources are identified, success criteria are established, and actions are planned to ensure that AI solutions meet the needs of stakeholders.

2. **Do**: This involves implementing the planned AI strategies and processes. During this phase, AI solutions are developed, tested, and integrated into existing business processes. It is a stage of direct action, where ideas and plans materialize through algorithm development, model building, and AI system execution.

3. **Check**: In this phase, the performance of AI systems is regularly monitored and evaluated to compare the results achieved with the objectives and expectations that were set during the planning phase. Checking involves collecting and analyzing data to assess the effectiveness and efficiency of AI solutions, identifying areas for improvement, and ensuring that AI systems are performing as expected.

4. **Act**: Based on the information obtained in the check phase, corrective actions are implemented to refine and improve AI processes and systems. This phase can involve adjustments to AI models, realignment of strategies, or changes to operational processes, always to continually improve the quality and effectiveness of AI solutions.

Adherence to the PDCA cycle within AI management allows organizations to develop a dynamic and adaptable AI practice, capable of responding to technological and market changes efficiently. By following this cycle, organizations can ensure that their AI initiatives remain aligned with strategic goals, achieve desired outcomes, and continually improve over time. The integration of the PDCA cycle, as advocated by ISO/IEC 42001, ensures that AI management is systematic, repeatable, and capable of sustaining long-term success.

The G³AI metamodel

The term *metamodel* is often used to describe an abstraction that defines the structure, rules, and interconnections between various models in a wider system. A metamodel is useful for explaining complex concepts in a simplified and structured way, establishing a pattern or template that can be replicated.

Let's take a look at this in the context of the G³AI framework:

- A metamodel makes it easier to understand how different components of the AI system interact and work together, providing a high-level view that is essential for strategic planning and implementation

- It defines how different elements, such as principles, processes, rules, practices, and tools, should be organized and used to create effective and accountable AI systems

The metamodel of this framework is a crucial tool that structures the approach to developing, implementing, and managing AI in dynamic and varied environments. It is made up of several components covering context, principles, actors, processes, rules, practices, and tools, each playing a vital role in ensuring that AI is developed and managed to a high standard of excellence and accountability.

Here are the components of the metamodel of the G³AI framework:

- **Principles**: The fundamental principles of the G³AI framework include transparency, accountability, and fairness. These principles guide all AI development and implementation activities, ensuring that solutions are developed ethically and fairly. They promote social welfare and ensure that AI systems respect fundamental rights, creating an environment of trust and integrity.

- **Context**: Using the **Cynefin Framework**, (`https://thecynefin.co`) the operating environment of AI systems is classified as Simple, Complicated, Complex, or Chaotic. This classification helps to identify the specific context in which AI will be applied, guiding the selection of the most appropriate strategies and tools for each scenario. Understanding the context is crucial to optimizing AI development and management approaches, allowing for more precise and effective adaptation to different operational situations.

- **Processes**: The detailed processes for implementing, monitoring, and continually reviewing AI systems are described in this component. Adaptable and agile, these processes allow for rapid adaptation to technological and market changes, ensuring that AI systems are continuously improved and aligned with the organization's strategic objectives.

- **Stakeholders**: This component of the metamodel clearly defines the roles and responsibilities, power, and influence of all the stakeholders involved in the AI ecosystem, from developers and operators to end users and regulators. Clarity in roles is essential for effective governance and responsible management of AI systems, facilitating efficient collaboration and effective communication between all stakeholders.

- **Rules**: This component includes regulatory norms and ethical standards that must be followed to ensure that AI operations are carried out safely and ethically. These rules are crucial for preventing problems such as algorithmic bias and guaranteeing the protection of personal data, contributing to a trustworthy and fair AI environment.

- **Connections**: This refers to the interrelationship and interaction between all the components of the framework, facilitating communication and effective cooperation between them. This component is crucial to ensuring that the various parts of the AI governance and management system operate in a cohesive and coordinated manner.

- **Practices**: This component presents best practices and recognized frameworks to promote compliance and effectiveness in AI development and management. It includes Agile methodologies, DevOps practices, and CI/CD techniques, which support the dynamic development and continuous operation of AI systems.

- **System**: The system component addresses the architecture and infrastructure needed to support AI systems. It includes aspects such as hardware and software configuration, integration of existing systems, and scalability. This component is crucial for ensuring that the technological infrastructure is capable of effectively supporting AI models in production and development.

- **Model**: This component focuses on the design, development, and validation of AI models. It includes modeling techniques, algorithm selection, model training and refinement, and performance evaluation. This layer is key to creating AI solutions that meet specific project needs and are optimized for efficiency, accuracy, and robustness.

- **Tools**: The range of artifacts that support the implementation and management of AI, such as specialized software, templates, management tools, and business models such as the Business Model Canvas (`https://www.strategyzer.com/library`), are described in this component. These tools are essential to facilitate the practical implementation of AI strategies and to support day-to-day operations.

This expanded and detailed metamodel of the G^3AI framework provides a solid foundation for AI specialists and web developers, ensuring that the development and management of AI systems is conducted in an ethical, responsible, and highly effective manner.

Having explored the comprehensive structure of the G^3AI framework, we now understand the multi-faceted approach required to manage AI effectively across different sectors and environments. This detailed understanding of the metamodel highlights the intricate interplay of principles, processes, and tools necessary for ethical and accountable AI governance and management.

As we recognize the critical importance of these components in shaping the operational integrity of AI systems, it is imperative to move forward from theoretical frameworks to practical applications. With this foundational knowledge in place, let's turn our focus toward the actionable steps involved in planning and implementing an AI governance and management system.

This next section will guide you through how to integrate these principles into your organizational strategies, ensuring that your AI initiatives are not only compliant but also strategically aligned with broader business objectives and ethical standards.

AI strategy

AI strategies are meticulously aligned with the international ISO/IEC 22989:2022 standard, which focuses on AI quality management. This alignment ensures that our AI initiatives are robust and meet our strategic and corporate objectives while being sustainable and effective. Here, we consider the needs of all stakeholders while planning resources and capabilities to address both current requirements and future challenges.

The strategy encompasses several key aspects:

- **Strategic objectives for AI**: We must define clear, strategic goals for the deployment and development of AI technologies. These objectives are crafted to enhance our operational efficiencies and innovate our services while aligning with our long-term business strategies.

- **Resource and capability planning**: Adequate resources and capabilities are planned to support our AI strategies. This involves allocating the necessary technological, human, and financial resources to ensure that our AI projects are sustainable and capable of adapting to future technological advancements and market changes.

- **Integration with organizational processes**: Our AI strategy considers how AI interacts with other technologies and business processes. By evaluating the organization's context as outlined in ISO/IEC 42001, Section 4.1, we ensure that AI systems are seamlessly integrated, supporting and enhancing existing processes rather than disrupting them.

- **Organizational impact assessment**: We must assess the potential impacts of AI across various facets of the organization. This includes evaluating how AI will affect operational workflows, employee roles, customer interactions, and overall service delivery. Assessing the potential impact of AI on various facets of the organization is essential. This includes the following:

  - **Operational workflows**: Identifying efficiency gains with AI implementation and evaluating the automation potential of processes

  - **Employee roles**: Planning the training and development of new skills for employees, as well as reconfiguring roles and responsibilities based on new AI technologies

  - **Customer interactions**: Improving the customer experience with personalized AI, using AI to personalize interactions and services

  - **Service delivery**: Enhancing the quality of delivered services, increasing the speed and accuracy of services

- **AI portfolio management and opportunity assessment**: Managing the AI portfolio involves prioritizing and managing AI initiatives strategically. This includes the following aspects:

  - **Developing business cases**: Creating business cases for each use case, evaluating feasibility and expected return

  - **Opportunity assessment**: Identifying opportunities for AI to be applied in both internal processes and products and services for customers

- **AI value management**: Ensuring that AI benefits are measurable and aligned with strategic objectives is crucial. Developing a value management framework allows you to measure and track the benefits that are delivered by AI initiatives, as well as conduct periodic reviews to adjust strategies and maximize delivered value.

- **AI planning and transformation**: Developing a detailed plan for implementing key activities in successive phases includes creating an implementation roadmap and strategies for managing organizational transition. Ensuring stakeholder acceptance and support is fundamental for the success of AI transformation.

- **AI benefit management**: This involves identifying and monitoring the expected benefits of AI initiatives, establishing KPIs to measure success, conducting post-implementation evaluations to identify lessons learned and ensure the sustainability of AI practices, and developing plans to continuously maintain and improve AI practices to ensure the organization adapts and thrives with technological changes.

- **Engagement with stakeholders**: Key to our strategy is the active engagement of stakeholders in defining the objectives and expectations related to AI. This includes internal stakeholders such as employees and management, as well as external parties such as customers, partners, and regulators.

- **Stakeholder feedback integration**: We must incorporate feedback from these engagements into our AI strategy to ensure that it remains aligned with stakeholder needs and expectations. This continuous loop of feedback and adaptation helps in fine-tuning our approach to AI deployment and management.

Rationale

ISO/IEC 22989:2022 provides guidance on establishing quality management systems for AI, ensuring that AI strategies are not only effective but also continuously improved upon to meet evolving demands.

Section 4.1 of ISO/IEC 42001 ensures that AI systems are seamlessly integrated, supporting and enhancing existing processes rather than disrupting them.

ISO/IEC 22989:2022 provides guidance on establishing quality management systems for AI, ensuring that AI strategies are not only effective but also continuously improved upon to meet evolving demands. Section 4.1 of ISO/IEC 42001 ensures that AI systems are seamlessly integrated, supporting and enhancing existing processes rather than disrupting them.

With a structured and comprehensive approach, organizations can develop and implement an AI strategy that not only meets stakeholder expectations but also aligns with strategic objectives, improves business processes, and ensures compliance with regulatory standards, providing significant and sustainable value. Now, let's move on to the practical aspects of AI governance.

AI governance

In this section, we will look at the governance of AI, a fundamental pillar for ensuring that the implementation of the technology reflects the highest ethical and regulatory standards.

As AI capabilities advance, our responsibility to manage these technologies fairly and transparently has never been more critical. In the subsequent sections, we will detail the essential components of **AI governance** that help guide organizations through this new technological territory.

Structuring internal controls

The effective governance and management of AI systems necessitate establishing robust internal controls. These controls ensure that AI systems operate within ethical and legal boundaries while achieving operational excellence. As AI auditors and specialists in AI governance, it is imperative to understand the intricacies of structuring these internal controls, drawing upon various standards such as **Committee of Sponsoring Organizations of the Treadway Commission (COSO)** and ISO/IEC 42001, particularly Sections 5.1 and 5.2.

> Rationale
>
> ISO/IEC 42001 *Sections 5.1* and *5.2* guide the commitment of leadership and the development of AI policies that enhance ethical integration and regulatory compliance.

Leadership must demonstrate a strong **commitment to the integration of AI**, which includes strict adherence to regulatory compliance and the development of AI policies that reflect ethical and legal responsibilities. According to ISO/IEC 42001, Sections 5.1 and 5.2, organizations are required to follow these policies:

- **Leadership commitment (Section 5.1)**: Ensure that top management demonstrates leadership and commitment to the AI management system. This includes establishing clear policies, providing necessary resources, and fostering an organizational culture that supports ethical AI practices.

- **AI policies (Section 5.2)**: Develop and implement policies for the AI management system that align with international standards. These policies must address ethical considerations and legal requirements and ensure responsible AI deployment.

These policies ensure that AI practices align with international standards and promote responsible behaviors.

To effectively manage AI systems, it is crucial to define the scope and applicability of the AI management system clearly. According to ISO/IEC 42001, Section 4.3, organizations must establish the boundaries of their AI management system, ensuring that all AI-related activities are covered. This includes identifying the processes, technologies, and personnel involved in AI operations, as well as understanding how AI interacts with other organizational processes.

A robust **AI risk management** system is essential for identifying, assessing, and mitigating risks associated with AI systems. The COSO framework, widely recognized for its comprehensive approach to risk management, provides valuable insights into establishing an effective risk management system. By integrating COSO's principles with ISO/IEC 42001, organizations can ensure that AI risks are systematically identified, evaluated, and mitigated. This involves doing the following:

- **Regular risk assessments**: Conducting frequent risk assessments to identify potential threats
- **Developing mitigation strategies**: Creating comprehensive strategies to address identified risks
- **Continuous monitoring**: Implementing ongoing monitoring processes to adapt to emerging threats

Implementing **internal controls** and safeguards is vital for maintaining the integrity and security of AI systems. This includes the following aspects:

- **Data governance policies**: Ensuring data quality, integrity, and privacy through strict data governance policies
- **Access controls**: Managing data access, sharing, and storage to comply with data protection regulations such as GDPR
- **Ethical guidelines**: Integrating ethical guidelines into AI development processes to prevent biases and ensure fairness

These controls are aligned with the requirements of ISO/IEC 42001, Sections 5.1 and 5.2, ensuring comprehensive governance and ethical management of AI systems.

Continuously monitoring and improving AI systems is critical for maintaining their effectiveness and compliance. Section 9.1 of ISO/IEC 42001 emphasizes the importance of regular monitoring, measurement, and analysis of AI systems. Organizations should do the following:

- **Track AI performance**: Implement mechanisms to monitor AI performance continuously
- **Identify areas for improvement**: Regularly assess the effectiveness of AI systems and identify opportunities for improvement
- **Adapt and enhance**: Make necessary adjustments to AI systems based on monitoring outcomes, aligning with the COSO framework's principle of continuous improvement

Investing in **training and development** is essential for building the necessary competencies for effective AI governance and management. Organizations should provide the following:

- **Continuous education programs**: Ensure that employees are well-versed in AI technologies, ethical considerations, and regulatory requirements

- **Skills development initiatives**: Enhance employees' skills to foster a culture of responsible AI use and strengthen the overall governance framework

In conclusion, structuring internal controls for AI governance involves a multifaceted approach that integrates ethical and legal responsibilities, clear scope definition, risk management, implementation of safeguards, continuous monitoring, and training. By leveraging standards such as ISO/IEC 42001 and COSO, organizations can establish a robust AI governance framework that promotes transparency, accountability, and operational excellence.

Having established a comprehensive understanding of structuring internal controls, the next step is to delve into the practical aspects of risk rating within AI systems. This involves assessing and classifying the risks associated with AI technologies to ensure that they are managed effectively. In the next section, we'll explore how to implement a robust risk rating system.

Risk rating

Implementing a rigorous risk analysis and classification system is crucial to ensuring that AI systems operate within safe and ethical boundaries. Each AI system is meticulously assessed to determine its risk level, with higher-risk systems subjected to stricter regulations. This structured approach not only minimizes potential threats but also ensures alignment with global best practices in risk management. *Table 18.1* outlines the risk categories defined by the EU's AI Act, providing a comprehensive overview of each category and the implications for AI system development:

Risk Category	Description	Examples of AI Systems	Compliance Measures
Unacceptable risk	Systems that pose a clear threat to safety, livelihoods, and fundamental rights	Mass surveillance systems, social scoring	Prohibited
High risk	Systems that can significantly affect the safety, health, or fundamental rights of individuals	Medical diagnostics, recruitment, critical infrastructure	Regular audits, high transparency, robust security protocols
Limited risk	Systems that require specific transparency requirements, such as informing users about their interaction with AI	Chatbots, virtual assistants	Mandatory disclosure of AI use, risk mitigation measures
Minimal risk	Systems that pose minimal or no risks to safety or fundamental rights	Spam filters, music recommendations	No specific compliance measures beyond standard security practices

Table 18.1 – Overview of the risk categories under the EU's AI Act

This table provides a clear overview of the risk categories under the EU's AI Act, describing the levels of risk, examples of AI systems in each category, and the associated compliance measures.

Under the guidance of the EU's AI Act and *Sections 6.1* to *6.3* of ISO/IEC 42001, AI risk assessment and management ranges from analyzing high-impact AI model releases to adversity testing, ensuring that all potential risks are identified and mitigated.

Reporting serious incidents to the European Commission and maintaining cyber security and energy efficiency are key to protecting against internal and external threats.

> **Rationale**
>
> The EU's AI Act outlines specific requirements for high-risk AI systems, ensuring that such systems undergo a thorough assessment and adhere to higher standards of accountability and transparency.

AI risk management

Risk identification and mitigation are continuous processes within our AI management framework. Through detailed analysis, we develop proactive strategies to address potential threats, ensuring that our AI systems remain safe and reliable.

> **Rationale**
>
> The EU's AI Act outlines specific measures for risk assessment and mitigation, particularly for high-risk AI applications, demanding regular testing and risk assessment throughout the life cycle of AI systems. It requires robust risk handling and mitigation strategies to be in place to address risks related to safety, privacy, and data protection.
>
> ISO/IEC 42001 supports these requirements by outlining a structure for setting up, executing, sustaining, and consistently enhancing an AI management system. This standard underscores the importance of managing AI risks, aligning with the need to ensure that AI systems operate within defined ethical and legal boundaries.

With a comprehensive understanding of risk rating and AI risk management, we can turn our attention to another critical aspect of AI governance: data governance. Effective data governance ensures that the data used in AI systems is managed responsibly and that its quality, integrity, and security are maintained. We'll explore the principles and practices of data governance in the next section.

Data governance

Our policies for the collection, security, and use of data are strictly enforced. We prioritize data quality and integrity, ensuring privacy and transparent access to data. This level of data governance is crucial for maintaining operational integrity and building trust among users.

> **Rationale**
>
> ISO/IEC 42001 emphasizes the importance of data security and privacy in AI systems, providing a framework for the responsible handling of data.

Having established the importance of robust data governance, we can now delve into another crucial aspect of AI governance: ethics and regulatory compliance. By adhering to ethical principles and regulatory requirements, we can ensure that our AI systems are developed and operated responsibly.

With the knowledge of what code assistants are, what benefits they offer, and how they differ from code generators under our belt, let's learn how to integrate them into a workflow.

Ethics and regulatory compliance

The development of an AI-specific code of ethics and rigorous regulatory compliance form the pillars of our governance framework. Additionally, we constantly evaluate the social and cultural impacts of AI, ensuring our technologies contribute positively to society. By integrating ethical guidelines and adhering to regulatory requirements, we ensure that our AI systems are not only innovative but also responsible and trustworthy.

To fully comprehend this stage of AI governance, *Chapter 3* provides valuable insights. That chapter delves into the practical challenges and opportunities associated with integrating AI into web development projects. It explores common obstacles developers may face and offers strategies for optimizing opportunities to leverage AI effectively. Topics such as data requirements, model selection, and ethical considerations are covered in detail, providing a comprehensive understanding of the landscape.

Additionally, the UNESCO Recommendation on the Ethics of Artificial Intelligence provides a detailed framework for ethical AI development. This recommendation emphasizes the importance of transparency, accountability, and fairness in AI systems, guiding developers to create technologies that respect human rights and promote social well-being.

AI auditing

Regular audits are conducted to assess the compliance, effectiveness, and safety of our AI systems. These audits are vital for the continuous improvement of our practices and systems, ensuring they always meet our high ethical and operational standards.

> **Rationale**
>
> The EU's AI Act and ISO/IEC 42001 both underscore the necessity of regular monitoring and reassessment of AI systems to ensure ongoing compliance and adaptation to new regulations.

With an understanding of these ethical and regulatory foundations, we can now examine the crucial aspects of transparency and accountability in AI governance.

Transparency and accountability

Our mechanisms for transparency ensure that all decisions that are made by AI systems are explainable. We maintain accountability in all operations, and our commitment to clear and effective communication of our AI practices helps build public trust and acceptance.

The EU's AI Act emphasizes the need for high transparency, especially for high-risk AI applications, requiring clear information about the logic involved and the meaning and consequences of AI processing. This regulation mandates that AI systems be designed to enable effective supervision and oversight, ensuring that users and stakeholders can understand and trust the decision-making processes.

ISO/IEC 42001 supports this objective by requiring AI management systems to include accountability and traceability measures. These standards ensure that AI systems not only comply with legal frameworks but are also capable of maintaining user trust through transparent practices.

For a deeper understanding of these principles, take a look at *Chapter 15*, which provides valuable insights. That chapter delved into the critical aspects of AI model governance, emphasizing trustworthiness, fairness, reliability, robustness, transparency, and data protection. Introducing the AI **Trust, Risk, and Security in Models (TRiSM)** framework, it explored the technological components and organizational governance needed to ensure ethical and responsible AI applications.

> **Rationale**
>
> The EU's AI Law stresses the need for high transparency, especially for high-risk AI applications, requiring clear information about the logic involved and the meaning and consequences of processing AI systems. It obliges AI systems to be designed in such a way as to enable effective supervision.
>
> ISO/IEC 42001 supports this objective by requiring AI management systems to include accountability and traceability measures. These standards ensure that AI systems not only comply with legal frameworks but are also able to maintain user trust through transparent practices.

By integrating the concepts from *Chapter 15*, we can reinforce the importance of transparency and accountability in AI governance. These principles not only enhance compliance with international standards but also foster trust and acceptance among users and stakeholders.

With an understanding of the importance of transparency and accountability in AI, let's move forward to the next critical aspect of AI governance: AI auditing. The next section will explore how regular audits ensure the continuous compliance, effectiveness, and safety of AI systems.

Performance evaluation and continuous improvement

Performance evaluation is continuous, as established in *Section 9.1* of ISO/IEC 42001, focusing on the effectiveness of the AI management system. Through regular monitoring and measurement, the organization can adapt and improve its AI practices, promoting continuous improvement that responds to technological and market changes.

The EU's AI Act emphasizes the necessity for ongoing assessment and adaptation of AI systems, particularly those categorized as high-risk. This legislation requires that AI systems undergo continuous evaluations to ensure they adhere to safety, privacy, and ethical standards throughout their operational life cycle. It mandates the following:

- **Regular testing and reassessment**: AI systems, especially those in high-risk categories, must be regularly tested against current standards and re-assessed to manage any emerging risks effectively

- **Adaptation to technological advancements**: It acknowledges the rapid development of AI technology and insists on continual updates and modifications to AI systems to keep them safe and effective

- **Documentation and reporting**: Maintaining detailed records of performance evaluations, including any incidents or near-misses, which are crucial for regulatory compliance and improvement processes

ISO/IEC 42001 provides a comprehensive framework that aligns with the continuous improvement cycle, famously known as the PDCA cycle, which is integral to quality management systems. This standard specifically addresses the following aspects:

- **Section 9.1 – Monitoring, Measurement, Analysis, and Evaluation**: This section requires organizations to establish systematic approaches to monitor and measure the performance of their AI systems. It includes the following areas:

  - **Performance metrics**: Developing specific metrics that reflect the effectiveness of the AI system in meeting its intended goals

  - **Regular reviews**: Conducting regular reviews of performance data to identify trends, opportunities for improvement, and areas of non-compliance

  - **Feedback mechanisms**: Implementing mechanisms to integrate feedback from these evaluations into the AI development and management processes

- **Section 10.1 – Nonconformity and Corrective Action**: This section reinforces the need to take prompt corrective actions when issues are identified, ensuring that AI systems continue to operate within the organization's risk tolerance and compliance requirements.

The combination of the EU's AI Act's stringent requirements for safety and risk management with ISO/IEC 42001's structured approach to continuous improvement offers a robust framework for managing AI systems.

By adhering to these standards, organizations can significantly enhance the reliability and safety of their AI systems. This is achieved through ongoing performance evaluations and a steadfast commitment to high standards of risk management. Furthermore, organizations are empowered to drive innovation responsibly. By ensuring that improvements and innovations in AI applications are conducted within a framework that emphasizes ethical practices and compliance, they can foster a culture of responsible development. Additionally, maintaining regulatory compliance becomes more manageable. By keeping AI systems aligned with evolving legal requirements and industry standards, organizations can ensure their operations remain lawful and ethical.

AI auditing

Regular audits are conducted to assess the compliance, effectiveness, and safety of our AI systems. These audits are vital for the continuous improvement of our practices and systems, ensuring they always meet our high ethical and operational standards. By following international standards such as ISO/IEC 42001 and the EU's AI Act, organizations can maintain alignment with evolving regulations and best practices, fostering trust and accountability in their AI technologies.

The Three Lines Model, developed by the **Institute of Internal Auditors (IIA)**, is a robust framework for effective AI governance and risk management. This model clarifies roles and responsibilities within an organization, promoting collaboration and enhancing overall risk management. Each "line" in the model represents a different aspect of the organization's defenses against risk.

First line – operational management

Operational management forms the foundation of the Three Lines Model. This line is responsible for managing risks directly through daily operations. Managers and employees in this line are tasked with maintaining effective controls and executing risk management procedures. The role of operational management includes the following aspects:

- **Implementation of controls**: Operational management is responsible for implementing and maintaining internal controls to manage and mitigate risks associated with AI systems

- **Continuous monitoring**: They continuously monitor AI systems, ensuring that they operate within established parameters and comply with regulatory requirements

- **Real-time adjustments**: This line is also tasked with making real-time adjustments to AI operations to address emerging risks and ensure ongoing compliance with ethical and legal standards

Here lies the critical role of developers, architects, database managers, infrastructure managers, security officers, AI engineers, and DevOps specialists. These professionals work collaboratively to implement, monitor, and adjust the AI systems, ensuring they are robust, compliant, and secure.

Second line – risk management and compliance

The second line focuses on establishing policies and procedures to manage and mitigate risks. This line provides oversight and ensures that the first line is effectively managing risks. It involves the following aspects:

- **Policy development**: This line develops comprehensive risk management policies and procedures tailored to AI systems

- **Risk assessments**: It conducts regular risk assessments to identify potential threats and vulnerabilities in AI operations

- **Compliance monitoring**: Ensuring that AI systems comply with relevant laws, regulations, and internal policies is a key responsibility

Collaboration is essential for effective risk management within an organization. The second line supports operational management by providing the tools and frameworks needed to manage risks effectively and works closely with internal audits to ensure that risk management practices are comprehensive and effective. This collaboration ensures a unified approach to risk management, enhancing the organization's ability to address potential threats proactively.

Third line – internal audit

The internal audit provides independent assurance that the organization's risk management, governance, and internal control processes are operating effectively. This line offers an objective evaluation of the effectiveness of the first and second lines. It involves the following aspects:

- **Independent assurance**: The internal audit evaluates the effectiveness of the organization's AI governance framework, risk management processes, and internal controls

- **Objective evaluations**: Comprehensive audits are conducted to ensure that AI systems are operating within the defined ethical and legal boundaries

- **Recommendations for improvement**: Based on their findings, internal auditors provide actionable recommendations to enhance AI governance and risk management practices

Collaboration is essential for effective risk management and governance within an organization. Internal auditors work closely with operational management and risk management to ensure that identified risks are adequately managed and that controls are effective. This collaborative approach creates a continuous feedback loop, promoting the ongoing improvement of AI systems and practices. By working together, these lines of defense enhance the organization's ability to address risks proactively and maintain robust, compliant AI operations.

> Rationale
>
> The EU's AI Act and ISO/IEC 42001 both underscore the necessity of regular monitoring and reassessment of AI systems to ensure ongoing compliance and adaptation to new regulations.

This section presented some of the essential processes of AI governance, taking advantage of corporate governance structures and establishing a model for other organizations to follow, promoting a future in which AI technology is developed and managed with maximum integrity and responsibility.

The EU's AI Act and ISO/IEC 42001 both underscore the necessity of regular monitoring and reassessment of AI systems to ensure ongoing compliance and adaptation to new regulations. This section presented some of the essential processes of AI governance, taking advantage of corporate governance structures and establishing a model for other organizations to follow, promoting a future in which AI technology is developed and managed with maximum integrity and responsibility.

With the knowledge of the Three Lines Model and its application in AI governance and risk management, let's delve into the specifics of AI management.

AI management

By exploring the management of **AI in web development**, we can immerse ourselves in a universe where technical precision and ethical strategy converge to shape digital futures. This section focuses on the meticulous practices and essential regulations that govern the effective implementation and management of AI, as established by ISO/IEC 42001 and the EU's AI Act.

In this phase, integrated AI loops (see *Figure 18.4*), as outlined in *Chapter 3*, play a crucial role. These loops provide a structured and iterative process that not only supports but enhances the management of AI in web development projects.

By adhering to these loops, developers can ensure that their AI systems are continuously refined and adjusted in line with the evolving standards and practices described by ISO/IEC 42001 and the EU's AI Act. This integration ensures a comprehensive management system that is both dynamic and compliant with the latest regulatory requirements.

This framework, depicted in *Figure 18.4* from G³ AI Global, outlines six interconnected cycles, each with a specific objective. Let's delve into each of these cycles in more detail:

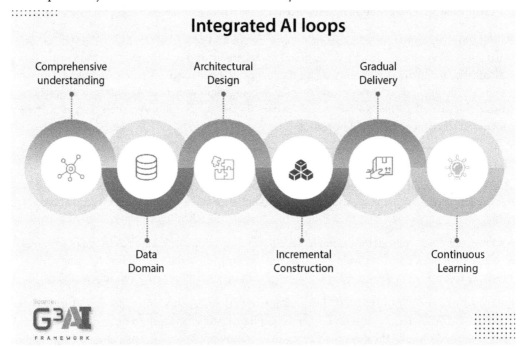

Figure 18.4 – Integrated AI loops (this image is from G³ AI Global)

The integrated AI loops pipeline (`https://g3ai.global/library`) is designed to provide a structured and iterative approach to efficiently and effectively developing and deploying AI models in web applications. By combining the best practices of AI and DevOps, this pipeline ensures that AI models meet user needs and business objectives, fostering an environment of continuous learning and improvement.

With the knowledge of what code assistants are, what benefits they offer, and how they differ from code generators under our belt, let's learn how to integrate them into a workflow.

Planning and implementing the AI management system

When planning and implementing management systems, they must be meticulously designed so that their technological capabilities align with the organization's strategic and regulatory objectives. According to *Section 4.3* of ISO/IEC 42001, it is essential to clearly define the boundaries and applicability of the AI management system, especially in the context of web development, to ensure that all AI activities are managed coherently and responsibly.

In this stage, it's highly recommended to utilize the **AYAI Framework**, as discussed in *Chapter 5*, to guide the definition of the scope and architecture of the AI solution. The AYAI Framework provides a structured approach to integrating AI systems within web development, ensuring that the planning and architectural design are in complete harmony with the strategic and regulatory requirements of the organization. This ensures that the AI management system is both effective and compliant, aligning with the broader objectives set out by the ISO/IEC 42001 standards.

This process of determining the scope of the AI management system is essential to ensure that all AI-related activities are managed effectively, aligning AI operations with the organization's strategic and compliance objectives.

Here's a detailed explanation of the importance and methodology for determining the scope as per this standard:

- **Clarifying boundaries**: Clearly establish the boundaries within which the management system will operate, thereby avoiding ambiguities that can lead to management failures and unanticipated risks

- **Ensuring adequate comprehensiveness**: Ensure that all the elements necessary for the effective management of AI, from human to technological resources, are included within the scope

- **Facilitate compliance and audit**: A well-defined scope facilitates the process of compliance with international regulations and facilitates audits by providing a clear framework for verifying management practices

According to ISO/IEC 42001, scope determination must follow a systematic process that includes the following aspects:

- **Requirements analysis**: Consider all legal, regulatory, and contractual requirements related to AI that the organization needs to comply with

- **Identification of assets and technologies**: Identify all AI assets and technologies that will be managed within the system, including hardware, software, data, and interfaces with other systems

- **Impact assessment**: Assess the potential impact of AI systems in terms of operations, security, and privacy, which will help define the level of control required

- **Stakeholder consultations**: Engage internal and external stakeholders to gain insight into expectations and requirements for AI management

- **Review and approval**: The proposed scope should be reviewed and approved by appropriate leadership to ensure that all critical areas are covered and that the scope is aligned with the organization's overall strategy

> **Rationale**
> Determining the scope of the AI management system is a fundamental process that establishes the boundaries and applicability of the management system, as outlined in *Section 4.3* of ISO/IEC 42001.

Determining the scope of the AI management system is a fundamental process that establishes the boundaries and applicability of the management system, as outlined in Section 4.3 of ISO/IEC 42001 (`https://www.iso.org/obp/ui/en/#iso:std:iso-iec:42001:ed-1:v1:en`).

With the knowledge of how to determine the scope of your AI management system, let's move forward to monitoring and reviewing AI systems, ensuring their effective and compliant integration into your organization's workflows.

Continuous integration/continuous deployment (CI/CD) in AI management

Incorporating CI/CD practices can significantly enhance the efficiency and reliability of AI system development and deployment. CI/CD practices involve automated processes that integrate and deploy code changes continuously, ensuring that updates are tested and deployed seamlessly and consistently:

- **CI**: This involves automatically integrating code changes from multiple contributors into a shared repository several times a day. Each integration is verified by an automated build, allowing teams to detect problems early. For AI systems, CI ensures that changes in algorithms, data processing pipelines, or model configurations are continuously validated against existing standards and performance benchmarks.

- **CD**: This extends CI by automatically deploying all code changes that pass the automated tests to the production environment. This practice minimizes manual intervention and ensures that new features, improvements, and bug fixes are delivered to users quickly and reliably. In the context of AI, CD ensures that models and algorithms are consistently updated and deployed without interrupting service availability or performance.

- **Automated testing**: Integral to both CI and CD, automated testing involves running predefined tests on code changes to ensure they do not introduce errors or degrade performance. For AI systems, this includes unit tests for individual components, integration tests for data pipelines, and performance tests for model accuracy and efficiency.

- **Monitoring and logging**: Continuously monitoring and logging AI system performance in real time helps identify issues promptly. Tools such as Prometheus, Grafana, and Elasticsearch, Logstash, Kibana (ELK) Stack can be used to monitor metrics such as response times, error rates, and resource usage. Logging detailed information about system operations and user interactions allows for comprehensive analysis and troubleshooting.

- **Feedback loops**: Establish feedback loops where insights from monitoring and user feedback are continuously fed back into the planning and development phases. This ensures that the AI system evolves based on actual performance and user needs, enhancing its relevance and effectiveness.

- **Regular audits and compliance checks**: Periodic audits and compliance checks ensure that the AI systems adhere to regulatory requirements and ethical standards. This involves reviewing data handling practices, model fairness, and transparency, and ensuring that any biases or ethical concerns are addressed promptly.

By integrating CI/CD practices within the AI loop, organizations can achieve a robust framework for AI management that supports continuous improvement, rapid adaptation to changes, and high standards of reliability and performance. This approach aligns with the principles of the G^3AI framework, ensuring that AI systems are developed and managed ethically, responsibly, and effectively.

This section provided insight into how to integrate robust AI management practices, from strategic conception through to operation and ongoing review, within the standards set by ISO/IEC 42001 and EU legislation, ensuring that AI development in the web environment is safe, ethical, and effective.

Summary

In this chapter, we navigated the complex landscape of AI regulations, specifically addressing the EU's AI Act and ISO/IEC 42001 standards. We started by providing an overview of AI regulations that shape the secure and ethical development of AI technologies. Through this exploration, you gained insights into how these frameworks ensure compliance with international guidelines and enhance AI system governance, including AI network communications and process mining for optimized security and efficiency.

Following this, we delved into how to plan and implement AI governance and management systems aligned with these standards. You learned how to design and implement effective AI governance systems that not only meet regulatory requirements but also support organizational goals. We covered the operationalization and support of AI systems, ensuring that you are equipped to manage AI operations efficiently and in compliance with regulations.

We also addressed AI risk assessment and management, teaching you how to conduct thorough risk assessments and implement strategies to mitigate potential threats, thereby ensuring ongoing compliance and security. Finally, we focused on performance evaluation and continuous improvement, providing you with strategies to foster responsible innovation and keep pace with technological and regulatory advancements.

As we conclude this chapter, and indeed, this book, *AI Strategy for Web Development*, we recognize the profound impact and transformative potential of AI in web development. Looking to the future, AI will continue to evolve, bringing new challenges and opportunities. Professionals equipped with the knowledge from this book are well-prepared to lead the charge in innovating, securing, and ethically guiding AI developments to reshape the digital landscape.

Further reading

- G³ AI Global. (2024). *Global Governance and Management AI (G³ AI) Framework*. Retrieved from `http://g3ai.global/library`.

- European Parliament. (2024). Regulation (EU) 2024/XXX of the European Parliament and of the Council of 13 March 2024 on harmonized rules for artificial intelligence (Artificial Intelligence Act) and amending certain Union Legislative Acts. Official Journal of the European Union, L XXX/XX. Available at `https://www.europarl.europa.eu/doceo/document/TA-9-2024-0138_EN.html`.

- European Parliament. (2024). *The AI Act Explorer | EU Artificial Intelligence Act*. Available at `https://artificialintelligenceact.eu/ai-act-explorer/`.

- IEEE. (2011). IEEE Guide-Adoption of ISO/IEC TR 24748-1:2010 Systems and Software Engineering–Life Cycle Management-Part 1: Guide for Life Cycle Management. In IEEE Std 24748-1-2011 (pp. 1-96).

- Google. (2021). *Machine Learning Glossary: Fairness*. Available at `https://developers.google.com/machine-learning/glossary/`.

- PwC. (2020). PwC Ethical AI Framework.

- IIA. (2017). The Institute of Internal Auditors artificial intelligence auditing framework: Practical applications Part A. In Global Perspectives and Insights.

- IAF. (2019). *Ethical data impact assessments and oversight models*. Information Accountability Foundation.

- ISO/IEC 42001:2023. (2023). *Information technology – Artificial intelligence – Management system. International Organization for Standardization (ISO) and International Electrotechnical Commission (IEC)*. Available at `https://www.iso.org/obp/ui/en/#iso:std:iso-iec:42001:ed-1:v1:en`.

- National Institute of Standards and Technology (NIST). (2024, April 29). *AI Risk Management Framework*. Available at `https://www.nist.gov/itl/ai-risk-management-framework`.

Index

X

Y

Z

Packtpub.com

Subscribe to our online digital library for full access to over 7,000 books and videos, as well as industry leading tools to help you plan your personal development and advance your career. For more information, please visit our website.

Why subscribe?

- Spend less time learning and more time coding with practical eBooks and Videos from over 4,000 industry professionals

- Improve your learning with Skill Plans built especially for you

- Get a free eBook or video every month

- Fully searchable for easy access to vital information

- Copy and paste, print, and bookmark content

Did you know that Packt offers eBook versions of every book published, with PDF and ePub files available? You can upgrade to the eBook version at packtpub.com and as a print book customer, you are entitled to a discount on the eBook copy. Get in touch with us at customercare@packtpub.com for more details.

At www.packtpub.com, you can also read a collection of free technical articles, sign up for a range of free newsletters, and receive exclusive discounts and offers on Packt books and eBooks.

Other Books You May Enjoy

If you enjoyed this book, you may be interested in these other books by Packt:

Building AI Applications with ChatGPT APIs

Martin Yanev

ISBN: 978-1-80512-756-7

- Develop a solid foundation in using the ChatGPT API for natural language processing tasks
- Build, deploy, and capitalize on a variety of desktop and SaaS AI applications
- Seamlessly integrate ChatGPT with established frameworks such as Flask, Django, and Microsoft Office APIs
- Channel your creativity by integrating DALL-E APIs to produce stunning AI-generated art within your desktop applications
- Experience the power of Whisper API's speech recognition and text-to-speech features
- Discover techniques to optimize ChatGPT models through the process of fine-tuning

The AI Product Manager's Handbook

Irene Bratsis

ISBN: 978-1-80461-293-4

- Build AI products for the future using minimal resources
- Identify opportunities where AI can be leveraged to meet business needs
- Collaborate with cross-functional teams to develop and deploy AI products
- Analyze the benefits and costs of developing products using ML and DL
- Explore the role of ethics and responsibility in dealing with sensitive data
- Understand performance and efficacy across verticals

Packt is searching for authors like you

If you're interested in becoming an author for Packt, please visit authors.packtpub.com and apply today. We have worked with thousands of developers and tech professionals, just like you, to help them share their insight with the global tech community. You can make a general application, apply for a specific hot topic that we are recruiting an author for, or submit your own idea.

Hi!

I am Anderson Soares Furtado Oliveira, author of *AI Strategies for Web Development*. I really hope you enjoyed reading this book and found it useful for increasing your productivity and efficiency.

It would really help me (and other potential readers!) if you could leave a review on Amazon sharing your thoughts on this book.

Go to the link below or scan the QR code to leave your review:

https://packt.link/r/1835886310

Your review will help us to understand what's worked well in this book, and what could be improved upon for future editions, so it really is appreciated.

Best wishes,

Anderson Soares Furtado Oliveira

Download a free PDF copy of this book

Thanks for purchasing this book!

Do you like to read on the go but are unable to carry your print books everywhere?

Is your eBook purchase not compatible with the device of your choice?

Don't worry, now with every Packt book you get a DRM-free PDF version of that book at no cost.

Read anywhere, any place, on any device. Search, copy, and paste code from your favorite technical books directly into your application.

The perks don't stop there, you can get exclusive access to discounts, newsletters, and great free content in your inbox daily

Follow these simple steps to get the benefits:

1. Scan the QR code or visit the link below

https://packt.link/free-ebook/978-1-83588-630-4

2. Submit your proof of purchase
3. That's it! We'll send your free PDF and other benefits to your email directly